# Good Housekeeping™

## BEST

# CHICKEN DISHES

### Plus Turkey & Other Poultry Recipes

# Good Housekeeping™

### BEST

# CHICKEN DISHES

## Plus Turkey & Other Poultry Recipes

Time Inc.
HOME ENTERTAINMENT

Hearst Communications, Inc.

# Good Housekeeping ™ (BEST) CHICKEN DISHES

GOOD HOUSEKEEPING

| | |
|---:|:---|
| *Editor in Chief:* | Ellen Levine |
| *Food Director:* | Susan Westmoreland |
| *Associate Food Director:* | Susan Deborah Goldsmith |
| *Food Associates:* | Lori Perlmutter, Mary Ann Svec, Lisa Troland |
| *Nutrition Director:* | Delia Hammock |
| *Food Appliances Director:* | Sharon Franke |
| *Art Director:* | Scott Yardley |
| *Photo Editor:* | Maya Kaimal |
| *Hearst Brand Development:* | Carrie Bloom, Jennifer Talansky |

TIME INC. HOME ENTERTAINMENT

| | |
|---:|:---|
| *President:* | David Gitow |
| *Director, Continuities and Single Sales:* | David Arfine |
| *Director, Continuities and Retention:* | Michael Barrett |
| *Director, New Products:* | Alicia Longobardo |
| *Group Product Manager:* | Jennifer McLyman |
| *Product Managers:* | Christopher Berzolla, Roberta Harris, Stacy Hirschberg, Kenneth Maehlum, Daniel Melore |
| *Manager, Retail and New Markets:* | Tom Mifsud |
| *Associate Product Managers:* | Carlos Jimenez, Daria Raehse, Dennis Sheehan, Betty Su Niki Viswanathan, Lauren Zaslansky, Cheryl Zukowski |
| *Assistant Product Managers:* | Victoria Alfonso, Jennifer Dowell, Meredith Shelley |
| *Editorial Operations Director:* | John Calvano |
| *Book Production Manager:* | Jessica McGrath |
| *Assistant Book Production Manager:* | Jonathan Polsky |
| *Book Production Coordinator:* | Kristen Travers |
| *Fulfillment Director:* | Michelle Gudema |
| *Assistant Fulfillment Director:* | Richard Perez |
| *Financial Director:* | Tricia Griffin |
| *Financial Manager:* | Amy Maselli |
| *Assistant Financial Manager:* | Steven Sandonato |
| *Marketing Assistant:* | Ann Gillespie |

GOOD HOUSEKEEPING BEST CHICKEN DISHES
Produced by Rebus, Inc.
New York, NY

First Edition
ISBN# 1-688-17172-9
Library of Congress Catalog Card Number: 98-71059
Good Housekeeping is a Registered Trademark of Hearst Communications, Inc.

Printed in the United States of America

We welcome your comments and suggestions about Good Housekeeping Books.
Please write us at: Good Housekeeping Books, Attention: Book Editors, P.O. Box 11016, Des Moines, IA 50336-1016

If you would like to order any of our Hard Cover Collector Edition books, please call us at 1-800-327-6388
(Monday through Friday, 7:00 a.m.–8:00 p.m. or Saturday, 7:00 a.m.–6:00 p.m. Central Time)

# Contents

*Welcome to Good Housekeeping's* collection of great recipes for chicken, turkey, capon, game hens, and goose. If, like many people, you already serve poultry several nights a week, you'll welcome this wonderful source of new ideas for dinner. The recipes were developed and triple-tested in the *Good Housekeeping* kitchens; and though some of the dishes feature exotic flavors, most are made with readily available market-shelf ingredients.

The great thing about making poultry your "meat" of choice is that there are so many different sizes, portions, parts, and cuts in the market. An unstuffed 3½-pound broiler/fryer, for instance, makes a perfect meal for four and will cook in an hour—just long enough to fill the house with appetizing aromas. A big juicy roaster, capon, or turkey, filled with a savory stuffing, may need more than four hours in the oven—but what a feast, with its big meaty breast, meal-sized drumsticks, and plenty of leftovers. Boneless, skinless chicken breasts are the "filet mignon" of the bird, and are very popular with cooks in a hurry. Lean, tender and delicately flavored, they take to sophisticated sauces and light marinades, and require only minutes in the skillet or on the grill; bone-in breasts cook more slowly and work with more robust flavorings. Dark meat —the thigh and drumstick—has a richer, fuller flavor that goes along with its higher fat content. These poultry parts can stand up to long simmering and dramatic seasoning. Turkey, no longer a once-yearly meal, is now sold whole, in parts, as bone-in or boneless breasts, breast fillets, and more. And there are the additional options of ground poultry and poultry sausages.

The recipes in *Best Chicken Dishes* were chosen by the Food editors of *Good Housekeeping* magazine to represent simple American home cooking, but with a nod to the hottest restaurant trends. So you'll find comforting main dishes like Creamy Chicken Stew, Chicken Cacciatore, and Bacon & Tomato Turkey Burgers—but also intriguing selections such as Raspberry-Chicken Salad with Caramelized Onions, Vietnamese Noodle Soup, Mahogany Chicken, and Thai Chicken Burritos. With over 375 recipes, *Best Chicken Dishes* can offer an inspiration for every day of the year!

# Soups & Sandwiches

# Vietnamese Noodle Soup

🐓 🐓 🐓

PREP: 20 MINUTES / COOK: 25 MINUTES

This is typically served with thin slices of beef, but our version is made with chicken.

4 ounces flat dried rice noodles or linguine
4 cans (14½ ounces each) reduced-sodium chicken
   broth or 7 cups homemade (page 11)
6 sprigs basil
6 sprigs cilantro
1 teaspoon coriander seeds
1 cinnamon stick (3 inches long)
2 garlic cloves, peeled
3 green onions, thinly sliced diagonally
2 large skinless, boneless chicken-breast halves
   (about 1 pound), cut into thin diagonal strips

4 medium mushrooms, sliced
Fresh cilantro leaves and lime wedges (optional)

**1** In large bowl, soak rice noodles in enough *warm water* to cover for 20 minutes. Drain noodles.

**2** Meanwhile, in 3-quart saucepan, heat chicken broth, basil, cilantro, coriander seeds, cinnamon stick, garlic, and one-third of green onions to boiling over high heat. Reduce heat to low; cover and simmer 10 minutes. Strain broth through sieve; discard solids and return broth to saucepan.

**3** Stir chicken, mushrooms, drained noodles, and remaining green onions into broth; heat to boiling over high heat. Reduce heat to low; cover and simmer 3 minutes or until chicken loses its pink color throughout. Serve with fresh cilantro leaves and lime wedges if you like. ***Makes about 9 cups or 4 main-dish servings.***

Each serving: About 255 calories, 32 g protein, 26 g carbohydrate, 2 g total fat (0 g saturated), 0.5 g fiber, 66 mg cholesterol, 1110 mg sodium.

*Vietnamese Noodle Soup*

# Greek Lemon Soup

### 🐓 🐓 🐓

PREP: 15 MINUTES / COOK: 35 MINUTES

Called *avgolemono* in Greek, this velvety-smooth chicken soup is thickened with eggs and rice. It's best served soon after you make it.

2 cans (14½ ounces each) chicken broth or
   3½ cups homemade (at right)
1 medium skinless, boneless chicken-breast half
   (about 6 ounces)
1 small onion, peeled and studded with
   2 whole cloves
1 medium carrot, peeled and cut into 2-inch pieces
1 medium celery stalk, cut into 2-inch pieces
⅔ cup regular long-grain rice
3 large eggs
⅓ cup fresh lemon juice (about 2 large lemons)
1 tablespoon margarine or butter
Chopped fresh chives for garnish

**1** In 3-quart saucepan, heat chicken broth, chicken breast, onion studded with cloves, carrot, celery, and *2½ cups water* to boiling over high heat. Reduce heat to low; cover and simmer 10 minutes.

**2** With slotted spoon, remove chicken and vegetables from saucepan; discard vegetables. Cool chicken until easy to handle, then shred into thin strips; set aside.

**3** Add rice to simmering broth; heat to boiling over high heat. Reduce heat to low; cover and simmer 15 to 20 minutes until rice is tender.

**4** Meanwhile, in large bowl, with wire whisk, mix eggs and lemon juice until combined.

**5** Slowly whisk 2 cups simmering broth into bowl with egg mixture, whisking constantly. Return broth mixture to saucepan; heat just to simmering, whisking constantly, about 5 minutes (do not boil or soup will curdle). Stir in shredded chicken and margarine or butter. Sprinkle with chopped chives if you like. *Makes about 7 cups or 6 first-course servings.*

Each serving: About 180 calories, 12 g protein, 19 g carbohydrate, 6 g total fat (2 g saturated), 0.5 g fiber, 123 mg cholesterol, 675 mg sodium.

# Homemade Chicken Broth

### 🐓 🐓 🐓

PREP: 15 MINUTES PLUS OVERNIGHT TO CHILL
COOK: 4 HOURS 15 MINUTES

We made our broth without salt so that it is versatile enough to use in a variety of recipes. If you want to serve the broth on its own, stir in 2 teaspoons salt (or to taste) after cooking.

1 whole chicken (about 3½ pounds)
2 carrots, peeled and cut into 2-inch pieces
1 celery stalk, cut into 2-inch pieces
1 medium onion, unpeeled and cut into quarters
5 parsley sprigs
1 garlic clove, unpeeled
½ teaspoon dried thyme
½ bay leaf

**1** In 8-quart Dutch oven or saucepot, place whole chicken with its neck (refrigerate or freeze giblets for use another day), carrots, celery, onion, parsley, garlic, thyme, and bay leaf. Add *3 quarts water*; heat to boiling over high heat. With slotted spoon, skim any foam from surface of broth. Reduce heat to low; cover and simmer 1 hour, turning chicken once and skimming foam occasionally.

**2** Remove Dutch oven from heat and transfer chicken to cutting board. When chicken is cool enough to handle, remove meat from bones (refrigerate or freeze meat for use another day). Return chicken bones, skin, and scraps to Dutch oven; heat to boiling over high heat. Reduce heat to low; simmer, uncovered, 3 hours.

**3** Drain broth through colander into large bowl. Then strain broth through sieve into another large bowl. Discard solids in sieve; cool broth slightly. Cover and refrigerate overnight.

**4** When cold, discard fat from surface of broth. *Makes about 5 cups broth.*

Each ½ cup: About 100 calories, 17 g protein, 2 g carbohydrate, 2 g total fat (1 g saturated), 0.5 g fiber, 53 mg cholesterol, 65 mg sodium.

## TURKEY-NOODLE SOUP

PREP: 10 MINUTES / COOK: 55 MINUTES

*1 cooked turkey-breast carcass with 2 cups*
*   meat left on*
*2 tablespoons vegetable oil*
*3 medium carrots, peeled and cut into ½-inch pieces*
*3 medium celery stalks, sliced ½ inch thick*
*1 large onion, diced*
*1 can (14½ to 16 ounces) stewed tomatoes*
*½ teaspoon salt*
*¼ teaspoon coarsely ground black pepper*
*¼ teaspoon dried thyme*
*1 package (8 ounces) egg noodles*
*1 package (10 ounces) frozen peas*

**1** Cut turkey-breast meat from carcass into bite-size pieces; cover and refrigerate. With kitchen shears, cut carcass in half.

**2** In 5-quart Dutch oven, heat oil over high heat. Add carrots, celery, and onion and cook until lightly browned, stirring occasionally. Add turkey carcass, stewed tomatoes with their liquid, salt, pepper, thyme, and *11 cups water*; heat to boiling, breaking up tomatoes with spoon. Reduce heat to low; cover and simmer 45 minutes, stirring soup occasionally.

**3** Remove carcass from broth; discard. Over high heat, heat broth mixture remaining in Dutch oven to boiling. Add noodles, reduce heat to medium and cook, stirring occasionally, until noodles are tender. Stir in frozen peas and turkey meat; heat through. Makes about 12 cups or 6 main-dish servings.

Each serving: About 340 calories, 24 g protein, 46 g carbohydrate, 7 g total fat (1 g saturated), 6 g fiber, 75 mg cholesterol, 470 mg sodium.

# Chicken & Barley Soup

PREP: 10 MINUTES / COOK: 1 HOUR 25 MINUTES

You can speed up this soup by using quick barley. It doesn't have the same chewy texture as regular barley, but it can shave about 40 minutes off the cooking time (it should be tender in 15 to 20 minutes).

1 tablespoon vegetable oil
3 medium carrots, peeled and sliced
3 medium celery stalks, chopped
½ pound mushrooms, sliced
1 large onion, chopped
1 whole chicken (about 3½ pounds), neck and
    gizzard reserved
2 cans (14½ ounces each) chicken broth or
    3½ cups homemade (page 11)
½ cup barley
½ teaspoon salt
½ teaspoon coarsely ground black pepper

**1** In 8-quart Dutch oven or saucepot, heat oil over medium-high heat. Add carrots, celery, mushrooms, onion, and *3 tablespoons water*; stirring frequently, until vegetables are golden.

**2** Add chicken, breast side down, to Dutch oven along with neck, gizzard, chicken broth, and *5 cups water*. Heat to boiling over high heat. Reduce heat to low; cover and simmer 35 minutes or until chicken loses its pink color throughout. Transfer chicken, neck, and gizzard to bowl. When cool enough to handle, pull meat from neck and chop gizzard. Discard bones, skin, and fat from chicken; cut chicken meat into bite-size pieces.

**3** Skim fat from liquid in Dutch oven. Add barley, salt, and pepper and heat to boiling over high heat. Reduce heat to low; cover and simmer 50 to 60 minutes, until barley is tender.

**4** When barley is tender, stir in chicken meat and gizzard; heat through. *Makes about 12 cups or 8 main-dish servings.*

Each serving: About 220 calories, 25 g protein, 16 g carbohydrate, 6 g total fat (1 g saturated), 4 g fiber, 75 mg cholesterol, 700 mg sodium.

# Chicken Minestrone

🐓 🐓 🐓

PREP: 15 MINUTES / COOK: 30 MINUTES

In Italian, a *minestra* is a hearty soup. And a *minestrone* is a "big" version of a *minestra*, made heartier by the addition of vegetables and typically a small soup pasta (such as tubetti) or rice.

½ cup tubetti or small elbow macaroni
1 tablespoon vegetable oil
¾ pound skinless, boneless chicken breasts, cut lengthwise in half, then crosswise into ¼-inch-thick strips
1 medium onion, chopped
1 medium carrot, peeled and chopped
2 large tomatoes, peeled, seeded, and diced
½ pound green beans, each cut diagonally in half
2 cans (14½ ounces each) chicken broth or 3½ cups homemade (page 11)
1 small yellow straightneck squash (about 8 ounces), cut lengthwise in half, then crosswise into ½-inch-thick pieces
1 can (16 to 19 ounces) white kidney beans (cannellini), rinsed and drained

1 package (10 ounces) frozen chopped spinach
Grated Parmesan cheese (optional)

**1** In large saucepot, prepare tubetti in *boiling water* as label directs; drain.

**2** Meanwhile, in 5-quart Dutch oven or saucepot, heat oil over medium-high heat until very hot. Add chicken strips and cook, stirring, just until they lose their pink color throughout. With slotted spoon, transfer chicken to bowl.

**3** Add onion and carrot to Dutch oven and cook until tender but not browned. Stir in tomatoes, green beans, chicken broth, and *2 cups water*; heat to boiling over high heat. Reduce heat to low; cover and simmer 5 minutes. Add yellow squash; simmer 5 minutes or until vegetables are tender.

**4** Stir in chicken strips, tubetti, white kidney beans, and frozen spinach. Cook over medium-high heat until heated through. If you like, pass Parmesan to sprinkle on each serving. ***Makes about 12 cups or 6 main-dish servings.***

Each serving without Parmesan cheese: About 250 calories, 23 g protein, 29 g carbohydrate, 5 g total fat (1 g saturated), 7 g fiber, 33 mg cholesterol, 785 mg sodium.

*Chicken Minestrone*

# Cream of Chicken Soup

🐓 🐓 🐓

PREP: 5 MINUTES / COOK: 30 MINUTES

If you have an immersible blender, use it to puree the soup right in the saucepan. The potatoes can be peeled or not, depending on how you feel about potato skin. If you choose to leave the skin on, be sure that the potatoes are very well scrubbed.

1 tablespoon vegetable oil
¾ pound skinless, boneless chicken-breast halves, each cut lengthwise in half, then crosswise into ¼-inch-thick strips
1 medium onion, finely chopped
4 medium potatoes (about 1½ pounds), cut into bite-size chunks
1 can (14½ ounces) chicken broth or 1¾ cups homemade (page 11)
½ pound spinach, trimmed and coarsely chopped
1 cup half-and-half or light cream
¾ teaspoon salt

1 In 4-quart saucepan, heat oil over medium-high heat until very hot. Add chicken strips and cook just until they lose their pink color throughout, stirring frequently. With slotted spoon, transfer chicken to bowl; set aside.

2 Add onion to saucepan and cook until golden and tender. Add potatoes, chicken broth, and *2½ cups water*. Heat to boiling over high heat. Reduce heat; cover and simmer until potatoes are tender, about 15 minutes.

## GREAT GO-WITHS

### SESAME PAN ROLLS

PREP: 40 MINUTES PLUS RISING TIME / BAKE: 15 TO 20 MINUTES

*⅓ cup sugar*
*1½ teaspoons salt*
*2 packages active dry yeast*
*About 4¾ cups all-purpose flour*
*5 tablespoons margarine or butter*
*2 large eggs*
*1 tablespoon sesame seeds*

1 In large bowl, combine sugar, salt, yeast, and 1½ cups flour. In 1-quart saucepan, heat 4 tablespoons margarine or butter (½ stick) and *1 cup water* until very warm (120° to 130°F.). Margarine or butter does not need to melt completely.

2 With mixer at low speed, gradually beat liquid into dry ingredients just until blended. Increase speed to medium; beat 2 minutes, occasionally scraping bowl with rubber spatula. In cup, refrigerate 1 tablespoon egg white for brushing on rolls later. Into flour mixture in bowl, beat in remaining eggs with ½ cup flour to make a thick batter; continue beating 2 minutes, scraping bowl often. With wooden spoon, stir in 2¼ cups flour to make a soft dough.

3 Turn dough onto lightly floured surface and knead until smooth and elastic, about 10 minutes, working in more flour (about ½ cup) while kneading. Shape dough into a ball; place in greased large bowl, turn-ing dough to grease top. Cover and let rise in warm place (80° to 85°F.) until doubled, about 1 hour.

4 Punch down dough. Turn dough onto lightly floured surface. Cut dough into 4 pieces; cover and let rest 15 minutes for easier handling.

5 Grease 13" by 9" metal baking pan. In small sauce-pan, melt remaining 1 tablespoon margarine or but-ter over low heat. Roll 1 piece of dough into a 16-inch-long rope. Cut rope into four equal pieces. Repeat with remaining dough to make 16 rolls in all. Brush rolls with melted margarine or butter and arrange in pan to make 2 lengthwise rows of 8 rolls each. Cover; let rise in warm place until doubled, about 30 minutes.

6 Preheat oven to 400°F. Mix reserved egg white with 1 teaspoon water. Brush rolls with egg-white mixture; sprinkle with sesame seeds. Bake rolls 15 to 20 min-utes until golden and rolls sound hollow when light-ly tapped with finger. Cool rolls in pan on wire rack 10 minutes. Place second rack on top of pan; invert rolls onto rack, then invert back onto first rack so rolls are right-side up. Serve rolls warm. Or, cool rolls to serve later. Reheat if desired. Makes 16 rolls.

Each roll: About 200 calories, 5 g protein, 33 g carbohydrate, 5 g total fat (1 g saturated), 1 g fiber, 27 mg cholesterol, 270 mg sodium.

**3** Spoon half of potato mixture into food processor or blender; cover (with center part of blender cover removed) and blend until smooth.

**4** Return soup to saucepan; stir in chicken, spinach, half-and-half, and salt. Over medium heat, heat soup until hot, stirring occasionally. *Makes about 8 cups or 4 main-dish servings.*

Each serving: About 370 calories, 27 g protein, 39 g carbohydrate, 12 g total fat (5 g saturated), 5 g fiber, 72 mg cholesterol, 1005 mg sodium.

# Chicken, Vegetable & Black Bean Soup

🐓 🐓 🐓

PREP: 10 MINUTES / COOK: 50 MINUTES

1 pound carrots
2 medium onions
1 whole chicken (about 3½ pounds)
1 large celery stalk, cut into ½-inch slices
2 tablespoons vegetable oil
1 small head green cabbage (about 1 pound), cut into ½-inch pieces
¾ teaspoon salt
2 cans (15 to 16 ounces each) black beans, rinsed and drained

**1** Peel 2 carrots and cut into ½-inch pieces. Cut 1 onion into ½-inch-thick pieces. Remove as much fat as possible from chicken.

**2** Place chicken, breast side down, in 4-quart saucepan. Add celery, carrot pieces, onion pieces, and *6 cups water.* Heat to boiling over high heat. Reduce heat to low; cover and simmer 30 minutes or until chicken loses its pink color throughout.

**3** Meanwhile, peel and cut remaining carrots into ¼-inch-thick slices. Coarsely chop remaining onion.

**4** In 5-quart Dutch oven or saucepot, heat oil over medium-high heat. Add sliced carrots, chopped onion, cabbage, and salt and cook 20 minutes or until tender and golden, stirring frequently.

**5** Transfer chicken and vegetables from saucepan to bowl; reserve cooking broth. When chicken is cool enough to handle, discard bones, skin, and fat; tear meat into bite-size pieces. Mash vegetables. Skim fat from cooking broth.

## DOUBLE-TURKEY SPLIT PEA SOUP

PREP: 10 MINUTES / COOK: 1 HOUR

Turkey from the deli is fine here, but if you have access to leftover roast turkey, try this with meat from the turkey drumstick, which has deeper flavor.

*2 tablespoons vegetable oil*
*2 medium carrots, peeled and diced*
*2 medium celery stalks, diced*
*1 medium onion, chopped*
*2 small turnips (about 6 ounces each), peeled and cut into ½-inch cubes*
*1 package (16 ounces) split peas, rinsed and picked over*
*¼ pound smoked turkey, diced*
*1 teaspoon salt*
*¼ teaspoon ground allspice*
*1 bay leaf*
*1 pound leftover roast turkey, cut into ½-inch pieces (about 3½ cups)*

**1** In 5-quart Dutch oven or saucepan, heat oil over medium-high heat. Add carrots, celery, onion, and turnips and cook until tender-crisp.

**2** Stir in split peas, smoked turkey, salt, allspice, bay leaf, and *8 cups water;* heat to boiling over high heat. Reduce heat to low; cover and simmer 45 minutes.

**3** Stir in roast turkey; cook 10 minutes longer to blend flavors. Makes about 12 cups or 6 main-dish servings.

Each serving: About 485 calories, 46 g protein, 54 g carbohydrate, 10 g total fat (2 g saturated), 7 g fiber, 68 mg cholesterol, 700 mg sodium.

**6** Pour reserved cooking broth through fine sieve into Dutch oven. Add chicken, mashed vegetables, black beans, and *2 cups water.* Heat to boiling over high heat. *Makes about 12 cups or 6 main-dish servings.*

Each serving: About 340 calories, 35 g protein, 30 g carbohydrate, 10 g total fat (2 g saturated), 9 g fiber, 89 mg cholesterol, 670 mg sodium.

*Chicken Piccata Sandwich with Red Pepper Sauce*

# Chicken Piccata Sandwiches with Red Pepper Sauce

🐓 🐓 🐓

PREP: 5 MINUTES / COOK: 15 MINUTES

1 large lemon
1 jar (7 ounces) roasted red peppers, drained
½ teaspoon sugar
3 tablespoons olive oil
½ teaspoon salt
4 medium skinless, boneless chicken-breast halves (about 1¼ pounds)
4 slices (½ inch thick) hearty country bread, toasted
Boston lettuce leaves

**1** Squeeze juice from lemon. In blender, blend 1 teaspoon lemon juice with roasted peppers, sugar, 2 tablespoons olive oil, and ¼ teaspoon salt until smooth.

**2** In nonstick 10-inch skillet, heat remaining 1 tablespoon olive oil over medium-high heat until very hot. Add chicken breasts and cook 4 to 5 minutes until golden brown. Turn chicken and sprinkle with remaining ¼ teaspoon salt. Reduce heat to medium and cook chicken until juices run clear when pierced with tip of knife, about 4 minutes longer. Stir in remaining lemon juice; heat through.

**3** To serve, spread toast with half of roasted red-pepper sauce, place on 4 dinner plates. Arrange lettuce leaves on toast; top with chicken and pour any juice in skillet over chicken. Spoon remaining red-pepper sauce over chicken. *Makes 4 sandwiches.*

Each sandwich: About 340 calories, 35 g protein, 20 g carbohydrate, 13 g total fat (2 g saturated), 1 g fiber, 82 mg cholesterol, 620 mg sodium.

# Chicken Gyros

### 🐓 🐓 🐓

PREP: 20 MINUTES / COOK: 15 MINUTES

For this take on a Greek *gyro* (which is traditionally made with lamb), sautéed chicken and a garlicky cucumber-yogurt sauce are rolled up in pitas. Be sure to warm the pitas in the oven as directed; this makes them pliable enough to roll up.

1¾ pounds skinless, boneless chicken breasts, cut into 1-inch chunks
3 tablespoons olive oil
1 teaspoon dried oregano
¾ teaspoon salt
1 medium cucumber, peeled and seeded
1 container (8 ounces) plain low-fat yogurt
1 garlic clove, minced
6 large pitas (8-inch diameter)
3 large onions, thinly sliced
1 cup thinly sliced iceberg lettuce, loosely packed
1 medium tomato, diced

**1** In bowl, toss chicken with olive oil, oregano, and ½ teaspoon salt.

**2** Coarsely shred cucumber onto paper towels. Roll paper towels with shredded cucumber and press to remove as much liquid as possible from cucumber. In small bowl, mix cucumber, yogurt, garlic, and remaining ¼ teaspoon salt; set aside.

**3** Wrap pitas in foil and warm in 300°F. oven. Meanwhile, in 12-inch skillet, cook chicken mixture over medium-high heat until chicken is lightly browned on the outside and loses its pink color throughout, about 5 minutes. With slotted spoon, transfer chicken to plate; keep warm.

**4** Add sliced onions to same skillet and cook over medium heat until just tender, about 10 minutes, stirring occasionally.

**5** To serve, spread cucumber mixture on warm (uncut) pitas; top with lettuce, then chicken, onion, and tomato. Roll pitas into a cone shape and wrap with napkin or foil to secure. *Makes 6 sandwiches.*

Each sandwich: About 520 calories, 42 g protein, 63 g carbohydrate, 10 g total fat (2 g saturated), 4 g fiber, 79 mg cholesterol, 870 mg sodium.

# Chicken Caesar Pockets

### 🐓 🐓 🐓

PREP: 20 MINUTES / COOK: 15 MINUTES

The salad lover's favorite, nestled in a pita. Just right for supper in the backyard or at the park.

¼ teaspoon salt
2 teaspoons plus 3 tablespoons olive oil
½ teaspoon coarsely ground black pepper
4 small skinless, boneless chicken-breast halves (about 1 pound)
3 tablespoons fresh lemon juice
3 tablespoons light mayonnaise
1 tablespoon Dijon mustard
1 teaspoon anchovy paste
1 small garlic clove, crushed with garlic press
½ cup grated Parmesan cheese
6 pitas (6- to 7-inch diameter)
8 cups sliced romaine lettuce (about ¾-pound head)

**1** Preheat broiler. In medium bowl, mix salt, 2 teaspoons olive oil, and ¼ teaspoon pepper. Add chicken and stir to coat. Place chicken on rack in broiling pan. Place pan in broiler at closest position to source of heat; broil chicken about 12 minutes, turning once, until juices run clear when thickest part is pierced with tip of knife. Transfer chicken to cutting board; cool 5 minutes or until easy to handle.

**2** Meanwhile, in large bowl, with fork, mix lemon juice, mayonnaise, mustard, anchovy paste, garlic, remaining 3 tablespoons olive oil, and remaining ¼ teaspoon pepper until blended; stir in Parmesan.

**3** With sharp knife, slit top third of each pita to form an opening. Thinly slice chicken. Add lettuce and chicken slices to dressing; toss well to coat. Fill pitas with salad. *Makes 6 sandwiches.*

Each sandwich: About 400 calories, 27 g protein, 36 g carbohydrate, 15 g total fat (3 g saturated), 2 g fiber, 52 mg cholesterol, 760 mg sodium.

## THAI CHICKEN BURRITOS

PREP: 15 MINUTES

A true fusion of Thai tastes and the convenience of the Mexican burrito.

*1 pound refrigerated roasted chicken breasts*
*¼ cup creamy peanut butter*
*2 tablespoons cayenne pepper sauce\**
*2 tablespoons honey*
*1 tablespoon Asian sesame oil*
*1 tablespoon soy sauce*
*1 tablespoon white wine vinegar*
*1 green onion, minced*
*2 medium plum tomatoes, diced*
*½ small cucumber, peeled and diced*
*4 (9-inch diameter) flour tortillas*
*2 cups thinly sliced iceberg lettuce*

**1** Discard skin and bones from chicken breasts; tear meat into shreds.

**2** In medium bowl, with wire whisk or fork, mix peanut butter, cayenne pepper sauce, honey, sesame oil, soy sauce, white wine vinegar, and green onion until blended. Stir in chicken, tomatoes, and cucumber.

**3** Top each tortilla with some sliced lettuce; spoon chicken mixture over lettuce down center of tortilla and roll tortilla to enclose filling.

*Cayenne pepper sauce is a milder variety of hot pepper sauce that adds tang and flavor, not just heat. Makes 4 burritos.

Each burrito: About 440 calories, 26 g protein, 41 g carbohydrate, 21 g total fat (4 g saturated), 3 g fiber, 72 mg cholesterol, 1240 mg sodium.

# Italian Chicken Sandwiches
🐓 🐓 🐓

PREP: 10 MINUTES / COOK: 5 MINUTES

1 small bunch arugula, stems trimmed (about
   1½ cups loosely packed)
½ cup mayonnaise
¼ cup freshly grated Parmesan or Romano cheese
½ teaspoon salt
¾ teaspoon coarsely ground black pepper
2 tablespoons all-purpose flour
6 large skinless, boneless chicken-breast halves
   (about 2¼ pounds)
2 tablespoons olive oil
6 large sandwich rolls
1 small head leaf lettuce, separated into leaves
1 jar (10 to 12 ounces) roasted red peppers,
   drained

**1** In food processor with knife blade attached or in blender, blend arugula, mayonnaise, Parmesan, ¼ teaspoon salt, and ¼ teaspoon pepper until arugula is finely chopped; set mixture aside.

**2** On waxed paper, mix flour, remaining ¼ teaspoon salt, and remaining ½ teaspoon pepper; use to coat chicken breasts.

**3** In 12-inch skillet, heat oil over medium-high heat until very hot. Add chicken and cook until lightly browned on both sides and juices run clear when pierced with tip of knife, about 5 minutes.

**4** To serve, slice each chicken breast horizontally in half. Slice each sandwich roll horizontally in half. Top bottom halves of rolls with lettuce leaves, sautéed chicken breasts, then roasted red peppers. Spread arugula mixture on top halves of sandwich rolls. *Makes 6 sandwiches.*

Each sandwich: About 660 calories, 49 g protein, 51 g carbohydrate, 29 g total fat (6 g saturated), 2 g fiber, 114 mg cholesterol, 1000 mg sodium.

# Spicy Guacamole & Chicken Roll-Ups

PREP: 30 MINUTES / COOK: 15 MINUTES

Don't miss this zesty guacamole—it's great with tortilla chips too.

2 teaspoons olive oil
4 small skinless, boneless chicken-breast halves
    (about 1 pound)
½ teaspoon salt
½ teaspoon coarsely ground black pepper
2 medium avocados (about 8 ounces each), peeled
    and cut into small chunks
1 medium tomato, diced
¼ cup loosely packed fresh cilantro leaves, coarsely
    chopped
4 teaspoons fresh lime juice
2 teaspoons finely chopped red onion
1 teaspoon adobo sauce from canned chipotle
    chiles* or 2 tablespoons green jalapeño sauce
4 burrito-size (10-inch diameter) flour tortillas,
    warmed
2 cups sliced iceberg lettuce

**1** In 10-inch skillet, heat olive oil over medium-high heat until very hot. Add chicken and sprinkle with ¼ teaspoon salt and ¼ teaspoon pepper. Cook chicken about 12 minutes, turning once, until juices run clear when thickest part is pierced with tip of knife. Transfer chicken to plate; cool 5 minutes or until easy to handle.

**2** Meanwhile, in medium bowl, with rubber spatula, gently stir avocados, tomato, cilantro, lime juice, red onion, adobo sauce, and remaining ¼ teaspoon salt and ¼ teaspoon pepper until blended.

**3** Pull chicken into thin shreds. Place tortillas on work surface; spread with guacamole. Place chicken, then lettuce on top of guacamole. Roll tortillas around filling. *Makes 4 sandwiches.*

*Canned chipotle chiles in adobo (smoked jalapeño chiles in a vinegary marinade) are available in some supermarkets and in Hispanic markets.

Each sandwich: About 475 calories, 33 g protein, 40 g carbohydrate, 21 g total fat (3 g saturated), 4 g fiber, 66 mg cholesterol, 745 mg sodium.

---

*Last-minute* DINNERS

## CHICKEN CUTLET HERO

PREP: 10 MINUTES / BAKE: 20 MINUTES

*1 long loaf Italian bread (8 ounces)*
*1 medium tomato*
*1 package (14 ounces) refrigerated, fully cooked,*
    *breaded chicken cutlets (4 cutlets)*
*1 cup bottled spaghetti sauce*
*¾ cup shredded mozzarella cheese*
*¼ cup large pitted Gaeta or Kalamata olives, sliced*

**1** Preheat oven to 400°F. Slice loaf of Italian bread horizontally in half. Wrap loaf in foil. Cut center part of tomato into thin slices; dice end pieces.

**2** Place chicken cutlets on ungreased cookie sheet. Bake chicken and Italian bread 15 minutes.

**3** Transfer chicken to plate. Unwrap Italian bread and return both halves to cookie sheet. Spread ½ cup spaghetti sauce on bottom half of bread. Alternately arrange tomato slices and chicken cutlets, overlapping, over spaghetti sauce, spooning 2 tablespoons spaghetti sauce on top of each chicken cutlet.

**4** Sprinkle cheese over hero; bake 5 minutes or until cheese melts. Sprinkle with sliced olives and diced tomato.

**5** Replace top half of bread. Cut hero into 4 pieces to serve. Makes 4 sandwiches.

Each serving: About 675 calories, 22 g protein, 61 g carbohydrate, 38 g total fat (10 g saturated), 3 g fiber, 52 mg cholesterol, 1840 mg sodium.

# Smoked Turkey & Mango Wraps

🐓 🐓 🐓

**PREP: 25 MINUTES PLUS CHILLING**

This sandwich is made with lahvash, the soft version of Armenian cracker bread, which ranges from 9 to 16 inches in diameter. The thin and pliable bread is especially good with creamy spreads, like goat cheese or guacamole. If you can't find lahvash, divide filling ingredients among four 8- to 10-inch flour tortillas.

1 large lime
¼ cup light mayonnaise
3 tablespoons mango chutney, chopped
½ teaspoon curry powder
⅛ teaspoon paprika
1 lahvash (half 14-ounce package soft Armenian flatbread)*
1 medium cucumber, peeled and thinly sliced
8 ounces thinly sliced smoked turkey breast
1 medium mango, peeled and finely chopped
6 large green-leaf-lettuce leaves

**1** Grate ¼ teaspoon peel and squeeze 1 tablespoon juice from lime. In small bowl, mix lime peel, lime juice, mayonnaise, chutney, curry, and paprika.

**2** Unfold lahvash; spread with mayonnaise mixture. Top with cucumber slices, smoked turkey, chopped mango, and lettuce. Roll lahvash jelly-roll fashion.

**3** Wrap lahvash roll in plastic wrap and refrigerate 2 to 4 hours to allow bread to soften.

*Smoked Turkey & Mango Wrap*

**4** To serve, trim ends, then cut lahvash roll into 4 pieces. *Makes 4 sandwiches.*

*If lahvash seems dry before filling, place between dampened paper towels 10 to 15 minutes to soften.

Each sandwich: About 375 calories, 18 g protein, 55 g carbohydrate, 7 g total fat (2 g saturated), 3 g fiber, 29 mg cholesterol, 940 mg sodium.

# Smoked Chicken & Apple Sandwiches

🐓🐓🐓

PREP: 15 MINUTES

If you can find chicken that's been smoked over applewood at your deli or specialty foods market, try making this sandwich with it. Or, if you can't find smoked chicken at all, make the sandwich with smoked turkey or smoked pork loin.

2 whole smoked boneless chicken breasts (about 1¼ pounds), skinned and torn into bite-size pieces
¼ cup drained hot-pepper rings*
2 tablespoons milk
⅓ cup plus 2 tablespoons mayonnaise
1 (12-inch diameter) round loaf unsliced whole-grain bread
1 medium red apple, peeled, cored, and cut into ¼-inch-thick slices
Lettuce leaves

**1** In medium bowl, stir together chicken, hot-pepper rings, milk, and ⅓ cup mayonnaise until chicken is well coated.

**2** Cut four ¾-inch-thick slices from center of loaf of bread. Reserve remaining bread for use another day.

**3** Place chicken salad on 2 slices of bread; top with apple slices and a few lettuce leaves. Spread each of the remaining 2 slices of bread with 1 tablespoon mayonnaise; place on top of sandwiches. Cut each sandwich in half. *Makes 4 sandwiches.*

*Hot-pepper rings are sold in jars and are available in the pickles section of the supermarket.

Each serving: About 500 calories, 32 g protein, 34 g carbohydrate, 27 g total fat (5 g saturated), 5 g fiber, 68 mg cholesterol, 1720 mg sodium.

## BACON & TOMATO TURKEY BURGERS

PREP: 20 MINUTES / COOK: 20 MINUTES

An unusual burger made from leftover turkey instead of ground turkey.

*6 slices bacon, diced*
*5 slices firm-textured white bread*
*2 cups finely minced cooked turkey (about ¾ pound)*
*¼ teaspoon salt*
*⅛ teaspoon coarsely ground black pepper*
*2 medium celery stalks, minced*
*1 small onion, grated*
*2 large eggs*
*3 tablespoons margarine or butter*
*6 kaiser rolls*
*Lettuce leaves*
*1 medium tomato, thinly sliced*

**1** In 12-inch skillet, cook bacon over medium-low heat until browned; transfer bacon to paper towels to drain; crumble bacon. Pour off all drippings from skillet; wipe skillet clean with paper towels; set aside.

**2** Tear 4 slices of bread into small pieces and place in large bowl. Add minced turkey, salt, pepper, celery, onion, eggs, and crumbled bacon; mix well. With hands, shape turkey mixture into six 3-inch-round patties.

**3** On waxed paper, chop remaining slice of bread into fine crumbs. Using hands, press crumbs onto patties to coat completely.

**4** In same skillet, melt margarine or butter over medium-high heat. Add patties and cook until lightly browned on both sides, about 10 minutes.

**5** To serve, slice each roll horizontally in half. Arrange lettuce leaves on bottom halves of rolls; top each with a burger and 1 or 2 tomato slices; replace tops of rolls. Makes 6 burgers.

Each burger: About 665 calories, 43 g protein, 66 g carbohydrate, 25 g total fat (6 g saturated), 4 g fiber, 180 mg cholesterol, 1145 mg sodium.

## LEMON-FLAVORED POTATO SALAD

PREP: 15 MINUTES / COOK: 30 MINUTES

Next time you bring the potato salad, surprise everyone with this lighter version that combines potatoes with cucumbers and spinach, dressed with a lemon-mustard vinaigrette.

*6 medium potatoes (about 2 pounds)*
*2 medium lemons*
*3 tablespoons extravirgin olive oil*
*1 tablespoon Dijon mustard*
*2 teaspoons sugar*
*1 teaspoon salt*
*½ teaspoon dried basil*
*½ teaspoon coarsely ground black pepper*
*2 medium cucumbers, each cut lengthwise in half,*
*    then crosswise into ¼-inch-thick slices*
*2 cups loosely packed spinach leaves*

1 In 5-quart Dutch oven or saucepot, heat unpeeled potatoes and enough *water* to cover to boiling over high heat. Reduce heat to low; cover and simmer 30 minutes or until potatoes are fork-tender. Drain; cool potatoes until easy to handle. Peel and cut potatoes into bite-size chunks.

2 Meanwhile, from lemons, grate 1 tablespoon peel and squeeze ¼ cup juice. In large bowl, with wire whisk or fork, mix lemon peel, lemon juice, olive oil, Dijon mustard, sugar, salt, basil, and ¼ teaspoon pepper.

3 Add potatoes, cucumbers, and spinach to dressing; toss to coat well. Spoon potato salad onto platter; sprinkle with remaining ¼ teaspoon pepper. Cover and refrigerate if not serving right away. Toss to serve. Makes 6 accompaniment servings.

Each serving: About 210 calories, 4 g protein, 33 g carbohydrate, 7 g total fat (1 g saturated), 4 g fiber, 0 mg cholesterol, 480 mg sodium.

# Chicken Burgers with Mustard Sauce

PREP: 25 MINUTES / COOK: 20 MINUTES

If you'd like, toast up some sandwich-size English muffins or some thick-sliced peasant bread to go with these burgers.

MUSTARD SAUCE:
¾ cup light mayonnaise
¼ cup chopped dill pickle
2 tablespoons prepared mustard
1 tablespoon ketchup
½ teaspoon hot pepper sauce

BURGERS:
2 tablespoons vegetable oil
1 medium celery stalk, minced
½ medium red or green pepper, minced
½ small onion, minced
1 pound ground chicken
1 large egg, separated
1 teaspoon Worcestershire sauce
¼ teaspoon salt
2 tablespoons plus ⅓ cup dried bread crumbs
¼ cup milk

1 Prepare Mustard Sauce: In small bowl, mix mayonnaise, dill pickle, prepared mustard, ketchup, and hot sauce; refrigerate.

2 Prepare Burgers: In nonstick 10-inch skillet, heat 1 tablespoon oil over medium heat. Add celery, pepper, and onion and cook until tender, stirring often. Set aside to cool slightly.

3 In large bowl, mix chicken, egg yolk, Worcestershire, salt, 2 tablespoons bread crumbs, and *1 tablespoon water*. Stir vegetable mixture into chicken mixture. Shape chicken mixture into four ¾-inch-thick patties.

4 In pie plate, mix milk and egg white. On waxed paper, place remaining ⅓ cup bread crumbs. Dip patties first into milk mixture, then into bread crumbs.

5 In nonstick 10-inch skillet, heat remaining 1 tablespoon oil over medium heat until very hot. Add patties and cook about 10 minutes or until cooked throughout, turning once. Serve patties with Mustard Sauce. *Makes 4 burgers.*

Each burger: About 485 calories, 24 g protein, 17 g carbohydrate, 35 g total fat (7 g saturated), 1 g fiber, 164 mg cholesterol, 1015 mg sodium.

# Turkey Burgers with Orange Teriyaki Sauce

🐓 🐓 🐓

PREP: 10 MINUTES / COOK: 15 MINUTES

Without buns, these tasty ground-turkey patties weigh in at a skinny 190 calories per portion, but if you'd prefer, serve the burgers on kaiser rolls or hamburger buns.

4 teaspoons olive oil
1 large celery stalk, minced
½ small onion, minced
½ teaspoon salt
½ teaspoon ground ginger
1 pound lean ground turkey breast
2 teaspoons prepared white horseradish
2 tablespoons chopped fresh parsley leaves
⅓ cup orange juice
1 tablespoon teriyaki sauce
⅓ teaspoon cornstarch

**1** In nonstick 12-inch skillet, heat 2 teaspoons oil over medium-high heat. Add celery, onion, salt, and ground ginger and cook until vegetables are tender. Set aside to cool slightly.

**2** In medium bowl, mix ground turkey, sautéed vegetable mixture, horseradish, and 1 tablespoon parsley until blended. With slightly dampened hands, shape turkey mixture into four 1-inch-thick round patties.

**3** In same skillet, heat remaining 2 teaspoons oil over medium-high heat until very hot. Add turkey patties and cook until golden brown on both sides and turkey loses its pink color throughout, about 10 minutes. Transfer turkey burgers to plate; keep warm.

**4** Meanwhile, in cup, mix orange juice, teriyaki sauce, cornstarch, remaining 1 tablespoon parsley, and *⅓ cup water* until smooth; stir into skillet. Heat to boiling over high heat, stirring to loosen browned bits; boil 1 minute. Serve turkey burgers with hot orange teriyaki sauce. *Makes 4 burgers.*

Each burger: About 190 calories, 29 g protein, 5 g carbohydrate, 5 g total fat (1 g saturated), 0.5 g fiber, 70 mg cholesterol, 530 mg sodium.

# Salsa Turkey Burgers with Sautéed Mushrooms

PREP: 10 MINUTES / BROIL: 10 MINUTES

Make a quick and easy corn salad to go with this burger. Drain a can of whole-kernel corn and toss it with chopped cilantro and a simple vinaigrette of equal parts olive oil and fresh lime juice. Season to taste with salt and pepper.

1 pound ground turkey breast
¼ cup plus ⅓ cup bottled mild to medium salsa
1 tablespoon vegetable oil
¾ pound mushrooms, sliced
¼ teaspoon salt
2 tablespoons mayonnaise
4 kaiser rolls or hamburger buns

**1** Preheat broiler. In bowl, mix ground turkey and ¼ cup salsa; shape into four ½-inch-thick round patties. Place patties on rack in broiling pan. Place pan in broiler at closest position to heat source; broil patties 8 to 10 minutes until they lose their pink color throughout, turning patties once.

**2** Meanwhile, in 10-inch skillet, heat oil over high heat. Add mushrooms and salt and cook until lightly browned, stirring frequently.

**3** In small bowl, mix mayonnaise and remaining ⅓ cup salsa.

**4** To serve, cut each kaiser roll horizontally in half. Spread mayonnaise mixture on bottom halves of rolls. Top with turkey burgers and sautéed mushrooms. *Makes 4 sandwiches.*

Each sandwich: About 405 calories, 35 g protein, 37 g carbohydrate, 12 g total fat (2 g saturated), 2 g fiber, 74 mg cholesterol, 920 mg sodium.

# Braises & Stews

# Buffalo Chicken Drumsticks

PREP: 5 MINUTES / COOK: 40 MINUTES

Serve these with celery stalks and a bottled blue-cheese salad dressing to dip them in.

12 medium chicken drumsticks (about 3 pounds)
3 tablespoons all-purpose flour
2 tablespoons vegetable oil
1 medium onion, minced
¾ cup bottled hot pepper sauce
1 teaspoon cornstarch

1 In sturdy plastic bag, toss chicken drumsticks, half at a time, with flour. In 12-inch skillet, heat oil over medium-high heat until very hot. Add drumsticks and cook until browned on all sides, transferring drumsticks to plate as they brown.

2 Add onion to skillet and cook until golden, about 5 minutes; return chicken to skillet. In 1-cup glass measuring cup, stir hot pepper sauce, cornstarch, and ¼ *cup water* until smooth. Pour pepper-sauce mixture over drumsticks; heat to boiling. Reduce heat to low; cover and simmer 25 minutes, occasionally spooning sauce over chicken, until drumsticks are fork-tender.

3 To serve, arrange drumsticks on platter; spoon sauce over. *Makes 6 main-dish servings.*

Each serving: About 320 calories, 30 g protein, 6 g carbohydrate, 18 g total fat (4 g saturated), 0.5 g fiber, 123 mg cholesterol, 915 mg sodium.

# Chicken Osso-Buco Style

PREP: 10 MINUTES / COOK: 40 MINUTES

Classic Italian *osso buco* is made with veal shanks braised in a flavorful tomato sauce. In our version, we made the same kind of sauce but substituted skinless chicken thighs for the veal shanks, so the dish is lighter but still excellent!

2 tablespoons vegetable oil
8 medium chicken thighs (about 2½ pounds), skin removed
½ teaspoon salt
8 ounces carrots, peeled and diced
1 large onion, diced
1 large celery stalk, diced
1 can (14½ to 16 ounces) stewed tomatoes
Chopped parsley and grated lemon peel for garnish

1 In 12-inch skillet, heat oil over medium-high heat until very hot. Add chicken thighs and salt and cook until chicken is golden on all sides. Transfer chicken to bowl.

2 Add carrots, onion, and celery to skillet and cook until lightly browned. Return chicken to skillet; stir in stewed tomatoes. Heat to boiling over high heat. Reduce heat to low; cover and simmer 25 minutes or until chicken is fork-tender and juices run clear when chicken is pierced with tip of knife. Sprinkle with chopped parsley and grated lemon peel. *Makes 4 main-dish servings.*

Each serving: About 330 calories, 34 g protein, 18 g carbohydrate, 14 g total fat (3 g saturated), 4 g fiber, 135 mg cholesterol, 700 mg sodium.

# Chicken Pot Roast

### ♦ ♦ ♦

PREP: 10 MINUTES / COOK: 50 MINUTES

Beef pot roast with vegetables is an easy one-dish dinner, but high in fat. We cut back on fat by pot-roasting a chicken (with the skin removed). Cooking in liquid keeps the chicken—even without skin—from drying out.

8 ounces small white onions
3 tablespoons all-purpose flour
1 teaspoon salt
3 tablespoons olive oil
1 whole chicken (about 3½ pounds), cut into eight pieces, skin removed
2 cans (14½ to 16 ounces each) stewed tomatoes
1 tablespoon sugar
1 teaspoon Worcestershire sauce
1 small rutabaga (about 12 ounces), peeled and cut into 1½-inch chunks
1 pound carrots, peeled and cut into 2" by ½" pieces
10 ounces mushrooms, each cut in half if large

**1** Peel onions, leaving a little of the root end to help them hold their shape during cooking; cut each lengthwise in half.

**2** In large bowl, combine flour and salt; add chicken and toss to coat.

**3** In 8-quart Dutch oven, heat 2 tablespoons oil over medium-high heat until very hot. Add chicken quarters and cook until browned on both sides; return chicken to bowl.

**4** Add remaining 1 tablespoon oil to Dutch oven. Add onions and cook until browned. Add stewed tomatoes, sugar, Worcestershire, rutabaga, carrots, mushrooms, and chicken with any juice in bowl. Heat to boiling over high heat. Reduce heat to low; cover and simmer 35 minutes or until chicken loses its pink color throughout and vegetables are tender. *Makes 6 main-dish servings.*

Each serving: About 520 calories, 48 g protein, 46 g carbohydrate, 17 g total fat (3 g saturated), 9 g fiber, 133 mg cholesterol, 1280 mg sodium.

---

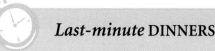

*Last-minute* DINNERS

# CHICKEN & SAUSAGE STEW

PREP: 10 MINUTES / COOK: 25 MINUTES

*1 tablespoon vegetable oil*
*1 pound fully cooked weisswurst (veal sausage) or bratwurst, cut into 2-inch pieces*
*1 can (14½ ounces) chicken broth or 1¾ cups homemade (page 11)*
*1 bag (16 ounces) frozen baby carrots*
*1 package (9 ounces) frozen cut green beans*
*½ teaspoon dried thyme*
*1 refrigerated roasted whole chicken (2½ to 3 pounds), skin removed, cut into 10 pieces*
*3 cans (16 to 19 ounces) white kidney beans (cannellini), undrained*

**1** In 5-quart Dutch oven, heat oil over medium-high heat. Add weisswurst and cook until well browned, about 10 minutes.

**2** Add broth, carrots, green beans, and thyme to pan; heat to boiling over high heat. Reduce heat to low; cover and simmer 10 minutes.

**3** Stir in chicken and white kidney beans with their liquid; heat to boiling over high heat. Reduce heat to low; cover and simmer 5 minutes longer or until chicken and beans are heated through. Makes 8 main-dish servings.

Each serving: About 485 calories, 33 g protein, 36 g carbohydrate, 23 g total fat (7 g saturated), 9 g fiber, 106 mg cholesterol, 1450 mg sodium.

# Chicken with Olives

PREP: 10 MINUTES / COOK: 45 MINUTES

An easy weeknight entrée that's impressive enough for company.

1 tablespoon olive oil
8 large skinless chicken thighs (about 2¼ pounds)
½ teaspoon salt
2 small onions (about 4 ounces each), each cut into 6 wedges
¾ cup chicken broth
½ cup Kalamata olives
1 teaspoon chopped fresh thyme or ¼ teaspoon dried thyme
2 teaspoons all-purpose flour

**1** In nonstick 12-inch skillet, heat olive oil over medium-high heat until very hot. Add chicken; sprinkle with ¼ teaspoon salt and cook until lightly browned. Transfer chicken to plate.

**2** Add onions to skillet and cook until golden, shaking skillet occasionally.

**3** Add chicken broth, olives, thyme, and chicken with any juices in plate. Reduce heat to low; cover and simmer 20 to 25 minutes until juices run clear when chicken is pierced with tip of knife.

**4** Transfer chicken to warm platter. In cup, mix flour, remaining ¼ teaspoon salt, and *1 tablespoon water* until smooth. Pour flour mixture into skillet, whisking constantly. Heat to boiling over medium-high heat; boil 1 minute until sauce thickens slightly. Pour sauce over chicken. ***Makes 4 main-dish servings.***

Each serving: About 335 calories, 38 g protein, 8 g carbohydrate, 16 g total fat (3 g saturated), 1 g fiber, 155 mg cholesterol, 950 mg sodium.

---

## GREAT GO-WITHS
## OLIVE & WALNUT BREAD

PREP: 25 MINUTES PLUS RISING TIME / BAKE: 35 TO 40 MINUTES

*1 package quick-rise yeast*
*1 teaspoon salt*
*1 teaspoon sugar*
*½ teaspoon coarsely ground black pepper*
*About 4½ cups all-purpose flour*
*2 tablespoons extravirgin olive oil*
*¾ cup pitted Kalamata olives, chopped*
*4 ounces walnuts, coarsely chopped and toasted*

**1** In large bowl, combine yeast, salt, sugar, pepper, and 2 cups flour. In saucepan, heat olive oil and *1½ cups water* over low heat until very warm (125° to 130°F.). With wooden spoon, stir liquid into dry ingredients until well blended. Stir in 2 cups flour to make a soft dough.

**2** Turn dough onto floured surface and knead until smooth and elastic, about 5 minutes, working in more flour (about ½ cup) while kneading. Shape dough into a ball; cover with plastic wrap and let rest 10 minutes for easier shaping. Grease large cookie sheet.

**3** With floured rolling pin, roll dough to 15" by 12" rectangle; sprinkle with olives and walnuts. From 12-inch side, tightly roll dough; pinch seam to seal; place, seam-side-down, on cookie sheet; tuck ends under.

*Olive & Walnut Bread*

**4** Preheat oven to 400°F. Cut diagonal slashes in top of loaf. Cover and let rise in warm place (80° to 85°F.) for 15 minutes. Dust top of loaf with flour. Bake 35 to 40 minutes until bread sounds hollow when lightly tapped and top is browned. Cool bread on wire rack slightly to serve warm. Or, cool completely. Makes 1 loaf or 16 servings.

Each serving: About 220 calories, 5 g protein, 31 g carbohydrate, 8 g total fat (1 g saturated), 1 g fiber, 0 mg cholesterol, 260 mg sodium.

# Chicken & Sausage with Artichokes

PREP: 10 MINUTES / COOK: 40 MINUTES

1 pound hot Italian turkey sausage links
1 whole chicken (about 3½ pounds), cut up
1 pound large mushrooms, each cut into quarters, skin removed
1 large onion, diced
4 bottled hot or mild cherry peppers
½ teaspoon salt
1 can (13¾ ounces) artichoke hearts, drained

**1** With fork, prick sausages several times. In 8-quart Dutch oven or 12-inch skillet, cook sausages over medium-high heat until browned on all sides. Transfer sausages to large bowl.

**2** Add chicken, half at a time, to Dutch oven and cook over medium-high heat until golden brown. Transfer chicken to bowl with sausages.

**3** Add mushrooms and onion to Dutch oven and cook, stirring frequently, until vegetables are brown; with slotted spoon, transfer vegetables to bowl with sausages and chicken.

**4** Discard any remaining drippings in Dutch oven. Return ingredients in bowl to Dutch oven. Stir in cherry peppers, salt, and *½ cup water*; heat to boiling over high heat. Reduce heat to low; cover and simmer 20 to 25 minutes until chicken is fork-tender and juices run clear when chicken is pierced with tip of knife. Stir in artichoke hearts; heat through.

**5** To serve, skim fat from liquid in Dutch oven. *Makes 6 main-dish servings.*

Each serving: About 405 calories, 34 g protein, 36 g carbohydrate, 15 g total fat (4 g saturated), 9 g fiber, 103 mg cholesterol, 1500 mg sodium.

# Dijon Chicken with Orzo

PREP: 10 MINUTES / COOK: 25 MINUTES

Although orzo makes an especially satisfying side dish, you could also make this with another small pasta shape (try acini di pepe or tubettini) or shift gears altogether and serve it with rice or couscous.

1 tablespoon vegetable oil
8 medium chicken thighs (about 2½ pounds), skin removed
1 cup milk
¼ cup Dijon mustard with seeds
2 tablespoons all-purpose flour
½ teaspoon salt
1¼ cups orzo
⅓ cup pimiento-stuffed olives, minced

**1** In nonstick 12-inch skillet, heat oil over medium-high heat until very hot. Add chicken thighs and cook 10 minutes or until browned.

**2** In 2-cup measuring cup, mix milk, Dijon mustard, flour, salt, and *1 cup water*. Stir mustard mixture into drippings in skillet and heat to boiling over high heat. Reduce heat to low; cover and simmer, stirring occasionally, until chicken thighs are fork-tender, about 15 minutes.

**3** Meanwhile, prepare orzo as label directs. Drain; stir in minced olives.

**4** Serve chicken and sauce on a bed of orzo. *Makes 4 main-dish servings.*

Each serving: About 500 calories, 41 g protein, 46 g carbohydrate, 14 g total fat (4 g saturated), 2 g fiber, 143 mg cholesterol, 1090 mg sodium.

# Mediterranean Chicken

PREP: 15 MINUTES / COOK: 40 MINUTES

The polenta for this Mediterranean dish is a perfect companion, but you could substitute rice or pasta.

2 tablespoons olive or vegetable oil
1 large onion, diced
2 tablespoons all-purpose flour
½ teaspoon dried basil
8 large chicken drumsticks (about 2¼ pounds), skin removed
1 can (14½ to 16 ounces) stewed tomatoes
¼ cup pimiento-stuffed olives, each cut in half
¼ cup Kalamata olives, pitted and coarsely chopped
1 medium tomato, diced
1 teaspoon salt
⅔ cup yellow cornmeal

1 In nonstick 12-inch skillet, heat 1 tablespoon olive oil over medium heat. Add onion and cook until tender. Transfer onion to bowl.

2 On waxed paper, mix flour and basil; use to coat chicken drumsticks. Add remaining 1 tablespoon olive oil to skillet and heat until very hot. Add chicken drumsticks and cook until lightly browned.

3 Add stewed tomatoes, pimiento-stuffed olives, Kalamata olives, diced tomato, sautéed onion, and ½ cup water to skillet; heat to boiling over mediu heat. Reduce heat to low; cover and simmer 20 minutes or until juices run clear when chicken is pierced with tip of knife.

4 Meanwhile, prepare polenta: In 3-quart saucepan, heat salt and 3½ cups water to boiling over high heat. With wire whisk, gradually stir in cornmeal, beating constantly until mixture is very thick. Reduce heat to low; simmer 1 minute, stirring constantly.

5 On 4 dinner plates, serve chicken drumsticks with sauce alongside of polenta. *Makes 4 main-dish servings.*

Each serving: About 420 calories, 33 g protein, 36 g carbohydrate, 16 g total fat (3 g saturated), 4 g fiber, 107 mg cholesterol, 1305 mg sodium.

---

CREATIVE LEFTOVERS

# QUICK CASSOULET

PREP: 10 MINUTES / COOK: 25 MINUTES

1 pound kielbasa, cut into ½-inch slices
3 teaspoons vegetable oil
1 pound carrots, peeled and cut into 1-inch pieces
2 large onions, sliced
2 medium celery stalks, sliced
2 cups bite-size pieces cooked chicken, preferably dark meat
3 cans (16 to 19 ounces each) white kidney beans (cannellini), rinsed and drained
1 can (14½ to 16 ounces) tomatoes
1 can (14½ ounces) chicken broth or 1¾ cups homemade (page 11)
1 bay leaf
½ cup fresh bread crumbs (1 slice white bread)
1 tablespoon plus ½ cup chopped fresh parsley leaves

1 In 5-quart Dutch oven or saucepot, cook kielbasa over medium heat until browned; transfer to plate.

2 Add 2 teaspoons oil to Dutch oven and heat over medium-high heat. Add carrots, onions, and celery and cook until browned and tender.

3 Return kielbasa to Dutch oven. Add chicken, white kidney beans, tomatoes with their juice, chicken broth, bay leaf, and 1¾ cups water. Heat to boiling over high heat. Reduce heat to low; simmer, uncovered, 15 minutes to blend flavors.

4 Meanwhile, in 1-quart saucepan, heat remaining 1 teaspoon oil over medium-high heat. Add bread crumbs and 1 tablespoon parsley and cook until bread crumbs are golden.

5 To serve, discard bay leaf. Stir remaining ½ cup parsley into bean mixture and sprinkle with toasted bread crumbs. Makes 8 main-dish servings.

Each serving: About 465 calories, 29 g protein, 37 g carbohydrate, 23 g total fat (7 g saturated), 11 g fiber, 72 mg cholesterol, 1230 mg sodium.

# Ragout of Chicken, White Beans & Tomatoes

PREP: 15 MINUTES / COOK: 45 MINUTES

2 tablespoons vegetable oil
6 large chicken thighs (about 2½ pounds), skin removed
¾ teaspoon salt
3 medium celery stalks, cut into 1-inch-thick slices
3 medium carrots, peeled and cut into ¼-inch-thick slices
1 large onion, chopped
¼ teaspoon coarsely ground black pepper
1 garlic clove, crushed with garlic press or finely minced
1 can (14½ to 16 ounces) stewed tomatoes
2 cans (16 ounces each) Great Northern beans, rinsed and drained
¼ cup chopped fresh basil leaves or 1½ teaspoons dried basil

1 In 8-quart Dutch oven, heat oil over medium-high heat until very hot. Add chicken thighs and ¼ teaspoon salt and cook until chicken is golden brown on all sides, transferring chicken thighs to plate as they brown.

2 Add celery, carrots, onion, pepper, and remaining ½ teaspoon salt to Dutch oven and cook, stirring occasionally, until vegetables are tender-crisp and golden brown. Stir in garlic; cook, stirring, 1 minute.

3 Add stewed tomatoes, using spoon to break up tomatoes. Return chicken thighs to Dutch oven; heat to boiling over high heat. Reduce heat to medium-low; cover and simmer 25 minutes or until chicken is tender and juices run clear when chicken is pierced with tip of knife.

4 Transfer chicken thighs to platter. Stir Great Northern beans and chopped basil into Dutch oven; heat through.

5 To serve, spoon white-bean and tomato mixture around chicken thighs on platter. *Makes 6 main-dish servings.*

Each serving: About 310 calories, 29 g protein, 27 g carbohydrate, 10 g total fat (2 g saturated), 7 g fiber, 90 mg cholesterol, 820 mg sodium.

# Chicken with Ragout of Summer Squash

PREP: 15 MINUTES / COOK: 50 MINUTES

1 whole chicken (about 3½ pounds), cut up, skin removed
¾ teaspoon salt
3 tablespoons vegetable oil
½ pound carrots, peeled and cut into 2½-inch-long pencil-thin strips
1 medium onion, cut into ¼-inch slices
1 medium zucchini (about 10 ounces), cut into 1½-inch chunks
1 medium yellow straightneck squash (about 10 ounces), cut into 1½-inch chunks
1 package (10 ounces) medium mushrooms, each cut in half if large
¼ cup orange juice
1 tablespoon all-purpose flour
1 can (14½ to 16 ounces) stewed tomatoes
2 tablespoons chopped fresh basil leaves

1 Sprinkle chicken with ½ teaspoon salt. In 12-inch skillet, heat 2 tablespoons oil over medium-high heat until very hot. Add chicken and cook until golden on all sides. Transfer chicken to plate.

2 Add remaining 1 tablespoon oil to skillet. Add carrots, onion, and ⅛ teaspoon salt and cook until vegetables are browned and tender-crisp. With slotted spoon, transfer carrot mixture to bowl. Add zucchini, yellow squash, mushrooms, and remaining ⅛ teaspoon salt and cook until vegetables are lightly browned and tender-crisp; transfer to bowl with carrots and onion.

3 In 1-cup measuring cup, with fork, stir together orange juice, flour, and ¾ cup water. Stir orange-juice mixture and stewed tomatoes into skillet; heat to boiling over high heat. Return chicken to skillet; heat to boiling. Reduce heat to low; cover and simmer 25 minutes.

4 Stir in vegetables; heat to boiling over high heat. Reduce heat to low; cover and simmer 5 to 10 minutes longer until vegetables are tender and juices run clear when chicken is pierced with a knife. Stir in chopped basil. *Makes 4 main-dish servings.*

Each serving: About 440 calories, 46 g protein, 28 g carbohydrate, 17 g total fat (3 g saturated), 6 g fiber, 134 mg cholesterol, 850 mg sodium.

# Chicken with Creamy Mustard Sauce

PREP: 15 MINUTES / COOK: 45 MINUTES

1 tablespoon margarine or butter
1 pound medium mushrooms, thinly sliced
3 teaspoons vegetable oil
1 large onion, diced
4 medium chicken-breast halves (about 2½ pounds), skin removed
½ teaspoon salt
1 package (9 ounces) frozen artichoke hearts, thawed
1 cup half-and-half or light cream
¼ cup Dijon mustard with seeds
1 tablespoon chopped fresh parsley leaves

**1** In nonstick 12-inch skillet, melt margarine or butter over medium-high heat. Add mushrooms and cook 15 minutes or until well browned and liquid evaporates from skillet. Transfer mushrooms to bowl.

**2** In same skillet, heat 1 teaspoon oil over medium heat. Add onion and cook until tender and golden. Transfer to bowl with mushrooms.

**3** In skillet, heat remaining 2 teaspoons oil over medium-high heat until very hot. Add chicken breasts, meat-side down, and cook, covered, 10 to 12 minutes until chicken is golden. Turn chicken breasts over. Add mushrooms, onion, salt, artichoke hearts, and *½ cup water*; heat to boiling. Reduce heat to medium and cook chicken breasts, covered, 5 minutes longer or until juices run clear when thickest part of chicken breast is pierced with tip of knife.

**4** Reduce heat to medium-low. Stir in half-and-half and Dijon mustard; heat through, occasionally spooning creamy mustard sauce in skillet over chicken (do not boil or mixture will curdle). Sprinkle chicken breasts with parsley. *Makes 4 main-dish servings.*

Each serving: About 425 calories, 49 g protein, 18 g carbohydrate, 16 g total fat (6 g saturated), 6 g fiber, 130 mg cholesterol, 865 mg sodium.

# Skillet Chicken with White Wine

PREP: 15 MINUTES / COOK: 30 MINUTES

1 tablespoon olive or vegetable oil
9 medium chicken thighs (3 pounds total), skin removed, each cut in half
2 jumbo onions (1 pound each), sliced
1 pound medium red potatoes, cut into 2-inch chunks
1 cup chicken broth
½ cup dry white wine
1 teaspoon dried thyme
½ teaspoon coarsely ground black pepper
8 Kalamata olives
1 small bunch spinach, tough stems trimmed

**1** In nonstick 12-inch skillet, heat oil over high heat until very hot. Add chicken thighs and cook until browned on both sides.

**2** Add onions, potatoes, chicken broth, white wine, thyme, pepper, and olives; heat to boiling over high heat. Reduce heat to low; cover and simmer about 20 minutes or until juices run clear when chicken is pierced with tip of knife and vegetables are tender.

**3** Stir in spinach; cook 1 to 2 minutes until spinach just wilts. *Makes 6 main-dish servings.*

Each serving: About 335 calories, 29 g protein, 29 g carbohydrate, 10 g total fat (2 g saturated), 4 g fiber, 107 mg cholesterol, 435 mg sodium.

*Chicken with Creamy Mustard Sauce* ➤

# Turkey & Shrimp Blanquette

🐔 🐔 🐔

PREP: 25 MINUTES / COOK: 1 HOUR 20 MINUTES

This creamy stew goes elegant when served in a chafing dish as a party-buffet entrée. Pair it with rice, noodles, or a basket of hot-from-the-oven biscuits so no one misses a drop of the delicious sauce.

3 medium onions
1 pound carrots
1 large celery stalk, cut into ½-inch-thick slices
1 turkey-breast half (about 2½ pounds)
½ cup dry white wine
10 black peppercorns
1 whole clove
2 tablespoons margarine or butter
12 ounces mushrooms, cut into ¼-inch-thick slices
½ teaspoon salt
⅓ cup all-purpose flour
2 cups milk
1½ pounds large shrimp, shelled and deveined
1 package (10 ounces) frozen peas
2 tablespoons chopped fresh dill

**1** Cut 1 onion and 1 carrot into ½-inch-thick slices. In 5-quart Dutch oven or saucepot, combine sliced onion, carrot, celery, turkey-breast half, wine, peppercorns, clove, and *4 cups water*. Heat to boiling over high heat. Reduce heat to low; cover and simmer 30 minutes or until turkey loses its pink color throughout, turning turkey breast occasionally.

**2** Meanwhile, dice remaining 2 onions. Cut remaining carrots diagonally into ⅛-inch-thick slices.

**3** Transfer turkey breast to bowl; set aside until cool enough to handle. Discard skin and bones from turkey. Cut turkey into bite-size chunks. Return turkey chunks to bowl.

**4** While turkey is cooling, strain turkey broth through sieve from Dutch oven into 4-quart saucepan; discard vegetable mixture. Set Dutch oven aside. Heat turkey broth to boiling over high heat. Reduce heat to medium; cook until turkey broth is reduced to 2 cups, about 30 minutes.

**5** In same Dutch oven, melt 1 tablespoon margarine or butter over high heat. Add carrots, mushrooms, and ¼ teaspoon salt and cook until mushrooms are golden and carrots are tender; transfer to bowl with turkey.

**6** Add remaining 1 tablespoon margarine or butter to Dutch oven and melt over medium heat. Add diced onions and remaining ¼ teaspoon salt and cook until onions are tender but not browned, about 15 minutes. Stir flour into onions; cook 1 minute.

**7** Gradually stir milk and turkey broth into onion mixture in Dutch oven; heat to boiling over high heat. Reduce heat to low; simmer, stirring occasionally,

---

**GREAT GO-WITHS**

## MARY'S SWEET DROP BISCUITS

PREP: 10 MINUTES / BAKE: 12 TO 15 MINUTES

*3 cups all-purpose flour*
*½ cup sugar*
*5 teaspoons baking powder*
*¾ teaspoon cream of tartar*
*½ teaspoon salt*
*¾ cup shortening*
*1¼ cups milk*
*2 teaspoons vanilla extract*

**1** Preheat oven to 425°F. Grease 2 cookie sheets.

**2** In large bowl, combine flour, sugar, baking powder, cream of tartar, and salt. With pastry blender or two knives used scissor-fashion, cut in shortening until mixture resembles coarse crumbs. Stir in milk and vanilla extract; quickly mix until just combined.

**3** Drop dough by ¼ cups, 2 inches apart, onto cookie sheets to make 16 biscuits.

**4** Place cookie sheets on 2 oven racks; bake biscuits 12 to 15 minutes until golden, rotating cookie sheets between upper and lower racks halfway through baking time. Serve warm. Or, if not serving right away, cool biscuits on wire rack. Store in tightly covered container to reheat before serving. Makes 16 biscuits.

Each biscuit: About 215 calories, 3 g protein, 26 g carbohydrate, 11 g total fat (3 g saturated), 0.5 g fiber, 3 mg cholesterol, 235 mg sodium.

until sauce thickens slightly, about 1 minute. Stir in shrimp, turkey chunks, carrots, mushrooms, and frozen peas; heat to boiling over high heat. Reduce heat to low; simmer 1 minute or until shrimp turn opaque throughout and blanquette is heated through. Stir in chopped dill. *Makes 10 main-dish servings.*

Each serving: About 285 calories, 39 g protein, 19 g carbohydrate, 6 g total fat (2 g saturated), 4 g fiber, 147 mg cholesterol, 345 mg sodium.

# Braised Chicken & Lentils

🐓 🐓 🐓

PREP: 15 MINUTES / COOK: 50 MINUTES

3 tablespoons olive or vegetable oil
4 large chicken legs (about 2½ pounds), skin removed
2 large carrots, peeled and diced
2 small celery stalks, diced
1 medium onion, diced
2 garlic cloves, minced
2 teaspoons curry powder
1 cup lentils
½ teaspoon salt
2 cans (14½ to 16 ounces each) stewed tomatoes
¼ cup chopped fresh parsley leaves

**1** In 5-quart Dutch oven, heat 2 tablespoons oil over medium-high heat until very hot. Add chicken legs and cook until browned on both sides. Transfer chicken to plate. Add remaining 1 tablespoon oil to Dutch oven. Add carrots, celery, onion, and garlic and cook until lightly browned. Stir in curry powder; cook 1 minute.

**2** Add lentils, salt, and *3 cups water*; heat to boiling over high heat. Reduce heat to low; cover and simmer 20 minutes or until lentils are almost tender.

**3** Stir in stewed tomatoes; return chicken to skillet. Heat to boiling over high heat. Reduce heat to low; cover and simmer 20 minutes or until lentils are tender and juices run clear when chicken is pierced with tip of knife. Stir in parsley. *Makes 4 main-dish servings.*

Each serving: About 590 calories, 56 g protein, 53 g carbohydrate, 19 g total fat (3 g saturated), 11 g fiber, 154 mg cholesterol, 970 mg sodium.

# Chicken Mole

🐓 🐓 🐓

PREP: 10 MINUTES / COOK: 45 MINUTES

Mole is a thick, rich, and spicy Mexican sauce traditionally made from a blend of chiles, ground seeds or nuts, spices, and a small amount of unsweetened chocolate. We've adapted the traditional mole sauce, using supermarket ingredients. Serve with rice.

1 can (14½ ounces) diced tomatoes
1 can (4 to 4½ ounces) chopped mild green chiles
½ cup whole blanched almonds
½ small onion, cut into chunks
1 small garlic clove
1 tablespoon chili powder
1 teaspoon ground cumin
1 teaspoon ground coriander
1 teaspoon salt
¾ teaspoon ground cinnamon
½ teaspoon sugar
1 tablespoon olive oil
3 pounds bone-in chicken parts such as thighs, drumsticks, and/or breast halves, skin removed
½ ounce (½ square) unsweetened chocolate, chopped
2 tablespoons chopped fresh cilantro

**1** In blender or food processor with knife blade attached, blend diced tomatoes, chopped chiles, almonds, onion, garlic, chili powder, cumin, coriander, salt, cinnamon, and sugar until smooth.

**2** In nonstick 12-inch skillet, heat oil over medium-high heat until very hot. Add chicken and cook until golden; transfer to plate.

**3** Add sauce, chopped chocolate, and *¼ cup water* to skillet; cook, stirring, until chocolate melts. Return chicken to skillet; heat to boiling. Reduce heat to low; cover and simmer 30 to 35 minutes until juices run clear when chicken is pierced with tip of knife. Sprinkle with cilantro to serve. *Makes 6 main-dish servings.*

Each serving: About 265 calories, 27 g protein, 9 g carbohydrate, 14 g total fat (3 g saturated), 3 g fiber, 76 mg cholesterol, 720 mg sodium.

# Chicken Ratatouille

🐓🐓🐓

PREP: 10 MINUTES / COOK: 50 MINUTES

3 tablespoons olive or vegetable oil

1 whole chicken (about 3½ pounds), cut up, skin removed

1 medium onion, diced

1 medium eggplant (about 1¼ pounds), cut into 1½-inch chunks

½ pound medium mushrooms, each cut in half

1 large yellow pepper, cut into 1½-inch pieces

1 medium zucchini, cut into 1½-inch chunks

1 can (14½ ounces) tomatoes

2 teaspoons sugar

1½ teaspoons salt

½ teaspoon dried oregano

½ teaspoon coarsely ground black pepper

1 can (10½ ounces) garbanzo beans, rinsed and drained

**1** In 8-quart Dutch oven, heat 1 tablespoon olive oil over medium-high heat until very hot. Add chicken and cook until browned on all sides, transferring pieces to plate as they brown.

**2** Add 1 tablespoon oil to Dutch oven. Add onion and cook until tender and golden. Add eggplant; cook, stirring frequently, about 5 minutes or until eggplant is tender-crisp. Transfer eggplant mixture to bowl.

**3** In same Dutch oven, heat remaining 1 tablespoon oil over high heat. Add mushrooms, yellow pepper, and zucchini and cook, stirring frequently, until tender-crisp and lightly browned, about 5 minutes.

**4** Add tomatoes with their juice, sugar, salt, oregano, black pepper, and *¼ cup water*. Return chicken and eggplant mixture to Dutch oven; heat to boiling over high heat. Reduce heat to low; cover and simmer 25 minutes or until chicken and eggplant are fork-tender, stirring mixture occasionally. Stir in garbanzo beans; heat through. ***Makes 6 main-dish servings.***

Each serving: About 320 calories, 32 g protein, 21 g carbohydrate, 12 g total fat (2 g saturated), 5 g fiber, 89 mg cholesterol, 855 mg sodium.

*Chicken Ratatouille*

# Balsamic Chicken with Baby Eggplants

🐓🐓🐓

PREP: 15 MINUTES / COOK: 45 MINUTES

3 tablespoons olive or vegetable oil
8 medium bone-in chicken thighs (about 3
   pounds), skin removed
12 ounces medium mushrooms, each cut in half
3 small onions, each cut into quarters
1 large yellow pepper, cut into 1-inch-wide strips
1 large red pepper, cut into 1-inch-wide strips
4 baby eggplants (about 1¼ pounds), each cut
   lengthwise in half
¼ cup balsamic vinegar or red wine vinegar
2 teaspoons sugar
1 teaspoon salt
½ teaspoon coarsely ground black pepper
¼ cup chopped fresh basil leaves

**1** In 8-quart Dutch oven, heat 1 tablespoon olive oil over medium-high heat until very hot. Add chicken thighs and cook until golden brown. Transfer chicken thighs to bowl.

**2** Add mushrooms and onions to Dutch oven and cook, stirring frequently, until vegetables are golden. With slotted spoon, transfer vegetables to bowl with chicken.

**3** Add 1 tablespoon oil to Dutch oven and heat over high heat. Add yellow and red peppers and cook, stirring constantly, until peppers begin to brown; transfer to bowl with chicken and vegetables.

**4** Add remaining 1 tablespoon oil to Dutch oven and cook baby eggplants, cut-sides down, until golden brown.

**5** Meanwhile, in cup, mix balsamic vinegar, sugar, salt, black pepper, and *2 tablespoons water*. Return chicken and vegetables to Dutch oven; stir in vinegar mixture. Heat to boiling over high heat. Reduce heat to low; cover and simmer 20 minutes, gently stirring occasionally, until chicken and vegetables are fork-tender and juices run clear when chicken is pierced with tip of knife.

**6** Stir in chopped basil; cover and simmer 5 minutes longer to blend flavors. *Makes 6 main-dish servings.*

Each serving: About 435 calories, 43 g protein, 26 g carbohydrate, 18 g total fat (3 g saturated), 6 g fiber, 161 mg cholesterol, 765 mg sodium.

# Chicken Paprika

🐓🐓🐓

PREP: 15 MINUTES / COOK: 1 HOUR 15 MINUTES

3 tablespoons vegetable oil
12 ounces medium mushrooms, each cut in half
1 teaspoon salt
3 tablespoons all-purpose flour
3 teaspoons paprika
1 whole chicken (about 3½ pounds), cut up, skin
   removed
1 medium onion, thinly sliced
1 cup chicken broth
½ cup sour cream
6 ounces wide egg noodles

**1** In 12-inch skillet, heat 1 tablespoon oil over medium heat. Add mushrooms and ¼ teaspoon salt and cook until mushrooms are tender and browned and all liquid evaporates. Transfer mushrooms to large bowl.

**2** In large plastic bag, mix flour, 1 teaspoon paprika, and remaining ¾ teaspoon salt. Add chicken pieces and shake to coat with flour mixture (reserve any flour mixture remaining in bag).

**3** In same skillet, heat 1 tablespoon oil over medium-high heat until very hot. Add half of chicken pieces at a time and cook until browned. Transfer chicken to bowl with mushrooms. Add remaining 1 tablespoon oil and onion and cook until tender and lightly browned. Stir in remaining 2 teaspoons paprika and any remaining flour mixture; cook 1 minute. Stir in chicken broth and sour cream.

**4** Return mushrooms and chicken to skillet; heat to boiling over high heat. Reduce heat to low; cover and simmer 40 minutes or until juices run clear when chicken is pierced with tip of knife.

**5** About 15 minutes before chicken is done, prepare noodles as label directs; drain.

**6** To serve, skim fat from liquid in skillet. Spoon chicken mixture and noodles onto large platter. *Makes 4 main-dish servings.*

Each serving: About 610 calories, 51 g protein, 45 g carbohydrate, 25 g total fat (7 g saturated), 3 g fiber, 187 mg cholesterol, 1020 mg sodium.

# Beer-Braised Chicken

PREP: 10 MINUTES / COOK: 50 MINUTES

1 tablespoon vegetable oil
1 whole chicken (about 3½ pounds), cut up, skin removed
3 large onions (about 1½ pounds), thinly sliced
2 tablespoons all-purpose flour
1 can or bottle (12 ounces) beer or nonalcoholic beer
1 small bay leaf
2 teaspoons brown sugar
¾ teaspoon salt
¼ teaspoon dried thyme
¼ teaspoon coarsely ground black pepper
2 tablespoons white wine vinegar

**1** In 12-inch skillet, heat oil over medium-high heat until very hot. Add chicken pieces and cook until browned on all sides. With slotted spoon, transfer chicken to large plate. Add onions to skillet and cook over medium heat, stirring occasionally, until tender and lightly browned. With slotted spoon, transfer onions to plate with chicken.

**2** Stir flour into drippings in skillet until blended; over medium heat, cook, stirring constantly, until flour is dark brown. Gradually stir in beer, cook until sauce boils and thickens slightly, stirring constantly. Stir in bay leaf, brown sugar, salt, thyme, and pepper. Return chicken and onions to skillet; heat to boiling over high heat. Reduce heat to low; cover and simmer 30 minutes or until chicken is fork-tender.

**3** Skim fat from sauce in skillet. Discard bay leaf. Stir in wine vinegar. *Makes 4 main-dish servings.*

Each serving: About 420 calories, 43 g protein, 24 g carbohydrate, 16 g total fat (4 g saturated), 3 g fiber, 142 mg cholesterol, 595 mg sodium.

# Shanghai Chicken

PREP: 15 MINUTES / COOK: 1 HOUR

3 medium leeks (about 1 pound)
1 whole chicken (about 4 pounds), cut up
4 medium carrots, peeled, cut crosswise in half, then lengthwise in half
⅓ cup dry sherry
⅓ cup soy sauce
1 slice peeled ginger, 1 inch in diameter and ½ inch thick

**1** Cut off roots and trim ends of leeks; cut each leek lengthwise in half and separate leaves. Rinse well with cold running water to remove any sand. Cut leeks crosswise in half.

**2** Place chicken pieces in 8-quart Dutch oven or saucepot, skin-side down. Add leeks, carrots, sherry, soy sauce, ginger, and ¾ *cup water*; heat to boiling over high heat. Reduce heat to low; cover and simmer 1 hour, turning chicken skin-side up halfway through cooking.

**3** To serve, discard ginger. Skim fat from liquid in Dutch oven. Serve from Dutch oven or in deep platter. *Makes 6 main-dish servings.*

Each serving: About 380 calories, 38 g protein, 13 g carbohydrate, 19 g total fat (5 g saturated), 2 g fiber, 116 mg cholesterol, 1030 mg sodium.

# Rosemary Chicken with Rotelle

PREP: 5 MINUTES / COOK: 20 MINUTES

2 tablespoons olive or vegetable oil
1¼ pounds skinless, boneless chicken breasts or thighs, cut into 2-inch chunks
½ teaspoon dried rosemary, crushed
¼ teaspoon salt
1 jar (14 to 15 ounces) marinara sauce
1 teaspoon sugar
1 pound rotelle pasta (corkscrews)
¼ cup pitted Kalamata olives, sliced

## PARMESAN POLENTA

PREP: 15 MINUTES / BROIL: 10 MINUTES

*2 cups milk*
*½ teaspoon salt*
*1 cup chicken broth*
*1 cup yellow cornmeal*
*½ cup grated Parmesan cheese*
*2 teaspoons olive oil*

**1** Line 8" by 8" baking pan with foil. In 3-quart saucepan, heat milk, salt, and chicken broth to boiling over medium-high heat. Gradually sprinkle in cornmeal, stirring constantly with wire whisk. Cook over medium heat, stirring to prevent polenta from burning, 5 to 8 minutes or until mixture is very thick. Remove saucepan from heat; stir in ¼ cup grated Parmesan. Spread cornmeal mixture (polenta) in foil-lined pan; set aside.

**2** Invert polenta onto cutting board; remove foil. Cut polenta into quarters; cut each quarter diagonally into 2 triangles. Place polenta triangles on greased cookie sheet; brush with oil and sprinkle with remaining ¼ cup Parmesan. Place cookie sheet on rack in broiler about 6 inches from source of heat; broil polenta 10 minutes or until cheese begins to brown. Keep warm. Makes 4 accompaniment servings.

Each serving: About 280 calories, 11 g protein, 33 g carbohydrate, 11 g total fat (5 g saturated), 2 g fiber, 25 mg cholesterol, 800 mg sodium.

**1** In nonstick 12-inch skillet, heat oil over medium-high heat until very hot. Add chicken, rosemary, and salt and cook until chicken is golden brown on all sides. Spoon off fat from skillet.

**2** Add marinara sauce, sugar, and *¼ cup water* to chicken in skillet, stirring to loosen brown bits from bottom; heat to boiling. Reduce heat to low; cover and simmer about 5 minutes or until chicken is cooked through, stirring occasionally.

**3** Meanwhile, in large saucepot, prepare pasta in *boiling water* as label directs, but do not use salt.

**4** Drain rotelle; arrange in warm deep bowl. Spoon chicken mixture over rotelle; sprinkle with olives. Toss before serving. ***Makes 6 main-dish servings.***

Each serving: About 490 calories, 33 g protein, 65 g carbohydrate, 11 g total fat (2 g saturated), 3 g fiber, 55 mg cholesterol, 695 mg sodium.

# Braised Chicken with Bacon & Mushrooms

🐓 🐓 🐓

PREP: 10 MINUTES / COOK: 1 HOUR 30 MINUTES

Serve the chicken, bacon, and mushroom mixture with triangles of Parmesan Polenta (at left).

3 slices bacon, cut into 1-inch pieces
10 ounces mushrooms, sliced
8 medium chicken thighs (about 2¼ pounds)
¾ cup chicken broth
1 tablespoon all-purpose flour

**1** In 12-inch skillet, cook bacon over medium-low heat until browned. With slotted spoon, transfer bacon to paper towels to drain.

**2** In bacon fat remaining in skillet, cook mushrooms over high heat, stirring occasionally, until tender and golden, about 10 minutes; transfer to bowl. In same skillet, cook chicken thighs over medium-high heat until browned on all sides, about 15 minutes. Spoon off fat from skillet.

**3** Add chicken broth to chicken in skillet, stirring to loosen brown bits from bottom of skillet; heat to boiling over high heat. Reduce heat to low; cover and simmer 20 minutes or until chicken is fork-tender.

**4** Return mushrooms to skillet with chicken. In small bowl, mix flour and *¼ cup water*; stir into liquid in skillet. Heat over high heat until mixture boils and sauce thickens slightly; boil 1 minute. Stir in bacon. ***Makes 4 main-dish servings.***

Each serving: About 450 calories, 36 g protein, 5 g carbohydrate, 31 g total fat (9 g saturated), 1 g fiber, 134 mg cholesterol, 425 mg sodium.

# Chicken & Potato Stew

PREP: 5 MINUTES / COOK: 25 MINUTES

2 tablespoons olive or vegetable oil
6 medium skinless, boneless chicken thighs (about
   1½ pounds), each cut in half
1 large onion, thinly sliced
¾ teaspoon salt
1 medium orange
¼ cup chicken broth
1 tablespoon all-purpose flour
4 medium red potatoes (about ¾ pound), cut into
   1½-inch chunks
1 teaspoon chopped fresh rosemary or
   ¼ teaspoon dried rosemary, crushed

**1** In 12-inch skillet, heat olive oil over medium-high heat until very hot. Add chicken thighs, onion, and ½ teaspoon salt and cook until onion is tender and thighs are browned and lose their pink color throughout, about 10 minutes. With fork, transfer chicken to bowl, leaving onions in skillet.

**2** Meanwhile, with vegetable peeler, cut two 2½" by ¾" strips of orange peel; reserve. Into 2-cup measuring cup, squeeze ¼ cup juice from orange; stir in chicken broth, flour, and ¾ *cup water*.

**3** Add potatoes, orange juice mixture, and remaining ¼ teaspoon salt to skillet; heat to boiling over high heat. Reduce heat to low; cover and simmer 10 minutes or until potatoes are almost tender.

**4** Return chicken thighs to skillet; stir in rosemary and cook until potatoes are tender and chicken is heated through. Cut reserved orange peel into thin strips. Garnish stew with orange peel. *Makes 4 main-dish servings.*

Each serving: About 370 calories, 36 g protein, 24 g carbohydrate, 14 g total fat (3 g saturated), 2 g fiber, 141 mg cholesterol, 655 mg sodium.

# Chicken & Sweet-Potato Stew

PREP: 20 MINUTES / COOK: 40 MINUTES

4 large chicken legs (about 2½ pounds), separated
   into drumsticks and thighs, skin removed
1 teaspoon salt
½ teaspoon coarsely ground black pepper
3 tablespoons vegetable oil
1 medium onion, coarsely chopped
1 small head Savoy cabbage (about 1½ pounds),
   thickly sliced
2 large sweet potatoes (about 1½ pounds), peeled
   and cut into 1½-inch chunks
½ pound large mushrooms, each cut in half
2 cups chicken broth, canned or homemade
   (page 11)
¼ teaspoon dried thyme
1 cup frozen peas
3 tablespoons all-purpose flour

**1** Rub chicken pieces with salt and pepper.

**2** In 8-quart Dutch oven, heat oil over medium-high heat until very hot. Add chicken and cook until browned on all sides, transferring pieces to plate as they brown.

**3** Add onion and cabbage to skillet and cook until lightly browned. Return chicken to Dutch oven; stir in sweet potatoes, mushrooms, chicken broth, and thyme; heat to boiling over high heat. Reduce heat to medium-low; cover and simmer 25 minutes or until vegetables are tender and juices run clear when chicken is pierced with tip of knife. Stir in frozen peas; heat through.

**4** In cup, with fork, mix flour and ¼ *cup water*. Stir flour mixture into simmering chicken mixture; heat over high heat until mixture boils and thickens. *Makes 4 main-dish servings.*

Each serving: About 555 calories, 43 g protein, 57 g carbohydrate, 18 g total fat (3 g saturated), 7 g fiber, 130 mg cholesterol, 1355 mg sodium.

# Quick Chicken Cacciatore with Pasta

PREP: 10 MINUTES / COOK: 50 MINUTES

3 tablespoons olive or vegetable oil
1 large green pepper, cut into bite-size pieces
1 pound mushrooms, sliced
1 large onion, diced
8 medium bone-in chicken thighs (about 3 pounds), skin removed
1 teaspoon salt
2 containers (15 ounces each) refrigerated plum tomato sauce
1 teaspoon sugar
1 pound perciatelloni or spaghetti

**1** In nonstick 12-inch skillet, heat 1 tablespoon oil over medium-high heat. Add green pepper and cook until tender and lightly browned. With slotted spoon, transfer green pepper to small bowl.

**2** Add 1 tablespoon oil to skillet. Add mushrooms and onion and cook over medium-high heat until all liquid has evaporated from pan and onions are tender, about 10 minutes. With slotted spoon, transfer mushroom mixture to another small bowl.

**3** Add remaining 1 tablespoon oil to skillet and heat over medium-high heat until very hot. Add chicken thighs and ½ teaspoon salt until chicken is lightly browned on both sides. Return mushroom mixture to skillet with chicken. Stir in plum tomato sauce, sugar, and remaining ½ teaspoon salt; heat to boiling over high heat. Reduce heat to low; cover and simmer until chicken thighs are fork-tender, about 20 to 25 minutes, turning chicken thighs once, and stirring sauce occasionally.

**4** Meanwhile, in large saucepot, prepare pasta in *boiling water* as label directs, but do not use salt; drain.

**5** To serve, arrange pasta on large platter; spoon chicken mixture and green pepper on pasta. *Makes 6 main-dish servings.*

Each serving: About 600 calories, 40 g protein, 73 g carbohydrate, 16 g total fat (2 g saturated), 4 g fiber, 107 mg cholesterol, 975 mg sodium.

*Quick Chicken Cacciatore with Pasta*

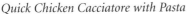

# Pulled Chicken
# with Mashed Potatoes
# & Peas

🐓 🐓 🐓

PREP: 20 MINUTES / COOK: 1 HOUR 20 MINUTES

If you don't want to go to the trouble of making the mashed potatoes to go with the pulled chicken, try it with the corn-studded Country Corn Bread (at right).

PULLED CHICKEN:

2 tablespoons vegetable oil
1 medium onion, chopped
1 medium green pepper, chopped
1 whole chicken (about 3½ pounds), cut into
    quarters and skin removed
⅓ cup cayenne pepper sauce*
½ cup orange juice
¼ cup packed dark brown sugar
¼ cup ketchup
1 tablespoon cider vinegar

MASHED POTATOES WITH PEAS:

6 medium potatoes (about 2 pounds), peeled and
    cut each into quarters
½ cup milk
2 tablespoons margarine or butter
½ teaspoon salt
1 cup frozen peas, thawed

1 Prepare Pulled Chicken: In 5-quart Dutch oven or saucepot, heat oil over medium heat. Add onion and green pepper and cook until tender and browned, about 20 minutes.

2 When vegetables are tender, add chicken quarters, cayenne pepper sauce, orange juice, brown sugar, ketchup, and vinegar. Reduce heat to low; cover and simmer 1 hour or until chicken is very tender.

3 Meanwhile, prepare Mashed Potatoes with Peas: In 3-quart saucepan, heat potatoes and enough *water* to cover to boiling over high heat. Reduce heat to low; cover and simmer 15 minutes or until potatoes are fork-tender. Drain potatoes; return to saucepan. Over medium heat, with potato masher, mash potatoes, milk, margarine or butter, and salt until potatoes are smooth. Stir in peas; cook until peas are heated through; keep warm.

4 With slotted spoon, transfer chicken to large plate; cool slightly. Skim fat from sauce in Dutch oven. Remove meat from bones; discard bones. With 2 forks, pull meat into large shreds. Return meat to Dutch oven; cook, uncovered, over medium-high heat until heated through. Serve chicken with mashed-potato mixture. ***Makes 4 main-dish servings.***

*Yes, we used ⅓ cup. Cayenne pepper sauce is a milder variety of hot sauce that adds tang and flavor, not just heat.

Each serving: About 625 calories, 48 g protein, 63 g carbohydrate, 20 g total fat (4 g saturated), 5 g fiber, 138 mg cholesterol, 1275 mg sodium.

---

## GREAT GO-WITHS

# COUNTRY CORN BREAD

PREP: 10 MINUTES / BAKE: 30 MINUTES

2½ cups yellow cornmeal
2 cups all-purpose flour
2 tablespoons sugar
1 tablespoon salt
1 tablespoon baking powder
1 teaspoon baking soda
4 large eggs
2½ cups buttermilk
½ cup vegetable oil
1 package (10 ounces) frozen whole-kernel corn,
    thawed

1 Preheat oven to 400°F. Grease 13" by 9" baking pan.

2 In large bowl, mix cornmeal, flour, sugar, salt, baking powder, and baking soda. In medium bowl, with wire whisk or fork, beat eggs, buttermilk, and oil until blended. Stir buttermilk mixture and corn into cornmeal mixture just until dry ingredients are moistened.

3 Spread batter evenly in pan. Bake 30 minutes or until golden and toothpick inserted in center comes out clean. Cut corn bread lengthwise into 3 strips, then cut each strip crosswise into 5 pieces. Serve warm. Or, cool in pan on wire rack to serve later; reheat if desired. Makes 15 servings.

Each serving: About 270 calories, 7 g protein, 39 g carbohydrate, 10 g total fat (2 g saturated), 2 g fiber, 58 mg cholesterol, 710 mg sodium.

# Chicken & Clams with Couscous

PREP: 15 MINUTES / COOK: 45 MINUTES

1 whole chicken (about 3½ pounds), cut up, skin removed
½ teaspoon coarsely ground black pepper
¾ teaspoon salt
2 tablespoons vegetable oil
1 can (14½ to 16 ounces) stewed tomatoes
1 can (4 to 4½ ounces) chopped mild green chiles
1 tablespoon chili powder
1 teaspoon sugar
1 dozen littleneck clams, well scrubbed
1 tablespoon chopped fresh parsley leaves
1 tablespoon margarine or butter
¼ teaspoon turmeric (optional)
1 cup couscous (Moroccan pasta)

**1** Sprinkle chicken with pepper and ¼ teaspoon salt.

**2** In 12-inch skillet, heat oil over medium-high heat until very hot. Add chicken and cook until browned on all sides; pour off fat in skillet. Stir in stewed tomatoes, green chiles with their liquid, chili powder, sugar, and *1 cup water*; heat to boiling over high heat. Reduce heat to low; cover and simmer 30 minutes.

**3** Add clams to skillet; cover and cook until shells open, about 8 to 10 minutes. Discard any unopened shells. Sprinkle chicken mixture with parsley.

**4** While clams are cooking, prepare couscous: In 2-quart saucepan, melt margarine or butter over high heat. Add turmeric (if using), remaining ½ teaspoon salt, and *1½ cups water* and heat to boiling. Stir in couscous. Cover saucepan and remove from heat; let stand 5 minutes. Fluff couscous with fork.

**5** Serve chicken and clams over couscous. *Makes 6 main-dish servings.*

Each serving: About 370 calories, 34 g protein, 32 g carbohydrate, 11 g total fat (2 g saturated), 2 g fiber, 95 mg cholesterol, 720 mg sodium.

# Mediterranean Chicken Stew

PREP: 5 MINUTES / COOK: 50 MINUTES

1 tablespoon vegetable oil
8 medium bone-in chicken thighs (about 2 pounds)
1 large onion, diced
2 tablespoons all-purpose flour
1½ pounds small red potatoes, each cut in half
¼ teaspoon salt
1 can (2 ounces) anchovy fillets, drained and chopped
1 package (9 ounces) frozen whole green beans
1 tablespoon fresh lemon juice

**1** In 8-quart Dutch oven, heat oil over medium-high heat until very hot. Add chicken thighs and cook until well browned on both sides; transfer to bowl.

**2** Add onion to Dutch oven and cook over medium heat until lightly browned. Stir in flour and cook, stirring constantly, until flour is lightly browned. Return chicken to Dutch oven; add potatoes, salt, and *3 cups water*. Heat to boiling over high heat. Reduce to low; cover and simmer 20 minutes, stirring occasionally.

**3** Stir in anchovies, frozen green beans, and lemon juice; cook 10 minutes longer or until green beans and chicken are tender, separating green beans with fork and stirring occasionally. Skim fat from pan gravy. *Makes 4 main-dish servings.*

Each serving: About 405 calories, 34 g protein, 44 g carbohydrate, 10 g total fat (2 g saturated), 5 g fiber, 114 mg cholesterol, 685 mg sodium.

# Hearty Chicken & Vegetable Stew

PREP: 45 MINUTES / COOK: 1 HOUR

2 tablespoons olive oil
2 tablespoons margarine or butter (¼ stick)
1 pound skinless, boneless chicken-breast halves,
    cut into 1½-inch pieces
½ pound mushrooms, thickly sliced
3 medium carrots (about 8 ounces), cut into 1-inch
    pieces
2 medium leeks (about 4 ounces each), cut into
    ¾-inch pieces
1 fennel bulb (about 1 pound), trimmed and cut
    into thin wedges
¾ pound red potatoes, cut into 1-inch pieces
1 bay leaf
¼ teaspoon dried tarragon
½ cup dry white wine
1 can (14½ ounces) chicken broth or 1¾ cups
    homemade (page 11)
1 cup half-and-half or light cream
3 tablespoons all-purpose flour
1 cup frozen peas, thawed
¾ teaspoon salt

1 In 5-quart Dutch oven or saucepot, heat 1 tablespoon olive oil over medium-high heat until hot. Add
1 tablespoon margarine or butter; melt. Add chicken
and cook until chicken is golden and just loses its pink
color throughout. With slotted spoon, transfer chick-
en to medium bowl.

2 Add mushrooms to Dutch oven and cook until
golden (do not overbrown). Transfer mushrooms to
bowl with chicken.

3 Add remaining 1 tablespoon olive oil to Dutch oven
and heat until hot. Add remaining 1 tablespoon margarine or butter; melt. Add carrots, leeks, fennel, potatoes, bay leaf, and tarragon. Cook vegetables 10 to 15
minutes, until fennel is translucent and leeks are wilt-
ed, stirring occasionally.

4 Add wine; cook 2 minutes, stirring. Add chicken
broth and ¼ *cup water*; heat to boiling over high heat.
Reduce heat to low; cover and simmer 20 minutes or
until vegetables are tender.

5 In cup, mix half-and-half and flour until smooth.
Stir half-and-half mixture into vegetable mixture; heat
to boiling over high heat. Reduce heat to medium;
cook 1 minute to thicken slightly. Stir in chicken,
mushrooms, peas, and salt; heat through. Discard bay
leaf. *Makes 4 main-dish servings.*

Each serving: About 550 calories, 36 g protein, 47 g carbohydrate,
22 g total fat (7 g saturated), 7 g fiber, 88 mg cholesterol, 1220 mg
sodium.

# Spaghetti with Chicken-Tomato Sauce

PREP: 15 MINUTES / COOK: 55 MINUTES

3 tablespoons olive or vegetable oil
1 pound ground chicken
1 pound medium mushrooms, thinly sliced
1 large onion, chopped
1 large garlic clove, minced
1 can (28 ounces) tomatoes in tomato puree
1 can (6 ounces) tomato paste
¾ cup chicken broth
1 tablespoon sugar
¼ cup chopped fresh basil or ½ teaspoon dried
    basil
¼ teaspoon dried oregano
¼ teaspoon coarsely ground black pepper
1 pound spaghetti
Crushed red pepper

1 In 5-quart Dutch oven, heat oil over high heat until
very hot. Add ground chicken, mushrooms, onion,
and garlic and cook, stirring occasionally, 15 to 20
minutes until all pan juices evaporate and chicken is
lightly browned.

2 Stir in tomatoes with puree, tomato paste, broth,
sugar, basil, oregano, and pepper; heat to boiling over
high heat. Reduce heat to low; cover and simmer 30
minutes to blend flavors, stirring occasionally.

3 Meanwhile, in large saucepot, prepare pasta in boiling salted water as label directs; drain.

4 To serve, place spaghetti in large deep bowl; pour
sauce over spaghetti. If you like, sprinkle with crushed
red pepper. Toss to serve. *Makes 6 main-dish servings.*

Each serving: About 560 calories, 27 g protein, 79 g carbohydrate,
15 g total fat (3 g saturated), 5 g fiber, 63 mg cholesterol, 635 mg
sodium.

◄ *Hearty Chicken & Vegetable Stew*

# Chicken & Vegetable Ragout

🐓🐓🐓

PREP: 15 MINUTES / COOK: 45 MINUTES

2 tablespoons vegetable oil
1 whole chicken (about 3½ pounds), cut into
    quarters, skin removed
¾ teaspoon salt
½ teaspoon dried thyme
¼ teaspoon coarsely ground black pepper
2 medium zucchini (about 10 ounces each), cut
    into ¾-inch chunks
3 medium carrots, peeled and coarsely chopped
1 large onion, coarsely chopped
2 teaspoons all-purpose flour
1 can (28 ounces) plum tomatoes
½ cup small pasta

**1** In nonstick 12-inch skillet, heat 1 tablespoon oil over medium-high heat until very hot. Add chicken; sprinkle with salt, thyme, and pepper and cook until chicken is browned on all sides. Remove chicken from skillet.

**2** Add zucchini to skillet and cook until browned and tender; transfer to bowl. Add remaining 1 tablespoon oil to skillet. Add carrots and onion and cook until they begin to brown.

**3** In cup, stir together flour and *2 tablespoons water.* Add tomatoes with their juice and flour mixture, stirring to break up tomatoes. Return chicken to skillet; heat to boiling over high heat. Reduce heat to low; cover and simmer 10 minutes. Stir in pasta and continue cooking 15 minutes longer or until pasta is just tender and juices run clear when chicken is pierced with tip of knife. Stir in zucchini; heat through. *Makes 4 main-dish servings.*

Each serving: About 440 calories, 47 g protein, 33 g carbohydrate, 14 g total fat (3 g saturated), 5 g fiber, 134 mg cholesterol, 930 mg sodium.

# Curried Chicken with Coconut Dumplings

🐓🐓🐓

PREP: 20 MINUTES / COOK: 50 MINUTES

12 chicken drumsticks (about 3½ pounds), skin
    removed
3 tablespoons all-purpose flour
3 tablespoons vegetable oil
1 large onion, diced
1 medium green pepper, diced
4 teaspoons curry powder
1 teaspoon salt
1 teaspoon ground ginger
1 can (28 ounces) plum tomatoes
4 large celery stalks, cut into 1½-inch lengths
1 medium Granny Smith apple, peeled and
    chopped
Coconut Dumplings (recipe follows)
3 tablespoons slivered almonds, toasted

**1** In large plastic bag, toss drumsticks with flour. In 12-inch skillet, heat 2 tablespoons oil over medium-high heat until very hot. Add drumsticks and cook until browned on all sides, transferring pieces to bowl as they brown.

**2** Add remaining 1 tablespoon oil to skillet. Add onion and pepper and cook until tender and lightly browned. Stir in curry powder, salt, and ginger; cook 1 minute. Stir in tomatoes with their juice, celery, and apple. Return chicken to skillet; heat to boiling over high heat. Reduce heat to low; cover and simmer 25 minutes, stirring occasionally.

**3** Meanwhile, prepare Coconut Dumplings.

**4** After chicken has cooked for 25 minutes, slightly push drumsticks to center of skillet. Drop dumpling dough by heaping tablespoons around edge of skillet into simmering liquid. Cook dumplings 10 minutes uncovered; then cover and cook 10 minutes longer or until dumplings are cooked through and juices run clear when chicken is pierced with tip of knife. Sprinkle dumplings with almonds. Serve chicken and dumplings in skillet. *Makes 6 main-dish servings.*

COCONUT DUMPLINGS: In 2-quart saucepan over medium-low heat, cook *½ cup flaked coconut* until toasted, stirring frequently. Transfer coconut to plate. In medium bowl, mix *1⅓ cups all-purpose flour, 2 teaspoons baking powder,* and *½ teaspoon salt*; stir in toasted coconut and *¼ cup chopped fresh parsley leaves.* In cup, combine ⅔ *cup milk* and *1 tablespoon vegetable oil*; slowly stir into flour mixture just until mixture forms a soft dough (stir as little as possible).

Each serving: About 505 calories, 37 g protein, 45 g carbohydrate, 20 g total fat (5 g saturated), 5 g fiber, 114 mg cholesterol, 1150 mg sodium.

# Simple Curried Chicken with Basmati Rice

🐓 🐓 🐓

PREP: 10 MINUTES / COOK: 20 MINUTES

Madras curry powder is a particularly hot type of curry powder, but you can just as easily make this dish with regular curry powder.

1 cup basmati rice
1 tablespoon Madras curry powder
½ teaspoon sugar
¼ teaspoon salt
1 tablespoon vegetable oil
1 medium onion, diced
4 medium skinless, boneless chicken-breast halves
    (about 1 pound), each cut into 8 pieces
⅓ cup golden raisins
¾ cup chicken broth
1 container (8 ounces) plain low-fat yogurt
2 tablespoons all-purpose flour
1 small Red Delicious apple, diced

**1** In 2-quart saucepan, prepare rice as label directs; keep warm.

**2** Meanwhile, in cup, mix curry powder, sugar, and salt.

**3** In nonstick 12-inch skillet, heat oil over medium-high heat. Add onion and cook until golden brown. Add chicken and curry-powder mixture and cook until chicken just loses its pink color throughout, 3 to 5 minutes.

**4** Stir in raisins and chicken broth; heat to boiling. Reduce heat to low. In small bowl, mix yogurt with flour until blended. Slowly stir yogurt mixture into liquid in skillet, stirring constantly until heated through (do not boil).

**5** Spoon rice and chicken mixture onto platter. Sprinkle with diced apple. *Makes 4 main-dish servings.*

Each serving: About 440 calories, 36 g protein, 62 g carbohydrate, 7 g total fat (2 g saturated), 3 g fiber, 69 mg cholesterol, 475 mg sodium.

---

**CREATIVE LEFTOVERS**

## CURRIED TURKEY

PREP: 10 MINUTES / COOK: 20 MINUTES

Serve over rice or egg noodles.

*3 tablespoons margarine or butter*
*1 medium onion, diced*
*1 green apple, peeled and cut into bite-size chunks*
*1 medium celery stalk, diced*
*1 tablespoon curry powder*
*1 tablespoon all-purpose flour*
*¼ teaspoon salt*
*⅛ teaspoon ground red pepper (cayenne)*
*2½ cups milk*
*3 cups diced cooked turkey*
*¾ cup chopped peanuts*

**1** In 4-quart saucepan, melt margarine or butter over medium heat. Add onion, apple, and celery and cook until tender, stirring. Stir in curry powder, flour, salt, and ground red pepper until blended; cook 1 minute, stirring.

**2** Gradually stir in milk; cook, stirring until mixture is thickened and smooth. Add turkey and peanuts; reduce heat to low; cover and simmer 10 minutes, stirring often. Makes 8 main-dish servings.

Each serving: About 280 calories, 22 g protein, 12 g carbohydrate, 16 g total fat (4 g saturated), 2 g fiber, 51 mg cholesterol, 205 mg sodium.

## PEPPER-THYME BISCUITS

PREP: 10 MINUTES / BAKE: 8 TO 10 MINUTES

Make these jumbo biscuits to serve with a stew, such as Creamy Chicken Stew, below.

*1½ cups buttermilk baking mix*
*½ teaspoon dried thyme*
*½ teaspoon coarsely ground black pepper*
*½ cup milk*
*Nonstick cooking spray*

**1** Preheat oven to 450°F. In medium bowl, with fork, mix baking mix, thyme, pepper, and milk until blended.

**2** Spray small cookie sheet with nonstick cooking spray; spoon biscuit batter into 4 mounds, about 3 inches apart, on cookie sheet, spreading each to about a 3-inch round. Bake biscuits 8 to 10 minutes until golden; remove biscuits to wire rack. Makes 4 large biscuits.

Each biscuit: About 215 calories, 4 g protein, 30 g carbohydrate, 8 g total fat (2 g saturated), 1 g fiber, 4 mg cholesterol, 565 mg sodium.

## Creamy Chicken Stew

🐓 🐓 🐓

PREP: 20 MINUTES / COOK: 15 MINUTES

Serve this hearty old-fashioned stew with Pepper-Thyme Biscuits (above). Slice the biscuits horizontally in half and spoon the stew over the bottom half of the biscuit. Place the top half of the biscuit over the stew.

2 tablespoons olive or vegetable oil
1½ pounds skinless, boneless chicken breasts, cut into 1-inch pieces
½ teaspoon salt
1 large carrot, peeled and thinly sliced
1 large celery stalk, thinly sliced
1 medium red pepper, diced
1 small onion, chopped
2 tablespoons all-purpose flour
2 cups milk
1 can (8¾ ounces) whole-kernel corn, drained
½ cup frozen peas

**1** In nonstick 12-inch skillet, heat olive oil until very hot. Add chicken and ¼ teaspoon salt and cook until chicken loses its pink color throughout. With slotted spoon, transfer chicken pieces to bowl.

**2** Add carrot, celery, red pepper, onion, and remaining ¼ teaspoon salt to skillet and cook, stirring frequently, until vegetables are tender.

**3** Meanwhile, in 2-cup measuring cup, with wire whisk or fork, mix flour and milk until blended.

**4** Return chicken to skillet with vegetable mixture; add corn, frozen peas, and milk mixture. Cook over high heat, stirring, until mixture boils and thickens; boil 1 minute. Serve hot. *Makes 4 main-dish servings.*

Each serving: About 410 calories, 47 g protein, 26 g carbohydrate, 14 g total fat (4 g saturated), 3 g fiber, 116 mg cholesterol, 590 mg sodium.

## Chicken & Shrimp Stroganoff

🐓 🐓 🐓

PREP: 20 MINUTES / COOK: 30 MINUTES

3 tablespoons margarine or butter
½ pound large shrimp, shelled and deveined
2 large skinless, boneless chicken-breast halves (about 1 pound), each cut into 6 pieces
4 medium skinless, boneless chicken thighs (about 1 pound), each cut into 4 pieces
¼ teaspoon salt
½ pound medium mushrooms, each cut in half
2 tablespoons dry sherry
2 tablespoons all-purpose flour
⅛ teaspoon coarsely ground black pepper
1 cup chicken broth, canned or homemade (page 11)
1 container (8 ounces) sour cream
1 tablespoon chopped fresh parsley leaves

**1** In 12-inch skillet, melt 2 tablespoons margarine or butter over medium-high heat. Add shrimp and cook, stirring frequently, until shrimp turn pink and are tender, about 5 minutes. With slotted spoon, transfer shrimp to bowl.

**2** In drippings in skillet, cook chicken with salt until chicken is lightly browned and juices run clear when pierced with tip of knife, about 6 minutes. With slotted spoon, transfer chicken to bowl with shrimp.

**3** Add remaining 1 tablespoon margarine or butter to skillet and melt over medium-high heat. Add mushrooms and sherry; cook, stirring frequently, until mushrooms are tender. In cup, with fork, stir flour, pepper, and chicken broth until blended; stir into mushrooms. Cook mushroom mixture, stirring constantly, until sauce boils and thickens. Reduce heat to low; stir in sour cream until blended.

**4** Return shrimp and chicken to skillet and cook over low heat, stirring, until heated through (do not boil); pour into serving bowl; sprinkle with parsley. *Makes 4 main-dish servings.*

Each serving: About 550 calories, 62 g protein, 9 g carbohydrate, 28 g total fat (11 g saturated), 1 g fiber, 256 mg cholesterol, 780 mg sodium.

# Chicken Meatball Chili

PREP: 25 MINUTES / COOK: 40 MINUTES

3 tablespoons vegetable oil
2 medium celery stalks, finely chopped
1 medium onion, finely chopped
3 slices white bread
2 pounds ground chicken
1 large egg
1¼ teaspoons salt
3 large carrots, peeled and thinly sliced
2 tablespoons chili powder
1 can (28 ounces) plum tomatoes
3 cans (16 to 19 ounces each) white kidney beans
   (cannellini), rinsed and drained

**1** In 5-quart Dutch oven, heat 1 tablespoon oil over medium heat. Add celery and onion and cook until tender, stirring occasionally.

**2** In blender or in food processor with knife blade attached, blend bread to make fine bread crumbs; place in large bowl.

**3** Add celery mixture to bread crumbs; mix in chicken, egg, 1 teaspoon salt, and *¼ cup water*. With wet hands, shape chicken mixture into 1½-inch meatballs.

**4** In same Dutch oven, heat remaining 2 tablespoons oil over medium heat. Add meatballs, half at a time, and cook until browned. Transfer meatballs to bowl as they brown.

**5** Add carrots to Dutch oven and cook over medium-high heat until tender-crisp. Stir in chili powder,

tomatoes with their juice, remaining ¼ teaspoon salt, and *2 cups water*. Heat to boiling over high heat.

**6** Return meatballs to Dutch oven. Reduce heat to low; cover and simmer 10 minutes. Stir beans into Dutch oven and heat through. *Makes 10 main-dish servings.*

Each serving: About 350 calories, 26 g protein, 30 g carbohydrate, 14 g total fat (3 g saturated), 9 g fiber, 97 mg cholesterol, 760 mg sodium.

# Linguine with Chicken & Vegetables

PREP: 10 MINUTES / COOK: 20 MINUTES

12 ounces linguine or spaghetti
Salt
2 tablespoons olive or vegetable oil
1 pound ground chicken
2 medium carrots, peeled and chopped
1 medium onion, chopped
1 garlic clove, minced
3 cups coarsely chopped broccoli
¼ teaspoon coarsely ground black pepper
1 can (14½ ounces) chicken broth or 1¾ cups
   homemade (page 11)
1 tablespoon soy sauce
1½ teaspoons cornstarch
Parmesan cheese (optional)

**1** In large saucepot, prepare linguine in *boiling salted water* as label directs; drain. Return linguine to pot.

**2** Meanwhile, in nonstick 12-inch skillet, heat olive oil over high heat. Add ground chicken, carrots, onion, garlic, broccoli, ¼ teaspoon salt, and pepper and cook, stirring frequently, until all pan juices evaporate and vegetables are tender.

**3** In small bowl, mix chicken broth, soy sauce, and cornstarch until smooth.

**4** Stir cornstarch mixture into chicken mixture in skillet; heat to boiling over high heat and boil 1 minute. Add cooked linguine to mixture in skillet; heat through, tossing to coat well. Serve with Parmesan, if you like. *Makes 6 main-dish servings.*

Each serving without Parmesan: About 410 calories, 23 g protein, 51 g carbohydrate, 13 g total fat (3 g saturated), 4 g fiber, 63 mg cholesterol, 815 mg sodium.

# Italian Turkey Meatballs

PREP: 15 MINUTES / COOK: 45 MINUTES

1 medium onion
2 slices white bread, finely chopped
1¼ pounds ground turkey
2 tablespoons grated Parmesan cheese
2 tablespoons chopped fresh basil leaves
1 large egg
1½ teaspoons salt
3 tablespoons olive oil
1 small eggplant (about 1 pound), cut into 1-inch
  chunks
2 small zucchini (about 6 ounces each), cut into
  1-inch chunks
1 can (28 ounces) plum tomatoes
½ teaspoon sugar

**1** Grate 1 tablespoon onion; chop remaining onion. In large bowl, combine grated onion, chopped bread, ground turkey, Parmesan, basil, egg, and 1 teaspoon salt. With wet hands, shape mixture into 15 meatballs.

**2** In nonstick 12-inch skillet, heat 1 tablespoon olive oil over medium heat. Add meatballs and cook until browned; remove to plate.

**3** In same skillet, heat remaining 2 tablespoons olive oil over medium-high heat. Add eggplant, zucchini, and chopped onion and cook 5 minutes, stirring frequently. Stir in *¼ cup water*. Reduce heat to medium-low; cover and cook 10 minutes, stirring occasionally.

**4** Add tomatoes with their juice, sugar, and remaining ½ teaspoon salt, stirring to break up tomatoes. Return meatballs to skillet; heat to boiling over high heat. Reduce heat to low; simmer, uncovered, 15 minutes or until meatballs are cooked through, gently stirring occasionally. *Makes 6 main-dish servings.*

Each serving: About 305 calories, 22 g protein, 19 g carbohydrate, 16 g total fat (4 g saturated), 3 g fiber, 106 mg cholesterol, 980 mg sodium.

# Chicken & White-Bean Chili

PREP: 10 MINUTES / COOK: 45 MINUTES

1 tablespoon olive or vegetable oil
12 large chicken drumsticks (about 3 pounds)
3 medium carrots, peeled and diced
1 large onion, diced
1 medium celery stalk, diced
2 tablespoons chili powder
½ teaspoon salt
¼ teaspoon crushed red pepper
1 cup chicken broth, canned or homemade
  (page 11)
2 cans (16 to 19 ounces each) white kidney beans
  (cannellini), rinsed and drained

**1** In 12-inch skillet, heat olive oil over medium-high heat until very hot. Add chicken drumsticks and cook until browned on all sides, about 15 minutes; transfer to plate.

**2** Discard all but 2 tablespoons fat from skillet. Add carrots, onion, and celery and cook over medium-high heat until browned and tender-crisp. Stir in chili powder, salt, and crushed red pepper; cook 1 minute, stirring constantly.

**3** Add chicken broth to skillet, stirring to loosen brown bits from bottom of pan. Return drumsticks to skillet. Heat to boiling over high heat. Reduce heat to low; cover and simmer 20 minutes or until drumsticks are fork-tender. Stir white kidney beans into mixture in skillet; heat through. *Makes 6 main-dish servings.*

Each serving: About 430 calories, 39 g protein, 27 g carbohydrate, 18 g total fat (5 g saturated), 9 g fiber, 101 mg cholesterol, 715 mg sodium.

*Italian Turkey Meatballs* ➤

# Chicken Meatballs

PREP: 10 MINUTES / COOK: 40 MINUTES

2 slices white bread, finely chopped
½ cup finely shredded carrots (about 2 medium)
1 tablespoon grated onion
1 pound ground chicken
½ teaspoon salt
2 tablespoons chopped fresh parsley leaves
½ pound medium mushrooms, each cut in half
2 cans (14½ ounces each) stewed tomatoes
1 cup frozen Italian-style green beans
1 cup frozen small white onions
Chopped pitted ripe olives for garnish
Italian bread (optional)

**1** Preheat oven to 400°F. Grease 13" by 9" metal baking pan. In large bowl, mix bread crumbs, carrots, onion, ground chicken, salt, and 1 tablespoon parsley.

**2** Shape chicken mixture into 20 meatballs. (Meatball mixture is very moist and sticky. For easier shaping, use wet hands.) Place meatballs in baking pan and bake 25 minutes or until meatballs are lightly browned and cooked through.

**3** Meanwhile, in 4-quart saucepan, combine mushroom halves and stewed tomatoes. Heat to boiling

*Chicken Meatballs*

over high heat. Reduce heat to low; cover and simmer 15 minutes.

**4** When meatballs are done, add to sauce with frozen Italian green beans and frozen onions; cover and simmer 10 minutes longer to blend flavors and cook vegetables until tender.

**5** Spoon meatball mixture into 4 dinner bowls. Garnish with chopped ripe olives and remaining parsley. Serve with Italian bread if you like. *Makes 4 main-dish servings.*

Each serving without garnish and Italian bread: About 335 calories, 26 g protein, 33 g carbohydrate, 12 g total fat (3 g saturated), 6 g fiber, 94 mg cholesterol, 920 mg sodium.

# Chili Chicken with Black Beans

PREP: 10 MINUTES / COOK: 20 MINUTES

1¼ cups regular long-grain rice
2 tablespoons vegetable oil
3 medium carrots, peeled and diced
1 pound skinless, boneless chicken-breast halves, cut into ½-inch strips
1 tablespoon chili powder
1 can (16 to 19 ounces) black beans, rinsed and drained
1 can (14½ to 16 ounces) stewed tomatoes

**1** Prepare rice as label directs; keep warm.

**2** Meanwhile, in 4-quart saucepan, heat oil over medium-high heat. Add carrots and cook until tender and lightly browned. Stir in chicken and chili powder; cook, stirring occasionally, until chicken is lightly browned.

**3** Stir in black beans, stewed tomatoes, and *¼ cup water*; heat to boiling. Reduce heat to low; cover and simmer 5 minutes or until chicken is cooked through. Spoon chicken mixture over rice on warm platter. *Makes 4 main-dish servings.*

Each serving: About 525 calories, 37 g protein, 71 g carbohydrate, 10 g total fat (1 g saturated), 7 g fiber, 66 mg cholesterol, 555 mg sodium.

# Turkey Chili

### ❦ ❦ ❦

PREP: 20 MINUTES / COOK: 40 MINUTES

Substituting ground turkey for ground beef reduces the fat and calories and makes this spicy vegetable-packed chili a healthy, hearty meal.

1 tablespoon olive or vegetable oil
¾ pound ground turkey
2 medium celery stalks, thinly sliced
2 medium carrots, peeled and thinly sliced
1 medium onion, chopped
1 small zucchini (6 ounces), diced
¾ teaspoon salt
¼ cup all-purpose flour
3 tablespoons chili powder
2 cans (14½ to 16 ounces each) stewed tomatoes
1 can (14½ ounces) chicken broth or 1¾ cups homemade (page 11)
1 can (11 ounces) vacuum-packed whole-kernel corn, drained
1 can (4 to 4½ ounces) chopped mild green chiles
1 tablespoon hot pepper sauce
2 cans (15¼ to 19 ounces each) red kidney beans, rinsed and drained

**1** In 5-quart Dutch oven or saucepot, heat olive oil over medium-high heat. Add ground turkey, celery, carrots, onion, zucchini, and salt and cook, stirring frequently, until any liquid evaporates and turkey and vegetables begin to brown, about 15 minutes.

**2** Stir in flour and chili powder and cook over medium heat for 1 minute, stirring constantly. Add stewed tomatoes, chicken broth, corn, green chiles with their liquid, hot pepper sauce, and *⅓ cup water.*

**3** Heat to boiling over high heat. Reduce heat to low; cover and simmer 15 minutes to blend flavors. Stir in beans; heat through. *Makes 6 main-dish servings.*

Each serving: About 385 calories, 24 g protein, 56 g carbohydrate, 9 g total fat (2 g saturated), 13 g fiber, 41 mg cholesterol, 1700 mg sodium.

---

## CREATIVE LEFTOVERS

# QUICK TURKEY CHILI WITH CHEESE

PREP: 10 MINUTES / COOK: 20 MINUTES

*1 tablespoon vegetable oil*
*1 medium green pepper, diced*
*1 small onion, diced*
*2 teaspoons chili powder*
*1 can (14½ to 16 ounces) tomatoes*
*1 can (15¼ to 19 ounces) red kidney beans, rinsed and drained*
*¾ cup chicken broth*
*2 cups diced cooked turkey*
*1 teaspoon sugar*
*½ teaspoon salt*
*½ teaspoon crushed red pepper*
*1 cup shredded Monterey Jack cheese (4 ounces)*

**1** In nonstick 12-inch skillet, heat oil over medium heat. Add green pepper and onion and cook until tender, stirring occasionally. Stir in chili powder and cook 1 minute.

**2** Stir in tomatoes with their juice, kidney beans, chicken broth, turkey, sugar, salt, and crushed red pepper; heat to boiling over high heat. Reduce heat to low; cover and simmer 10 minutes to blend flavors, stirring occasionally.

**3** Serve in soup bowls with shredded cheese. Makes 6 main-dish servings.

Each serving: About 255 calories, 24 g protein, 15 g carbohydrate, 11 g total fat (4 g saturated), 4 g fiber, 56 mg cholesterol, 680 mg sodium.

## HERBED POLENTA TRIANGLES

PREP: 25 MINUTES / BROIL: 5 TO 10 MINUTES

*4½ cups chicken broth, canned or homemade (page 11)*
*2 cups milk*
*1½ teaspoons salt*
*1 teaspoon minced fresh rosemary or ¼ teaspoon dried rosemary, crushed*
*½ teaspoon minced fresh sage or ¼ teaspoon dried sage*
*2 tablespoons olive or vegetable oil*
*2 cups yellow cornmeal*

**1** Line 15½" by 10½" jelly-roll pan with plastic wrap. In 4-quart saucepan, heat chicken broth, milk, salt, rosemary, sage, and 1 tablespoon olive oil to boiling over medium-high heat. Reduce heat to low; gradually sprinkle in cornmeal, stirring constantly with wire whisk or spoon to prevent lumping. Cook 5 to 8 minutes until mixture is thick and all liquid is absorbed. Spoon cornmeal mixture evenly into jelly-roll pan; set aside 10 minutes or until polenta is set and firm. If not serving right away, cover and refrigerate.

**2** Preheat broiler. Remove polenta from jelly-roll pan; discard plastic wrap. Cut polenta lengthwise into thirds; cut each third crosswise into 4 pieces. Then cut each piece diagonally crisscross into 4 triangles (48 triangles in all).

**3** To garnish polenta triangles, brush triangles with remaining 1 tablespoon olive oil. Place triangles on 2 large cookie sheets.

**4** With rack about 5 to 7 inches from source of heat, broil polenta 5 to 10 minutes until lightly browned and heated through. Makes 12 accompaniment servings.

Each serving: About 140 calories, 4 g protein, 20 g carbohydrate, 5 g total fat (1 g saturated), 1 g fiber, 6 mg cholesterol, 705 mg sodium.

# Chicken Provençal

🐔 🐔 🐔

PREP: 30 MINUTES / COOK: 1 HOUR

A melt-in-your-mouth stew flavored with orange peel and fennel seed.

2 teaspoons olive oil
2 pounds skinless, boneless chicken thighs, each cut into quarters
¾ teaspoon salt
2 medium red peppers, cut into ¼-inch-thick slices
1 medium yellow pepper, cut into ¼-inch-thick slices
1 jumbo onion (1 pound), thinly sliced
3 garlic cloves, crushed with garlic press
1 can (28 ounces) Italian-style plum tomatoes
¼ teaspoon dried thyme
¼ teaspoon fennel seeds, crushed
3 strips (3" by 1" each) orange peel
½ cup loosely packed fresh basil leaves, chopped

**1** In nonstick 5-quart Dutch oven, heat 1 teaspoon olive oil over medium-high heat until hot. Add half of chicken and ¼ teaspoon salt and cook until lightly browned on all sides, about 10 minutes. Transfer chicken to plate. Repeat with remaining oil, chicken, and ¼ teaspoon salt.

**2** Add peppers, onion, and remaining ¼ teaspoon salt to Dutch oven and cook, stirring frequently, until tender and lightly browned, about 20 minutes. Add garlic and cook 1 minute.

**3** Return chicken to Dutch oven. Add tomatoes with their juice, thyme, fennel seeds, and orange peel, stirring to break up tomatoes with spoon; heat to boiling. Reduce heat to low; cover and simmer 15 minutes or until chicken is tender.

**4** Sprinkle with basil to serve. *Makes 8 main-dish servings.*

Each serving: About 200 calories, 24 g protein, 11 g carbohydrate, 6 g total fat (1 g saturated), 3 g fiber, 94 mg cholesterol, 475 mg sodium.

# Turkey Sausage & Hominy Chili

PREP: 5 MINUTES / COOK: 20 MINUTES

I pound hot or sweet Italian-style turkey-sausage
  links, casings removed
I pound ground turkey
I large onion, chopped
I medium green pepper, chopped
¼ cup chili powder
I can (28 ounces) tomatoes
I can (16 ounces) white hominy, drained
I can (6 ounces) tomato paste
I tablespoon sugar
½ teaspoon salt
¾ teaspoon dried oregano
Shredded Monterey Jack cheese (optional)

**1** In 5-quart Dutch oven, cook turkey sausage and
ground turkey over high heat, stirring occasionally,
about 5 minutes.

**2** Add onion and pepper to Dutch oven and continue
cooking until meat is lightly browned and onion and
green pepper are tender. Skim fat.

**3** Stir in chili powder; cook 1 minute. Stir in tomatoes
with their juice, hominy, tomato paste, sugar, salt, and
oregano; heat to boiling. Reduce heat to low; cover
and simmer 10 minutes. Serve with shredded cheese,
if you like. *Makes 8 main-dish servings.*

Each serving without cheese: About 285 calories, 23 g protein,
24 g carbohydrate, 12 g total fat (3 g saturated), 5 g fiber, 72 mg
cholesterol, 1060 mg sodium.

# Stuffed Napa Cabbage

PREP: 25 MINUTES / COOK: 40 MINUTES

I large head Napa cabbage (Chinese cabbage),
  about 3 pounds
I pound ground chicken
½ pound firm tofu, chopped
¼ pound mushrooms, chopped
¼ cup soy sauce
I tablespoon grated, peeled fresh ginger
I cup chicken broth, canned or homemade
  (page 11)
I tablespoon margarine or butter
¼ cup chopped chives

**1** Fill 5-quart saucepot three-fourths full of *water*;
heat to boiling over high heat. Meanwhile, remove 12
large leaves from cabbage (if some leaves are very
small, remove several additional ones to use together
later to make rolls). Finely chop enough remaining
cabbage to measure 1 cup. Refrigerate any leftover
cabbage to use another day.

**2** Add cabbage leaves to boiling water; cook 2 to 3
minutes until leaves soften. Drain in colander.

**3** In large bowl, mix ground chicken, tofu, mushrooms, soy sauce, ginger, and chopped cabbage.

**4** At stem end of each cabbage leaf, place rounded ¼
cup chicken mixture. Roll leaves, jelly-roll fashion.
Place rolls, seam-side down, in 12-inch skillet. Pour
chicken broth over rolls. Heat to boiling over high
heat. Reduce heat to low; cover and simmer 20 minutes or until chicken loses its pink color.

**5** With slotted spoon, place rolls on warm platter;
keep warm. Over low heat, stir margarine or butter
into chicken broth until margarine melts. Stir in
chopped chives. Pour sauce over rolls. *Makes 4 main-
dish servings.*

Each serving: About 350 calories, 34 g protein, 14 g carbohydrate,
19 g total fat (4 g saturated), 3 g fiber, 94 mg cholesterol, 1450 mg
sodium.

# Sautés & Stir-Fries

# Chicken Breasts in Orange Sauce

🐔🐔🐔

PREP: 15 MINUTES / COOK: 30 MINUTES

Use sweet seedless oranges for this flavorful entrée.

4 large navel oranges
4 medium bone-in chicken-breast halves (about 2½ pounds), skin removed
½ teaspoon salt
½ teaspoon coarsely ground black pepper
¼ teaspoon dried thyme
1 tablespoon olive oil
½ cup chicken broth
¼ cup orange marmalade
1 teaspoon cornstarch

**1** With vegetable peeler, remove four 3-inch-long strips peel (about ¾ inch wide each) from 1 orange. Cut peel lengthwise into very thin slivers. Squeeze enough juice from 2 oranges to equal ⅔ cup. Cut peel and white pith from remaining 2 oranges. Cut each orange in half from stem to blossom end, then cut each half crosswise into ¼-inch-thick slices; set aside.

**2** Rub chicken breasts with salt, pepper, and thyme. In nonstick 12-inch skillet, heat olive oil over medium-high heat until hot. Add chicken breasts and cook until golden, about 6 minutes, turning once. Add orange juice, orange-peel strips, and chicken broth; heat to boiling. Reduce heat to low; cover and simmer 20 minutes or until juices run clear when chicken is pierced with tip of knife.

**3** In cup, mix orange marmalade and cornstarch until blended. Transfer chicken breasts to warm platter; keep warm. To same skillet, add marmalade mixture; heat to boiling. Cook, stirring constantly, 1 minute, until sauce thickens slightly. Stir in orange slices; heat through. Spoon sauce over chicken breasts on platter. *Makes 4 main-dish servings.*

Each serving: About 350 calories, 44 g protein, 29 g carbohydrate, 6 g total fat (1 g saturated), 2 g fiber, 107 mg cholesterol, 555 mg sodium.

# Balsamic Chicken & Pears

🐔🐔🐔

PREP: 10 MINUTES / COOK: 20 MINUTES

2 teaspoons vegetable oil
4 small skinless, boneless chicken-breast halves (about 1 pound)
2 Bosc pears, unpeeled and each cut into 8 wedges
1 cup chicken broth
3 tablespoons balsamic vinegar
2 teaspoons cornstarch
1½ teaspoons sugar
¼ cup dried cherries or raisins
Rosemary sprigs for garnish

**1** In nonstick 12-inch skillet, heat 1 teaspoon oil over medium-high heat. Add chicken breasts and cook 8 to 10 minutes, turning once, until juices run clear when pierced with tip of knife. Transfer chicken to bowl.

**2** Add remaining 1 teaspoon oil to skillet. Add pear wedges and cook until lightly browned and tender.

**3** In cup, with fork, mix chicken broth, balsamic vinegar, cornstarch, and sugar until blended. Add chicken-broth mixture and dried cherries to skillet with pears. Heat to boiling; boil 1 minute. Return chicken to skillet; heat through. Garnish with rosemary to serve. *Makes 4 main-dish servings.*

Each serving: About 235 calories, 27 g protein, 22 g carbohydrate, 4 g total fat (1 g saturated), 2 g fiber, 66 mg cholesterol, 340 mg sodium.

*Balsamic Chicken & Pears* ➤

## *Last-minute* DINNERS

# SALSA CHICKEN

PREP: 5 MINUTES / COOK: 20 MINUTES

*1 teaspoon olive oil*
*4 medium skinless, boneless chicken-breast halves*
  *(about 1¼ pounds)*
*1 can (15 ounces) black beans, rinsed and drained*
*1 jar (10 ounces) thick-and-chunky salsa*
*1 can (8¾ ounces) whole-kernel corn, drained*
*1 tablespoon chopped fresh cilantro leaves*

**1** In 12-inch nonstick skillet, heat oil over medium-high heat until very hot. Add chicken breasts and cook until golden, 8 to 10 minutes. Transfer chicken to plate.

**2** Add black beans, salsa, corn, cilantro, and ¼ *cup water*. Cook 1 minute to heat through. Pour sauce over chicken. Makes 4 main-dish servings.

Each serving: About 305 calories, 39 g protein, 26 g carbohydrate, 4 g total fat (1 g saturated), 5 g fiber, 82 mg cholesterol, 1150 mg sodium.

# Chicken Breasts with Peanut Sauce

PREP: 5 MINUTES / COOK: 15 MINUTES

1 tablespoon vegetable oil
4 medium skinless, boneless chicken-breast halves
  (about 1¼ pounds)
1 bunch radishes
¼ cup creamy peanut butter
2 tablespoons soy sauce
1 teaspoon white wine vinegar
⅛ teaspoon crushed red pepper

**1** In 10-inch skillet, heat oil over medium-high heat until very hot. Add chicken breasts and cook 7 to 10 minutes until juices run clear when pierced with tip of knife, turning once. Transfer chicken to warm platter.

**2** Meanwhile, coarsely chop half of radishes; reserve remaining radishes for garnish.

**3** Stir peanut butter, soy sauce, vinegar, crushed red pepper, and ⅔ *cup water* into drippings in skillet; stir until smooth and heated through. Pour sauce over chicken on platter; sprinkle with chopped radishes. Garnish platter with remaining radishes. *Makes 4 main-dish servings.*

Each serving: About 295 calories, 38 g protein, 5 g carbohydrate, 14 g total fat (2 g saturated), 2 g fiber, 82 mg cholesterol, 690 mg sodium.

# Chicken with Sautéed Pears & Dill Sauce

PREP: 20 MINUTES / COOK: 25 MINUTES

2 tablespoons margarine or butter
3 medium pears, each cut crosswise into
  3 or 4 thick slices
1 tablespoon light brown sugar
6 large skinless, boneless chicken-breast halves
  (about 2¼ pounds)
1 large egg
1½ cups fresh bread crumbs (about 3 slices bread)
½ teaspoon salt
8 tablespoons all-purpose flour
2 tablespoons vegetable oil
1½ cups chicken broth, canned or homemade
  (page 11)
2 tablespoons minced fresh dill
1 cup half-and-half or light cream

**1** In 10-inch skillet, melt 1 tablespoon margarine or butter over medium heat. Add pears and brown sugar and cook until pears are tender, about 10 minutes.

**2** Place the chicken-breast halves between 2 sheets of waxed paper and with the flat side of a small skillet or meat pounder, pound the chicken to a ¼-inch thickness. In pie plate, with fork, beat egg and *1 tablespoon water*. On 1 sheet of waxed paper, mix bread crumbs, salt, and 3 tablespoons flour. On another sheet of waxed paper, place 3 tablespoons flour. Dip cutlets in plain flour, then egg mixture, then coat with bread-crumb mixture.

**3** In nonstick 12-inch skillet, heat oil and remaining 1 tablespoon margarine or butter over medium heat until butter is melted. Add cutlets in batches and cook until browned on both sides and cooked through, 3 to 4 minutes; transfer to plate; keep warm.

**4** In small bowl, with fork, stir broth and remaining 2 tablespoons flour until smooth. Stir broth mixture into drippings in skillet. Cook over high heat, stirring constantly, until sauce boils and thickens slightly.

**5** Stir minced dill and half-and-half into sauce in skillet; heat through.

**6** To serve, arrange chicken cutlets and pears on warm large platter; spoon some sauce over chicken. Pass remaining sauce in gravy boat. *Makes 6 main-dish servings.*

Each serving: About 460 calories, 44 g protein, 31 g carbohydrate, 17 g total fat (5 g saturated), 3 g fiber, 149 mg cholesterol, 695 mg sodium.

# Apple-Curry Chicken

🐓 🐓 🐓

PREP: 5 MINUTES / COOK: 20 MINUTES

3 teaspoons olive oil
4 medium skinless, boneless chicken-breast halves
    (about 1¼ pounds)
1 small onion, chopped
1 Golden Delicious apple, peeled and diced
1½ teaspoons curry powder
¼ teaspoon salt
½ cup mango chutney
½ cup frozen peas, thawed

**1** In nonstick 12-inch skillet, heat 1 teaspoon oil over medium-high heat until very hot. Add chicken breasts and cook until golden, 8 to 10 minutes. Transfer chicken to plate.

**2** Add remaining 2 teaspoons oil to skillet. Add onion and apple and cook over medium heat until tender. Stir in curry powder and salt; cook 1 minute. Stir in mango chutney, peas, and *½ cup water*; boil 1 minute. Pour sauce over chicken. *Makes 4 main-dish servings.*

Each serving: About 350 calories, 34 g protein, 38 g carbohydrate, 5 g total fat (1 g saturated), 2 g fiber, 82 mg cholesterol, 595 mg sodium.

# Chicken Breasts with Tarragon Sauce

🐓 🐓 🐓

PREP: 10 MINUTES / COOK: 20 MINUTES

2 teaspoons plus 1 tablespoon olive or vegetable
    oil
2 large shallots, thinly sliced
1 teaspoon salt
1 tablespoon fresh tarragon leaves, chopped, or
    ½ teaspoon dried tarragon
5 tablespoons all-purpose flour
4 medium bone-in chicken-breast halves (about
    2½ pounds), skin removed
1½ cups chicken broth, canned or homemade
    (page 11)

**1** In nonstick 12-inch skillet, heat 2 teaspoons olive oil over medium heat. Add shallots and cook until tender and lightly browned. With slotted spoon, transfer shallots to bowl.

**2** On waxed paper, mix salt, tarragon, and 3 tablespoons flour; use to coat chicken breasts. Add remaining 1 tablespoon oil to skillet and heat until very hot. Add chicken breasts and cook until golden brown, turning once. Reduce heat to medium-low; cover and continue cooking about 10 minutes or until juices run clear when chicken is pierced with tip of knife. Place chicken on 4 dinner plates.

**3** In small bowl, with fork, mix remaining 2 tablespoons flour with chicken broth. Add broth mixture and sautéed shallots to skillet; heat to boiling over high heat, stirring to loosen any brown bits from bottom of skillet. Boil 1 minute. Pour sauce over chicken. *Makes 4 main-dish servings.*

Each serving: About 305 calories, 44 g protein, 9 g carbohydrate, 9 g total fat (2 g saturated), 0.5 g fiber, 107 mg cholesterol, 1100 mg sodium.

*Chicken Breasts with Tomato & Olive Sauce*

# Chicken Breasts with Tomato & Olive Sauce

🐓 🐓 🐓

PREP: 10 MINUTES / COOK: 20 MINUTES

1 tablespoon olive or vegetable oil
4 medium skinless, boneless chicken-breast halves
 (about 1¼ pounds)
1 medium onion, finely chopped
1 tablespoon red wine vinegar
6 large plum tomatoes (about 1 pound) or 3
 medium tomatoes, peeled, seeded, and chopped
½ cup pitted Kalamata olives

**1** In 12-inch skillet, heat olive oil over medium-high heat until very hot. Add chicken breasts and cook until golden and juices run clear when chicken is pierced with tip of knife, about 8 minutes. Transfer chicken to plate.

**2** Add onion to skillet and cook until tender-crisp. Add red wine vinegar and cook until onion is very tender; stir in tomatoes and olives. Heat to boiling over high heat.

**3** Return chicken to skillet; heat through. *Makes 4 main-dish servings.*

Each serving:  About 275 calories, 34 g protein, 11 g carbohydrate, 10 g total fat (2 g saturated), 2 g fiber, 82 mg cholesterol, 410 mg sodium.

# Cheese-Stuffed Mexican Chicken

🐔 🐔 🐔

PREP: 20 MINUTES / COOK: 30 MINUTES

6 ounces Monterey Jack cheese with jalapeño
   chiles
6 medium skinless, boneless chicken-breast halves
   (about 1¾ pounds)
¼ cup all-purpose flour
1¼ teaspoons salt
1 large egg
¼ cup milk
¾ cup yellow cornmeal
1 tablespoon vegetable oil
1 jar (12 ounces) thick-and-chunky hot salsa
1 jar (8 ounces) hot or mild taco sauce

**1** Cut half of cheese into 6 slices; shred remaining cheese.

**2** Make a 2½-inch horizontal cut in meatier part of each chicken-breast half to make a deep pocket. Place 1 slice of cheese in each pocket, cutting cheese to fit.

**3** On waxed paper, combine flour and salt. In bowl, mix egg and milk; place cornmeal on another sheet of waxed paper. Dip each chicken-breast half into flour, then into egg mixture, then into cornmeal.

**4** In nonstick 12-inch skillet, heat oil over medium-high heat until very hot. Add chicken breasts and brown on both sides, about 5 minutes. Transfer to plate.

**5** Add salsa, taco sauce, and *⅓ cup water* to skillet; heat to boiling over high heat. Arrange chicken breasts in sauce; reduce heat to low and simmer, uncovered, 15 minutes. Sprinkle with shredded cheese; cover and cook until cheese melts. *Makes 6 main-dish servings.*

Each serving: About 410 calories, 41 g protein, 27 g carbohydrate, 14 g total fat (6 g saturated), 1 g fiber, 144 mg cholesterol, 1655 mg sodium.

# Chicken with Beurre Blanc

PREP: 10 MINUTES / COOK: 20 MINUTES

6 medium skinless, boneless chicken-breast halves
   (about 1¾ pounds)
2 tablespoons all-purpose flour
½ teaspoon salt
5 tablespoons cold butter (do not use margarine)
1 medium red onion, diced
⅓ cup white wine vinegar
¼ teaspoon cracked black pepper

**1** Place the chicken breasts between 2 sheets of waxed paper and with the flat side of a small skillet or meat pounder, pound the chicken to a ½-inch thickness.

**2** On waxed paper, mix flour and salt. Dip each chicken cutlet in flour mixture to coat.

**3** In nonstick 12-inch skillet, melt 2 tablespoons butter over medium heat. Add 3 chicken breasts at a time and cook about 5 minutes, turning once, until juices run clear when thickest part is pierced with tip of knife. Transfer cutlets to warm platter; keep warm.

**4** In butter remaining in skillet, cook onion until just tender, about 5 minutes. Add vinegar and cracked pepper to skillet and heat to boiling over high heat. Boil until vinegar mixture is slightly reduced, about 1 minute. Reduce heat to medium; gradually add remaining 3 tablespoons cold butter, 2 teaspoons at a time, beating constantly with wire whisk until butter melts and sauce thickens slightly. Pour sauce over chicken. *Makes 6 main-dish servings.*

Each serving: About 255 calories, 31 g protein, 5 g carbohydrate, 11 g total fat (6 g saturated), 0.5 g fiber, 103 mg cholesterol, 380 mg sodium.

# Chili Chicken with Vegetable Hash

PREP: 10 MINUTES / COOK: 30 MINUTES

5 small red potatoes (about 1 pound), cut into
  ½-inch pieces
2 tablespoons vegetable oil
1 medium red pepper, diced
1 medium green pepper, diced
2 medium green onions, cut into ½-inch slices
3 teaspoons chili powder
1 teaspoon salt
1 tablespoon all-purpose flour
4 medium skinless, boneless chicken-breast halves
  (about 1¼ pounds)

**1** In 2-quart saucepan, heat potatoes and enough *water* to cover to boiling over high heat. Reduce heat to low; cover and simmer 5 to 10 minutes until the potatoes are almost tender; drain.

**2** Meanwhile, in nonstick 12-inch skillet, heat 1 tablespoon oil over medium-high heat. Add red and green peppers and cook until peppers are lightly browned, stirring frequently.

**3** Stir in cooked potatoes, green onions, 1 teaspoon chili powder, and ½ teaspoon salt. Continue cooking until potatoes are golden brown and tender, stirring mixture frequently; remove vegetable hash to warm platter; keep warm. Wash and dry skillet.

**4** On waxed paper, mix flour, remaining 2 teaspoons chili powder, and remaining ½ teaspoon salt. Coat chicken breasts with flour mixture.

**5** Add remaining 1 tablespoon oil to skillet and heat over medium-high heat until very hot. Add chicken breasts and cook 6 to 8 minutes, until lightly browned on both sides and juices run clear when pierced with tip of knife, turning chicken occasionally. Arrange the chicken on platter with the vegetable hash. *Makes 4 main-dish servings.*

Each serving: About 335 calories, 36 g protein, 26 g carbohydrate, 9 g total fat (1 g saturated), 3 g fiber, 82 mg cholesterol, 705 mg sodium.

# Chicken with Curry-Peach Sauce

PREP: 10 MINUTES / COOK: 20 MINUTES

2 tablespoons vegetable oil
4 medium skinless, boneless chicken-breast halves
  (about 1¼ pounds)
¾ teaspoon salt
1 medium onion, chopped
1½ teaspoons curry powder
1 can (16 ounces) sliced peaches in extralight
  syrup
⅓ cup mango chutney
1 tablespoon soy sauce

**1** In nonstick 12-inch skillet, heat 1 tablespoon oil over medium-high heat until very hot. Add chicken breasts and salt and cook until chicken is browned on

---

## GREAT GO-WITHS

### RICE TIMBALES

PREP: 10 MINUTES / COOK: 20 MINUTES

Here is an unbelievably simple way to dress up any plate. Just press hot cooked rice into a small cup (like a custard cup), then invert onto a plate. Magically, the rice will hold the shape of the cup.

*1 tablespoon olive oil*
*1 medium onion, chopped*
*1 medium carrot, peeled and diced*
*1 cup regular long-grain rice*
*¾ teaspoon salt*
*1 tablespoon chopped fresh parsley leaves*

**1** In 2-quart saucepan, heat oil over medium-high heat. Add onion and carrot and cook until tender but not browned. Stir in rice and salt and cook, stirring frequently, until rice grains are opaque. Add *2 cups water*; heat to boiling over high heat. Reduce heat to low; cover and simmer 20 minutes or until rice is tender and all liquid is absorbed.

**2** Remove saucepan from heat and stir in parsley. Grease six 4-ounce timbale molds or custard cups. Pack hot rice firmly into molds. Unmold to serve. Makes 4 accompaniment servings.

Each serving: About 235 calories, 4 g protein, 43 g carbohydrate, 5 g total fat (1 g saturated), 2 g fiber, 0 mg cholesterol, 445 mg sodium.

both sides. Reduce heat to medium; cover and cook until chicken is tender and juices run clear when chicken is pierced with tip of knife. Transfer chicken to plate; keep warm.

**2** Add remaining 1 tablespoon oil to skillet. Add onion and cook until browned and tender. Stir in curry powder; cook 1 minute. Stir in sliced peaches with their syrup, mango chutney, and soy sauce; boil 1 minute.

**3** Return chicken to skillet with any accumulated juices in plate and heat through. *Makes 4 main-dish servings.*

Each serving: About 365 calories, 34 g protein, 36 g carbohydrate, 9 g total fat (1 g saturated), 1 g fiber, 82 mg cholesterol, 1020 mg sodium.

# Chinese Ginger Chicken

🐓 🐓 🐓

PREP: 5 MINUTES / COOK: 20 MINUTES

2 teaspoons olive oil
4 medium skinless, boneless chicken-breast halves (about 1¼ pounds)
1 medium red pepper, thinly sliced
2 tablespoons soy sauce
2 tablespoons seasoned rice vinegar
1 tablespoon grated, peeled fresh ginger
Chopped green onions for garnish

**1** In nonstick 12-inch skillet, heat 1 teaspoon oil over medium-high heat until very hot. Add chicken breasts and cook until golden, 8 to 10 minutes. Transfer chicken to plate.

**2** Add remaining 1 teaspoon oil and red pepper, and cook over medium heat until tender-crisp. Stir in ½ *cup water*, soy sauce, vinegar, and ginger; boil 1 minute. Pour sauce over chicken. Sprinkle with green onions. *Makes 4 main-dish servings.*

Each serving: About 195 calories, 33 g protein, 4 g carbohydrate, 4 g total fat (1 g saturated), 0.5 g fiber, 82 mg cholesterol, 755 mg sodium.

# Chicken with Canadian Bacon & Provolone

 🐓 🐓 🐓

PREP: 10 MINUTES / COOK: 15 MINUTES

1 tablespoon all-purpose-flour
½ teaspoon salt
¼ teaspoon coarsely ground black pepper
4 large skinless, boneless chicken-breast halves (about 1½ pounds)
1 tablespoon margarine or butter
4 teaspoons Dijon mustard with seeds
4 slices Provolone cheese, each cut crosswise in half
4 slices Canadian bacon

**1** On waxed paper, mix flour, salt, and pepper; use to coat chicken breasts.

**2** In 10-inch skillet, melt margarine or butter over medium-high heat. Add chicken breasts and cook until browned and juices run clear when pierced with tip of knife, 8 to 10 minutes.

**3** Spread chicken breasts with mustard. Place half of cheese over chicken breasts; top with Canadian bacon, then with remaining cheese. Cover; cook 1 to 2 minutes to melt cheese. *Makes 4 main-dish servings.*

Each serving: About 370 calories, 53 g protein, 3 g carbohydrate, 15 g total fat (7 g saturated), 0 g fiber, 133 mg cholesterol, 1200 mg sodium.

# Golden Chicken with Marsala Mushrooms

PREP: 5 MINUTES / COOK: 20 MINUTES

1 tablespoon olive or vegetable oil
4 large boneless chicken-breast halves (about
   2 pounds with skin)
¼ teaspoon coarsely ground black pepper
½ teaspoon salt
1 pound medium mushrooms, each cut into
   quarters
¼ cup dry Marsala wine

**1** In nonstick 12-inch skillet, heat olive oil over medium-high heat until very hot. Add chicken breasts, skin-side down, and cook until golden brown, about 5 minutes. Turn chicken; sprinkle with pepper and ¼ teaspoon salt. Reduce heat to medium; cook chicken until juices run clear when pierced with tip of knife, about 5 minutes longer. Transfer chicken to plate.

**2** Add mushrooms and remaining ¼ teaspoon salt to skillet and cook until mushrooms are golden brown and all liquid has evaporated, stirring frequently. Add Marsala wine to mushrooms, stirring to loosen any brown bits from bottom of skillet. Return chicken breasts to mushroom mixture; heat through.

**3** To serve, spoon chicken on 4 dinner plates; top with mushrooms. *Makes 4 main-dish servings.*

Each serving: About 390 calories, 40 g protein, 6 g carbohydrate, 21 g total fat (5 g saturated), 2 g fiber, 116 mg cholesterol, 410 mg sodium.

# Curried Chicken Breasts with Walnut-Raisin Sauce

PREP: 15 MINUTES / COOK: 25 MINUTES

1 teaspoon curry powder
¼ teaspoon coarsely ground black pepper
⅛ teaspoon ground cinnamon
2 teaspoons plus 1 tablespoon all-purpose flour
¾ teaspoon salt
4 large skinless, boneless chicken-breast halves
   (about 1½ pounds)
2 tablespoons vegetable oil
1 small onion, finely chopped
1 small yellow pepper, cut into matchstick-thin
   strips
1 cup chicken broth, canned or homemade
   (page 11)
1 teaspoon sugar
¼ cup walnuts, toasted and coarsely chopped
¼ cup dark seedless raisins

**1** On sheet of waxed paper, mix curry powder, pepper, cinnamon, 2 teaspoons flour, and ½ teaspoon salt. Use to coat chicken breasts.

**2** In 10-inch skillet, heat 1 tablespoon oil over medium-high heat until very hot. Add chicken breasts and cook, turning once, until golden brown on both sides and juices run clear when chicken is pierced with tip of knife, about 6 minutes; transfer to plate.

**3** Add remaining 1 tablespoon oil to skillet. Add onion, yellow pepper, and remaining ¼ teaspoon salt and cook, stirring occasionally, until vegetables are golden brown and tender.

**4** In cup, with fork, mix broth, sugar, and remaining 1 tablespoon flour until blended; stir broth mixture, toasted walnuts, and raisins into vegetable mixture in skillet. Heat to boiling over high heat; boil 1 minute.

**5** To serve, spoon sauce over chicken. *Makes 4 main-dish servings.*

Each serving: About 360 calories, 42 g protein, 16 g carbohydrate, 14 g total fat (2 g saturated), 2 g fiber, 99 mg cholesterol, 815 mg sodium.

*Greek Chicken*

# Greek Chicken

🐔 🐔 🐔

PREP: 20 MINUTES / COOK: 20 MINUTES

1 cup crumbled feta cheese (about 4 ounces)
1 tablespoon fresh lemon juice
1 teaspoon dried oregano
6 large skinless, boneless chicken-breast halves
   (about 2 pounds)
½ teaspoon salt
¼ teaspoon coarsely ground black pepper
2 tablespoons all-purpose flour
2 tablespoons olive oil
1 cup chicken broth, canned or homemade
   (page 11)
1 medium tomato, diced
2 cups loosely packed sliced spinach

**1** In small bowl, with fork, mix feta cheese, lemon juice, and oregano until smooth.

**2** Place the chicken breasts between 2 sheets of waxed paper and with the flat side of a small skillet or meat pounder, pound the chicken to a ½-inch thickness.

**3** With knife or small metal spatula, spread cheese mixture over each breast half to within ½ inch of edge. Fold chicken breasts crosswise in half to enclose filling; secure with toothpick.

**4** On sheet of waxed paper, mix salt, pepper, and 1 tablespoon flour; use to coat chicken.

**5** In 12-inch skillet, heat olive oil over medium-high heat until very hot. Add chicken and cook until golden brown on both sides, turning once.

**6** Meanwhile, in cup, mix chicken broth and remaining 1 tablespoon flour until smooth. Add broth mixture, tomato, and spinach to skillet; heat to boiling over high heat. Reduce heat to low; cover and simmer 8 to 10 minutes until chicken is fork-tender and loses its pink color throughout. Remove and discard toothpicks to serve chicken. ***Makes 6 main-dish servings.***

Each serving: About 275 calories, 39 g protein, 4 g carbohydrate, 11 g total fat (4 g saturated), 1 g fiber, 105 mg cholesterol, 700 mg sodium.

# Dijon Chicken with Grapes

PREP: 5 MINUTES / COOK: 20 MINUTES

1 teaspoon olive oil
4 medium skinless, boneless chicken-breast halves
  (about 1¼ pounds)
½ cup half-and-half or light cream
2 tablespoons Dijon mustard with seeds
¾ cup seedless red or green grapes, each cut in
  half

**1** In nonstick 12-inch skillet, heat olive oil over medium-high heat until very hot. Add chicken breasts and cook until golden, 8 to 10 minutes. Transfer chicken to plate.

**2** Add half-and-half, mustard, and grapes, and cook 1 minute. To serve, pour sauce over chicken. *Makes 4 main-dish servings.*

Each serving: About 235 calories, 34 g protein, 7 g carbohydrate, 7 g total fat (3 g saturated), 0.5 g fiber, 93 mg cholesterol, 285 mg sodium.

# Herbed Chicken with Avocado Salsa

PREP: 20 MINUTES / COOK: 10 MINUTES

1 large tomato, chopped
1 small onion, finely chopped
1 can (4 to 4½ ounces) chopped mild green chiles
2 tablespoons fresh lime juice
1 tablespoon chopped fresh cilantro leaves
¼ teaspoon coarsely ground black pepper
2 tablespoons olive oil
½ teaspoon salt
1 small avocado, peeled and cut into ½-inch chunks
4 medium skinless, boneless chicken-breast halves
  (about 1¼ pounds)
1 tablespoon dried oregano
1 teaspoon paprika
1 teaspoon chili powder

**1** In medium bowl, combine tomato, onion, chiles with their liquid, lime juice, cilantro, pepper, 1 table-spoon olive oil, and ¼ teaspoon salt. Gently stir avocado into tomato mixture.

**2** Place the chicken breasts between 2 sheets of waxed paper and with the flat side of a small skillet or meat pounder, pound the chicken to a ¼-inch thickness.

**3** On waxed paper, combine oregano, paprika, chili powder, and remaining ¼ teaspoon salt. Dip chicken into spice mixture to coat both sides.

**4** In nonstick 12-inch skillet, heat remaining 1 table-spoon olive oil over medium-high heat until very hot. Add chicken breasts and cook until tender and golden, 8 to 10 minutes.

**5** To serve, spoon avocado salsa on platter with chicken. *Makes 4 main-dish servings.*

Each serving: About 315 calories, 35 g protein, 12 g carbohydrate, 15 g total fat (2 g saturated), 3 g fiber, 82 mg cholesterol, 580 mg sodium.

# Indonesian Chicken & Rice

PREP: 15 MINUTES / COOK: 30 MINUTES

1 cup regular long-grain rice
4 large skinless, boneless chicken-breast halves
  (about 1½ pounds)
½ cup white vinegar
1 teaspoon cornstarch
2 tablespoons vegetable oil
1 medium onion, diced
5 teaspoons hot curry powder
1 tablespoon grated peeled fresh ginger
¾ teaspoon salt
⅓ cup sugar
¼ cup dark seedless raisins
¼ cup shredded coconut

**1** Prepare rice as label directs.

**2** Meanwhile, with knife held in slanting position, almost parallel to cutting surface, slice each chicken breast across width into ⅛-inch-thick slices. In cup, mix vinegar, cornstarch, and *½ cup water* until blended; set aside.

**3** In 12-inch skillet, heat oil over medium heat. Add onion and cook until tender. Increase heat to high; add chicken, curry powder, ginger, and salt and cook, stirring constantly, until chicken just loses its pink color, about 3 minutes.

**4** Stir cornstarch mixture to blend; stir into mixture in skillet. Add sugar and stir to loosen brown bits from bottom of skillet; boil 1 minute.

**5** Remove skillet from heat; stir in hot cooked rice. Spoon chicken mixture onto warm serving platter. Sprinkle with raisins and coconut. *Makes 6 main-dish servings.*

Each serving: About 375 calories, 29 g protein, 47 g carbohydrate, 7 g total fat (2 g saturated), 2 g fiber, 66 mg cholesterol, 375 mg sodium.

# Lemon-Rosemary Chicken

🐔 🐔 🐔

PREP: 10 MINUTES / COOK: 10 MINUTES

2 medium lemons
1 tablespoon chopped fresh rosemary or
  ½ teaspoon dried rosemary, crushed
2 teaspoons olive oil
½ teaspoon salt
¼ teaspoon coarsely ground black pepper
1 garlic clove, minced
4 small skinless, boneless chicken-breast halves
  (about 1 pound)

**1** From 1 lemon, grate 2 teaspoons peel. Thinly slice half of second lemon; reserve slices for garnish. Squeeze juice from remaining 3 lemon halves into small bowl. Stir in lemon peel, rosemary, olive oil, salt, pepper, and garlic.

**2** Spray heavy 12-inch skillet with nonstick cooking spray. Heat skillet over medium-high heat until very hot.

**3** Meanwhile, toss chicken breasts with lemon-juice mixture.

**4** Place chicken breasts in hot skillet; cook 5 minutes, brushing with remaining lemon-juice mixture in bowl. Turn chicken over and cook 5 minutes longer until juices run clear when thickest part of chicken breast is pierced with tip of knife. Garnish with lemon slices. *Makes 4 main-dish servings.*

Each serving: About 155 calories, 27 g protein, 3 g carbohydrate, 4 g total fat (1 g saturated), 0 g fiber, 66 mg cholesterol, 365 mg sodium.

---

## GREAT GO-WITHS

# ROSEMARY BISCUIT MUFFINS

PREP: 25 MINUTES / BAKE: 15 MINUTES

*2 teaspoons dried rosemary, crushed*
*½ teaspoon coarsely ground black pepper*
*¾ cup (1½ sticks) margarine or butter*
*4 cups all-purpose flour*
*1 tablespoon baking powder*
*1½ teaspoons salt*
*½ teaspoon baking soda*
*1½ cups buttermilk\**

**1** In 1-quart saucepan, heat rosemary, pepper, and 4 tablespoons margarine or butter (½ stick) over low heat just until margarine begins to brown slightly; remove saucepan from heat. With pastry brush, brush insides of twelve 2½" by 1¼" muffin-pan cups with some rosemary mixture.

**2** Preheat oven to 400°F. In large bowl, mix flour, baking powder, salt, and baking soda. With pastry blender or two knives used scissor-fashion, cut in remaining ½ cup margarine or butter (1 stick) until mixture resembles coarse crumbs. With fork, stir buttermilk into flour mixture just until ingredients are blended.

**3** Turn dough onto lightly floured surface. Shape dough into ball. With floured knife, cut ball into 12 pieces; gently shape each into a ball. Place 1 dough ball in each muffin-pan cup. Brush tops with remaining rosemary mixture.

**4** Bake muffins 15 minutes or until golden brown. Serve muffins warm. Or, cool on wire rack; wrap in single layer in foil. Just before serving, reheat if desired. Makes 12 muffins.

\*Or, instead of buttermilk, add *⅓ cup buttermilk powder* to dry ingredients and use *1½ cups water* when liquid buttermilk is called for.

Each muffin: About 270 calories, 6 g protein, 34 g carbohydrate, 12 g total fat (2 g saturated), 1 g fiber, 1 mg cholesterol, 630 mg sodium.

# Skillet Lemon Chicken

PREP: 15 MINUTES / COOK: 15 MINUTES

4 medium skinless, boneless chicken-breast halves
  (about 1¼ pounds)
2 tablespoons plus 1½ teaspoons all-purpose flour
½ teaspoon salt
1 large egg
2 teaspoons olive oil
2 tablespoons margarine or butter
3 garlic cloves, crushed with side of chef's knife
½ lemon, thinly sliced
½ cup chicken broth
¼ cup dry white wine
2 tablespoons fresh lemon juice
2 tablespoons drained capers
1 tablespoon chopped fresh parsley leaves
Lemon leaves for garnish

1 Between 2 sheets plastic wrap, with meat mallet or rolling pin, pound chicken breasts to flatten slightly. On waxed paper, mix 2 tablespoons flour with salt. In pie plate, with fork, beat egg. Coat chicken with flour mixture, then dip in egg.

2 In nonstick 12-inch skillet, heat olive oil over medium-high heat until hot. Stir in 1 tablespoon margarine or butter until melted. Add chicken; cook 5 minutes. Reduce heat to medium; turn chicken and cook about 8 to 10 minutes longer, until juices run clear when thickest part of chicken is pierced with tip of knife. Transfer chicken to warm platter.

3 Add garlic and lemon slices to drippings in skillet; cook until golden. In cup, mix chicken broth, wine, lemon juice, and 1½ teaspoons flour until smooth; stir into mixture in skillet. Heat sauce to boiling; boil 1 minute. Stir in capers and remaining 1 tablespoon margarine or butter until margarine or butter melts. Discard garlic. Arrange lemon slices over and between chicken breasts. Pour sauce over chicken. Sprinkle with chopped parsley. Garnish platter with lemon leaves. *Makes 4 main-dish servings.*

Each serving: About 285 calories, 35 g protein, 7 g carbohydrate, 11 g total fat (2 g saturated), 0 g fiber, 135 mg cholesterol, 785 mg sodium.

# Orange Chicken & Beets

PREP: 10 MINUTES / COOK: 40 MINUTES

8 medium beets (about 1½ pounds, without tops)
1 tablespoon vinegar
½ teaspoon sugar
¾ teaspoon salt
2 medium oranges
1 tablespoon vegetable oil
1 medium onion, cut into thin slices
4 medium skinless, boneless chicken-breast halves
  (about 1¼ pounds)
¼ teaspoon coarsely ground black pepper
1 bunch watercress, tough stems trimmed

1 In 4-quart saucepan, heat beets and enough *water* to cover beets to boiling over high heat. Reduce heat to low; cover and simmer 30 minutes or until beets are fork-tender. Drain beets; peel and cut into wedges. Place beets in large bowl with vinegar, sugar, and ½ teaspoon salt.

2 Meanwhile, from oranges, grate 1 teaspoon peel and squeeze ½ cup juice.

3 In nonstick 10-inch skillet, heat oil over medium-high heat. Add onion and cook until golden brown. Push onion to side of skillet. Add chicken breasts and cook until browned on one side, about 3 minutes. Turn chicken breasts; add orange juice, pepper, and remaining ¼ teaspoon salt. Reduce heat to low; cover and simmer 5 minutes or until juices run clear when chicken is pierced with tip of knife.

4 Arrange watercress on platter. Place chicken over watercress on one side of platter. Spoon onions in skillet and half of sauce over chicken. Pour remaining sauce over beets in bowl; toss to coat. Arrange beets on platter with chicken; sprinkle beets with grated orange peel. *Makes 4 main-dish servings.*

Each serving: About 275 calories, 36 g protein, 20 g carbohydrate, 6 g total fat (1 g saturated), 3 g fiber, 82 mg cholesterol, 635 mg sodium.

◄ *Skillet Lemon Chicken*

# Paprika Chicken with Chopped Salad

🐔 🐔 🐔

PREP: 25 MINUTES / COOK: 10 MINUTES

Light and Easy. Boneless chicken dusted with spices, browned, and served with a vegetable salad—a breeze to make.

3 cups loosely packed chopped romaine lettuce
1 medium tomato, seeded and diced
1 medium yellow pepper, diced
½ medium cucumber, seeded and diced
¼ cup light mayonnaise
2 tablespoons low-fat (1%) milk
1 tablespoon chopped fresh dill
½ teaspoon sugar
3 tablespoons fresh lemon juice
¾ teaspoon salt
½ teaspoon coarsely ground black pepper
¾ teaspoon paprika
4 medium skinless, boneless chicken-breast halves
    (about 1¼ pounds)
1 tablespoon olive oil

1  In medium bowl, mix romaine lettuce, tomato, yellow pepper, and cucumber. In small bowl, mix mayonnaise, milk, dill, sugar, 1 tablespoon lemon juice, and ¼ teaspoon salt. Set aside.

2  On sheet of waxed paper, mix black pepper, paprika, and remaining ½ teaspoon salt. Use to coat the chicken breasts.

3  In nonstick 10-inch skillet, heat oil over medium-high heat until very hot. Add chicken breasts and cook until golden and juices run clear when pierced with tip of knife, 6 to 7 minutes, turning them once. Sprinkle chicken breasts with remaining 2 tablespoons lemon juice.

4  To serve, toss chopped vegetables with dressing; arrange salad on 4 dinner plates and top with hot chicken breasts. ***Makes 4 main-dish servings.***

Each serving: About 240 calories, 28 g protein, 8 g carbohydrate, 10 g total fat (2 g saturated), 2 g fiber, 71 mg cholesterol, 640 mg sodium.

# Potato-Crisp Chicken

🐔 🐔 🐔

PREP: 20 MINUTES / COOK: 20 MINUTES

4 large skinless, boneless chicken-breast halves
    (about 1½ pounds)
2 large baking potatoes (about 10 ounces each),
    peeled
½ teaspoon salt
1 tablespoon vegetable oil
¼ teaspoon coarsely ground black pepper

1  Place chicken breasts between 2 sheets of waxed paper and, with flat side of a small skillet or meat pounder, pound chicken to a ¼-inch thickness.

2  With very sharp knife, cut the middle, wide portion of each potato crosswise into 24 paper-thin slices (or slice potato in food processor with thin slicing blade attached), placing potato slices in bowl of cold water as soon as cut to prevent discoloration. When all potato slices are cut (there should be a total of 48); drain; pat dry with paper towels. Reserve any leftover potato for making mashed potatoes another day.

3  On work surface, arrange 6 potato slices to match size of a chicken-breast half, overlapping the potato slices to fit. Arrange chicken breast on top of potato slices; sprinkle chicken with ⅛ teaspoon salt. Top chicken with another 6 slices of potato to enclose chicken. Repeat with remaining chicken breasts and potato slices, using ⅛ teaspoon salt for each.

4  In nonstick 12-inch skillet, heat oil over medium-high heat until very hot. Add chicken and cook until potatoes are golden on bottom. Reduce heat to medium and cook 2 to 3 minutes. With metal spatula, carefully turn chicken; sprinkle with pepper. Cook over medium-high heat until potatoes are golden on other side. Reduce heat to medium and cook 2 to 3 minutes longer until potatoes are nicely browned and fork-tender. ***Makes 4 main-dish servings.***

Each serving: About 300 calories, 42 g protein, 19 g carbohydrate, 6 g total fat (1 g saturated), 2 g fiber, 99 mg cholesterol, 405 mg sodium.

# Parmesan-Crusted Chicken Breasts

PREP: 10 MINUTES / COOK: 15 MINUTES

¼ cup fresh bread crumbs (1 slice bread)
2 tablespoons freshly grated Parmesan cheese
4 medium skinless, boneless chicken-breast halves
  (about 1¼ pounds)
2 tablespoons olive oil
1 jar (4 ounces) pimientos, sliced
½ cup chicken broth
1 tablespoon chopped fresh parsley leaves
⅛ teaspoon coarsely ground black pepper

**1** On waxed paper, mix bread crumbs and Parmesan. Dip each chicken breast in bread-crumb mixture to coat.

**2** In nonstick 12-inch skillet, heat olive oil over medium-high heat until very hot. Add chicken breasts and cook until golden brown on one side, about 5 min-utes. Turn chicken; reduce heat to medium and cook until juices run clear when chicken is pierced with tip of knife, about 5 minutes longer. Transfer chicken to platter; keep warm.

**3** Add pimientos, chicken broth, parsley, and pepper to skillet, stirring to loosen any brown bits from bottom of skillet. Pour sauce over chicken on platter. *Makes 4 main-dish servings.*

Each serving: About 245 calories, 35 g protein, 3 g carbohydrate, 10 g total fat (2 g saturated), 0 g fiber, 84 mg cholesterol, 290 mg sodium.

## GREAT GO-WITHS

### GARBANZO SALAD

PREP: 10 MINUTES

*2 tablespoons red wine vinegar*
*2 tablespoons olive oil*
*1 teaspoon Dijon mustard*
*¼ teaspoon salt*
*3 small ripe tomatoes (about ¾ pound), each cut*
  *into 8 wedges*
*½ cup pitted Kalamata olives, coarsely chopped*
*1 green onion, thinly sliced*
*1 can (15 to 19 ounces) garbanzo beans, rinsed and*
  *drained*

In medium bowl, with wire whisk or fork, mix red wine vinegar, olive oil, Dijon mustard, and salt. Add tomato wedges, olives, green onion, and garbanzo beans; toss to mix well. Makes 4 accompaniment servings.

Each serving: About 215 calories, 5 g protein, 19 g carbohydrate, 13 g total fat (2 g saturated), 4 g fiber, 0 mg cholesterol, 620 mg sodium.

# Provençal Chicken

PREP: 5 MINUTES / COOK: 20 MINUTES

2 teaspoons olive oil
4 medium skinless, boneless chicken-breast halves
  (about 1¼ pounds)
1 medium onion, chopped
1 can (14½ ounces) chunky tomatoes with olive
  oil, garlic, and spices
½ cup pitted Kalamata olives, each cut in half
1 tablespoon drained capers

**1** In nonstick 12-inch skillet, heat 1 teaspoon olive oil over medium heat until very hot. Add chicken and cook for 8 to 10 minutes until golden. Transfer chicken to plate.

**2** Add remaining 1 teaspoon oil and onion to pan and cook until tender. Stir in chunky tomatoes, olives, capers, and *¼ cup water*; cook 1 minute to heat through. Pour sauce over chicken. *Makes 4 main-dish servings.*

Each serving: About 280 calories, 34 g protein, 7 g carbohydrate, 10 g total fat (1 g saturated), 2 g fiber, 82 mg cholesterol, 1015 mg sodium.

# Sautéed Chicken with Asparagus & Radicchio

🐓 🐓 🐓

PREP: 10 MINUTES / COOK: 20 MINUTES

½ teaspoon salt
¼ teaspoon coarsely ground black pepper
1 tablespoon plus 2 teaspoons all-purpose flour
4 large skinless, boneless chicken-breast halves
   (about 1½ pounds)
2 tablespoons margarine or butter
1 pound asparagus, trimmed and cut diagonally into
   2½-inch pieces
½ cup chicken broth
1 small head radicchio, thinly sliced

1 On waxed paper, mix salt, pepper, and 1 tablespoon flour; use to coat chicken breasts.

2 In 10-inch skillet, melt margarine or butter over medium-high heat. Add chicken and cook until lightly browned on both sides and juices run clear when pierced with tip of knife, about 5 minutes. Transfer chicken to platter; keep warm.

3 Add asparagus and ¼ *cup water* to skillet; heat to boiling over high heat. Reduce heat to low; cover and simmer 5 minutes or until asparagus is tender-crisp.

4 In 1-cup glass measuring cup, mix chicken broth and remaining 2 teaspoons flour until smooth. Add broth mixture to asparagus mixture in skillet; heat to boiling over high heat. Boil 1 minute. Remove saucepan from heat; stir in radicchio. Spoon asparagus, radicchio, and sauce over chicken. ***Makes 4 main-dish servings.***

Each serving: About 280 calories, 43 g protein, 7 g carbohydrate, 8 g total fat (2 g saturated), 1 g fiber, 99 mg cholesterol, 605 mg sodium.

*Sautéed Chicken with Asparagus & Radicchio*

# Prosciutto-Stuffed Chicken Rolls

🐓🐓🐓

PREP: 35 MINUTES / COOK: 25 MINUTES

If you'd like, you can use the sauce for this dish as a light coating sauce for pasta. Prepare 1 pound of strand pasta such as spaghetti as the label directs and toss it with the sauce.

4 ounces thinly sliced prosciutto or cooked ham, minced
¼ cup grated Parmesan cheese
¼ cup plain dried bread crumbs
2 tablespoons minced fresh parsley leaves
½ teaspoon dried oregano
4 small skinless, boneless chicken-breast halves (about 1 pound)
2 tablespoons vegetable oil
¼ teaspoon salt
1 can (14½ ounces) chicken broth or 1¾ cups homemade (page 11)
2 medium tomatoes, peeled and diced

**1** In small bowl, stir together prosciutto, Parmesan, bread crumbs, parsley, and oregano.

**2** Holding knife parallel to work surface and starting from a long side, cut each chicken-breast half in two, cutting almost but not all the way through. Spread chicken breasts open and place between 2 sheets of waxed paper. With the flat side of a small skillet or meat pounder, pound the chicken breasts to an even thickness.

**3** Sprinkle each breast with 1 heaping tablespoon prosciutto mixture; reserve remaining mixture. Starting from a long side, roll each breast jelly-roll fashion; secure with toothpicks.

**4** In 12-inch skillet, heat oil over medium-high heat until very hot. Add chicken rolls and salt and cook until chicken is browned on all sides and loses its pink color throughout, about 10 minutes. Transfer chicken to plate; keep warm.

**5** Add chicken broth and diced tomatoes to skillet and heat to boiling, stirring to loosen brown bits from bottom of skillet. Stir remaining prosciutto mixture into skillet. Reduce heat to low; cover and simmer 5 minutes to blend flavors. Return chicken rolls to skillet and heat through.

**6** Discard toothpicks from chicken rolls and cut rolls into ½-inch-thick slices. Spoon some sauce onto dinner plates and top with sliced chicken rolls. *Makes 6 main-dish servings.*

Each serving: About 215 calories, 25 g protein, 6 g carbohydrate, 10 g total fat (2 g saturated), 1 g fiber, 62 mg cholesterol, 895 mg sodium.

# Sautéed Chicken with Lemon-Dill Dressing

🐓🐓🐓

PREP: 20 MINUTES / COOK: 10 MINUTES

¾ cup plain low-fat yogurt
2 tablespoons fresh lemon juice
1 tablespoon chopped fresh dill
1¼ teaspoons sugar
1 teaspoon salt
2 cups chopped romaine lettuce
2 cups chopped radicchio
1 small cucumber, seeded and diced
1 can (8 ounces) garbanzo beans, rinsed and drained
1 tablespoon all-purpose flour
¼ teaspoon coarsely ground black pepper
4 medium skinless, boneless chicken-breast halves (about 1¼ pounds)
1 tablespoon olive oil

**1** In small bowl, mix yogurt, lemon juice, dill, sugar, and ½ teaspoon salt until blended. Cover and refrigerate dressing until ready to use.

**2** In large bowl, mix romaine, radicchio, cucumber, and garbanzo beans; cover and refrigerate.

**3** On sheet of waxed paper, mix flour, pepper, and remaining ½ teaspoon salt; use to coat chicken breasts. In 10-inch skillet, heat oil over medium-high heat until very hot. Add chicken breasts and cook, turning once, until golden on both sides and fork-tender, 6 to 8 minutes.

**4** To serve, toss lettuce mixture with half of lemon-dill dressing. Arrange chopped salad on platter; top with sautéed chicken breasts. Drizzle chicken with remaining dressing. *Makes 4 main-dish servings.*

Each serving: About 280 calories, 38 g protein, 15 g carbohydrate, 7 g total fat (1 g saturated), 3 g fiber, 85 mg cholesterol, 775 mg sodium.

# Sautéed Chicken with Onion Gravy

PREP: 10 MINUTES / COOK: 30 MINUTES

½ teaspoon salt
¼ teaspoon coarsely ground black pepper
2 tablespoons all-purpose flour
4 large skinless, boneless chicken-breast halves
    (about 1½ pounds)
2 tablespoons vegetable oil
4 small onions, each cut into 6 wedges
1 cup chicken broth, canned or homemade
    (page 11)
¼ cup dry sherry

**1** On waxed paper, mix salt, pepper, and 1 tablespoon flour; use to coat chicken breasts.

**2** In nonstick 12-inch skillet, heat 1 tablespoon oil over medium-high heat until very hot. Add chicken breasts and cook until golden and juices run clear when pierced with tip of knife, turning them once, about 8 to 10 minutes. Transfer chicken breasts to large platter.

**3** Add remaining 1 tablespoon oil to skillet and heat over medium heat. Add onions and cook until tender and golden, stirring frequently, about 15 minutes.

**4** Meanwhile, in small bowl, mix broth, sherry, and remaining 1 tablespoon flour until smooth.

**5** Add sherry mixture to skillet. Heat to boiling over high heat; boil 1 minute. Spoon sauce over chicken on platter. *Makes 4 main-dish servings.*

Each serving: About 330 calories, 41 g protein, 14 g carbohydrate, 10 g total fat (2 g saturated), 2 g fiber, 99 mg cholesterol, 670 mg sodium.

# Stir-Fried Chicken & Asian Vegetables

PREP: 15 MINUTES PLUS SOAKING / COOK: 15 MINUTES

1½ ounces dried tree ear mushrooms (optional)
4 large skinless, boneless chicken-breast halves
    (about 1½ pounds)
2 tablespoons dry sherry
1 tablespoon soy sauce
½ teaspoon salt
3 tablespoons vegetable oil
2 medium carrots, peeled and cut into 3-inch-long
    matchsticks
4 green onions, cut into 1-inch pieces
½ pound snow peas, strings removed, cut into
    matchstick-thin strips
4 ounces shiitake mushrooms, stems trimmed, caps
    thinly sliced
1 tablespoon cornstarch
½ cup chicken broth
3 pieces peeled fresh ginger, each about 1 inch in
    diameter and ¼ inch thick
2 tablespoons blanched whole almonds, toasted

**1** If using dried tree ear mushrooms, place in bowl; add *boiling water* to cover. Let soak 30 minutes. Drain tree ear mushrooms; discard soaking liquid. Rinse tree ears with running cold water to remove any sand. If tree ear mushrooms are large, cut into bite-size pieces.

**2** Meanwhile, with knife held in slanting position, almost parallel to the cutting surface, slice each chicken breast across width into ⅛-inch-thick slices. In medium bowl, combine chicken, sherry, soy sauce, and ¼ teaspoon salt.

**3** In 12-inch skillet, heat 1 tablespoon oil over medium-high heat. Add carrots and green onions and cook 2 minutes, stirring quickly and frequently. Add snow peas, shiitakes, tree ears, and remaining ¼ teaspoon salt, stirring quickly and frequently, until vegetables are tender-crisp, about 5 minutes; transfer to bowl.

**4** In cup, mix cornstarch and chicken broth; set aside.

**5** Wash and dry skillet. In same skillet, heat remaining 2 tablespoons oil over medium-high heat. Add ginger and cook until golden brown. Discard ginger. Stir chicken mixture into hot oil in skillet; cook over high heat, stirring constantly, until chicken is tender and just loses its pink color, about 3 minutes. Stir broth mixture; add to chicken, stirring until chicken mixture is slightly thickened. Return vegetables to skillet; toss to mix well. Spoon chicken mixture into serving bowl. Garnish with toasted almonds. *Makes 6 main-dish servings.*

Each serving: About 250 calories, 29 g protein, 9 g carbohydrate, 10 g total fat (1 g saturated), 3 g fiber, 66 mg cholesterol, 540 mg sodium.

---

## CREATIVE LEFTOVERS

# CHICKEN STIR-FRY

PREP: 20 MINUTES / COOK: 15 MINUTES

*1 tablespoon vegetable oil*
*1 bunch green onions, cut into 1-inch pieces*
*1 medium red pepper, cut into ¼-inch-thick slices*
*¾ pound mushrooms, sliced*
*1 tablespoon grated, peeled fresh ginger*
*1 garlic clove, finely chopped*
*½ pound snow peas, strings removed*
*3 tablespoons soy sauce*
*1 tablespoon cornstarch*
*¾ pound cooked chicken, cut into 2" by ½" strips (about 2 cups)*
*1 can (15 ounces) baby corn, drained*

**1** In nonstick 12-inch skillet, heat oil over high heat. Add green onions and red pepper and cook, stirring frequently, until they begin to brown. Stir in mushrooms, ginger, and garlic; cook 5 minutes or until any liquid in skillet evaporates and mushrooms are golden. Stir in snow peas; cook, stirring occasionally, until snow peas are tender-crisp.

**2** In cup, with whisk, mix soy sauce, cornstarch, and *¾ cup water*. Stir soy-sauce mixture, chicken, and baby corn into skillet; heat to boiling. Reduce heat to low; simmer 1 minute or until heated through and sauce thickens slightly. Makes 4 main-dish servings.

Each serving: About 290 calories, 31 g protein, 18 g carbohydrate, 11 g total fat (2 g saturated), 6 g fiber, 76 mg cholesterol, 870 mg sodium.

---

# Sweet & Sour Chicken with Cashews

PREP: 15 MINUTES / COOK: 20 MINUTES

Lean, tender chicken, vitamin-rich vegetables, and a sprinkle of crunchy cashews. This kind of Chinese food is good to eat and good for you!

4 large skinless, boneless chicken-breast halves
   (about 1½ pounds)
¼ cup soy sauce
2 tablespoons balsamic vinegar
2 teaspoons brown sugar
2 tablespoons vegetable oil
5 medium carrots, peeled and thinly sliced
   diagonally
2 large red peppers, cut into 1½-inch pieces
1 bunch green onions, cut into 1-inch pieces
⅓ cup cashews, coarsely chopped

**1** With knife held in slanting position, almost parallel to the cutting surface, slice each chicken breast across width into ⅛-inch-thick slices. In small bowl, combine soy sauce, balsamic vinegar, and brown sugar.

**2** In nonstick 12-inch skillet, heat 1 tablespoon oil over high heat until very hot. Add chicken and cook, stirring quickly and frequently, until chicken just loses its pink color throughout. Transfer chicken to bowl.

**3** Add remaining 1 tablespoon oil to skillet and heat over medium-high heat. Add carrots and red peppers and cook 4 minutes, stirring frequently. Add green onions and cook, stirring, until vegetables are tender-crisp.

**4** Return chicken and any accumulated juices in bowl to skillet; stir in soy-sauce mixture; cook 1 minute to heat through.

**5** To serve, sprinkle chicken with cashews. *Makes 4 main-dish servings.*

Each serving: About 395 calories, 44 g protein, 22 g carbohydrate, 15 g total fat (3 g saturated), 5 g fiber, 99 mg cholesterol, 1180 mg sodium.

# Stuffed Chicken Rolls Marinara

PREP: 25 MINUTES / COOK: 45 MINUTES

½ (10-ounce) package frozen chopped broccoli,
   thawed and squeezed dry
2 tablespoons grated Parmesan cheese
¼ teaspoon coarsely ground black pepper
1 teaspoon salt
2 cups shredded part-skim mozzarella cheese
   (8 ounces)
6 large skinless, boneless chicken-breast halves
   (about 2¼ pounds)
2 tablespoons vegetable oil
1 medium onion, chopped
½ pound medium mushrooms, sliced
1 can (28 ounces) plum tomatoes
1 can (6 ounces) tomato paste
2 teaspoons sugar
½ teaspoon dried basil

**1** In food processor with knife blade attached, blend broccoli, Parmesan, pepper, ¼ teaspoon salt, and half of shredded mozzarella until finely chopped.

**2** Place the chicken breasts between 2 sheets of waxed paper and with the flat side of a small skillet or meat pounder, pound the chicken to a ¼-inch thickness.

**3** Place one-sixth of broccoli mixture at narrow end of a chicken breast. Roll chicken breast jelly-roll fashion; secure with toothpicks. Repeat with remaining broccoli mixture and chicken breasts to make 6 rolls in all.

**4** In nonstick 12-inch skillet, heat 1 tablespoon oil over medium-high heat until very hot. Add chicken rolls and cook until lightly browned on all sides; transfer to plate.

**5** Add remaining 1 tablespoon oil to skillet. Add onion and mushrooms and cook until golden and tender and liquid from mushrooms evaporates. Reduce heat to medium; stir in tomatoes with their juice, tomato paste, sugar, basil, remaining ¾ teaspoon salt, and ½ *cup water*. Heat to boiling over high heat, stirring to break up tomatoes.

**6** Add chicken rolls. Reduce heat to low; cover and simmer 25 minutes. Sprinkle with remaining mozzarella cheese. Cover and simmer 10 minutes longer until chicken is tender and cheese melts. *Makes 6 main-dish servings.*

Each serving: About 415 calories, 53 g protein, 19 g carbohydrate, 14 g total fat (5 g saturated), 4 g fiber, 122 mg cholesterol, 1155 mg sodium.

## GREAT GO-WITHS

### BUTTERNUT SQUASH & PEAS

PREP: 10 MINUTES / COOK: 15 MINUTES

*2 small butternut squash (about 1½ pounds each)*
*¼ cup light brown sugar*
*½ teaspoon salt*
*⅛ teaspoon grated nutmeg*
*1 tablespoon margarine or butter*
*1 package (10 ounces) frozen peas*

**1** Cut butternut squash lengthwise in half; discard seeds. Cut each half crosswise into 1-inch-thick slices; cut off peel.

**2** In 3-quart saucepan, heat squash and enough *water* to cover to boiling over high heat. Reduce heat to low; cover and simmer 15 minutes or until squash is very tender. Drain squash well; return to saucepan. Add brown sugar, salt, and nutmeg. With potato masher, mash squash with margarine or butter until smooth; keep warm.

**3** Meanwhile, prepare peas as label directs; gently fold into mashed squash. Makes 6 accompaniment servings.

Each serving: About 175 calories, 4 g protein, 38 g carbohydrate, 2 g total fat (0 g saturated), 5 g fiber, 0 mg cholesterol, 280 mg sodium.

# Chicken au Poivre

🐓 🐓 🐓

PREP: 5 MINUTES / COOK: 20 MINUTES

3 tablespoons all-purpose flour
¾ teaspoon salt
1½ teaspoons coarsely ground black pepper
6 medium chicken cutlets (about 1½ pounds)
2 tablespoons vegetable oil
½ small onion, minced
½ cup chicken broth
2 tablespoons dry Marsala wine or dry sherry
    (optional)

**1** On waxed paper, combine 2 tablespoons flour and salt. Pat pepper onto chicken cutlets; then coat with flour mixture.

**2** In 12-inch skillet, heat oil over medium-high heat until very hot. Add chicken cutlets, half at a time, and cook 5 minutes or until they lose their pink color throughout, turning once halfway through cooking. Transfer cutlets them to warm large platter as they are done.

**3** Add onion to skillet and cook over medium heat until tender and golden.

**4** In 1-cup measuring cup, with fork, combine chicken broth and remaining 1 tablespoon flour until smooth. Stir broth mixture and Marsala, if you like, into skillet. Heat to boiling over high heat, stirring to loosen brown bits from bottom of skillet. Reduce heat to low; simmer 2 minutes, stirring occasionally. Pour sauce over chicken cutlets. *Makes 6 main-dish servings.*

Each serving: About 185 calories, 27 g protein, 4 g carbohydrate, 6 g total fat (1 g saturated), 0.5 g fiber, 66 mg cholesterol, 455 mg sodium.

# Chicken Cutlets with Easy Vegetable Sauté

🐓 🐓 🐓

PREP: 10 MINUTES / COOK: 35 MINUTES

Chicken and vegetables in light sauce with a splash of balsamic vinegar.

4 teaspoons plus 1 tablespoon olive oil
1 medium zucchini, thickly sliced
½ pound mushrooms, thickly sliced
6 medium chicken cutlets (about 1½ pounds)
2 tablespoons all-purpose flour
1 medium onion, chopped
1 can (14½ to 16 ounces) tomatoes
3 tablespoons balsamic vinegar or red wine vinegar
½ teaspoon salt

**1** In nonstick 12-inch skillet, heat 2 teaspoons oil over medium-high heat. Add zucchini and cook until tender-crisp and lightly browned; transfer to plate.

**2** Add 2 teaspoons oil to skillet and heat over medium-high heat. Add mushrooms and cook until browned; transfer to bowl.

**3** Coat chicken with flour. Add remaining 1 tablespoon oil to skillet and heat until very hot. Add chicken and cook until lightly browned and juices run clear when pierced with tip of knife, about 10 minutes. Transfer to bowl with mushrooms.

**4** Add onion to skillet and cook until tender and browned. Stir in *½ cup water.*

**5** Return chicken and vegetables to skillet; add tomatoes, vinegar, and salt; heat to boiling over high heat. Reduce heat to low and simmer, uncovered, 5 minutes. Add zucchini and cook until heated through. *Makes 6 main-dish servings.*

Each serving: About 220 calories, 29 g protein, 10 g carbohydrate, 7 g total fat (1 g saturated), 2 g fiber, 66 mg cholesterol, 390 mg sodium.

# Chicken Cutlets with Summer Vegetable Sauce

PREP: 10 MINUTES / COOK: 20 MINUTES

Our lighter version of an old Italian recipe—all the flavor is still there, but the calories per serving now total a mere 225!

1 medium lemon
2 tablespoons all-purpose flour
½ teaspoon salt
¾ pound chicken cutlets, cut crosswise in half
3 tablespoons margarine or butter
1 medium onion, diced
2 medium zucchini, cut into bite-size chunks
2 medium plum tomatoes, diced
½ cup chicken broth
¼ cup sliced fresh basil leaves or ½ teaspoon dried basil

**1** From lemon, grate peel and squeeze 2 teaspoons juice.

**2** On waxed paper, mix flour and salt; use to coat chicken cutlets.

**3** In nonstick 12-inch skillet, melt 2 tablespoons margarine or butter over medium-high heat. Add cutlets, half at a time, and cook until browned on both sides, transferring cutlets to warm plate as they brown.

**4** Add remaining 1 tablespoon margarine to skillet and melt over medium-high heat. Add onion and cook until golden. Add zucchini and cook, stirring occasionally, until golden and tender-crisp. Stir in tomatoes, lemon juice, lemon peel, and chicken broth. Heat to boiling over high heat; boil 1 minute, stirring to loosen browned bits from bottom of skillet. Stir in sliced basil.

**5** To serve, spoon sauce over cutlets. *Makes 4 main-dish servings.*

Each serving: About 225 calories, 22 g protein, 11 g carbohydrate, 10 g total fat (2 g saturated), 2 g fiber, 49 mg cholesterol, 580 mg sodium.

# Chicken Roulades

PREP: 30 MINUTES / COOK: 20 MINUTES

Serve on a bed of mini bow-tie pasta.

1 bunch basil
4 medium skinless, boneless chicken-breast halves (about 1¼ pounds)
½ jar (7 ounces) roasted red peppers, drained and sliced
2 ounces herb-and-garlic goat cheese, crumbled
¼ teaspoon salt
¼ teaspoon coarsely ground black pepper
1 tablespoon olive oil

**1** Measure ½ cup loosely packed basil leaves. Reserve remaining basil for garnish.

**2** Holding knife parallel to work surface and starting from a long side, cut each chicken-breast half almost in half, making sure not to cut all the way through. Spread chicken breasts open. Place the chicken breasts between 2 sheets of waxed paper and with the flat side of a small skillet or meat pounder, pound to a ¼-inch thickness.

**3** Place one-fourth of red-pepper slices, goat cheese, and basil leaves on each breast half. Starting from a long side, roll each breast jelly-roll fashion; secure with toothpicks.

**4** Sprinkle chicken roulades with salt and pepper. In nonstick 12-inch skillet, heat olive oil over medium-high heat until very hot. Add chicken roulades and cook until chicken is browned on all sides. Reduce heat to medium; cover and cook until chicken loses its pink color throughout, 12 to 15 minutes longer. Discard toothpicks. Slice roulades crosswise into diagonal slices to serve. Garnish with basil. *Makes 4 main-dish servings.*

Each serving: About 230 calories, 35 g protein, 3 g carbohydrate, 8 g total fat (3 g saturated), 1 g fiber, 97 mg cholesterol, 345 mg sodium.

*Chicken Roulades* ➤

# Chicken Cutlets with Sherried Mushrooms

PREP: 20 MINUTES / COOK: 20 MINUTES

4 medium skinless, boneless chicken-breast halves
   (about 1¼ pounds)
¼ teaspoon dried thyme
4 tablespoons all-purpose flour
¾ teaspoon salt
3 tablespoons olive oil
¾ pound mushrooms, each cut into quarters
¼ cup dry sherry
1 can (14½ ounces) chicken broth or 1¾ cups
   homemade (page 11)
2 tablespoons chopped fresh parsley leaves

**1** Holding knife almost parallel to work surface, cut each chicken breast crosswise into 3 or 4 thin slices. Place the slices between 2 sheets of waxed paper and with the flat side of a small skillet or meat pounder, pound to a ⅛-inch thickness.

**2** On waxed paper, combine thyme, 3 tablespoons flour, and ½ teaspoon salt. Dip each chicken piece into flour mixture to coat.

**3** In nonstick 12-inch skillet, heat 2 tablespoons oil over medium-high heat until very hot. Add chicken, a few pieces at a time, and cook until lightly browned, about 4 minutes, turning once. Transfer chicken to plate.

**4** Add remaining 1 tablespoon oil, mushrooms, and remaining ¼ teaspoon salt to skillet and cook until lightly browned, about 5 minutes. In cup, stir together sherry and remaining 1 tablespoon flour. Stir sherry mixture and chicken broth into mushrooms in skillet; heat to boiling over high heat. Reduce heat to low; simmer 1 minute or until sauce boils and thickens slightly, stirring occasionally. Return chicken to skillet. Stir in parsley and heat through. *Makes 4 main-dish servings.*

Each serving: About 325 calories, 36 g protein, 11 g carbohydrate, 13 g total fat (2 g saturated), 1 g fiber, 82 mg cholesterol, 980 mg sodium.

# Chicken in Pimiento Cream

PREP: 10 MINUTES / COOK: 20 MINUTES

6 medium skinless, boneless chicken thighs (about
   1½ pounds), each cut horizontally in half
½ teaspoon salt
1 tablespoon olive oil
1 jar (6½ ounces) pimientos, drained
¾ cup half-and-half or light cream
1 tablespoon dried basil
¼ teaspoon hot pepper sauce or ¼ teaspoon
   ground red pepper (cayenne)

**1** Sprinkle chicken with salt.

**2** In nonstick 12-inch skillet, heat oil over medium-high heat until very hot. Add chicken and cook until well browned on both sides, turning once. Transfer chicken to bowl. Discard fat in skillet.

**3** Meanwhile, in blender or food processor with knife blade attached, blend pimientos, half-and-half, and basil until smooth.

**4** Return chicken to skillet; add hot pepper sauce and pimiento cream. Cook over medium-low heat until chicken and pimiento cream are heated through, stirring occasionally. *Makes 4 main-dish servings.*

Each serving: About 305 calories, 35 g protein, 5 g carbohydrate, 15 g total fat (5 g saturated), 0 g fiber, 158 mg cholesterol, 470 mg sodium.

# Sautéed Chicken & Shrimp in White Wine-Caper Sauce

🐓 🐓 🐓

PREP: 25 MINUTES / COOK: 25 MINUTES

3 tablespoons all-purpose flour
1 teaspoon salt
1 pound chicken cutlets, cut into 3" by 2" pieces
3 teaspoons plus 2 tablespoons olive oil
1 package (10 ounces) large mushrooms, sliced
1 pound large shrimp, shelled and deveined
1 shallot or small onion, minced
¼ cup dry white wine
2 tablespoons capers (optional)

**1** On waxed paper, combine 2 tablespoons flour and ½ teaspoon salt. Dip chicken pieces into flour mixture to coat.

**2** In nonstick 12-inch skillet, heat 2 teaspoons oil over medium-high heat. Add mushrooms and cook until golden. With slotted spoon, transfer mushrooms to large bowl.

**3** Add 1 teaspoon oil to skillet and heat over medium-high heat. Add shrimp and shallot and cook until shrimp turn opaque throughout. Transfer to bowl with mushrooms.

**4** Add 1 tablespoon oil to skillet and heat until very hot. Add chicken cutlets, half at a time, and cook 2 to 3 minutes until chicken loses its pink color throughout; transfer to same bowl.

**5** Add remaining 1 tablespoon oil to skillet. Stir in remaining 1 tablespoon flour; cook until flour begins to brown slightly, about 30 seconds, stirring constantly. Gradually stir in wine, remaining ½ teaspoon salt, and 1¼ cups water. Heat over high heat until sauce boils and thickens slightly; boil 1 minute.

**6** Return the chicken mixture to skillet; stir in the capers and heat through. *Makes 6 main-dish servings.*

Each serving: About 250 calories, 31 g protein, 6 g carbohydrate, 10 g total fat (2 g saturated), 1 g fiber, 137 mg cholesterol, 530 mg sodium.

# Turkey with Roasted Pepper Purée

PREP: 20 MINUTES / COOK: 20 MINUTES

1 pound turkey cutlets
1 medium lemon
½ jar (7 ounces) roasted red peppers
¾ teaspoon salt
¼ teaspoon coarsely ground black pepper
2 tablespoons margarine or butter
½ small onion, finely chopped
¼ teaspoon sugar
¼ cup crumbled feta cheese (1 ounce)
1 tablespoon chopped fresh parsley leaves

**1** Place the turkey cutlets between 2 sheets of waxed paper and with the flat side of a small skillet or meat pounder, pound the turkey to a ⅛-inch thickness.

**2** From lemon, grate 1 teaspoon peel and squeeze 2 teaspoons juice. In blender, blend roasted red peppers, lemon peel, lemon juice, and *½ cup water* until smooth.

**3** Sprinkle turkey cutlets with ½ teaspoon salt and black pepper. In nonstick 12-inch skillet, melt 1 tablespoon butter or margarine over medium-high heat. Add turkey cutlets, half at a time, and cook until golden and turkey loses its pink color throughout, transferring cutlets to plate as they are done.

**4** Add remaining 1 tablespoon margarine or butter to skillet. Add onion and cook until tender. Stir in puréed roasted-pepper mixture, sugar, and remaining ¼ teaspoon salt; boil 1 minute.

**5** Spoon roasted-pepper sauce onto 4 warm dinner plates. Arrange turkey over sauce. Sprinkle with feta cheese and parsley. *Makes 4 main-dish servings.*

Each serving: About 215 calories, 29 g protein, 6 g carbohydrate, 8 g total fat (2 g saturated), 0.5 g fiber, 77 mg cholesterol, 705 mg sodium.

# Turkey Cutlets with Fruit Sauce

PREP: 15 MINUTES / COOK: 15 MINUTES

¼ cup dried apricots, coarsely chopped
2 tablespoons dried currants or raisins
¼ cup light mayonnaise
2 tablespoons mango chutney
1 teaspoon curry powder
4 turkey cutlets (about 1 pound)
2 tablespoons all-purpose flour
½ teaspoon salt
¼ teaspoon coarsely ground black pepper
2 tablespoons vegetable oil
1 small onion, thinly sliced

**1** In small bowl, combine apricots, currants, and *½ cup hot tap water*; set aside.

**2** In another small bowl, mix mayonnaise, chutney (chopping any large pieces), and curry powder; set aside.

**3** If turkey cutlets are thick, place them between 2 sheets of waxed paper and with the flat side of a small skillet or meat pounder, pound to a ⅛-inch thickness. On waxed paper, combine flour, salt, and pepper. Dip each turkey cutlet in flour mixture to coat.

**4** In nonstick 12-inch skillet, heat 1 tablespoon oil over medium-high heat until very hot. Add turkey cutlets, 2 at a time, until they lose their pink color throughout, about 2 minutes per side. Transfer cutlets to warm platter.

**5** Add remaining 1 tablespoon oil to skillet. Add onion and cook until golden. Stir in fruit mixture and mayonnaise mixture and heat through. Spoon sauce over cutlets. *Makes 4 main-dish servings.*

Each serving: About 325 calories, 29 g protein, 22 g carbohydrate, 13 g total fat (2 g saturated), 2 g fiber, 75 mg cholesterol, 550 mg sodium.

*Turkey Cutlets with Fruit Sauce*

# Turkey Cutlets with Provolone, Basil & Roasted Peppers

🐔 🐔 🐔

PREP: 15 MINUTES / COOK: 15 MINUTES

4 turkey cutlets (6 ounces each), each ¼ inch thick
1 cup shredded provolone or mozzarella cheese
   (4 ounces)
4 tablespoons chopped roasted red peppers
4 tablespoons finely slivered fresh basil
3 tablespoons dried bread crumbs
2 tablespoons grated Parmesan cheese
½ teaspoon salt
½ teaspoon coarsely ground black pepper
2 tablespoons milk
2 tablespoons olive oil

**1** On half of each turkey cutlet, arrange one-fourth each of shredded cheese, chopped roasted peppers, and basil. Fold other half of turkey cutlets over filling. Press edges of turkey cutlets together to seal slightly.

**2** On waxed paper, combine bread crumbs, Parmesan, salt, and black pepper. Pour milk into pie plate. Dip turkey cutlets, one at a time, into milk, then into bread-crumb mixture.

**3** In nonstick 12-inch skillet, heat olive oil over medium heat until very hot. Add cutlets and cook about 10 minutes or until golden brown and fork-tender and cheese melts, turning once. *Makes 4 main-dish servings.*

Each serving: About 390 calories, 51 g protein, 6 g carbohydrate, 17 g total fat (7 g saturated), 0.5 g fiber, 128 mg cholesterol, 730 mg sodium.

# Lemony Turkey Cutlets with Artichokes

PREP: 10 MINUTES / COOK: 30 MINUTES

1 package (9 ounces) frozen artichoke hearts
1 large lemon
3 tablespoons plus 1 teaspoon all-purpose flour
¾ teaspoon salt
1 pound turkey cutlets (⅛ inch thick), cut into
   3" by 3" pieces
2 tablespoons vegetable oil
1 large red pepper, sliced
1 small onion, thinly sliced
½ cup chicken broth

**1** Prepare artichoke hearts as label directs. From lemon, grate 1 teaspoon peel and squeeze 1 tablespoon juice.

**2** On waxed paper, combine lemon peel, 3 tablespoons flour, and ½ teaspoon salt; use to coat turkey.

**3** In nonstick 12-inch skillet, heat 1 tablespoon oil over medium-high heat until very hot. Add turkey cutlets, half at a time, and cook 2 to 3 minutes until lightly browned and they lose their pink color throughout; transfer to bowl.

**4** Add remaining 1 tablespoon oil to skillet. Add red pepper, onion, and remaining ¼ teaspoon salt and cook until vegetables are lightly browned. Stir in artichoke hearts; continue cooking until pepper and onion are tender-crisp.

**5** In small bowl, with whisk, mix chicken broth, lemon juice, and remaining 1 teaspoon flour. Add to vegetable mixture, stirring until sauce boils and thickens slightly; boil 1 minute. Return cutlets to skillet; heat through. Spoon mixture onto warm platter. *Makes 4 main-dish servings.*

Each serving: About 255 calories, 31 g protein, 15 g carbohydrate, 8 g total fat (1 g saturated), 5 g fiber, 70 mg cholesterol, 655 mg sodium.

# Turkey Cutlets with Curried Apricot Sauce

🐓 🐓 🐓

PREP: 15 MINUTES / COOK: 15 MINUTES

1¼ pounds turkey cutlets
¼ teaspoon salt
¼ teaspoon coarsely ground black pepper
4 teaspoons olive oil
1 small onion, chopped
1 teaspoon curry powder
½ teaspoon ground coriander
1 cup chicken broth, canned or homemade
  (page 11)
1 teaspoon cornstarch
½ cup dried apricots or pitted prunes

**1** Sprinkle turkey cutlets with salt and pepper. In nonstick 12-inch skillet, heat 2 teaspoons olive oil over medium-high heat until very hot. Add turkey cutlets and cook 3 to 5 minutes, turning cutlets once, until lightly browned on the outside and they just lose their pink color on the inside. Transfer cutlets to platter.

**2** Add remaining 2 teaspoons olive oil to skillet and heat over medium heat until hot. Add onion and cook 6 to 8 minutes, until onion is golden and tender, stirring occasionally.

**3** Increase heat to medium-high. Add curry powder and coriander; cook 1 minute, stirring. In cup, with fork, mix chicken broth and cornstarch until smooth. Add broth mixture and apricots or prunes to skillet; heat to boiling. Cook 1 minute. To serve, spoon sauce over turkey cutlets. *Makes 4 main-dish servings.*

Each serving: About 260 calories, 36 g protein, 14 g carbohydrate, 6 g total fat (1 g saturated), 2 g fiber, 88 mg cholesterol, 480 mg sodium.

# Turkey Cutlets with Cranberry Sauce

🐓 🐓 🐓

PREP: 15 MINUTES / COOK: 15 MINUTES

3 tablespoons all-purpose flour
¾ teaspoon salt
1 pound turkey cutlets (⅛ inch thick), cut into 3"
  by 3" pieces
2 tablespoons olive or vegetable oil
1 cup chicken broth, canned or homemade
  (page 11)
1 teaspoon cornstarch
⅔ cup whole-berry cranberry sauce
1 tablespoon fresh lemon juice

**1** On waxed paper, combine flour and ½ teaspoon salt. Dip turkey pieces into flour mixture to coat.

**2** In nonstick 12-inch skillet, heat olive oil over medium-high heat until very hot. Add turkey cutlets, half at a time, and cook 2 to 3 minutes until turkey cutlets are lightly browned and lose their pink color throughout; transfer to bowl.

**3** In cup, with fork, mix chicken broth and cornstarch until smooth. Add broth mixture, cranberry sauce, lemon juice, and remaining ¼ teaspoon salt to skillet, and cook, stirring constantly, until sauce boils and thickens slightly. Return turkey cutlets to skillet; heat through. Spoon mixture onto warm platter. *Makes 4 main-dish servings.*

Each serving: About 290 calories, 29 g protein, 24 g carbohydrate, 8 g total fat (1 g saturated), 1 g fiber, 70 mg cholesterol, 780 mg sodium.

◀ *Turkey Cutlets with Curried Apricot Sauce*

# Breaded Turkey Cutlets with Lemon-Butter Sauce

PREP: 25 MINUTES / COOK: 35 MINUTES

Lightly coated with bread crumbs, these tasty cutlets are sautéed until golden and simmered in a delicate lemon sauce.

2 pounds small turkey cutlets (about 8)
2 large eggs
2 tablespoons milk
3½ cups fresh bread crumbs (about 8 slices white bread)
4 tablespoons margarine or butter (½ stick)
2 small lemons
1½ cups chicken broth, canned or homemade (page 11)
½ teaspoon salt

**1** Place the turkey cutlets between 2 sheets of waxed paper and with the flat side of a small skillet or meat pounder, pound the turkey to a ⅛-inch thickness.

**2** In pie plate, with fork, beat eggs with milk until well blended. Place bread crumbs on waxed paper. Dip cutlets in egg mixture, then in crumbs, to coat both sides.

**3** In nonstick 12-inch skillet, melt 2 tablespoons margarine or butter over medium-high heat. Add half of turkey cutlets and cook until browned on both sides, transferring them to plate as they brown. Repeat with remaining turkey cutlets and remaining 2 tablespoons margarine or butter. Keep cutlets warm.

**4** Reduce heat to low. Squeeze juice of 1 lemon into drippings in skillet; stir in chicken broth and salt, scraping to loosen brown bits from bottom of skillet. Return turkey cutlets to skillet; heat to boiling over high heat. Reduce heat to low; cover and simmer mixture 5 minutes or until cutlets are fork-tender.

**5** To serve, thinly slice the remaining lemon; arrange cutlets slightly overlapping, on warm large platter and garnish with lemon slices. Pour lemon-butter sauce over cutlets. *Makes 8 main-dish servings.*

Each serving: About 260 calories, 32 g protein, 12 g carbohydrate, 9 g total fat (2 g saturated), 0.5 g fiber, 125 mg cholesterol, 580 mg sodium.

# Turkey Cutlets with Chopped Arugula Salad

PREP: 15 MINUTES / COOK: 15 MINUTES

1 green onion, thinly sliced
2 tablespoons grated Parmesan cheese
1 tablespoon red wine vinegar
½ teaspoon Dijon mustard
¼ teaspoon salt
¼ teaspoon coarsely ground black pepper
3 tablespoons olive oil
4 large plum tomatoes (about 1 pound), cut into ¾-inch chunks
2 bunches arugula, well washed and coarsely chopped
4 large turkey cutlets (about 1 pound)
⅓ cup seasoned dried bread crumbs

**1** In medium bowl, with wire whisk or fork, mix green onion with Parmesan, vinegar, mustard, salt, pepper, and 2 tablespoons olive oil. Add tomatoes and arugula; gently toss to mix well.

**2** If turkey cutlets are thick, pound them to a ¼-inch thickness. Coat turkey cutlets with bread crumbs.

**3** In nonstick 12-inch skillet, heat remaining 1 tablespoon oil over medium-high heat until very hot. Add 2 turkey cutlets at a time and cook until golden on both sides and they lose their pink color throughout.

**4** Place turkey cutlets on 4 dinner plates. Pile chopped salad on top of cutlets. *Makes 4 main-dish servings:*

Each serving: About 305 calories, 33 g protein, 15 g carbohydrate, 13 g total fat (2 g saturated), 3 g fiber, 72 mg cholesterol, 550 mg sodium.

*Chicken Amalfi*

# Chicken Amalfi

PREP: 10 MINUTES / COOK: 40 MINUTES

2 tablespoons olive or vegetable oil
4 medium chicken legs (about 2¼ pounds), separated into drumsticks and thighs, skin removed
½ teaspoon salt
1 medium onion, thinly sliced
¼ cup Kalamata or Niçoise olives, pitted and coarsely chopped
3 medium plum tomatoes, seeded and diced
3 tablespoons capers, drained and chopped
½ cup chicken broth
½ teaspoon dried rosemary, crushed
2 tablespoons fresh lemon juice
1 tablespoon chopped fresh parsley leaves

**1** In 12-inch skillet, heat oil over medium-high heat until very hot. Add chicken pieces and salt and cook until chicken is golden brown on all sides, transferring chicken pieces to plate as they brown.

**2** Add onion to skillet and cook until golden, stirring frequently. Stir in olives, tomatoes, capers, chicken broth, rosemary, lemon juice, and ⅓ *cup water.*

**3** Return chicken to skillet; heat to boiling over high heat. Reduce heat to low; cover and simmer 25 to 30 minutes, occasionally spooning olive mixture over chicken, until juices run clear when chicken is pierced with tip of knife.

**4** To serve, arrange chicken drumsticks and thighs on platter; spoon olive mixture over. Sprinkle with chopped parsley. *Makes 4 main-dish servings.*

Each serving: About 290 calories, 30 g protein, 8 g carbohydrate, 15 g total fat (3 g saturated), 1 g fiber, 116 mg cholesterol, 985 mg sodium.

# Chicken Thighs with Ginger-Lime Sauce

🐓🐓🐓

PREP: 10 MINUTES / COOK: 25 MINUTES

3 tablespoons all-purpose flour
½ teaspoon salt
¼ teaspoon coarsely ground black pepper
6 medium bone-in chicken thighs (about 2 pounds), skin removed, each cut in half
1 tablespoon vegetable oil
1 teaspoon minced, peeled fresh ginger

1 garlic clove, minced
1 small lime
2 tablespoons soy sauce
2 tablespoons honey
1 tablespoon Asian sesame oil

**1** On waxed paper, combine flour, salt, and pepper; use to coat chicken thighs.

**2** In nonstick 10-inch skillet, heat oil over medium-high heat until very hot. Add chicken thighs and cook until browned on both sides. Reduce heat to medium; add ginger and garlic; cover and cook about 20 minutes or until chicken is fork-tender.

**3** Meanwhile, grate peel from lime; reserve for garnish. Squeeze juice from lime.

**4** Add lime juice, soy sauce, honey, and sesame oil to skillet and heat to boiling over medium heat, turning chicken thighs occasionally to coat with sauce in skillet. Garnish with grated lime peel to serve. *Makes 4 main-dish servings.*

Each serving: About 275 calories, 27 g protein, 15 g carbohydrate, 12 g total fat (2 g saturated), 0 g fiber, 107 mg cholesterol, 915 mg sodium.

---

## CREATIVE LEFTOVERS

### THAI TURKEY

PREP: 10 MINUTES / COOK: 15 MINUTES

*1 garlic clove, minced*
*2 tablespoons soy sauce*
*1 tablespoon chopped fresh cilantro leaves*
*1 tablespoon honey*
*1½ teaspoons curry powder*
*1 teaspoon Asian sesame oil*
*½ teaspoon cornstarch*
*¼ teaspoon crushed red pepper*
*1 tablespoon vegetable oil*
*3 green onions, thinly sliced*
*1 medium red pepper, cut into 2-inch-long thin strips*
*3 cups shredded leftover turkey breast meat (about 12 ounces)*

**1** In small bowl, mix garlic, soy sauce, cilantro, honey, curry powder, sesame oil, cornstarch, crushed red pepper, and *⅓ cup water* until well blended.

**2** In 10-inch skillet, heat oil over high heat. Add green onions and red pepper and cook, stirring frequently, until vegetables are tender and golden. Stir in soy-curry mixture and shredded turkey meat and cook, stirring to coat turkey well, until heated through. Makes 4 main-dish servings.

Each serving: About 190 calories, 27 g protein, 8 g carbohydrate, 5 g total fat (1 g saturated), 1 g fiber, 71 mg cholesterol, 560 mg sodium.

---

# Chicken with Buttermilk Gravy

🐓🐓🐓

PREP: 10 MINUTES / COOK: 25 MINUTES

8 medium bone-in chicken thighs (about 2½ pounds), skin removed
1 cup buttermilk
1 teaspoon chopped fresh thyme or ½ teaspoon dried thyme
½ teaspoon salt
½ cup plus 1 tablespoon all-purpose flour
1 tablespoon vegetable oil
1 cup chicken broth, canned or homemade (page 11)

**1** In bowl, mix chicken thighs with ½ cup buttermilk. On waxed paper, mix thyme, salt, and ½ cup flour. Dip thighs into mixture to coat.

**2** In nonstick 12-inch skillet, heat oil over medium-high heat until very hot. Add chicken thighs and cook until golden. Reduce heat to medium-low; cook until juices run clear when chicken is pierced with tip of knife, turning chicken occasionally, about 15 minutes longer. Transfer chicken to platter.

**3** In 2-cup measuring cup, with fork, mix remaining 1 tablespoon flour and chicken broth. Stir mixture into skillet, scraping up any browned bits; heat over medium-high heat until mixture boils and thickens; boil 1 minute. Remove from heat; stir in remaining ½ cup buttermilk. Serve gravy with chicken. *Makes 4 main-dish servings.*

Each serving: About 320 calories, 36 g protein, 17 g carbohydrate, 11 g total fat (3 g saturated), 0.5 g fiber, 137 mg cholesterol, 755 mg sodium.

# Country Chicken

PREP: 10 MINUTES / COOK: 40 MINUTES

3 tablespoons all-purpose flour
1 teaspoon salt
½ teaspoon coarsely ground black pepper
6 medium skinless, boneless chicken thighs (about 1½ pounds), each cut in half
1 tablespoon olive or vegetable oil
5 medium red potatoes (1 pound), each cut in half
1 medium red pepper, cut into bite-size pieces
1 medium yellow pepper, cut into bite-size pieces
2 tablespoons brown sugar
2 tablespoons cider vinegar

**1** On waxed paper, mix flour, ½ teaspoon salt, and ¼ teaspoon black pepper. Coat chicken thighs with flour mixture.

**2** In nonstick 12-inch skillet, heat oil over medium-high heat until very hot. Add chicken thighs and cook until golden brown. Transfer chicken to bowl.

**3** Add potatoes, red and yellow peppers, remaining ½ teaspoon salt, and remaining ¼ teaspoon black pepper and cook until vegetables are golden brown. Return chicken to skillet. Reduce heat to medium; cover and continue cooking until juices run clear when chicken is pierced with tip of knife and potatoes are fork-tender, stirring often.

**4** Stir in brown sugar and cider vinegar; heat through. *Makes 4 main-dish servings.*

Each serving: About 385 calories, 37 g protein, 35 g carbohydrate, 10 g total fat (2 g saturated), 3 g fiber, 141 mg cholesterol, 740 mg sodium.

# Asian Glazed Chicken & Eggplant

PREP: 10 MINUTES / COOK: 35 MINUTES

6 medium baby eggplants (about 2 pounds) or 2 small eggplants (about 1 pound each)
2 tablespoons vegetable oil
6 medium skinless, boneless chicken-breast halves (about 1¾ pounds), cut lengthwise into ½-inch-wide strips
1 garlic clove, minced
1 tablespoon grated, peeled fresh ginger or 1 teaspoon ground ginger
¼ cup soy sauce
¼ cup red wine vinegar
3 tablespoons sugar
1 tablespoon Asian sesame oil
2 teaspoons cornstarch
¼ teaspoon crushed red pepper

**1** Cut each baby eggplant lengthwise in half. (If using regular eggplants, cut each crosswise in half, then lengthwise into 1-inch-wide strips.)

**2** In 12-inch skillet, heat oil over high heat until very hot. Add chicken and cook until lightly browned and it loses its pink color throughout. With slotted spoon, transfer chicken to bowl.

**3** Add eggplant, garlic, ginger, and *½ cup water* to skillet and heat to boiling over high heat. Reduce heat to medium-low; cover and cook, stirring occasionally, until liquid evaporates and eggplant is very tender, about 20 minutes.

**4** Meanwhile, in cup, with fork, mix soy sauce, vinegar, sugar, sesame oil, and cornstarch until blended.

**5** Add chicken, soy-sauce mixture, and crushed red pepper to eggplant in skillet; heat to boiling over high heat. Reduce heat to medium and cook, stirring, until sauce boils and thickens slightly. *Makes 6 main-dish servings.*

Each serving: About 280 calories, 33 g protein, 18 g carbohydrate, 9 g total fat (1 g saturated), 2 g fiber, 77 mg cholesterol, 780 mg sodium.

# Sautéed Turkey Cutlets with Mushroom Sauce

PREP: 15 MINUTES / COOK: 15 MINUTES

1¼ pounds turkey cutlets
¼ teaspoon salt
¼ teaspoon coarsely ground black pepper
4 teaspoons olive oil
1 garlic clove, crushed with garlic press
1 pound mushrooms, sliced
¼ teaspoon dried thyme
1 cup chicken broth, canned or homemade
   (page 11)
1 teaspoon cornstarch

**1** Sprinkle turkey cutlets with salt and pepper. In nonstick 12-inch skillet, heat 2 teaspoons olive oil over medium-high heat until very hot. Add turkey cutlets and cook 3 to 5 minutes, turning cutlets once, until lightly browned on the outside and they just lose their pink color on the inside. Transfer cutlets to platter.

**2** Add remaining 2 teaspoons olive oil to skillet and heat over medium heat until hot. Add garlic and cook 10 seconds. Add mushrooms and thyme and cook 10

*Sautéed Turkey Cutlets with Mushroom Sauce*

minutes longer or until mushrooms are golden and liquid evaporates. In cup, mix chicken broth and cornstarch until smooth. Add broth mixture to skillet and heat to boiling. Cook 2 minutes. Spoon sauce over cutlets. *Makes 4 main-dish servings.*

Each serving: About 235 calories, 38 g protein, 7 g carbohydrate, 6 g total fat (1 g saturated), 2 g fiber, 88 mg cholesterol, 480 mg sodium.

# Chicken & Artichokes with Pasta

PREP: 20 MINUTES / COOK: 30 MINUTES

4 teaspoons plus 1 tablespoon olive oil
2 large red peppers, cut into ½-inch slices
2 large yellow peppers, cut into ½-inch slices
Salt
1 pound large mushrooms, each cut in half
1 medium onion, chopped
1 pound skinless, boneless chicken breasts, cut
   crosswise into ¾-inch slices
1 pound penne or rigate pasta
2 jars (6 ounces each) marinated artichoke hearts
3 tablespoons balsamic vinegar or red wine vinegar
½ teaspoon coarsely ground black pepper
½ teaspoon dried basil
½ teaspoon sugar

**1** In nonstick 12-inch skillet, heat 2 teaspoons oil over medium-high heat. Add red and yellow peppers and ⅛ teaspoon salt and cook, stirring frequently, until tender and golden. With slotted spoon, transfer peppers to large bowl.

**2** Add 2 teaspoons oil to skillet along with mushrooms, onion, and ⅛ teaspoon salt and cook until vegetables are tender and golden, stirring frequently. Transfer mushroom mixture to bowl with peppers.

**3** Add remaining 1 tablespoon oil to skillet and heat over medium-high heat until very hot. Add chicken and ⅛ teaspoon salt and cook until chicken is golden brown and loses its pink color throughout.

**4** Meanwhile, in large saucepot, prepare pasta in *boiling salted water* as label directs; drain. Return pasta to saucepot; keep warm.

**5** Drain artichoke hearts, reserving marinade from 1 jar. In small bowl, combine artichoke marinade, balsamic vinegar, black pepper, basil, sugar, and ¼ teaspoon salt.

**6** Return vegetables to skillet with chicken. Add artichoke hearts and balsamic-vinegar mixture, tossing to coat well; heat through.

**7** In large bowl, toss pasta with chicken mixture. *Makes 8 main-dish servings.*

Each serving: About 385 calories, 23 g protein, 54 g carbohydrate, 9 g total fat (1 g saturated), 5 g fiber, 33 mg cholesterol, 570 mg sodium.

# Peanut Chicken

PREP: 10 MINUTES / COOK: 10 MINUTES

Here is a simple weeknight chicken dish. Serve it with basmati rice.

1 can (14½ ounces) diced tomatoes
¼ cup packed fresh cilantro leaves
¼ cup creamy peanut butter
2 garlic cloves
½ teaspoon salt
¼ teaspoon crushed red pepper
1 teaspoon ground cumin
¼ teaspoon ground cinnamon
1 pound chicken breast tenders
1 tablespoon vegetable oil

**1** Drain tomatoes and reserve juice. In blender at high speed or in food processor with knife blade attached, blend tomato juice, cilantro, peanut butter, garlic, salt, and crushed red pepper until pureed.

**2** In medium bowl, mix cumin and cinnamon; stir in chicken tenders.

**3** In nonstick 12-inch skillet, heat vegetable oil over medium-high heat until hot. Add chicken and cook, turning once, until browned, about 5 minutes.

**4** Pour peanut-butter mixture and diced tomatoes over chicken; heat to boiling. Reduce heat to low; simmer, uncovered, 5 minutes to blend flavors. *Makes 4 main-dish servings.*

Each serving: About 275 calories, 32 g protein, 8 g carbohydrate, 13 g total fat (2 g saturated), 2 g fiber, 66 mg cholesterol, 610 mg sodium.

# Balsamic Chicken with Potatoes & Arugula

PREP: 10 MINUTES / COOK: 25 MINUTES

6 large skinless, boneless chicken thighs (about 1¼ pounds), each cut in half
2 tablespoons all-purpose flour
½ teaspoon salt
1 tablespoon vegetable oil
3 garlic cloves, peeled and each cut lengthwise in half
1 pound medium red potatoes, each cut into quarters
2 tablespoons brown sugar
2 tablespoons balsamic or red wine vinegar
2 tablespoons soy sauce
2 bunches arugula, well washed

**1** In bowl, toss chicken with flour and salt.

**2** In nonstick 12-inch skillet, heat oil over medium heat until very hot. Add chicken thighs and garlic and cook, covered, 20 minutes or until chicken is browned and juices run clear when chicken is pierced with tip of knife, turning once halfway through cooking time.

**3** Meanwhile, in 2-quart saucepan, heat potatoes and enough *water* to cover to boiling over high heat. Reduce heat to low; cover and simmer 7 to 10 minutes until potatoes are just tender; drain and keep warm.

**4** In cup, with fork, stir brown sugar, balsamic vinegar, and soy sauce. When chicken is done, add vinegar mixture to skillet, tossing to coat chicken well. Remove skillet from heat; add potatoes and half of arugula, tossing to mix well. Arrange remaining arugula on platter or 4 dinner plates; top with chicken mixture. *Makes 4 main-dish servings.*

Each serving: About 355 calories, 33 g protein, 34 g carbohydrate, 10 g total fat (2 g saturated), 3 g fiber, 118 mg cholesterol, 955 mg sodium.

# Chicken, Spinach & Mushrooms with Linguine

🐓 🐓 🐓

PREP: 10 MINUTES / COOK: 20 MINUTES

Salt
1 pound linguine
2 tablespoons vegetable oil
1 pound chicken cutlets, cut crosswise into thin
    strips
1 medium onion, diced
½ pound shiitake mushrooms or regular
    mushrooms, thinly sliced
1 can (14½ ounces) chicken broth or 1¾ cups
    homemade (page 11)
6 ounces reduced-fat cream cheese (Neufchâtel)
1 medium bunch spinach, coarsely chopped
1 teaspoon coarsely ground black pepper

**1** In large saucepot, prepare pasta in *boiling salted water* as label directs; drain. Return linguine to saucepan; keep warm.

**2** Meanwhile, in nonstick 12-inch skillet, heat 1 tablespoon oil over medium-high heat until very hot. Add chicken and ½ teaspoon salt and cook until chicken is lightly browned and just loses its pink color throughout, about 5 minutes. With slotted spoon, transfer chicken to bowl.

**3** Add remaining 1 tablespoon oil to skillet. Add onion and cook until almost tender, about 5 minutes. Add mushrooms and ¼ teaspoon salt; cook until onion and mushrooms are golden.

**4** Add chicken broth and cream cheese. Heat to boiling over high heat, stirring until cream cheese melts; boil 2 minutes. Return chicken to skillet and stir in spinach and pepper; heat through. Toss linguine with chicken mixture. *Makes 6 main-dish servings.*

Each serving: About 510 calories, 33 g protein, 63 g carbohydrate, 13 g total fat (5 g saturated), 4 g fiber, 64 mg cholesterol, 760 mg sodium.

---

**CREATIVE LEFTOVERS**

# MOO SHU TURKEY

PREP: 20 MINUTES / COOK: 15 MINUTES

The Rosemary Roast Turkey Breast (page 163) adds an especially nice and unexpected flavor to this Asian-inspired dish. However, any leftover skinless roast turkey meat would be fine.

*8 (6-inch diameter) flour tortillas*
*3 tablespoons hoisin sauce*
*2 tablespoons soy sauce*
*¾ teaspoon Asian sesame oil*
*3 teaspoons olive oil*
*1 package (8 ounces) sliced mushrooms*
*1 package (16 ounces) shredded cabbage mix for*
    *coleslaw*
*½ medium red pepper, thinly sliced*
*3 green onions, thinly sliced*
*1 garlic clove, crushed with garlic press*
*2 teaspoons grated, peeled fresh ginger*
*¾ pound leftover skinless Rosemary Roast Turkey*
    *meat (page 163), pulled into shreds (2 cups)*

**1** Warm tortillas as label directs.

**2** Meanwhile, in small bowl, mix hoisin sauce, soy sauce, and sesame oil until smooth; set aside.

**3** In nonstick 12-inch skillet, heat 1 teaspoon olive oil over medium-high heat. Add mushrooms and cook until all liquid evaporates and mushrooms are browned, about 8 minutes; transfer mushrooms to bowl.

**4** Add remaining 2 teaspoons olive oil to skillet. Add cabbage mix, red pepper, and sliced green onions and cook 3 minutes, stirring constantly. Add garlic and ginger; cook 1 minute, stirring constantly. Stir in shredded turkey, hoisin-sauce mixture, and mushrooms; heat through.

**5** To serve, spoon turkey mixture onto warm tortillas and roll up. Makes 4 main-dish servings.

Each serving: About 400 calories, 32 g protein, 41 g carbohydrate, 12 g total fat (2 g saturated), 3 g fiber, 66 mg cholesterol, 1030 mg sodium.

---

# Chicken & Bok Choy Stir-Fry with Wide Noodles

PREP: 20 MINUTES / COOK: 30 MINUTES

1 tablespoon cornstarch
3 tablespoons soy sauce
2 tablespoons white vinegar
1 tablespoon Asian sesame oil
1 tablespoon grated, peeled fresh ginger
1½ teaspoons sugar
¼ teaspoon crushed red pepper
1 garlic clove, minced
1 pound skinless, boneless chicken breasts, cut crosswise into ¼-inch-wide strips
8 ounces fettuccine or tagliatelli noodles (wide ribbons)
2 tablespoons vegetable oil
1 medium head bok choy, cut crosswise into ½-inch-thick slices
¼ pound snow peas, strings removed
1 medium red pepper, cut into ¼-inch-wide strips
4 green onions, thinly sliced
¼ cup salted roasted cashews

**1** In medium bowl, mix cornstarch, soy sauce, vinegar, sesame oil, ginger, sugar, crushed red pepper, and garlic. Add chicken, tossing to coat; set aside.

**2** In large saucepot, prepare fettuccine in *boiling water* as label directs; do not use salt in water.

**3** Meanwhile, in nonstick 12-inch skillet, heat 1 tablespoon oil over high heat. Add bok choy and cook, stirring constantly, until bok choy is tender-crisp. With slotted spoon, transfer bok choy to bowl.

**4** Add snow peas and red pepper and cook, stirring occasionally, until vegetables are tender-crisp. Transfer to bowl with bok choy.

**5** With slotted spoon, remove chicken strips from soy-sauce mixture, reserving soy-sauce mixture. Add remaining 1 tablespoon oil to skillet and heat over medium-high heat until very hot. Add chicken and green onions and cook, stirring frequently, until chicken loses its pink color throughout. Return veg-

etables to skillet. Stir in reserved soy-sauce mixture; heat to boiling over high heat. Boil 1 minute.

**6** Drain fettuccine. Add fettuccine to chicken mixture, tossing to coat well. Spoon mixture onto platter; sprinkle with cashews. *Makes 4 main-dish servings.*

Each serving: About 545 calories, 39 g protein, 59 g carbohydrate, 17 g total fat (3 g saturated), 5 g fiber, 66 mg cholesterol, 1020 mg sodium.

# Chicken with Peas & Artichokes

PREP: 10 MINUTES / COOK: 20 MINUTES

¼ teaspoon coarsely ground black pepper
2 tablespoons plus 1 teaspoon all-purpose flour
¾ teaspoon salt
1 pound skinless, boneless chicken breasts, cut into 2-inch chunks
1 package (9 ounces) frozen artichoke hearts
1 tablespoon olive or vegetable oil
2 tablespoons balsamic vinegar
4 ounces smoked ham, cut into 2" by ¼" strips
1 package (10 ounces) frozen peas

**1** On waxed paper, mix pepper, 2 tablespoons flour, and ½ teaspoon salt; use to coat chicken chunks.

**2** Prepare frozen artichoke hearts as label directs; drain.

**3** Meanwhile, in nonstick 12-inch skillet, heat oil over medium-high heat until very hot. Add chicken and cook until golden brown and it just loses its pink color throughout.

**4** In cup, with fork, mix balsamic vinegar, remaining 1 teaspoon flour, remaining ¼ teaspoon salt, and ½ *cup water*. Stir balsamic-vinegar mixture, ham, artichoke hearts, and frozen peas into skillet; heat to boiling. *Makes 4 main-dish servings.*

Each serving: About 290 calories, 38 g protein, 19 g carbohydrate, 7 g total fat (1 g saturated), 7 g fiber, 79 mg cholesterol, 1025 mg sodium.

# Chicken with Peppers & Onions

PREP: 10 MINUTES / COOK: 20 MINUTES

2 tablespoons vegetable oil
4 medium red and/or yellow peppers, cut into
½-inch strips
2 medium onions, cut into wedges
¾ teaspoon salt
½ cup pitted ripe olives, sliced
8 medium skinless, boneless chicken thighs (about
1½ pounds), each cut in half

**1** In nonstick 12-inch skillet, heat 1 tablespoon oil over medium-high heat. Add peppers, onions, and ¼ teaspoon salt and cook until vegetables are tender and lightly browned. Stir in ripe olives and ¼ *cup water*; transfer to bowl.

**2** Add remaining 1 tablespoon oil to skillet and heat over high heat until very hot. Add chicken with remaining ½ teaspoon salt and cook until lightly brown, about 4 minutes. Cover, reduce heat to medium, and cook 5 minutes longer or until juices run clear when chicken is pierced with tip of knife.

**3** Return vegetable mixture to skillet; heat through. *Makes 4 main-dish servings.*

Each serving: About 335 calories, 35 g protein, 13 g carbohydrate, 16 g total fat (3 g saturated), 3 g fiber, 141 mg cholesterol, 735 mg sodium.

# Spicy Thai Chicken

PREP: 20 MINUTES / COOK: 10 MINUTES

Asian fish sauce (*nuoc nam*) brings a special salty undertone to Thai and Vietnamese cooking. The thin, translucent brown liquid—extracted from salted, fermented fish—can be purchased in the Asian section of some grocery stores, but if you can't find it, increase the soy sauce to 2 tablespoons.

3 tablespoons Asian fish sauce (nuoc nam)
1 tablespoon soy sauce
1 tablespoon brown sugar
4 small skinless, boneless chicken-breast halves
(4 ounces each), sliced crosswise into ¼-inch-
thick slices
2 teaspoons vegetable oil
1 large onion (12 ounces), cut into ¼-inch-thick
slices
2 red or green chiles (serrano or jalapeño), seeded
and cut into matchstick-thin strips
2 teaspoons minced, peeled fresh ginger
2 garlic cloves, crushed with garlic press
1½ cups loosely packed fresh basil leaves
Basil sprigs for garnish

**1** In medium bowl, combine fish sauce, soy sauce, and brown sugar; stir in chicken slices to coat. Let marinate 5 minutes.

**2** In nonstick 12-inch skillet, heat vegetable oil over medium-high heat until very hot. Add chicken with marinade and cook, stirring occasionally, until chicken slices lose their pink color throughout, about 3 to 4 minutes. With slotted spoon, remove chicken to plate.

**3** Add onion to marinade remaining in skillet and cook, stirring occasionally, until tender-crisp, about 4 minutes. Stir in chiles, ginger, and garlic; cook 1 minute longer.

**4** Return chicken to skillet; heat through. Stir in basil leaves just before serving. Garnish with basil sprigs. *Makes 4 main-dish servings.*

Each serving: About 325 calories, 35 g protein, 39 g carbohydrate, 7 g total fat (1 g saturated), 1 g fiber, 66 mg cholesterol, 795 mg sodium.

*Spicy Thai Chicken* ➤

# Sweet & Sour Chicken

PREP: 20 MINUTES / COOK: 30 MINUTES

2 tablespoons vegetable oil
1 bunch green onions, cut diagonally into 1-inch
    pieces
1 large red pepper, cut into ½-inch-thick slices
10 medium skinless, boneless chicken thighs (about
    2¼ pounds), each cut in thirds
½ teaspoon salt
1 can (20 ounces) pineapple chunks in juice
¼ cup sugar
¼ cup cider vinegar
2 tablespoons ketchup
1 teaspoon cornstarch
4 teaspoons soy sauce

1 In nonstick 12-inch skillet, heat 1 tablespoon oil over medium-high heat. Add green onions and red pepper and cook until tender-crisp, stirring frequently; transfer to bowl.

2 Add remaining 1 tablespoon oil to skillet and heat over medium-high heat until very hot. Add chicken thighs and salt, half at a time, and cook until chicken is cooked through, about 15 minutes, transferring chicken to plate when it is done; discard any fat remaining in skillet.

3 Meanwhile, drain pineapple chunks, reserving ¼ cup pineapple juice. In cup, mix reserved pineapple juice with sugar, vinegar, ketchup, cornstarch, and soy sauce.

4 Return chicken to skillet; stir in pineapple-juice mixture, stirring to loosen any brown bits from bottom of skillet. Cook until mixture thickens slightly and coats chicken.

5 Stir in green-onion mixture and pineapple chunks; heat through. *Makes 6 main-dish servings.*

Each serving: About 355 calories, 35 g protein, 28 g carbohydrate, 11 g total fat (2 g saturated), 2 g fiber, 141 mg cholesterol, 635 mg sodium.

# Chicken with Sesame Noodles

PREP: 10 MINUTES / COOK: 25 MINUTES

Salt
8 ounces linguine or spaghetti
2 tablespoons cornstarch
1 pound skinless, boneless chicken breasts, cut
    crosswise into 1-inch-thick strips
1 tablespoon vegetable oil
¼ cup creamy peanut butter
3 tablespoons soy sauce
1 tablespoon Asian sesame oil
1 tablespoon white vinegar
2 teaspoons sugar
1 medium red pepper, cut into matchstick-thin
    strips
1 medium cucumber, cut into matchstick-thin strips
1 green onion, thinly sliced
¼ teaspoon crushed red pepper (optional)

1 In large saucepot, prepare pasta in *boiling salted water* as label directs; drain.

2 Meanwhile, in medium bowl, combine cornstarch and ½ teaspoon salt. Toss chicken strips in cornstarch mixture to coat. In nonstick 12-inch skillet, heat vegetable oil over medium-high heat until very hot. Add chicken pieces and cook, stirring quickly and constantly, until lightly browned and chicken loses its pink color throughout. Transfer chicken to plate.

3 Add peanut butter, soy sauce, sesame oil, vinegar, sugar, and *¾ cup water* to skillet; cook, stirring constantly, until mixture is smooth. Stir in linguine and heat through.

4 Spoon linguine mixture onto warm platter. Top with red-pepper and cucumber strips, then chicken strips and green onion. If you like, sprinkle with crushed red pepper. Toss to serve. *Makes 4 main-dish servings.*

Each serving: About 535 calories, 39 g protein, 55 g carbohydrate, 17 g total fat (3 g saturated), 3 g fiber, 66 mg cholesterol, 1120 mg sodium.

# Indonesian Chicken

### 🐓 🐓 🐓

PREP: 10 MINUTES PLUS MARINATING / COOK: 15 MINUTES

3 teaspoons vegetable oil
1 medium green onion, thinly sliced
1 garlic clove, minced
1 medium lime
1 medium orange
2 tablespoons soy sauce
1 tablespoon honey
½ teaspoon crushed red pepper
½ teaspoon ground cumin
½ teaspoon ground coriander
1 pound skinless, boneless chicken breasts, cut
   crosswise into ½-inch-wide strips
1 teaspoon cornstarch

**1** In nonstick 12-inch skillet, heat 1 teaspoon oil over medium heat. Add green onion and garlic and cook 2 to 3 minutes until just beginning to brown. Spoon green-onion mixture into large bowl.

**2** Grate peel and squeeze juice from lime and orange. Set aside orange juice. Add lime and orange peels and lime juice to bowl with green onion; stir in soy sauce, honey, crushed red pepper, cumin, and coriander.

**3** Add chicken to spice mixture in bowl. Cover and let marinate about 15 minutes.

**4** With slotted spoon, remove chicken from marinade; reserve marinade. In same nonstick skillet, heat remaining 2 teaspoons oil over high heat until very hot. Add chicken and cook, stirring quickly and constantly, 5 minutes or until chicken just loses its pink color throughout. Remove chicken from skillet.

**5** In cup, with whisk, mix cornstarch with orange juice. Add cornstarch mixture and reserved chicken marinade to skillet; cook over medium heat until mixture boils and thickens slightly; boil 1 minute. Return chicken to skillet; heat through. *Makes 4 main-dish servings.*

Each serving: About 200 calories, 27 g protein, 10 g carbohydrate, 5 g total fat (1 g saturated), 0 g fiber, 66 mg cholesterol, 590 mg sodium.

# Thai Chicken & Vegetables

### 🐓 🐓 🐓

PREP: 10 MINUTES / COOK: 30 MINUTES

1 tablespoon vegetable oil
6 medium skinless, boneless chicken thighs (about
   1½ pounds), each cut into 6 pieces
1 tablespoon minced, peeled fresh ginger
1 large carrot, peeled and cut into pencil-thin strips
1 small zucchini (about 8 ounces), cut into pencil-
   thin strips
2 large green onions, thinly sliced
⅓ cup soy sauce
¼ cup creamy peanut butter
3 tablespoons chili sauce
3 tablespoons seasoned rice vinegar
¼ teaspoon coconut extract
Peanuts for garnish

**1** In nonstick 12-inch skillet, heat oil over medium-high heat until very hot. Add chicken thighs, half at a time, and cook until golden brown, transferring thighs to plate as they brown.

**2** Add ginger and carrot to skillet and cook until carrot is lightly browned. Stir in zucchini and green onions and continue cooking until vegetables are tender. Transfer vegetable mixture to small bowl.

**3** Stir soy sauce, peanut butter, chili sauce, rice vinegar, coconut extract, and *1¼ cups water* into skillet until well blended. Return chicken thighs to skillet with peanut sauce; heat to boiling over high heat. Reduce heat to low; cover and simmer until chicken loses its pink color throughout, about 5 minutes.

**4** To serve, spoon carrot mixture over chicken; garnish with peanuts. Toss to serve. *Makes 6 main-dish servings.*

Each serving without peanuts: About 260 calories, 27 g protein, 10 g carbohydrate, 12 g total fat (2 g saturated), 2 g fiber, 94 mg cholesterol, 1325 mg sodium.

# Grills & Broils

# Apple-Glazed Cornish Hens

PREP: 10 MINUTES / BROIL: 35 MINUTES

3 Rock Cornish hens (1¾ pounds each), each cut
  in half
½ teaspoon dried thyme
¼ teaspoon coarsely ground black pepper
1¼ teaspoons salt
½ cup apple jelly
1 tablespoon fresh lemon juice

**1** Preheat broiler. Rub hens with thyme, pepper, and salt. Place hen halves, skin-side down, in broiling pan (do not use rack).

**2** With broiling pan 5 to 7 inches from source of heat, broil hens 20 minutes. Turn hen halves skin-side up; broil about 15 minutes longer or until juices run clear when thickest part of hen is pierced with tip of knife, brushing with pan drippings occasionally.

**3** Meanwhile, in 1-quart saucepan, melt apple jelly and lemon juice over medium-low heat. During last few minutes of broiling, brush hens with apple-jelly mixture; broil until golden, about 1 minute.

**4** To serve, arrange hens on platter. Skim fat from drippings in broiling pan and discard. Serve pan drippings with Cornish hens. *Makes 6 main-dish servings.*

Each serving: About 505 calories, 37 g protein, 18 g carbohydrate, 31 g total fat (8 g saturated), 0 g fiber, 219 mg cholesterol, 600 mg sodium.

# Broiled Cornish Hens with Lemon & Rosemary

PREP: 15 MINUTES / BROIL: 30 MINUTES

2 Rock Cornish hens (1½ pounds each), each cut
  in half
¾ teaspoon salt
½ teaspoon dried rosemary, crushed
¼ teaspoon coarsely ground black pepper
2 tablespoons fresh lemon juice
2 tablespoons chopped fresh parsley leaves
Lemon slices for garnish

**1** Preheat broiler. In small roasting pan (about 14" by 10"), arrange hen halves, skin-side down; sprinkle with ¼ teaspoon salt. With roasting pan 5 to 7 inches from source of heat, broil hens 15 minutes.

**2** In cup, with fork, mix rosemary, pepper, and remaining ½ teaspoon salt. Turn hens; sprinkle with herb mixture. Broil hens 15 minutes longer, basting once or twice with pan drippings, until golden brown and juices run clear when thickest part of hen is pierced with tip of knife.

**3** Transfer hens to warm large platter; skim fat from drippings in roasting pan. Add lemon juice to roasting pan, stirring to loosen brown bits; stir in parsley. Spoon sauce over hens on platter. Garnish with lemon slices. *Makes 4 main-dish servings.*

Each serving: About 375 calories, 32 g protein, 1 g carbohydrate, 26 g total fat (7 g saturated), 0 g fiber, 187 mg cholesterol, 530 mg sodium.

# SALSA SAMPLER

Salsa—the perfect companion to grilled or broiled chicken. After making any of these salsas, cover and refrigerate at least 1 hour to blend flavors. Most salsas can be kept in the refrigerator 2 to 3 days, though those made with very wet ingredients will get diluted.

## Cherry Salsa

In medium bowl, mix *1 pound cherries*, pitted and chopped, *⅓ cup diced yellow pepper*, *1 chopped green onion*, *2 tablespoons seasoned rice vinegar*, *1 teaspoon grated, peeled fresh ginger*, and *⅛ teaspoon salt*, stirring gently to combine. Makes about 3 cups.

Each ¼ cup: About 30 calories, 0 g protein, 6 g carbohydrate, 0 g total fat (0 g saturated), 0.5 g fiber, 0 mg cholesterol, 75 mg sodium.

## Plum Salsa

In medium bowl, mix *1½ pounds ripe plums (6 to 8 medium)*, pitted and coarsely chopped, *1 green onion, chopped*, *1 tablespoon coarsely chopped fresh basil*, *2 tablespoons balsamic vinegar*, and *⅛ teaspoon salt*, stirring gently to combine. Makes about 3 cups.

Each ¼ cup: About 30 calories, 0 g protein, 7 g carbohydrate, 0 g total fat (0 g saturated), 1 g fiber, 0 mg cholesterol, 25 mg sodium.

## Peach Salsa

In medium bowl, mix *1¾ pounds ripe peaches (about 6 medium)*, peeled, pitted, and coarsely chopped, *2 tablespoons minced red onion*, *1 tablespoon chopped fresh mint*, *1 tablespoon fresh lime juice*, *1 teaspoon seeded, finely chopped jalapeño chile*, and *⅛ teaspoon salt*, stirring gently to combine. Makes about 3 cups.

Each ¼ cup: About 25 calories, 0 g protein, 6 g carbohydrate, 0 g total fat (0 g saturated), 1 g fiber, 0 mg cholesterol, 50 mg sodium.

## Pineapple-Cranberry Salsa

In 3-quart saucepan, heat *1 tablespoon olive oil* over medium heat. Add *1 small onion, chopped*, and cook until tender, stirring occasionally. Stir in *1 bag (12 ounces) cranberries*, *¾ cup packed light brown sugar*, *¼ teaspoon salt*, and *2 tablespoons water*. Cook over medium-high heat, stirring, until cranberries pop and mixture boils and thickens slightly. Remove pan from heat; stir in *1 can (8 ounces) sliced pineapple*, drained

*Clockwise from top left: cherry, peach, tomato, plum, and watermelon salsas*

and chopped, and *1 can (4 to 4½ ounces) chopped mild green chiles*. Makes about 3½ cups.

Each ¼ cup: About 80 calories, 0 g protein, 18 g carbohydrate, 1 g total fat (0 g saturated), 1 g fiber, 0 mg cholesterol, 100 mg sodium.

## Watermelon Salsa

In medium bowl, mix *1 piece watermelon (about 2½ pounds)*, seeds and rind removed and melon coarsely chopped, *1 tablespoon finely chopped red onion*, *1 tablespoon chopped fresh cilantro leaves*, *2 tablespoons fresh lime juice*, *2 teaspoons seeded, finely chopped jalapeño chile*, and *⅛ teaspoon salt*, stirring gently to combine. Makes about 3 cups.

Each ¼ cup: About 15 calories, 0 g protein, 4 g carbohydrate, 0 g total fat (0 g saturated), 0 g fiber, 0 mg cholesterol, 25 mg sodium.

## Tomato Salsa

From *1 large lime*, grate ½ teaspoon peel and squeeze 2 tablespoons juice. In medium bowl, mix lime peel and juice with *1½ pounds ripe tomatoes*, diced, *1 small jalapeño chile*, seeded and finely diced, *2 tablespoons chopped fresh cilantro leaves*, *¾ teaspoon salt*, and *¼ teaspoon coarsely ground black pepper*, stirring gently to combine. Makes about 3 cups.

Each ¼ cup: About 15 calories, 1 g protein, 3 g carbohydrate, 0 g total fat (0 g saturated), 1 g fiber, 0 mg cholesterol, 150 mg sodium.

# Grilled Apricot-Glazed Cornish Hens

PREP: 15 MINUTES / GRILL: 35 MINUTES

4 large apricots (1 pound), pitted
1 garlic clove, peeled
1 piece (1" by ½") peeled fresh ginger or
  ½ teaspoon ground ginger
¼ cup apricot preserves
2 tablespoons soy sauce
4 Rock Cornish hens (1½ pounds each), each cut
  in half

**1** In blender or in food processor with knife blade attached, blend apricots, garlic, ginger, apricot preserves, and soy sauce until smooth.

**2** Place hen halves on grill over medium heat; cook 35 minutes, turning hens often. Brush hens frequently with apricot mixture during last 10 minutes of grilling. *Makes 8 main-dish servings.*

**TO BROIL IN OVEN:** Preheat broiler. Place hen halves, skin-side down, in large broiling pan. With pan in broiler 7 to 9 inches from source of heat, broil hens 25 minutes or until golden. Brush hens generously with some apricot mixture; broil 2 to 3 minutes. Turn hens skin-side up; broil 15 minutes longer or until fork-tender, brushing with remaining apricot mixture during last 10 minutes of cooking.

Each serving: About 425 calories, 33 g protein, 13 g carbohydrate, 26 g total fat (7 g saturated), 1 g fiber, 187 mg cholesterol, 355 mg sodium.

# Cornish Hens with Fruit Salsa

PREP: 30 MINUTES / GRILL: 35 MINUTES

2 medium limes
2 medium kiwifruit, peeled
2 medium peaches, peeled and diced
1 large jalapeño chile, seeded and minced
1 can (8 ounces) crushed pineapple in its own
  juice, drained
1 tablespoon minced fresh cilantro leaves
½ teaspoon sugar
1 teaspoon salt
2 garlic cloves, minced
4 teaspoons chili powder
1 tablespoon olive oil
2 Rock Cornish hens (1½ pounds each), each cut
  in half

**1** Grate peel from 1 lime. Squeeze juice from both limes to equal 3 tablespoons.

**2** Dice 1 kiwifruit. In bowl, with fork, coarsely crush remaining kiwifruit. Stir in peaches and diced kiwifruit, jalapeño chile, pineapple, cilantro, sugar, ¼ teaspoon salt, lime peel, and 2 tablespoons lime juice. Cover and refrigerate until serving time.

**3** In cup, mix garlic, chili powder, olive oil, remaining 1 tablespoon lime juice, and remaining ¾ teaspoon salt. Rub garlic mixture on hen halves.

**4** Place hens on grill over medium heat; cook 35 minutes, turning hens often, until juices run clear when hens are pierced with tip of knife.

**5** To serve, arrange hens on platter. Serve fruit salsa in bowl with hens. *Makes 4 main-dish servings.*

Each serving: About 505 calories, 33 g protein, 26 g carbohydrate, 30 g total fat (8 g saturated), 4 g fiber, 187 mg cholesterol, 705 mg sodium.

# Honey & Spice Cornish Hens

🐔 🐔 🐔

PREP: 10 MINUTES / GRILL: 35 MINUTES

1¾ teaspoons Chinese five-spice powder
1¼ teaspoons salt
2 Rock Cornish hens (1½ pounds each)
2 tablespoons honey

**1** In cup, mix five-spice powder and salt. Rub mixture on hen halves.

**2** Place hen halves on grill over medium heat; cook 30 minutes, turning hens occasionally, until juices run clear when thickest part is pierced with tip of knife. Brush hens with honey; grill 2 to 3 minutes longer until hens are golden. *Makes 4 main-dish servings.*

Each serving: About 410 calories, 32 g protein, 10 g carbohydrate, 26 g total fat (7 g saturated), 0 g fiber, 187 mg cholesterol, 820 mg sodium.

# All-American BBQ Chicken

🐔 🐔 🐔

PREP: 60 MINUTES / GRILL: 40 TO 45 MINUTES

Try our sweet and spicy sauce on pork spareribs too.

1 tablespoon olive oil
1 large onion, chopped
2 cans (15 ounces each) tomato sauce
1 cup red wine vinegar
½ cup light molasses
¼ cup Worcestershire sauce
⅓ cup packed brown sugar
¾ teaspoon ground red pepper (cayenne)
2 whole chickens (about 3½ pounds each), each
   cut into quarters

**1** In nonstick 10-inch skillet, heat olive oil over medium heat. Add onion and cook until tender, about 10 minutes. Stir in tomato sauce, vinegar, molasses, Worcestershire, brown sugar, and ground red pepper; heat to boiling over high heat. Reduce heat to medi-

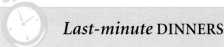

## Last-minute DINNERS

## BROILED BUFFALO DRUMSTICKS

PREP: 5 MINUTES / BROIL: 25 MINUTES

For a change of pace, try this with green hot pepper sauce made with jalapeños; it's not quite as sharp in flavor.

⅓ cup bottled hot pepper sauce
3 tablespoons Worcestershire sauce
1 tablespoon chili powder
12 large chicken drumsticks (about 3¾ pounds)

**1** Preheat broiler. In small bowl, mix hot pepper sauce, Worcestershire, and chili powder.

**2** Brush chicken drumsticks with pepper-sauce mixture; arrange drumsticks on rack in broiling pan. With broiling pan 5 to 7 inches from source of heat, broil drumsticks 25 minutes, turning frequently and brushing with remaining pepper-sauce mixture, or until chicken drumsticks are fork-tender and juices run clear when pierced with tip of knife. Makes 6 main-dish servings.

Each serving: About 305 calories, 37 g protein, 2 g carbohydrate, 15 g total fat (4 g saturated), 0 g fiber, 122 mg cholesterol, 560 mg sodium.

um-low and cook, uncovered, 45 minutes or until sauce thickens slightly. If not using sauce right away, cover and refrigerate to use within 2 weeks.

**2** Reserve 1½ cups sauce to serve with grilled chicken. Place chicken quarters on grill over medium heat; cook 20 to 25 minutes, turning chicken once. Generously brush chicken with some of the remaining barbecue sauce; cook 20 minutes longer, turning pieces often and brushing with sauce frequently until juices run clear when chicken is pierced with tip of knife. Serve with reserved barbecue sauce. *Makes 8 main-dish servings.*

Each serving: About 545 calories, 49 g protein, 28 g carbohydrate, 26 g total fat (7 g saturated), 0.5 g fiber, 154 mg cholesterol, 260 mg sodium.

# Barbecued Chicken with Creole Sauce

PREP: 25 MINUTES / GRILL: 35 MINUTES

1 tablespoon olive or vegetable oil
1 medium onion, chopped
1 medium green pepper, chopped
1 garlic clove, minced
1 cup ketchup
2 tablespoons light brown sugar
3 tablespoons red wine vinegar
1¼ teaspoons salt
½ teaspoon hot pepper sauce
2 whole chickens (about 3½ pounds each), each
    cut into quarters

**1** In 2-quart saucepan, heat oil over medium-high heat. Add onion and green pepper and cook until vegetables are tender; add garlic and cook, stirring, 1 minute. Stir in ketchup, brown sugar, red wine vinegar, salt, hot pepper sauce, and *2 tablespoons water*; heat to boiling over high heat. Reduce heat to low; cover and simmer 5 minutes to blend flavors. Transfer half of sauce to bowl for brushing on chicken quarters while grilling; keep remaining sauce warm.

**2** Place chicken on grill over medium heat; cook until golden on both sides, about 10 minutes. Then, to avoid charring, stand pieces upright, leaning one against the other. Rearrange pieces from time to time and cook until fork-tender, about 25 minutes longer. During last 10 minutes of cooking, brush chicken pieces frequently with barbecue sauce. Serve chicken with reserved barbecue sauce. *Makes 8 main-dish servings.*

**TO BROIL IN OVEN:** Preheat broiler. Place chicken, skin-side down, on rack in broiling pan. With pan 5 to 7 inches from source of heat, broil chicken 20 minutes or until golden. Brush generously with sauce; broil 1 to 2 minutes longer. Turn chicken pieces skin-side up; broil 10 minutes. Brush generously with sauce; broil 5 minutes. Brush with remaining sauce and continue broiling about 5 minutes longer or until chicken is fork-tender and juices run clear when chicken is pierced with tip of knife.

Each serving:  About 490 calories, 49 g protein, 14 g carbohydrate, 26 g total fat (7 g saturated), 1 g fiber, 154 mg cholesterol, 870 mg sodium.

# Citrus-Sage Chicken

PREP: 25 MINUTES PLUS 2 HOURS TO MARINATE
GRILL: 30 TO 35 MINUTES

The tangy marinade doesn't just taste good—it makes the chicken tender too.

2 large oranges
2 large lemons
¼ cup chopped fresh sage leaves
2 tablespoons olive oil
2 teaspoons salt
¾ teaspoon coarsely ground black pepper
2 whole chickens (about 3½ pounds each), each
    cut into 8 pieces, skin removed
Fresh sage leaves for garnish

**1** Grate 1 tablespoon peel and squeeze 3 tablespoons juice from oranges. Grate 1 tablespoon peel and squeeze 3 tablespoons juice from lemons.

**2** In large bowl, with wire whisk or fork, combine orange and lemon peels, orange and lemon juices, chopped sage, olive oil, salt, and pepper. Add chicken, turning to coat. Cover and refrigerate 2 hours, turning pieces 3 or 4 times.

**3** Place chicken, meat-side down, on grill over medium heat. Cook chicken 20 minutes. Turn chicken and cook 10 to 15 minutes longer until juices run clear when chicken is pierced with tip of knife.

**4** Place chicken in large serving dish; garnish with sage leaves. *Makes 8 main-dish servings.*

Each serving:  About 305 calories, 41 g protein, 2 g carbohydrate, 14 g total fat (3 g saturated), 0 g fiber, 127 mg cholesterol, 705 mg sodium.

*Citrus-Sage Chicken* ➤

# Prosciutto-Stuffed Chicken Breasts with Lemon Dressing

PREP: 20 MINUTES / GRILL: 10 MINUTES

6 large skinless, boneless chicken-breast halves (about 2¼ pounds)
¼ pound thinly sliced prosciutto or cooked ham
3 large plum tomatoes (about ½ pound), cut lengthwise into ¼-inch-thick slices
6 large basil leaves plus 1 tablespoon chopped fresh basil
1 tablespoon plus ¼ cup olive oil
2 tablespoons fresh lemon juice
½ teaspoon salt
¼ teaspoon coarsely ground black pepper
1 tablespoon grated Parmesan cheese

**1** With tip of knife, cut a 2-inch opening along side of each breast half to form a deep pocket. Into each pocket, place one-sixth of prosciutto (folding to fit, if necessary), 1 or 2 slices of tomato, and 1 basil leaf. With finger, press pockets closed; fasten with toothpicks. Rub breasts with 1 tablespoon olive oil.

**2** In small bowl, mix chopped basil, lemon juice, salt, pepper, and remaining ¼ cup olive oil; set aside.

**3** Place chicken breasts on grill over medium heat; cook 10 minutes or until chicken loses its pink color throughout and is golden on both sides, turning chicken occasionally.

**4** To serve, carefully remove toothpicks from chicken. Arrange chicken on large platter. Spoon lemon dressing over chicken and sprinkle with Parmesan. *Makes 6 main-dish servings.*

**TO BROIL IN OVEN:** Preheat broiler. Place chicken on rack in broiling pan. With pan at closest position to source of heat, broil chicken about 10 minutes, turning once, until chicken loses pink color throughout.

Each serving: About 345 calories, 45 g protein, 2 g carbohydrate, 16 g total fat (3 g saturated), 0.5 g fiber, 115 mg cholesterol, 670 mg sodium.

# Grilled Mushroom-Stuffed Chicken Breasts

PREP: 25 MINUTES / GRILL: 35 MINUTES

For a really simple side dish, grill jumbo mushrooms along with the chicken. Toss them with some oil and salt before putting them on the grill.

1 teaspoon plus 2 tablespoons olive or vegetable oil
¾ pound medium mushrooms, finely chopped
2 teaspoons plus 3 tablespoons soy sauce
6 large bone-in chicken-breast halves, with skin (about 3½ pounds)
2 green onions, finely chopped
¼ teaspoon coarsely ground black pepper

**1** In nonstick 12-inch skillet, heat 1 teaspoon olive oil over medium-high heat. Add chopped mushrooms and cook until golden and all liquid evaporates, stirring occasionally. Stir in 2 teaspoons soy sauce.

**2** Loosen skin on each chicken-breast half; spoon mushroom mixture between meat and skin.

**3** In small bowl, mix green onions, pepper, remaining 3 tablespoons soy sauce, and remaining 2 tablespoons olive oil; set basting mixture aside.

**4** Place chicken breasts on grill over medium heat; cook about 10 minutes until golden on both sides. Then, to avoid charring, stand chicken pieces upright, leaning one against the other. Rearrange pieces from time to time and cook 20 to 25 minutes longer until chicken is fork-tender and juices run clear when chicken is pierced with tip of knife.

**5** During last 10 minutes of cooking, brush chicken frequently with soy-sauce basting mixture. *Makes 6 main-dish servings.*

TO BROIL IN OVEN: Preheat broilers. Place chicken breasts, skin-side down, on rack in broiling pan. With pan 5 to 7 inches from source of heat, broil chicken 20 minutes. Brush chicken with some soy-sauce mixture; turn chicken skin-side up. Broil 15 to 20 minutes, brushing chicken occasionally with remaining soy-sauce mixture, until chicken is fork-tender and juices run clear when chicken is pierced with a knife.

Each serving:  About 350 calories, 44 g protein, 4 g carbohydrate, 17 g total fat (4 g saturated), 1 g fiber, 120 mg cholesterol, 735 mg sodium.

## GREAT GO-WITHS

### GRILLED SWEET CORN WITH FRESH HERBS

PREP: 10 MINUTES PLUS SOAKING / GRILL: 40 MINUTES

*8 medium ears of corn with husks*
*8 teaspoons olive oil*
*Several sprigs each of basil, rosemary, sage, and*
*   thyme*

1 Into 8-quart saucepot or kettle, place corn with husks and enough *water* to cover; let soak 15 minutes. (Soaking corn with husks in water keeps husks from burning on grill.)

2 Remove corn from water and drain well. Gently pull back husks three-fourths way down; remove silk. With pastry brush, brush each ear of corn with 1 teaspoon olive oil. Tuck in several sprigs of herb next to kernels. Rewrap corn with husks, removing 1 strip of husk from each ear of corn and tying tops of corn with strip of extra husk.

3 Place corn on grill over medium heat; grill 30 to 40 minutes, turning occasionally, until tender. Makes 8 accompaniment servings.

Each ear of corn:  About 165 calories, 5 g protein, 27 g carbohydrate, 6 g total fat (1 g saturated), 5 g fiber, 0 mg cholesterol, 20 mg sodium.

# Chili-Broiled Chicken Breasts

PREP: 15 MINUTES / BROIL: 10 MINUTES

1 tablespoon olive or vegetable oil
1 small onion, minced
½ medium green pepper, minced
1½ teaspoons chili powder
¼ cup orange juice
1 tablespoon brown sugar
2 tablespoons hot pepper sauce
1 tablespoon tomato paste
½ teaspoon salt
4 medium skinless, boneless chicken-breast halves
   (about 1¼ pounds)

1 In 2-quart saucepan, heat olive oil over medium-high heat. Add onion and green pepper and cook until browned, stirring occasionally. Add chili powder and cook 1 minute, stirring constantly.

2 Preheat broiler. Add orange juice, brown sugar, hot pepper sauce, tomato paste, and salt to saucepan, stirring until well blended; heat to boiling over high heat. Boil 2 minutes to blend flavors; remove from heat.

3 Add chicken breasts to saucepan; turn to coat with sauce. Arrange chicken breasts on rack in broiling pan. With broiling pan about 5 inches from source of heat, broil chicken 3 minutes. Turn chicken and spoon on remaining sauce. Broil 5 minutes longer or until juices run clear when chicken is pierced with tip of knife. *Makes 4 main-dish servings.*

Each serving:  About 225 calories, 34 g protein, 9 g carbohydrate, 5 g total fat (1 g saturated), 1 g fiber, 82 mg cholesterol, 620 mg sodium.

# Orange-Rosemary
# Mixed Grill

🐔🐔🐔

PREP: 10 MINUTES / GRILL: 35 MINUTES

½ cup orange marmalade
2 tablespoons fresh lemon juice
1 teaspoon dried rosemary, crushed
¾ teaspoon salt
6 fully cooked bratwurst or knockwurst
1 whole chicken (about 3½ pounds), cut into
    quarters
Tomato wedges for garnish

**1** In small bowl, mix orange marmalade, lemon juice, rosemary, and salt.

**2** Cut a few slashes in each bratwurst to prevent them from bursting while cooking.

**3** Place chicken quarters on grill over medium heat; cook until golden on both sides, about 10 minutes. Then to avoid charring, stand chicken pieces upright, leaning one against the other. Rearrange pieces from time to time and cook until fork-tender and juices run clear when pierced with knife, about 25 minutes longer. During last 10 minutes of cooking, place bratwurst on same grill. Brush chicken quarters and bratwurst frequently with orange-rosemary mixture.

**4** Garnish with tomato wedges to serve. *Makes 6 main-dish servings.*

Each serving without tomatoes: About 690 calories, 48 g protein, 21 g carbohydrate, 45 g total fat (15 g saturated), 0 g fiber, 171 mg cholesterol, 1035 mg sodium.

# Spice-Marinated
# Chicken

🐔🐔🐔

PREP: 10 MINUTES PLUS MARINATING / BROIL: 15 MINUTES

1 small onion, grated
1 cup plain low-fat yogurt
1 tablespoon vegetable oil
1 teaspoon salt
2 teaspoons grated, peeled fresh ginger
½ teaspoon ground cumin
¼ teaspoon chili powder
¼ teaspoon ground turmeric
¼ teaspoon ground cinnamon
4 large skinless, boneless chicken-breast halves
    (about 1½ pounds)

**1** In 11" by 7" glass baking dish, mix onion, yogurt, oil, salt, ginger, cumin, chili powder, turmeric, and cinnamon. Add chicken breasts, turning to coat. Cover with plastic wrap and refrigerate at least 3 hours.

**2** Preheat broiler. Spray rack in broiling pan with nonstick cooking spray. Arrange chicken breasts on rack. Spread any yogurt mixture remaining in baking dish over chicken; set aside.

**3** With broiling pan about 5 inches from source of heat, broil chicken for 12 to 15 minutes, without turning, until lightly browned and juices run clear when pierced with tip of knife. With knife held in slanting position almost parallel to cutting surface, slice each chicken-breast half into 5 pieces. *Makes 4 main-dish servings.*

Each serving: About 265 calories, 43 g protein, 7 g carbohydrate, 7 g total fat (2 g saturated), 0.5 g fiber, 102 mg cholesterol, 735 mg sodium.

*Orange-Rosemary Mixed Grill* ➤

# Yogurt-Broiled Chicken

🐔 🐔 🐔

PREP: 20 MINUTES / BROIL: 10 MINUTES

½ cup plain low-fat yogurt
1 green onion, chopped
1 teaspoon dried oregano
1 tablespoon olive or vegetable oil
1 tablespoon white wine vinegar
¾ teaspoon salt
⅛ teaspoon coarsely ground black pepper
4 large skinless, boneless chicken-breast halves
   (about 1½ pounds)

1 In large bowl, mix yogurt, green onion, oregano, olive oil, vinegar, salt, and pepper. Add chicken breasts and toss to mix well. Let chicken stand 15 minutes, turning chicken breasts occasionally.

## ▰▰▰ GREAT GO-WITHS ▰▰▰

### COUSCOUS SALAD

PREP: 15 MINUTES / COOK: 10 MINUTES

1 package (10 ounces) couscous (Moroccan pasta)
1 can (14½ ounces) chicken broth or 1¾ cups
   homemade (page 11)
1 bunch radishes, coarsely chopped
1 cup frozen peas, thawed
1 cup frozen whole-kernel corn, thawed
3 tablespoons olive oil
1 teaspoon grated lemon peel
½ teaspoon salt

1 Prepare couscous as label directs but use chicken broth plus *water* to equal amount of water called for on label, and do not use margarine or butter or salt.

2 In large bowl, mix radishes, peas, corn, olive oil, lemon peel, and salt. Stir in couscous until mixed. Cover and refrigerate if not serving right away. Makes 8 accompaniment servings.

Each serving: About 220 calories, 6 g protein, 35 g carbohydrate, 6 g total fat (1 g saturated), 3 g fiber, 0 mg cholesterol, 400 mg sodium.

2 Preheat broiler. Place chicken breasts on rack in broiling pan. With pan at closest position to source of heat, broil chicken 4 minutes. Turn chicken, brushing with any yogurt mixture remaining in bowl, and broil 5 to 6 minutes longer until chicken is fork-tender and lightly browned. *Makes 4 main-dish servings.*

Each serving: About 240 calories, 41 g protein, 3 g carbohydrate, 6 g total fat (1 g saturated), 0 g fiber, 100 mg cholesterol, 565 mg sodium.

# Chicken Olé

🐔 🐔 🐔

PREP: 10 MINUTES / BROIL: 10 MINUTES

2 tablespoons vegetable oil
1 large green onion, chopped
1 medium plum tomato, chopped
4 tablespoons minced fresh cilantro leaves
½ teaspoon dried oregano
¼ teaspoon ground cumin
¼ teaspoon salt
¼ teaspoon coarsely ground black pepper
4 small skinless, boneless chicken-breast halves
   (about 1 pound)

1 Preheat broiler. In cup, with fork, mix oil, green onion, tomato, 2 tablespoons cilantro, oregano, cumin, salt, and pepper. Place chicken breasts in 13" by 9" baking pan; brush tops with some oil from tomato mixture.

2 With pan at closest position to source of heat, broil chicken 3 minutes. Turn breasts; spread remaining tomato mixture on top; broil 3 to 4 minutes longer until chicken is fork-tender.

3 Pour any drippings in pan over chicken. Sprinkle with remaining 2 tablespoons cilantro. *Makes 4 main-dish servings.*

Each serving: About 190 calories, 26 g protein, 1 g carbohydrate, 8 g total fat (1 g saturated), 0.5 g fiber, 66 mg cholesterol, 220 mg sodium.

# Apricot-Ginger Chicken Legs

🐓 🐓 🐓

PREP: 10 MINUTES / GRILL: 35 MINUTES

2 green onions, chopped
½ cup apricot preserves
⅓ cup ketchup
2 tablespoons cider vinegar
1 tablespoon plus 1 teaspoon grated, peeled
   fresh ginger
1 tablespoon plus 1 teaspoon soy sauce
6 large chicken legs (about 3¾ pounds)

**1** In small bowl, mix green onions, apricot preserves, ketchup, vinegar, ginger, and soy sauce.

**2** Place chicken legs on grill over medium heat; cook until golden on both sides, about 10 minutes. Then to avoid charring, stand chicken legs upright, leaning one against the other. Rearrange pieces from time to time and cook until fork-tender and juices run clear when pierced with knife, about 25 minutes longer.

*Apricot-Ginger Chicken Legs (above) on a bed of Couscous Salad (opposite page).*

During last 10 minutes of cooking, brush chicken legs frequently with apricot mixture. *Makes 6 main-dish servings.*

Each serving: About 410 calories, 37 g protein, 22 g carbohydrate, 19 g total fat (5 g saturated), 0.5 g fiber, 129 mg cholesterol, 520 mg sodium.

# Chili-Spiced Chicken Legs

PREP: 10 MINUTES / BROIL: 50 MINUTES

1 bottle (12 ounces) chili sauce
1 small onion, grated
1 garlic clove, crushed with garlic press or finely
   minced
3 tablespoons light brown sugar
1 tablespoon white wine vinegar
1 tablespoon olive or vegetable oil
2 teaspoons chili powder
1 teaspoon salt
½ teaspoon hot pepper sauce
3 tablespoons chopped fresh parsley leaves
8 medium chicken legs (about 4½ pounds)

**1** Preheat broiler. In small bowl, mix chili sauce, onion, garlic, brown sugar, vinegar, olive oil, chili powder, salt, hot pepper sauce, 2 tablespoons chopped parsley, and *1 tablespoon water* until blended.

**2** Arrange chicken legs skin-side down on rack in large broiling pan; brush chicken with some chili mixture. With pan 5 to 7 inches from source of heat, broil chicken legs 25 minutes.

**3** Turn chicken legs; broil 20 to 25 minutes longer, brushing occasionally with chili mixture, until chicken is fork-tender and juices run clear when chicken is pierced with tip of knife. Sprinkle chicken legs with remaining 1 tablespoon chopped parsley. *Makes 8 main-dish servings.*

Each serving: About 380 calories, 34 g protein, 17 g carbohydrate, 19 g total fat (5 g saturated), 0.5 g fiber, 116 mg cholesterol, 985 mg sodium.

# Chutney Chicken Breasts

### 🐔 🐔 🐔

PREP: 15 MINUTES / GRILL: 12 MINUTES

For a refreshing and flavorful accompaniment, grill thick slices of pineapple when you grill the chicken.

4 large skinless, boneless chicken-breast halves
   (about 1½ pounds)
1 jar (8½ ounces) mango chutney, coarsely
   chopped
1 can (8 to 8¼ ounces) crushed pineapple, drained
1 tablespoon curry powder
1 tablespoon fresh lime or lemon juice
1 tablespoon vegetable oil
Lime slices for garnish

**1** With tip of knife, cut a horizontal slit in thickest part of each chicken-breast half to form a pocket.

**2** In medium bowl, mix chutney, pineapple, curry powder, and lime juice. Transfer half of chutney mixture to bowl to serve with chicken breasts later.

**3** Stir oil into remaining chutney mixture. Place 1 tablespoon chutney-oil mixture in each chicken-breast pocket. Coat chicken breasts with remaining chutney-oil mixture.

**4** Place chicken breasts on grill over medium heat; cook 10 to 12 minutes, turning occasionally, until lightly browned and juices run clear when chicken is pierced with tip of knife.

**5** Arrange chicken breasts on 4 dinner plates. Serve with reserved chutney mixture. Garnish with lime slices. *Makes 4 main-dish servings.*

Each serving: About 450 calories, 40 g protein, 55 g carbohydrate, 6 g total fat (1 g saturated), 1 g fiber, 99 mg cholesterol, 650 mg sodium.

# Lemon Chicken Italiano

### 🐔 🐔 🐔

PREP: 10 MINUTES PLUS MARINATING / BROIL: 40 MINUTES

1 large lemon
6 medium chicken legs (about 3 pounds)
½ teaspoon salt
⅛ teaspoon coarsely ground black pepper
5 drained, oil-packed, sun-dried tomatoes (about
   ¼ cup), minced
¼ cup chopped fresh parsley leaves
2 tablespoons grated Parmesan cheese

**1** From lemon, grate peel and squeeze juice. In 13" by 9" baking dish, toss chicken legs with lemon juice. Cover and refrigerate 30 minutes.

**2** Preheat broiler. Sprinkle chicken legs with salt and pepper; place skin-side down in broiling pan. With pan 7 to 9 inches from source of heat, broil chicken legs 20 minutes. Turn chicken and broil 15 minutes longer or until juices run clear when pierced with tip of knife, basting occasionally with pan drippings.

**3** Meanwhile, in small bowl, combine sun-dried tomatoes, parsley, and Parmesan.

**4** When chicken is done, sprinkle with tomato mixture. Return chicken to oven; broil 2 minutes or until parsley is crisp.

**5** To serve, arrange chicken legs on platter; sprinkle with reserved grated lemon peel. *Makes 6 main-dish servings.*

Each serving: About 305 calories, 30 g protein, 2 g carbohydrate, 19 g total fat (5 g saturated), 0 g fiber, 104 mg cholesterol, 540 mg sodium.

*Chutney Chicken Breasts* ➤

# Grilled Turkey Cutlets with Pineapple & Oranges

🐓🐓🐓

PREP: 40 MINUTES / GRILL: 10 MINUTES

1 medium pineapple
2 large oranges, cut into ½-inch-thick slices
2 tablespoons light brown sugar
1 jar (10 ounces) orange marmalade
2 tablespoons curry powder
1 tablespoon Worcestershire sauce
1 tablespoon vegetable oil
1¼ teaspoons salt
6 turkey cutlets, each about ½-inch thick (about 1½ pounds)

**1** Cut off crown and stem end of pineapple; cut pineapple, with rind still on, lengthwise into quarters. Cut off the core along the tops of the quarters; score each quarter crosswise into 1-inch-thick slices. Sprinkle pineapple and oranges with brown sugar.

**2** In small bowl, with fork, mix orange marmalade, curry powder, Worcestershire, oil, and salt.

**3** Arrange turkey cutlets and fruit on grill over medium heat. Cook 5 to 7 minutes, brushing turkey frequently with marmalade mixture and turning turkey and fruit occasionally, until turkey just loses its pink color throughout and fruit is hot and browned.

**4** To serve, arrange turkey and fruit on platter, tucking orange slices in between cutlets. *Makes 6 main-dish servings*

TO BROIL IN OVEN: Preheat broiler. Arrange fruit, with pineapple cut-side up, on rack in large broiling pan. With pan at closest position to source of heat, broil fruit about 5 to 7 minutes until browned and bubbly. Transfer fruit to platter. Arrange turkey cutlets on same broiling pan. With pan at closest position to source of heat, broil turkey 5 to 7 minutes, brushing frequently with marmalade mixture and turning once, until turkey just loses its pink color throughout.

Each serving: About 400 calories, 30 g protein, 70 g carbohydrate, 4 g total fat (1 g saturated), 4 g fiber, 70 mg cholesterol, 600 mg sodium.

# Grilled Chicken with Quick Barbecue Sauce

PREP: 5 MINUTES / COOK: 40 MINUTES

½ cup apricot preserves
¼ cup soy sauce
¼ cup ketchup
1 tablespoon brown sugar
6 medium chicken drumsticks (about 1½ pounds)
12 chicken wings (about 2 pounds)

**1** In small bowl, mix apricot preserves, soy sauce, ketchup, and brown sugar.

**2** Place chicken drumsticks on grill over medium heat; cook 20 minutes, turning occasionally. Add chicken wings to grill; cook 10 minutes longer, turning pieces occasionally.

**3** Generously brush chicken with barbecue sauce; cook 10 minutes longer, turning pieces often and brushing with sauce frequently, until juices run clear when chicken is pierced with tip of knife. *Makes 6 main-dish servings.*

TO BROIL IN OVEN: Preheat broiler. Place drumsticks on rack in broiling pan. With pan 5 to 7 inches from source of heat, broil drumsticks 20 minutes, turning once. Add chicken wings to rack; broil 10 minutes, turning chicken pieces once. Generously brush apricot glaze onto chicken; broil 10 minutes longer, turning chicken pieces once and brushing with any remaining glaze, until juices run clear when chicken is pierced with a knife.

Each serving: About 375 calories, 31 g protein, 23 g carbohydrate, 17 g total fat (5 g saturated), 0.5 g fiber, 97 mg cholesterol, 910 mg sodium.

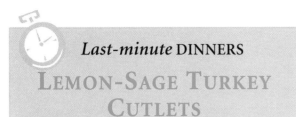

## *Last-minute* DINNERS

# LEMON-SAGE TURKEY CUTLETS

PREP: 5 MINUTES / GRILL: 7 MINUTES

2 medium lemons
1 tablespoon chopped fresh sage or ¾ teaspoon
   dried sage
1 tablespoon vegetable oil
½ teaspoon salt
¼ teaspoon coarsely ground black pepper
1 garlic clove, crushed with a press
1 pound turkey cutlets
Lemon slices and sage leaves for garnish

**1** From lemons, grate 2 teaspoons peel. Cut each lemon in half; squeeze juice from 3 halves into small bowl.

**2** Stir lemon peel, sage, oil, salt, pepper, and garlic into lemon juice.

**3** Place turkey cutlets on grill over high heat. Cook cutlets 5 to 7 minutes, brushing with lemon mixture often and turning them once until turkey just loses its pink color throughout.

**4** Arrange turkey cutlets on dinner plates. Squeeze juice from remaining lemon half over turkey cutlets. Garnish each serving with lemon slices and sage leaves. Makes 4 main-dish servings.

Each serving: About 165 calories, 28 g protein, 3 g carbohydrate, 4 g total fat (1 g saturated), 0 g fiber, 70 mg cholesterol, 345 mg sodium.

# Grilled Turkey Cutlets, Indian-Style

PREP: 15 MINUTES / GRILL: 5 TO 7 MINUTES

Delicious with a squeeze of fresh lime or with some Peach Salsa (page 103).

2 large limes
⅓ cup plain low-fat yogurt
1 tablespoon vegetable oil
2 teaspoons minced, peeled fresh ginger
1 teaspoon ground cumin
1 teaspoon ground coriander
1 teaspoon salt
1 garlic clove, crushed with garlic press
1½ pounds turkey cutlets
Cilantro sprigs for garnish

**1** From 1 lime, grate 1 teaspoon peel and squeeze 1 tablespoon juice. Cut the remaining lime into wedges; reserve wedges for squeezing juice over cooked cutlets. In large bowl, mix lime peel, lime juice, yogurt, oil, ginger, cumin, coriander, salt, and garlic until blended.

**2** Just before grilling, add turkey cutlets to bowl with yogurt mixture, stirring to coat cutlets. (Do not let cutlets marinate in yogurt mixture, their texture will become mealy.)

**3** Place turkey cutlets on grill over medium heat; cook 5 to 7 minutes until cutlets just lose their pink color throughout. Serve with lime wedges. Garnish with cilantro sprigs. ***Makes 6 main-dish servings.***

Each serving: About 160 calories, 29 g protein, 2 g carbohydrate, 3 g total fat (1 g saturated), 0 g fiber, 71 mg cholesterol, 455 mg sodium.

# Grilled Chicken Cutlets with Tomato-Olive Relish

PREP: 15 MINUTES / GRILL: 10 TO 12 MINUTES

Our tasty no-cook relish was inspired by Italian puttanesca sauce.

2 medium tomatoes, diced
¼ cup Kalamata olives, pitted and coarsely
  chopped
2 tablespoons minced red onion
2 tablespoons drained capers
1 teaspoon red wine vinegar
3 teaspoons olive oil
4 small skinless, boneless chicken-breast halves
  (about 1 pound)
¼ teaspoon salt
¼ teaspoon coarsely ground black pepper
Kalamata olives for garnish

**1** In small bowl, mix tomatoes, chopped olives, red onion, capers, vinegar, and 1 teaspoon olive oil; set aside.

**2** In medium bowl, toss chicken breasts with salt, pepper, and remaining 2 teaspoons olive oil to coat.

**3** Place chicken on grill over medium heat; cook 5 to 6 minutes per side or until juices run clear when thickest part is pierced with tip of knife, turning once. Serve chicken topped with relish and garnish with olives. *Makes 4 main-dish servings.*

Each serving: About 200 calories, 27 g protein, 5 g carbohydrate, 7 g total fat (1 g saturated), 1 g fiber, 66 mg cholesterol, 565 mg sodium.

# Sweet & Sour Chicken Wings

PREP: 10 MINUTES / GRILL: 30 MINUTES

¼ cup red wine vinegar
¼ cup soy sauce
¼ cup sugar
1 tablespoon cornstarch
2 tablespoons Asian sesame oil
2 pounds chicken wings (about 12)
½ teaspoon salt
¼ teaspoon coarsely ground black pepper
1 green onion, chopped for garnish

**1** In 1-quart saucepan, combine vinegar, soy sauce, sugar, cornstarch, sesame oil, and *¼ cup water*. Heat over medium-high heat until sauce boils and thickens; boil 1 minute. Remove saucepan from heat. Sprinkle chicken wings with salt and pepper.

**2** Place wings on grill over medium heat; cook 25 to 30 minutes until wings are tender and golden, turning frequently and brushing with sweet-and-sour sauce during last 10 minutes of cooking.

**3** Transfer wings to platter; sprinkle with chopped green onion. *Makes 4 main-dish servings.*

TO BROIL IN OVEN: Preheat broiler. Place chicken wings on rack in broiling pan. With pan 5 to 7 inches from source of heat, broil wings 25 to 30 minutes until wings are tender and golden, turning occasionally and brushing with sweet-and-sour sauce during last 10 minutes of broiling.

Each serving: About 380 calories, 24 g protein, 17 g carbohydrate, 24 g total fat (6 g saturated), 0 g fiber, 72 mg cholesterol, 1390 mg sodium.

◀ *Grilled Chicken Cutlets with Tomato-Olive Relish*

# Portuguese Mixed Grill

PREP: 30 MINUTES PLUS 30 MINUTES TO MARINATE
GRILL: 20 TO 25 MINUTES

Marinating the chicken in a vinaigrette seasoned with fresh chopped oregano leaves adds robust flavor.

¼ cup red wine vinegar
1 teaspoon salt
½ teaspoon coarsely ground black pepper
3 tablespoons olive oil
2 tablespoons chopped fresh oregano leaves
8 large bone-in chicken thighs (about 3½ pounds), skin removed
3 medium red onions
¾ pound fully cooked chorizo-sausage links, each cut crosswise in half
⅓ cup assorted olives such as Kalamata, cracked green, and Picholine (optional)
Oregano sprig for garnish

1 In large bowl, combine vinegar, salt, pepper, 2 tablespoons olive oil, and 1 tablespoon chopped oregano; add chicken thighs, tossing to coat. Refrigerate 30 minutes to marinate.

2 Meanwhile, cut each red onion into 6 wedges; thread onto 3 metal skewers.

3 Place red-onion skewers on grill over medium heat; brush with remaining 1 tablespoon olive oil. Cook 5 minutes. Place chicken thighs on grill with onions; cook about 20 minutes longer, turning onions and chicken once until onions are browned and tender and juices run clear when chicken thighs are pierced with tip of knife.

4 About 10 minutes before onions and chicken are done, add chorizo pieces to grill and cook, turning chorizo occasionally, until lightly browned and heated through.

5 To serve, place red-onion skewers on platter with chicken and chorizo. Sprinkle with remaining 1 tablespoon chopped oregano. Serve with olives, if you like. Garnish with oregano. *Makes 6 main-dish servings.*

Each serving without olives: About 465 calories, 38 g protein, 9 g carbohydrate, 30 g total fat (9 g saturated), 1 g fiber, 850 mg cholesterol, 1190 mg sodium.

# Caribbean Chicken Kabobs

PREP: 30 MINUTES / BROIL: 10 MINUTES

The tang of green onions, soy sauce, ginger, and allspice adds a burst of island flavor to these juicy low-fat kabobs.

1½ bunches green onions
1 tablespoon sugar
2 tablespoons soy sauce
1 tablespoon Worcestershire sauce
1 tablespoon vegetable oil
1 teaspoon salt
2 teaspoons grated, peeled fresh ginger
¼ teaspoon crushed red pepper
25 whole allspice
1½ pounds skinless, boneless chicken breasts, cut into 1½-inch chunks
1 large red pepper, cut into 1-inch pieces

1 Soak twelve 8-inch bamboo skewers in water for 15 minutes.

2 Meanwhile, coarsely cut up 1 bunch green onions. In blender or in food processor with knife blade attached, blend cut-up green onions, sugar, soy sauce, Worcestershire, oil, salt, ginger, crushed red pepper, and allspice until puréed.

3 Cut remaining green onions into 2-inch-long pieces.

4 Preheat broiler. In bowl, toss chicken with puréed spice mixture to coat. Alternately thread chicken, red pepper, and green onion pieces onto skewers.

5 Place kabobs on rack in broiling pan. Brush any remaining spice mixture on chicken. With broiling pan at closest position to source of heat, broil kabobs 10 minutes or until chicken just loses its pink color throughout, turning skewers once halfway through cooking time. *Makes 6 main-dish servings.*

Each serving: About 175 calories, 27 g protein, 7 g carbohydrate, 4 g total fat (1 g saturated), 1 g fiber, 66 mg cholesterol, 840 mg sodium.

*Portuguese Mixed Grill* ➤

# Chicken Saté

🐓 🐓 🐓

PREP: 10 MINUTES PLUS MARINATING / BROIL: 5 MINUTES

4 large skinless, boneless chicken-breast halves
  (about 1½ pounds)
¼ cup soy sauce
1 tablespoon vegetable oil
1 tablespoon light molasses
¼ teaspoon crushed red pepper
1 garlic clove, crushed with garlic press
4 tablespoons fresh lemon juice
½ cup creamy peanut butter

1 Place chicken breasts between 2 sheets of waxed paper and with the flat side of a small skillet or meat pounder, pound to a ½-inch thickness. Cut chicken breasts lengthwise into 1-inch-wide strips.

2 In bowl, mix chicken strips, soy sauce, oil, molasses, crushed red pepper, garlic, and 2 tablespoons lemon juice. Cover and refrigerate chicken in marinade 2 hours, stirring occasionally. Meanwhile, soak twelve 8-inch-long bamboo skewers in water to prevent charring when broiling.

3 Preheat broiler. Thread chicken strips on bamboo skewers. Place bamboo skewers on rack in broiling pan. Brush generously with marinade. With broiling pan at closest position to source of heat, broil chicken 4 to 5 minutes until chicken just loses its pink color and is tender, turning skewers once and brushing the chicken with remaining marinade frequently.

*Chicken Saté*

**4** Meanwhile, in bowl, with fork, mix peanut butter, remaining 2 tablespoons lemon juice, and *½ cup hot water* until smooth. Serve chicken with peanut sauce. *Makes 6 main-dish servings.*

Each serving: About 290 calories, 33 g protein, 8 g carbohydrate, 15 g total fat (3 g saturated), 1 g fiber, 66 mg cholesterol, 860 mg sodium.

# Peanut-Glazed Turkey Skewers

PREP: 15 MINUTES / BROIL: 5 MINUTES

2 tablespoons sugar
3 tablespoons soy sauce
3 tablespoons red wine vinegar
2 tablespoons creamy peanut butter
1 tablespoon grated, peeled fresh ginger
6 turkey cutlets, each ¼-inch thick (about
   1 pound), cut lengthwise into
   1½-inch-wide strips

**1** Preheat broiler. In medium bowl, with fork, mix sugar, soy sauce, vinegar, peanut butter, and ginger. Add turkey strips to soy-sauce mixture; toss to coat.

**2** On each of twelve metal skewers, thread 1 turkey strip, accordion-style. Place skewers in broiling pan with rack removed. Brush some remaining soy-sauce mixture over turkey strips.

**3** With broiling pan at closest position to source of heat, broil turkey 5 minutes or until it just loses its pink color throughout, turning skewers once and brushing with any remaining soy-sauce mixture.

**4** To serve, spoon any pan juices over turkey. *Makes 4 main-dish servings.*

Each serving: About 210 calories, 31 g protein, 9 g carbohydrate, 5 g total fat (1 g saturated), 0.5 g fiber, 70 mg cholesterol, 865 mg sodium.

# Caribbean-Style Chicken

PREP: 30 MINUTES / GRILL: 5 MINUTES

1 tablespoon vegetable oil
½ small onion, grated
2 tablespoons brown sugar
2 tablespoons chili sauce
1 tablespoon fresh lime juice
½ teaspoon salt
½ teaspoon ground allspice
½ teaspoon dried thyme
¼ teaspoon ground red pepper (cayenne)
4 small skinless, boneless chicken-breast halves
   (about 1 pound), each cut into 8 pieces

**1** In small saucepan, heat oil over medium-high heat. Add onion and cook 2 minutes. Stir in brown sugar, chili sauce, lime juice, salt, allspice, thyme, and ground red pepper. Heat to boiling over medium heat; boil 1 minute to blend flavors. Set spice mixture aside to cool.

**2** Preheat broiler. Soak eight 6" to 8" bamboo skewers in water for 15 minutes.

**3** Add chicken to spice mixture; toss to coat. Thread 4 chicken pieces on each bamboo skewer. Arrange skewers on rack in broiling pan. With pan at closest position to source of heat, broil 5 minutes or until chicken loses its pink color throughout, turning once and brushing with any remaining spice mixture halfway through cooking time. *Makes 4 main-dish servings.*

Each serving: About 200 calories, 27 g protein, 11 g carbohydrate, 5 g total fat (1 g saturated), 0 g fiber, 66 mg cholesterol, 480 mg sodium.

# Jamaican Jerk Island Kabobs

The marinade, punched up with chile, ginger, and green onions, is ready in minutes. Try serving kabobs with black beans and rice. If you like spicy-hot food, leave some or all of the seeds in the jalapeño chile.

2 green onions, chopped
1 jalapeño chile, seeded and chopped
1 tablespoon chopped, peeled fresh ginger
2 tablespoons white wine vinegar
2 tablespoons Worcestershire sauce
1 teaspoon ground allspice
1 teaspoon dried thyme
3 teaspoons vegetable oil
½ teaspoon plus ⅛ teaspoon salt
1 pound skinless, boneless chicken breasts, cut into
   12 pieces
2 medium red peppers, cut into 1-inch pieces

**1** In blender, blend green onions, jalapeño chile, ginger, vinegar, Worcestershire, allspice, thyme, 2 teaspoons oil, and ½ teaspoon salt until combined. Place chicken pieces in small bowl or zip-tight plastic bag with green-onion mixture, turning to coat. Marinate in refrigerator 30 minutes.

**2** Meanwhile, in small bowl, toss pepper pieces with remaining 1 teaspoon oil and ⅛ teaspoon salt; set aside.

**3** Preheat broiler. On 4 metal skewers, alternately thread chicken and peppers.

**4** Place kabobs on rack in broiling pan. Brush kabobs with any remaining marinade. With broiling pan at closest position to source of heat, broil kabobs 10 minutes or until chicken is no longer pink inside, turning once. *Makes 4 main-dish servings.*

Each serving: About 180 calories, 27 g protein, 6 g carbohydrate, 5 g total fat (1 g saturated), 1 g fiber, 66 mg cholesterol, 525 mg sodium.

# Curried Chicken Kabobs

If you make rice to go with this, stir a handful of chopped peanuts and raisins into it.

½ cup plain low-fat yogurt
1 tablespoon curry powder
1 tablespoon fresh lemon juice
1 teaspoon salt
4 small skinless, boneless chicken-breast halves
   (about 1 pound), each cut into 6 chunks
1 bunch green onions, cut into 2-inch lengths

**1** In medium bowl, mix yogurt, curry powder, lemon juice, and salt. Add chicken chunks to yogurt mixture; toss to coat.

**2** Preheat broiler. On eight 6- to 7-inch-long metal skewers, alternately thread chicken chunks and green onions. Place skewers on rack in broiling pan. With pan at closest position to source of heat, broil kabobs 8 minutes or until chicken is fork-tender, turning skewers once. *Makes 4 main-dish servings.*

Each serving: About 160 calories, 28 g protein, 5 g carbohydrate, 2 g total fat (1 g saturated), 1 g fiber, 68 mg cholesterol, 680 mg sodium.

◄ *Jamaican Jerk Island Kabobs*

# Roasts

# Stuffed Cornish Hens with Roasted Turnips

PREP: 35 MINUTES / ROAST: 1 HOUR 30 MINUTES

Raisin-Bread & Pear Stuffing (recipe follows)
4 Rock Cornish hens (about 1¼ pounds each)
1 tablespoon apple jelly
1 teaspoon ground sage
1 teaspoon salt
6 large turnips (about 2 pounds), peeled and cut
  into quarters
1 tablespoon vegetable oil
Pan Gravy (page 142)

**1** Prepare Raisin-Bread & Pear Stuffing.

**2** Preheat oven to 350°F. Remove giblets and neck from hens; refrigerate for use another day. Rinse hens with cold running water and drain well; pat dry with paper towels.

**3** Spoon some stuffing lightly into body cavity of each hen.* Fold neck skin to back; lift wings toward neck, then fold them under back of hens so they stay in place. With string, tie legs and tail of each hen together. In cup, mix apple jelly, sage, and ½ teaspoon salt.

Rub hens with apple-jelly mixture. Place hens, breast-side up, on small rack in large roasting pan.

**4** In large bowl, toss turnips with oil and remaining ½ teaspoon salt. Add to roasting pan with hens. Roast hens in 350°F. oven about 1½ hours, brushing hens occasionally with drippings in pan and stirring turnips occasionally, until turnips are fork-tender and juices run clear when hens are pierced with tip of knife.

**5** When hens are done, place on warm large platter. Transfer turnips to platter with hens; keep warm.

**6** Prepare Pan Gravy and pour into gravy boat. Serve hens with gravy, stuffing, and turnips. *Makes 8 main-dish servings.*

*Bake any leftover stuffing in covered greased small casserole during last 30 minutes of roasting time.

RAISIN-BREAD & PEAR STUFFING: In 5-quart Dutch oven, melt *4 tablespoons margarine or butter (½ stick)* over medium heat. Add *1 large celery stalk*, diced, and *1 medium onion*, diced, and cook until tender, stirring occasionally. Remove Dutch oven from heat; add *1 can (16 ounces) sliced pears*, drained and chopped, *1 loaf (16 ounces) raisin bread with cinnamon*, cubed, ½ cup water, and ½ teaspoon poultry seasoning. Toss to mix.

Each serving: About 650 calories, 36 g protein, 49 g carbohydrate, 34 g total fat (9 g saturated), 5 g fiber, 175 mg cholesterol, 755 mg sodium.

## TO SKIN OR NOT TO SKIN

Chicken skin gets 80 percent of its calories from fat, so it makes sense to serve your bird without it. But you don't have to remove the skin before cooking. According to the U.S. Department of Agriculture (USDA), it makes little difference in the fat content whether the skin is removed before or after cooking. But tastewise, especially when roasting whole chickens, you'll get a moister, more tender result if you cook with the skin still intact. Some skin-removal incentives:

| | Calories | Fat g | Saturated Fat g |
|---|---|---|---|
| Breast, | | | |
| WITH SKIN | 197 | 8 | 2 |
| WITHOUT SKIN | 165 | 4 | 1 |
| Drumstick and thigh, | | | |
| WITH SKIN | 232 | 13 | 4 |
| WITHOUT SKIN | 191 | 8 | 2 |

*All figures are for a 3½-ounce cooked serving.*

# Cornish Hens Provençale

PREP: 10 MINUTES / ROAST: 50 MINUTES

1 tablespoon olive oil
1 small garlic clove, minced
½ teaspoon dried thyme
¼ teaspoon coarsely ground black pepper
½ teaspoon salt
3 Rock Cornish hens (about 1¼ pounds each)
2 large onions, each cut into quarters
10 pitted Kalamata olives, coarsely chopped
3 large tomatoes, each cut into quarters

**1** Preheat oven to 425°F. In cup, mix olive oil, garlic, thyme, pepper, and salt.

**2** Remove giblets and neck from hens; refrigerate for

use another day. Rinse hens with cold running water and drain well; pat dry with paper towels.

**3** Lift wings toward neck, then fold them under back of hens so they stay in place. With string, tie legs of each hen together. Place hens, breast side up, in large roasting pan (17" by 11½"). Rub with oil mixture.

**4** Arrange onions and olives around Cornish hens and bake, uncovered, 35 minutes, brushing hens occasionally with drippings in pan. Add tomatoes and cook 10 to 15 minutes longer or until juices run clear when hens are pierced with tip of knife. *Makes 6 main-dish servings.*

Each serving: About 445 calories, 31 g protein, 13 g carbohydrate, 29 g total fat (7 g saturated), 3 g fiber, 174 mg cholesterol, 460 mg sodium.

# Cornish Hens with Roasted Winter Squash

🐓 🐓 🐓

PREP: 15 MINUTES / ROAST: 1 HOUR 15 MINUTES

2 medium acorn squash (about 1¼ pounds each)
3 Rock Cornish hens (about 1¼ pounds each)
¾ teaspoon salt
½ teaspoon coarsely ground black pepper
1 cup apple cider or apple juice
½ cup pitted prunes (3 ounces)
2 cinnamon sticks (each 3 inches long)

**1** Preheat oven to 375°F. Cut each acorn squash lengthwise in half; remove and discard seeds. Cut each half lengthwise into 3 wedges; cut each wedge diagonally in half.

**2** Remove giblets and neck from hens; refrigerate for use another day. Rinse hens with cold running water and drain well; pat dry with paper towels.

**3** Lift wings toward neck, then fold them under back of hens so they stay in place. With string, tie legs of each hen together. Place hens, breast-side up, in large roasting pan (17" by 11½"); rub with salt and pepper. Arrange squash in roasting pan around hens.

**4** Bake hens and squash 30 minutes. Add apple cider, prunes, and cinnamon sticks. Bake 45 minutes longer, basting with pan juices occasionally, until squash is tender and juices run clear when fork is inserted between leg and body cavity of hens.

**5** To serve, arrange hens, squash, prunes, and cinnamon sticks on large platter. Skim and discard fat from pan juices; serve pan juices with hens. *Makes 6 main-dish servings.*

Each serving: About 460 calories, 28 g protein, 29 g carbohydrate, 26 g total fat (7 g saturated), 6 g fiber, 160 mg cholesterol, 375 mg sodium.

# Plum-Glazed Chicken

🐓 🐓 🐓

PREP: 10 MINUTES / ROAST: 1 HOUR

1 whole chicken (about 3½ pounds)
¼ cup plum jam
¾ teaspoon Chinese five-spice powder
½ teaspoon salt
2 tablespoons margarine or butter, softened
¼ teaspoon coarsely ground black pepper

**1** Preheat oven to 450°F. Remove giblets and neck from chicken; refrigerate for use another day. Rinse chicken with cold running water and drain well; pat dry with paper towels.

**2** In small bowl, stir plum jam with ½ teaspoon five-spice powder and ¼ teaspoon salt. In another small bowl, stir margarine or butter with pepper, remaining ¼ teaspoon five-spice powder, and remaining ¼ teaspoon salt until blended. With fingertips, gently separate skin from meat on breast and thighs. Rub margarine mixture on meat under skin.

**3** With breast side up, lift wings up toward neck, then fold wing tips under back of chicken so wings stay in place. Tie legs together. Place chicken, breast side up, on rack in small roasting pan (14" by 10").

**4** Roast chicken about 1 hour, brushing occasionally with plum-jam mixture during last 10 minutes. Chicken is done when temperature on meat thermometer reaches 175° to 180°F. and juices run clear when thickest part of thigh is pierced with tip of knife.

**5** Place chicken on warm platter; let stand 10 minutes to set juices for easier carving. *Makes 4 main-dish servings.*

Each serving: About 520 calories, 48 g protein, 13 g carbohydrate, 30 g total fat (8 g saturated), 0 g fiber, 154 mg cholesterol, 510 mg sodium.

# Chicken with Port-Wine Sauce

### 🐓 🐓 🐓

PREP: 45 MINUTES / ROAST: 3 HOURS 30 MINUTES

Port is a sweet fortified wine that adds incredible depth of flavor to the sauce for this roast chicken. A fortified wine is one that has had brandy added to it in order to increase its alcohol content without reducing its natural sweetness. Other examples of fortified wines (which you could also try in this recipe) are Madeira, a Portuguese wine, and Marsala, from Italy.

Aromatic Rice Stuffing (opposite page)
1 large chicken (about 8 pounds)
2 teaspoons salt
½ teaspoon dried thyme
2 cups cranberry-raspberry juice
2 tablespoons brown sugar
¼ cup cranberries, sliced
¼ cup port wine or chicken broth
2 teaspoons cornstarch
⅓ cup chicken broth

1 Prepare Aromatic Rice Stuffing.

2 Preheat oven to 350°F. Remove giblets and neck from chicken; refrigerate for use another day. Rinse chicken with cold running water and drain well; pat dry with paper towels.

3 Spoon some stuffing into neck cavity. Fold neck skin over stuffing; fasten neck skin to back with 1 or 2 skewers. With chicken breast side up, lift wings toward neck, then fold them under back of chicken so they stay in place.

4 Spoon remaining stuffing into body cavity.* Close by folding skin lightly over opening; skewer closed if necessary. With string, tie legs and tail together.

5 Place chicken, breast side up, on rack in medium roasting pan (15½" by 10½"). Rub chicken all over with salt and thyme. Roast chicken 3 to 3½ hours. Chicken is done when temperature on meat thermometer reaches 175° to 180°F. and juices run clear when thickest part of thigh is pierced with tip of knife. (Stuffing temperature should reach 160° to 165°F.) Start checking for doneness during last half hour of roasting.

6 Meanwhile, prepare glaze: In 3-quart saucepan, heat cranberry-raspberry juice and brown sugar to boiling over high heat. Cook, uncovered, 15 minutes or until mixture has reduced to ⅓ cup. Cover and set aside.

7 Place chicken on warm platter; let stand 10 minutes to allow juices to set for easier carving.

8 Prepare sauce: Remove rack from roasting pan. Skim and discard fat from drippings. Add ½ cup water to roasting pan, stirring until brown bits are loosened; pour through sieve into 1-quart saucepan; stir in cranberries and ¼ cup prepared glaze. Heat to boiling over high heat; boil 1 minute to cook cranberries. In 1-cup measuring cup, stir together port wine, cornstarch, and broth. Stir cornstarch mixture into sauce; heat to boiling. Boil 1 minute or until thickened; pour into gravy boat.

9 To serve, brush chicken with remaining glaze. Serve with sauce and stuffing. *Makes 8 main-dish servings.*

*Bake any leftover stuffing in greased covered casserole during last 30 minutes of roasting.

Each serving: About 750 calories, 59 g protein, 46 g carbohydrate, 35 g total fat (9 g saturated), 1 g fiber, 178 mg cholesterol, 1180 mg sodium.

# RICE STUFFINGS FOR SMALL BIRDS

Rice stuffings are perfect for birds whose body cavities are on the small side. These recipes make enough to stuff a 7- to 9-pound bird. Any extra stuffing should be baked in a greased covered casserole during the last 30 minutes of roasting.

## Rice & Spinach Stuffing

In 3-quart saucepan, heat *1 tablespoon vegetable oil* over medium heat. Add *1 medium onion*, diced, and cook until golden brown. Add *1 cup regular long-grain rice* and prepare as label directs (but do not use butter). When rice is done, add *1 package (10 ounces) frozen chopped spinach*, thawed and squeezed dry, and *2 tablespoons fresh lemon juice*; toss to mix well. Makes about 6 cups stuffing.

Each ½ cup: About 80 calories, 2 g protein, 15 g carbohydrate, 1 g total fat (1 g saturated), 1 g fiber, 0 mg cholesterol, 20 mg sodium.

## Wild-Rice Stuffing

In 3-quart saucepan, heat *3½ cups chicken broth* (canned or homemade, page 11), *1 package (4 ounces) wild rice*, and *1 cup water* to boiling over high heat. Reduce heat to low; cover and simmer 25 minutes. Stir in *¾ cup regular long-grain rice*; heat to boiling over high heat. Reduce heat to low; cover and simmer 15 to 20 minutes until liquid is absorbed and rices are tender. Meanwhile, in 10-inch skillet, melt *3 tablespoons margarine or butter* over medium-high heat. Add *1 pound carrots*, peeled and diced, *2 medium celery stalks*, diced, *2 large onions*, diced, and *¾ teaspoon salt* and cook until lightly browned and tender, about 15 minutes. Stir sautéed vegetables and *¼ cup chopped parsley* into cooked rice. Makes about 8 cups stuffing.

Each ½ cup: About 105 calories, 3 g protein, 18 g carbohydrate, 3 g total fat (1 g saturated), 2 g fiber, 0 mg cholesterol, 380 mg sodium.

## Aromatic Rice Stuffing

In 3-quart saucepan, prepare *1½ cups Texmati, Jasmine, or other aromatic rice* as label directs using *¾ teaspoon salt*. Meanwhile, in 10-inch skillet, heat *2 tablespoons vegetable oil* over medium heat. Add *3 medium celery stalks*, cut into thin slices, *1 medium onion*, minced, and *½ teaspoon salt* and cook until vegetables are lightly browned. Add *½ cup water* to skillet; heat to boiling over high heat. Reduce heat to low; simmer, uncovered, until water evaporates and vegetables are tender. Stir vegetables and *⅓ cup dried currants or raisins* into rice. Makes about 6 cups stuffing.

Each ½ cup: About 115 calories, 2 g protein, 22 g carbohydrate, 2 g total fat (0 g saturated), 0.5 g fiber, 0 mg cholesterol, 250 mg sodium.

## Rice & Vegetable Stuffing

In 3-quart saucepan, heat *4 cups chicken broth* (canned or homemade, page 11) to boiling over high heat. Stir in *2 cups regular long-grain rice*; heat to boiling. Reduce heat to low; cover and simmer 20 minutes or until rice is tender and liquid is absorbed. Meanwhile, in 12-inch skillet, heat *2 tablespoons vegetable oil* over over medium-high heat. Add *2 large celery stalks*, diced, *2 medium carrots*, diced, *1 large onion*, chopped, *1 teaspoon poultry seasoning*, *½ teaspoon salt*, and *½ teaspoon pepper*, stirring frequently, until vegetables are tender and golden. Add *1 pound spinach*, coarsely chopped, and cook, stirring, until spinach wilts. When rice is done, stir rice into vegetable mixture. Makes about 8 cups stuffing.

Each ½ cup: About 125 calories, 3 g protein, 22 g carbohydrate, 2 g total fat (0 g saturated), 2 g fiber, 0 mg cholesterol, 370 mg sodium.

## Barley & Brown Rice Stuffing

In 4-quart saucepan, heat *1 can (14½ ounces) chicken broth* and enough *water* to equal 5½ cups liquid, *1 cup barley*, and *1 teaspoon salt* to boiling over high heat. Reduce heat to low, cover, and simmer 15 minutes. Stir in *¾ cup brown rice*; cover pan and continue cooking 45 minutes or until barley and brown rice are tender and all liquid is absorbed. Meanwhile, in 12-inch skillet, heat *2 tablespoons olive oil* over medium-high heat. Add *10 ounces mushrooms*, sliced, *3 medium carrots*, peeled and diced, *3 medium celery stalks*, sliced, *1 large onion*, diced, *½ teaspoon salt*, and *¼ teaspoon coarsely ground black pepper* and cook until vegetables are tender, about 10 minutes, stirring occasionally. Stir vegetable mixture into barley mixture. Toss to mix well. Makes about 8 cups stuffing.

Each ½ cup: About 105 calories, 3 g protein, 19 g carbohydrate, 3 g total fat (0 g saturated), 3 g fiber, 0 mg cholesterol, 345 mg sodium.

# Apple & Thyme Chicken

PREP: 20 MINUTES / ROAST: 1 HOUR

1 whole chicken (about 3½ pounds)
1 bunch thyme
¾ teaspoon salt
¼ teaspoon coarsely ground black pepper
⅛ teaspoon ground allspice
1 jumbo onion (about 1 pound), cut into thin
   wedges
2 teaspoons olive oil
2 large Granny Smith apples, each cut into quarters
2 tablespoons applejack or Calvados
½ cup chicken broth

**1** Preheat oven to 450°F. Remove giblets and neck from chicken; refrigerate for use another day. Rinse chicken with cold running water and drain well; pat dry with paper towels.

**2** Reserve 2 thyme sprigs; chop enough remaining thyme leaves to equal 1 tablespoon. With fingertips, gently separate skin from meat on chicken breast. Place 1 thyme sprig under skin of each breast half. In cup, mix chopped thyme, salt, pepper, and allspice.

**3** With chicken breast-side up, lift wings up toward neck, then fold wing tips under back of chicken so wings stay in place. With string, tie legs together.

**4** In medium roasting pan (15½" by 10½"), stir onion wedges with olive oil, chopped thyme mixture, and ¼ *cup water*. Push onion mixture to sides of roasting pan. Place chicken, breast side up, on small rack in center of roasting pan.

**5** Roast chicken and onion wedges 40 minutes. Add apples to pan; roast about 20 minutes longer. Chicken is done when temperature on meat thermometer reaches 175° to 180°F. and juices run clear when thickest part of thigh is pierced with tip of knife.

**6** Place chicken on warm platter; let stand 10 minutes to allow juices to set for easier carving.

**7** Meanwhile, remove rack from roasting pan. With slotted spoon, transfer onions to platter with chicken. Skim fat from drippings in pan. Add applejack to pan and cook 1 minute over medium heat, stirring. Add chicken broth; heat to boiling. Serve pan-juice mixture with chicken. *Makes 4 main-dish servings.*

Each serving: About 640 calories, 49 g protein, 24 g carbohydrate, 36 g total fat (10 g saturated), 4 g fiber, 162 mg cholesterol, 715 mg sodium.

# Fennel-Rubbed Roast Chicken

PREP: 20 MINUTES / ROAST: 1 HOUR

1 whole chicken (about 3½ pounds)
1 tablespoon fennel seeds, crushed
1 teaspoon grated orange peel
1 teaspoon salt
½ teaspoon coarsely ground black pepper
1 medium fennel bulb (about 1½ pounds), trimmed
   and cut into ½-inch wedges
1½ pounds medium red potatoes, unpeeled and
   cut into 1-inch chunks
1 large red onion, cut into 8 wedges
2 teaspoons olive oil

**1** Preheat oven to 450°F. Remove giblets and neck from chicken; refrigerate for use another day. Rinse chicken with cold running water and drain well; pat dry with paper towels.

**2** In cup, mix fennel seeds, orange peel, ½ teaspoon salt, and ¼ teaspoon pepper. With fingertips, gently separate skin from meat on chicken breast and thighs. Rub half of spice mixture on meat under skin. Rub outside of chicken with remaining spice mixture.

**3** With breast side up, lift wings up toward neck, then fold wing tips under back of chicken so wings stay in place. With string, tie legs together.

**4** In large roasting pan (17" by 11½"), toss fennel, potatoes, and red onion with olive oil and remaining ½ teaspoon salt and ¼ teaspoon pepper. Push vegetable mixture to sides of roasting pan. Place chicken, breast side up, on small rack in center of roasting pan.

**5** Roast chicken and vegetables about 1 hour. Chicken is done when temperature on meat thermometer reaches 175° to 180°F. and juices run clear when thickest part of thigh is pierced with tip of knife.

**6** Place chicken on warm platter; let stand 10 minutes to set juices for easier carving.

**7** Meanwhile, remove rack from roasting pan. With slotted spoon, transfer vegetables to platter with chicken. *Makes 4 main-dish servings.*

Each serving: About 790 calories, 56 g protein, 41 g carbohydrate, 44 g total fat (12 g saturated), 6 g fiber, 203 mg cholesterol, 930 mg sodium.

*Apple & Thyme Chicken* ➤

# Lemon-Rosemary Roast Chicken

PREP: 10 MINUTES / ROAST: 1 HOUR

Scented with lemon juice and fresh rosemary, this simple dish is a good choice for beginners.

1 whole chicken (about 3½ pounds)
1 lemon, cut in half
1 bunch rosemary
¾ teaspoon salt
½ teaspoon coarsely ground black pepper
¼ cup chicken broth

**1** Preheat oven to 450°F. Remove giblets and neck from chicken; refrigerate for use another day. Rinse chicken with cold running water and drain well; pat dry with paper towels.

**2** Squeeze juice from lemon halves; set juice and lemon halves aside. Reserve 4 rosemary sprigs; chop enough remaining rosemary to equal 1 tablespoon. Place lemon halves and rosemary sprigs inside cavity of chicken. In cup, mix chopped rosemary with ¼ teaspoon salt and ¼ teaspoon pepper. With fingertips, gently separate skin from meat on chicken breast and thighs. Rub rosemary mixture on meat under skin. Sprinkle outside of chicken with remaining salt and pepper.

**3** With breast side up, lift wings up toward neck, then fold wing tips under back of chicken so wings stay in place. With string, tie legs together. Place chicken, breast side up, on rack in small roasting pan (14" by 10"). Pour lemon juice over chicken.

**4** Roast chicken about 1 hour. Chicken is done when temperature on meat thermometer reaches 175° to 180°F. and juices run clear when thickest part of thigh is pierced with tip of knife.

**5** Place chicken on warm platter; let stand 10 minutes to set juices for easier carving.

**6** Meanwhile, remove rack from roasting pan. Skim and discard fat from drippings in pan. Add chicken broth to pan drippings; heat to boiling over medium heat, stirring to loosen brown bits. Serve chicken with pan-juice mixture. *Makes 4 main-dish servings.*

Each serving: About 425 calories, 48 g protein, 1 g carbohydrate, 24 g total fat (7 g saturated), 0 g fiber, 154 mg cholesterol, 645 mg sodium.

# Moroccan-Style Roast Chicken

PREP: 15 MINUTES / ROAST: 1 HOUR

A low-stress dish for a busy weeknight—serve with quick sides like couscous and peas.

1 whole chicken (about 3½ pounds)
1 tablespoon margarine or butter, softened
1½ teaspoons ground cumin
1½ teaspoons ground coriander
¼ teaspoon ground cinnamon
¼ teaspoon ground allspice
¼ teaspoon coarsely ground black pepper
½ teaspoon salt
1 can (14½ to 16 ounces) tomatoes, drained and coarsely chopped
1 tablespoon minced fresh cilantro leaves

**1** Preheat oven to 450°F. Remove giblets and neck from chicken; refrigerate for use another day. Rinse chicken with cold running water and drain well; pat dry with paper towels.

**2** In small bowl, stir margarine or butter with cumin, coriander, cinnamon, allspice, pepper, and salt. With fingertips, gently separate skin from meat on breast and thighs. Rub spice mixture on meat under skin.

**3** With breast side up, lift wings up toward neck, then fold wing tips under back of chicken so wings stay in place. With string, tie legs together. Place chicken, breast side up, on rack in small roasting pan (14" by 10").

**4** Roast chicken 40 minutes. Add tomatoes; roast about 20 minutes longer. Chicken is done when temperature on meat thermometer reaches 175° to 180°F. and juices run clear when thickest part of thigh is pierced with tip of knife.

**5** Place chicken on warm platter; let stand 10 minutes to set juices for easier carving.

**6** Meanwhile, remove rack from roasting pan. Skim and discard fat from pan. Transfer tomatoes to bowl; stir in cilantro. Serve chicken with tomato mixture. *Makes 4 main-dish servings.*

Each serving: About 470 calories, 49 g protein, 5 g carbohydrate, 27 g total fat (7 g saturated), 1 g fiber, 154 mg cholesterol, 645 mg sodium.

# Roast Chicken Provençal

### 🐓 🐓 🐓

PREP: 20 MINUTES / ROAST: 1 HOUR

It's cooked on a bed of red peppers and onions and seasoned with fresh basil, garlic, and olives.

1 whole chicken (about 3½ pounds)
1 head garlic, separated into cloves, unpeeled, with loose papery skin discarded
½ teaspoon salt
¼ teaspoon coarsely ground black pepper
2 medium red peppers, cut into 1½-inch-wide slices
1 jumbo onion (about 12 ounces), cut into ½-inch-wide wedges
1 teaspoon olive oil
½ cup Mediterranean olives, such as Kalamata, Picholine, or Niçoise
½ cup chicken broth
2 tablespoons chopped fresh basil leaves

1 Preheat oven to 450°F. Remove giblets and neck from chicken; refrigerate for use another day. Rinse chicken with cold running water and drain well; pat dry with paper towels.

2 Place garlic cloves inside cavity of chicken. Sprinkle outside of chicken with salt and pepper.

3 With breast side up, lift wings up toward neck, then fold wing tips under back of chicken so wings stay in place. With string, tie legs together.

4 Place peppers and onion in small roasting pan (14" by 10"); stir in olive oil and ¼ cup water. Place chicken, breast side up, on vegetables.

5 Roast chicken and vegetables 45 minutes. Stir olives into vegetable mixture and roast about 15 minutes longer. Chicken is done when temperature on meat thermometer reaches 175° to 180°F. and juices run clear when thickest part of thigh is pierced with tip of knife.

6 Place chicken on warm platter; let stand 10 minutes to set juices for easier carving.

7 Meanwhile, with slotted spoon, transfer vegetable mixture to platter with chicken. Skim and discard fat from drippings in pan. Add chicken broth, basil, and ½ cup water to pan; heat to boiling over medium heat, stirring to loosen brown bits. Serve with vegetables and pan juices. *Makes 4 main-dish servings.*

Each serving: About 600 calories, 50 g protein, 16 g carbohydrate, 36 g total fat (9 g saturated), 2 g fiber, 159 mg cholesterol, 875 mg sodium.

# Roast Chicken with Herb Butter

###

PREP: 10 MINUTES / ROAST: 1 HOUR

1 whole chicken (about 3½ pounds)
3 tablespoons margarine or butter, softened
2 tablespoons chopped fresh chives
1 tablespoon chopped fresh parsley leaves
¼ teaspoon salt
¼ teaspoon coarsely ground black pepper

1 Preheat oven to 450°F. Remove giblets and neck from chicken; refrigerate for use another day. Rinse chicken with cold running water and drain well; pat dry with paper towels.

2 In cup, mix margarine or butter, chives, and parsley until blended. With fingertips, gently separate skin from meat on chicken breast and thighs. Rub herb mixture on meat under skin. Sprinkle outside of chicken with salt and pepper.

3 With breast side up, lift wings up toward neck, then fold wing tips under back of chicken so wings stay in place. With string, tie legs together. Place chicken, breast side up, on rack in small roasting pan (about 14" by 10").

4 Roast chicken about 1 hour. Chicken is done when temperature on meat thermometer reaches 175° to 180°F. and juices run clear when thickest part of thigh is pierced with tip of knife.

5 Place chicken on warm platter; let stand 10 minutes to set juices for easier carving. *Makes 4 main-dish servings.*

Each serving: About 495 calories, 48 g protein, 0 g carbohydrate, 32 g total fat (8 g saturated), 0 g fiber, 154 mg cholesterol, 390 mg sodium.

# MASHED POTATOES

Our foolproof recipe for fluffy potatoes—plus 5 easy flavor variations—follows. (If you use a ricer or food mill, process potatoes first, then transfer them to a bowl and add the margarine or butter, salt, and milk.)

*3 pounds all-purpose potatoes, peeled and cut into*
    *1-inch chunks*
*4 tablespoons margarine or butter (½ stick)*
*1 teaspoon salt*
*1 cup hot milk*

**1** In 3-quart saucepan, heat potatoes and enough *water* to cover to boiling over high heat. Reduce heat to low; cover and simmer 15 minutes or until potatoes are fork-tender; drain.

**2** Return potatoes to pan. With potato masher, mash potatoes with margarine or butter and salt. Gradually add milk; mash until mixture is smooth and well blended. Keep warm. **Makes 8 accompaniment servings.**

Each serving: About 170 calories, 4 g protein, 24 g carbohydrate, 7 g total fat (2 g saturated), 2 g fiber, 4 mg cholesterol, 380 mg sodium.

**Mashed Potatoes with Onion & Bacon** In 10-inch skillet, cook *4 slices bacon*, chopped, over medium-low heat until browned. With slotted spoon, transfer bacon to paper towels to drain. Add *1 large onion*, chopped, to bacon fat in skillet and cook over medium heat, stirring occasionally, until tender, about 15 minutes. Meanwhile, prepare basic mashed potatoes through step 1 but add *1 bay leaf* to water (discard before proceeding). Mash potatoes as directed in step 2 and add *¼ teaspoon coarsely ground black pepper*. Stir in onion and bacon.

Each serving: About 245 calories, 5 g protein, 27 g carbohydrate, 13 g total fat (4 g saturated), 3 g fiber, 12 mg cholesterol, 460 mg sodium.

**Mashed Potatoes with Sour Cream & Chives** Prepare basic mashed potatoes but add *¼ teaspoon coarsely ground black pepper, 1 container (8 ounces) sour cream*, and *3 tablespoons chopped fresh chives*; use only *½ cup milk*.

Each serving: About 220 calories, 4 g protein, 25 g carbohydrate, 12 g total fat (5 g saturated), 2 g fiber, 15 mg cholesterol, 390 mg sodium.

*Mashed Potatoes with Garlic & Lemon*

**Mashed Potatoes with Garlic & Lemon** Prepare basic mashed potatoes through step 1. Meanwhile, with garlic press, press *2 cloves garlic* into 1-quart saucepan with the margarine or butter and salt called for in step 2; heat over low heat 2 to 3 minutes until margarine melts. Add garlic mixture to potatoes with the milk; mash. Stir in *2 tablespoons finely chopped fresh parsley leaves* and *1 teaspoon grated lemon peel*.

Each serving: About 170 calories, 4 g protein, 25 g carbohydrate, 7 g total fat (2 g saturated), 2 g fiber, 4 mg cholesterol, 380 mg sodium.

**Mashed Potatoes with Horseradish** Prepare basic mashed potatoes but add *2 tablespoons undrained prepared white horseradish* with the milk.

Each serving: About 170 calories, 4 g protein, 25 g carbohydrate, 7 g total fat (2 g saturated), 2 g fiber, 4 mg cholesterol, 385 mg sodium.

**Mashed Potatoes with Parsnips** Prepare basic mashed potatoes but substitute *1 pound parsnips*, peeled and cut into 1-inch pieces, for 1 pound potatoes and use only *¾ cup milk*.

Each serving: About 170 calories, 3 g protein, 25 g carbohydrate, 7 g total fat (1 g saturated), 4 g fiber, 3 mg cholesterol, 380 mg sodium.

# Roast Chicken with Orange Peel & Bay Leaves

🐓🐓🐓

PREP: 10 MINUTES / ROAST: 1 HOUR

The chicken is rubbed with our special orange butter, and the bay leaves are tucked under the skin before roasting.

1 whole chicken (about 3½ pounds)
2 tablespoons margarine or butter, softened
1½ teaspoons finely grated orange peel
¼ teaspoon coarsely ground black pepper
½ teaspoon salt
6 bay leaves

**1** Preheat oven to 450°F. Remove giblets and neck from chicken; refrigerate for use another day. Rinse chicken with cold running water and drain well; pat dry with paper towels.

**2** In small bowl, stir margarine or butter with orange peel, pepper, and ¼ teaspoon salt until blended. With fingertips, gently separate skin from meat on chicken breast and thighs. Rub margarine mixture on meat under skin. Place 1 bay leaf under skin of each breast half. Place remaining 4 bay leaves inside cavity of chicken. Sprinkle outside of chicken with remaining ¼ teaspoon salt.

**3** With breast side up, lift wings up toward neck, then fold wing tips under back of chicken so wings stay in place. With string, tie legs together. Place chicken, breast side up, on rack in small roasting pan (about 14" by 10").

**4** Roast chicken about 1 hour. Chicken is done when temperature on meat thermometer reaches 175° to 180°F. and juices run clear when thickest part of thigh is pierced with tip of knife.

**5** Place chicken on warm platter; let stand 10 minutes to set juices for easier carving. Discard bay leaves. *Makes 4 main-dish servings.*

Each serving: About 475 calories, 48 g protein, 1 g carbohydrate, 30 g total fat (8 g saturated), 0 g fiber, 154 mg cholesterol, 500 mg sodium.

# Roast Chicken with Basil Gremolata

🐓🐓🐓

PREP: 15 MINUTES / ROAST: 1 HOUR

Gremolata, a flavorful Italian garnish, is usually made with garlic, lemon, and parsley; using basil makes it special.

1 whole chicken (about 3½ pounds)
10 large basil leaves
1 whole head garlic
1 lemon, cut into thin slices
½ teaspoon salt
¼ teaspoon coarsely ground black pepper
½ teaspoon finely grated lemon peel

**1** Preheat oven to 450°F. Remove giblets and neck from chicken; refrigerate for use another day. Rinse chicken with cold running water and drain well; pat dry with paper towels.

**2** With fingertips, gently separate skin from meat on breast. Place 2 basil leaves under the skin of each breast half. Remove 1 garlic clove from head of garlic; reserve for making gremolata. Cut head of garlic horizontally in half; place inside cavity of chicken with lemon slices. Sprinkle chicken with salt and pepper.

**3** With breast side up, lift wings up toward neck, then fold wing tips under back of chicken so wings stay in place. With string, tie legs together. Place chicken, breast side up, on rack in small roasting pan (14" by 10").

**4** Roast chicken about 1 hour. Chicken is done when temperature on meat thermometer reaches 175° to 180°F. and juices run clear when thickest part of thigh is pierced with tip of knife.

**5** Meanwhile, prepare gremolata: Mince together grated lemon peel, reserved garlic clove, and remaining 6 basil leaves.

**6** Place chicken on warm platter; let stand 10 minutes to set juices for easier carving. Sprinkle with gremolata to serve. *Makes 4 main-dish servings.*

Each serving: About 435 calories, 49 g protein, 4 g carbohydrate, 24 g total fat (7 g saturated), 0 g fiber, 154 mg cholesterol, 435 mg sodium.

# Southwestern Chicken

PREP: 20 MINUTES / ROAST: 2 HOURS 15 MINUTES

CHICKEN:
1 whole chicken (about 6 pounds)
1 teaspoon salt
½ teaspoon ground red pepper (cayenne)
½ teaspoon ground cumin
2 tablespoons vegetable oil

BLACK BEAN & CORN SALAD:
1 small lemon
3 tablespoons white wine vinegar
½ teaspoon sugar
½ teaspoon salt
½ teaspoon coarsely ground black pepper
¼ cup olive oil
1 can (16 ounces) black beans, rinsed and drained
1 can (11 ounces) whole-kernel corn, drained
1 medium tomato, diced
1 small cucumber, seeded and diced

1 Preheat oven to 350°F. Remove giblets and neck from chicken; refrigerate for use another day. Rinse chicken with cold running water and drain well; pat dry with paper towels.

2 Working with chicken breast side up, lift wings toward neck, then fold them under back of chicken so they stay in place. Sprinkle inside body cavity of chicken with ½ teaspoon salt. Tie legs together. Place chicken, breast side up, on rack in roasting pan.

3 In cup, mix ground red pepper, cumin, oil, and remaining ½ teaspoon salt. Brush chicken generously with oil mixture. Roast chicken 2 hours 15 minutes. Chicken is done when temperature on meat thermometer reaches 175° to 180°F. and juices run clear when thickest part of thigh is pierced with tip of knife.

4 Meanwhile, prepare Black Bean & Corn Salad: From lemon, grate peel and squeeze 2 teaspoons juice. In medium bowl, with fork, mix lemon peel and juice, vinegar, sugar, salt, black pepper, and oil until blended. Stir in black beans, corn, tomato, and cucumber.

5 Place chicken on platter; keep warm. Skim fat from drippings in pan. Stir ½ cup water into roasting pan and heat to boiling over high heat, stirring to loosen brown bits from bottom of pan. Serve chicken with gravy and bean salad. *Makes 6 main-dish servings.*

Each serving: About 680 calories, 59 g protein, 16 g carbohydrate, 42 g total fat (10 g saturated), 3 g fiber, 176 mg cholesterol, 945 mg sodium.

# Roast Chicken with Pears & Sage

PREP: 15 MINUTES / ROAST: 1 HOUR

If you can't get fresh sage, used dried whole leaf sage. Crumble the leaves that are mixed with the margarine; the leaves that go into the chicken cavity can be left whole.

1 whole chicken (about 3½ pounds)
1 teaspoon thinly sliced fresh sage leaves plus 6 sprigs
¼ teaspoon coarsely ground black pepper
2 tablespoons plus 1 teaspoon margarine or butter, softened
½ teaspoon salt
1 medium red onion, cut into ½-inch-thick slices
2 medium Bosc or Anjou pears, peeled, cored, and each cut into quarters

1 Preheat oven to 450°F. Remove giblets and neck from chicken; refrigerate for use another day. Rinse chicken with cold running water and drain well; pat dry with paper towels.

2 In small bowl, stir sliced sage, pepper, 2 tablespoons margarine or butter, and ¼ teaspoon salt. With fingertips, gently separate skin from meat on breast and thighs. Sprinkle herb mixture on meat under skin. Place sage sprigs inside cavity of chicken. Sprinkle outside of chicken with remaining ¼ teaspoon salt.

3 With breast side up, lift wings up toward neck, then fold wing tips under back of chicken so wings stay in place. With string, tie legs together.

4 In small roasting pan (14" by 10"), melt remaining 1 teaspoon margarine or butter in oven. Remove pan from oven; stir in onion and ¼ cup water. Place chicken, breast side up, on rack in roasting pan with onion. Roast chicken 30 minutes. Add pears and roast 30 minutes longer. Chicken is done when meat thermometer reaches 175° to 180°F. and juices run clear when thickest part of thigh is pierced with tip of knife.

5 Place chicken on warm platter; let stand 10 minutes to set juices for easier carving.

6 Meanwhile, remove rack from pan. Skim and discard fat from pear mixture. Transfer pear mixture to platter with chicken. *Makes 4 main-dish servings.*

Each serving: About 600 calories, 49 g protein, 17 g carbohydrate, 37 g total fat (10 g saturated), 3 g fiber, 160 mg cholesterol, 515 mg sodium.

# Tarragon Chicken

### ♨ ♨ ♨

PREP: 20 MINUTES / ROAST: 1 HOUR

1 whole chicken (about 3½ pounds)
2 tablespoons chopped fresh tarragon leaves
1 tablespoon margarine or butter, softened
½ teaspoon salt
¼ teaspoon coarsely ground black pepper
3 shallots, peeled
1 carrot, peeled and cut into 1-inch pieces
1 celery stalk, cut into 1-inch pieces
1 medium onion, cut into 8 wedges
1 teaspoon olive oil
1 cup chicken broth, canned or homemade
   (page 11)
⅓ cup dry white wine

**1** Preheat oven to 450°F. Remove giblets and neck from chicken; refrigerate for use another day. Rinse chicken with cold running water and drain well; pat dry with paper towels.

**2** In cup, mix 1 tablespoon tarragon with margarine or butter until well blended. With fingertips, gently separate skin from meat on chicken breast and thighs. Rub tarragon mixture on meat under skin of chicken. Sprinkle outside of chicken with salt and pepper. Place 2 shallots inside cavity of chicken. Mince remaining shallot; set aside.

**3** With breast side up, lift wings up toward neck, then fold wing tips under back of chicken so wings stay in place. With string, tie legs together.

**4** In small roasting pan (about 14" by 10"), stir carrot, celery, onion, oil, and ¼ cup water. Push vegetables to sides of pan. Place chicken, breast side up, on small rack in center of pan. Roast chicken about 1 hour. Chicken is done when temperature on meat thermometer reaches 175° to 180°F. and juices run clear when thickest part of thigh is pierced with tip of knife.

**5** Place chicken on warm platter; let stand 10 minutes to set juices for easier carving.

**6** Meanwhile, remove rack from roasting pan. Discard vegetables. Skim all but 2 tablespoons fat from pan. Add minced shallot and cook over medium heat 2 minutes, stirring. Add broth and wine to pan; heat to boiling and cook 2 minutes, stirring to loosen brown bits. Stir in remaining 1 tablespoon tarragon. Serve chicken with pan juices. *Makes 4 main-dish servings.*

Each serving: About 620 calories, 49 g protein, 8 g carbohydrate, 41 g total fat (11 g saturated), 2 g fiber, 165 mg cholesterol, 745 mg sodium.

# Roast Capon with Wild-Rice Stuffing

### ♨ ♨ ♨

PREP: 1 HOUR / ROAST: 3 HOURS

Wild-Rice Stuffing (page 131)
1 whole capon or large chicken (7 pounds)
1 teaspoon dried thyme
2 teaspoons vegetable oil
½ teaspoon coarsely ground black pepper
1 teaspoon salt
Giblet Gravy (page 142)

**1** Prepare Wild-Rice Stuffing.

**2** Preheat oven to 325°F. Remove giblets and neck from capon; reserve for making gravy. Rinse capon with cold running water and drain well. With capon breast side up, lift wings toward neck, then fold them under back of capon so they stay in place. Spoon rice mixture lightly into body cavity.* Close cavity by folding skin lightly over opening; skewer closed if necessary. With string, tie legs and tail together.

**3** Place capon, breast side up, on rack in medium roasting pan (15½" by 10½"). In cup, mix thyme, oil, pepper, and salt. Rub capon all over with herb mixture. Roast capon 2½ to 3 hours until temperature on meat thermometer reaches 180° to 185°F. and juices run clear when thickest part of thigh is pierced with tip of knife, brushing capon occasionally with pan drippings for an attractive sheen. When capon turns golden, cover loosely with a tent of foil. Place capon on warm large platter; keep warm.

**4** While capon is roasting, prepare giblets and giblet broth for gravy. When capon is done, prepare Giblet Gravy and pour into gravy boat. Serve capon with gravy and Wild-Rice Stuffing. *Makes 8 main-dish servings.*

*Bake leftover stuffing in greased covered small casserole during last 30 minutes of roasting time.

Each serving: About 680 calories, 63 g protein, 37 g carbohydrate, 30 g total fat (8 g saturated), 4 g fiber, 191 mg cholesterol, 1180 mg sodium.

# Twin Chickens with Raisin Bread Stuffing

🐓🐓🐓

PREP: 45 MINUTES / ROAST: 1 HOUR 30 MINUTES

Instead of one big bird, roast two small ones! They're a time-saver, and there's more of everything to choose from—drumsticks, white meat, wings! Another time-saver: Prepare the stuffing the day before, refrigerate, then stuff the chickens just before roasting them.

Raisin-Bread Stuffing (at right)
2 whole chickens (4 pounds each)
1 tablespoon olive or vegetable oil
1 teaspoon salt
½ teaspoon coarsely ground black pepper
Pan Gravy (page 142)
2 tablespoons apple jelly

1 Prepare Raisin-Bread Stuffing.

2 Preheat oven to 350°F. Remove giblets and necks from chickens; refrigerate for use another day. Rinse chickens with cold running water and drain well; pat dry with paper towels.

3 Spoon some stuffing lightly into body cavity of each chicken.* Close by folding skin lightly over opening; skewer closed if necessary. With string, tie legs together. Fold neck skin to back; lift wings toward neck, then fold them under back of chickens so they stay in place. In cup, mix olive oil, salt, and pepper. Rub chickens with oil mixture.

4 Place chickens, breast side up, on rack in large roasting pan (17" by 11½"). Roast chickens 1½ hours, brushing chickens occasionally with drippings in pan. Chicken is done when temperature on meat thermometer reaches 175° to 180°F. and juices run clear when thickest part of thigh is pierced with tip of knife.

5 Place chickens on warm platter; let stand 10 minutes to set juices for easier carving.

6 Prepare Pan Gravy. Pour into gravy boat.

7 To serve, in small saucepan, melt apple jelly over low heat; brush onto chickens. Serve chickens with gravy and stuffing. ***Makes 12 main-dish servings.***

*Bake any leftover stuffing in covered greased small casserole during last 30 minutes of roasting time.

**RAISIN-BREAD STUFFING:** In 5-quart Dutch oven, heat *3 tablespoons vegetable oil* over medium heat. Add *2 large onions*, diced, *2 large celery stalks*, diced, and *½ teaspoon salt* and cook until vegetables are tender and lightly browned. Stir in *1 large Golden Delicious apple*, peeled and diced, and cook 3 minutes longer, stirring occasionally; remove from heat. Into vegetable mixture in Dutch oven, stir *1 loaf (16 ounces) raisin bread*, cut into cubes, *⅔ cup water*, *2 tablespoons chopped fresh parsley leaves*, and *¾ teaspoon salt*.

Each serving: About 500 calories, 40 g protein, 29 g carbohydrate, 24 g total fat (6 g saturated), 2 g fiber, 117 mg cholesterol, 705 mg sodium.

# Barbecued Roast Chicken

🐓🐓🐓

PREP: 40 MINUTES / ROAST: 2 HOURS 30 MINUTES

4 tablespoons margarine or butter (½ stick)
3 large onions, diced, plus 1 small onion, minced
2 large celery stalks, diced
1 package (8 ounces) corn-bread-stuffing mix
1 whole chicken (about 7 pounds)
½ teaspoon salt
1 tablespoon vegetable oil
1 small green pepper
1 bottle (4½ ounces) hot pepper sauce (½ cup)
3 tablespoons honey
2 tablespoons orange juice
1 teaspoon Worcestershire sauce
½ teaspoon dry mustard

1 In 5-quart Dutch oven or saucepot, melt margarine or butter over medium heat. Add diced onions and celery and cook until tender, about 20 minutes, stirring occasionally. Stir in corn-bread-stuffing mix and 1⅓ cups water. Set stuffing aside to cool slightly.

2 Preheat oven to 350°F. Remove giblets and neck from chicken; refrigerate for use another day. Rinse chicken with running cold water and drain well. Pat dry with paper towels.

3 Spoon some stuffing lightly into neck cavity. Fold neck skin over stuffing; fasten neck skin to back with 1 or 2 skewers. With chicken breast side up, lift wings up toward neck, then fold under back of chicken so they stay in place. Spoon stuffing into body cavity.* Close

by folding skin lightly over opening; skewer closed if necessary. With string, tie legs together.

**4** Place chicken, breast side up, on rack in medium roasting pan (15½" by 10½"). Sprinkle chicken with salt. Roast chicken 2½ hours.

**5** Meanwhile, prepare barbecue sauce: In 3-quart saucepan, heat oil over medium-high heat. Add green pepper and minced onion and cook until tender and browned. Measure out and set aside 2 tablespoons green-pepper mixture. Add hot pepper sauce, honey, orange juice, Worcestershire, dry mustard, and ¼ cup water to saucepan; heat to boiling over high heat. Reduce heat to low; simmer sauce 1 minute to blend flavors. Keep warm.

**6** When chicken turns golden, cover loosely with a tent of foil. Remove foil during last 20 minutes of roasting time. With pastry brush, baste chicken occasionally with some barbecue sauce and sprinkle with reserved green-pepper mixture. Chicken is done when temperature on meat thermometer reaches 175° to 180°F. and juices run clear when thickest part of thigh is pierced with tip of knife.

**7** Place chicken on warm platter; let stand 10 minutes to set juices for easier carving. Serve with remaining barbecue sauce. *Makes 8 main-dish servings.*

*Bake any leftover stuffing in covered, greased small casserole during last 30 minutes of roasting time.

Each serving: About 660 calories, 52 g protein, 37 g carbohydrate, 32 g total fat (8 g saturated), 2 g fiber, 154 mg cholesterol, 1115 mg sodium.

*Barbecued Roast Chicken*

# GOOD GRAVY

All you need to make a good gravy are the rich caramelized meat juices from a roast chicken or turkey. In the first step in making a gravy, the roasting pan is "deglazed" by stirring a liquid into the pan drippings to incorporate the brown bits of caramelized meat juices. The simplest deglazing liquid is water, but you could also use wine or broth (chicken, turkey, or giblet). In the Pan Gravy, below, the deglazed meat juices are then thickened with flour. In Giblet Gravy, the giblets are used to make a broth to deglaze the roasting pan. The cooked giblets are then chopped and added to the gravy. Note that the liver is not added to the giblet broth until the end of the cooking. The reason for this is that you need to cook the liver to include it in the gravy, but you don't want its flavor to overpower the broth.

## Pan Gravy

Remove rack from roasting pan. Pour pan drippings into 4-cup measure. Add *2 cups water* to roasting pan; stir until brown bits are loosened. Add deglazed pan juices to pan drippings in measuring cup. Let juices stand a few seconds until fat rises to top. Skim fat and discard. (You can also do this step with a gravy separator.) Pour into 2-quart saucepan. Measure out a small amount to mix with *3 tablespoons all-purpose flour*, then stir the flour mixture back into the meat juices until smooth. Cook over medium heat, stirring, until mixture boils and thickens. Makes about 3 cups.

Each ¼ cup: About 20 calories, 1 g protein, 2 g carbohydrate, 0 g total fat (0 g saturated), 0 g fiber, 1 mg cholesterol, 0 mg sodium.

## Giblet Broth

In 2-quart saucepan, heat *1 small carrot*, coarsely chopped, *1 small celery stalk*, coarsely chopped, *1 small onion*, cut into quarters, *1 bay leaf, gizzard, heart, neck*, and *2 cups water* to boiling over high heat. Reduce heat to low; cover and simmer 45 minutes. Add *liver*; cook 15 minutes longer or until giblets are tender. Strain giblet broth into 4-cup measure. Remove giblets and neck from strainer; cool slightly. Chop giblets; pull meat from neck and coarsely chop. Discard bones and remaining contents in strainer. Cover and refriger-

ate giblets (and neck meat) and broth separately until ready to make gravy. Makes about 1½ cups.

Each ¼ cup: About 15 calories, 1 g protein, 0 g carbohydrate, 1 g total fat (0 g saturated), 0 g fiber, 1 mg cholesterol, 15 mg sodium.

## Giblet Gravy

While bird is roasting, make Giblet Broth (at left). Remove rack from roasting pan. Pour pan drippings into 4-cup measure. Add *1 cup Giblet Broth* to roasting pan and stir until brown bits are loosened. Add deglazed pan juices to pan drippings in measuring cup. Let drippings stand a few seconds until fat rises to top. Skim fat and discard. (You can also do this step with a gravy separator.) Add remaining Giblet Broth and enough *water* to meat juices in cup to equal 3½ cups. Pour into 2-quart saucepan. Measure out a small amount to mix with *3 tablespoons all-purpose flour*, then stir the flour mixture back into the meat juices until smooth. Cook over medium heat, stirring, until mixture boils and thickens. Stir in reserved giblets and neck meat; heat through. Makes about 4½ cups.

Each ¼ cup: About 20 calories, 2 g protein, 2 g carbohydrate, 1 g total fat (0 g saturated), 0 g fiber, 12 mg cholesterol, 30 mg sodium.

# Asian Sesame Chicken

PREP: 15 MINUTES / ROAST: 1 HOUR

Intense, exotic sesame oil, made from roasted sesame seeds, takes chicken from ordinary to out-of-this-world.

1 whole chicken (about 3½ pounds)
2 green onions, minced
1 tablespoon minced, peeled fresh ginger
1 garlic clove, minced
2 tablespoons Asian sesame oil
½ teaspoon salt
¼ teaspoon coarsely ground black pepper

**1** Preheat oven to 450°F. Remove giblets and neck from chicken; refrigerate for use another day. Rinse chicken with cold running water and drain well; pat dry with paper towels.

**2** In small bowl, stir green onions with ginger, garlic, and 1 tablespoon sesame oil until mixed. With fingertips, gently separate skin from meat on breast and thighs. Rub green-onion mixture on breast meat under skin.

**3** With breast side up, lift wings up toward neck, then fold wing tips under back of chicken so wings stay in place. With string, tie legs together. Sprinkle chicken with salt and pepper. Place chicken, breast side up, on rack in small roasting pan (14" by 10").

**4** Roast chicken 50 minutes. Brush with remaining 1 tablespoon sesame oil and roast about 10 minutes longer. Chicken is done when temperature on meat thermometer reaches 175° to 180°F. and juices run clear when thickest part of thigh is pierced with tip of knife.

**5** Place chicken on warm platter; let stand 10 minutes to set juices for easier carving. *Makes 4 main-dish servings.*

Each serving: About 485 calories, 48 g protein, 1 g carbohydrate, 31 g total fat (8 g saturated), 0.5 g fiber, 154 mg cholesterol, 435 mg sodium.

# Caribbean Roast Chicken

PREP: 15 MINUTES / ROAST: 1 HOUR

Jerk seasonings bring a taste of the tropics to your table.

1 whole chicken (about 3½ pounds)
2 green onions, coarsely chopped
2 tablespoons white wine vinegar
2 tablespoons Worcestershire sauce
1 jalapeño chile, seeded and coarsely chopped
1 tablespoon chopped, peeled fresh ginger
1 teaspoon ground allspice
1 teaspoon dried thyme
¾ teaspoon salt

**1** Preheat oven to 450°F. Remove giblets and neck from chicken; refrigerate for use another day. Rinse chicken with cold running water and drain well; pat dry with paper towels.

**2** In blender at high speed, blend all ingredients except chicken until smooth. With fingertips, gently separate skin from meat on chicken breast and thighs. Spread half of green-onion mixture on meat under skin (mixture will be thin).

**3** With breast side up, lift wings up toward neck, then fold wing tips under back of chicken so wings stay in place. With string, tie legs together. Place chicken, breast side up, on rack in small roasting pan (14" by 10").

**4** Roast chicken 40 minutes. Brush remaining green-onion mixture on skin; roast about 15 minutes longer. Chicken is done when temperature on meat thermometer reaches 175° to 180°F. and juices run clear when thickest part of thigh is pierced with tip of knife.

**5** Place chicken on warm platter; let stand 10 minutes to set juices for easier carving. *Makes 4 main-dish servings.*

Each serving: About 435 calories, 48 g protein, 3 g carbohydrate, 24 g total fat (7 g saturated), 0.5 g fiber, 154 mg cholesterol, 665 mg sodium.

# Couscous-Stuffed Chicken

### 🐓 🐓 🐓

PREP: 40 MINUTES / ROAST: 2 HOURS 30 MINUTES

1 large bunch basil or parsley
¼ cup walnuts, finely chopped
1 tablespoon honey
1 tablespoon olive oil
1 small onion, minced
1 can (14½ ounces) chicken broth
1 cup couscous (Moroccan pasta)
½ cup golden raisins
1 whole chicken (about 7 pounds)
1 teaspoon salt
Pan Gravy (page 142)

1 Coarsely chop enough basil from bunch to measure ¼ cup lightly packed. Mince enough basil from bunch to measure 1 tablespoon. Reserve remaining basil for garnish later. In cup, stir minced basil, chopped walnuts, and honey.

2 In 10-inch skillet, heat olive oil over medium heat. Add onion and cook until tender. Add chicken broth and heat to boiling over high heat. Stir in couscous and raisins. Remove skillet from heat and let stand 5 minutes. Stir in coarsely chopped basil.

3 Preheat oven to 350°F. Remove giblets and neck from chicken; refrigerate for use another day. Rinse chicken with cold running water and drain well; pat dry with paper towels.

4 Spoon some stuffing lightly into neck cavity of chicken. Fold neck skin over stuffing; fasten neck skin to back with 1 or 2 skewers. With chicken breast-side up, lift wings toward neck, then fold them under back of chicken so they stay in place. Spoon remaining stuffing lightly into body cavity. Close by folding skin lightly over opening; skewer closed if necessary. With string, tie legs and tail together.

5 Place chicken, breast side up, on rack in medium roasting pan (15½" by 10½"); sprinkle with salt. Roast chicken for about 2½ hours, brushing occasionally with pan drippings. Chicken is done when thermometer reaches 175° to 180°F. and juices run clear when thickest part of thigh is pierced with tip of knife. During last 20 minutes of roasting time, spread walnut mixture over chicken.

6 Place chicken on warm platter; let stand 10 minutes to set juices for easier carving.

7 Meanwhile, prepare Pan Gravy. Pour into gravy boat.

8 To serve, garnish chicken with reserved basil. Serve chicken with gravy. *Makes 8 main-dish servings.*

Each serving: About 765 calories, 55 g protein, 32 g carbohydrate, 45 g total fat (12 g saturated), 2 g fiber, 203 mg cholesterol, 710 mg sodium.

# Peking Chicken

### 🐓 🐓 🐓

PREP: 20 MINUTES / ROAST: 1 HOUR

It's glazed with a fragrant honey-soy sauce mixture near the end of roasting.

1 whole chicken (about 3½ pounds)
2 tablespoons honey
2 tablespoons soy sauce
1 tablespoon minced, peeled fresh ginger
2 garlic cloves, crushed with garlic press
1 teaspoon seasoned rice vinegar
⅛ teaspoon ground red pepper (cayenne)
1 package (10 ounces) 8-inch flour tortillas
¼ cup chicken broth
¼ cup hoisin sauce
2 green onions, each cut crosswise into thirds, then sliced lengthwise into thin strips

1 Preheat oven to 450°F. Remove giblets and neck from chicken; refrigerate for use another day. Rinse chicken with cold running water and drain well.

2 With breast side up, lift wings up toward neck, then fold wing tips under back of chicken so wings stay in place. With string, tie legs together.

3 Place chicken, breast side up, on rack in sink. Pour *1 quart boiling water* over chicken. Turn chicken over; pour *1 quart boiling water* over back of chicken. (This process allows fat to render easily from chicken and helps skin get crispy during roasting.)

4 Place chicken, breast side up, on rack in small roasting pan (14" by 10"). Roast chicken 50 minutes.

**5** Meanwhile, in cup, combine honey, soy sauce, ginger, garlic, rice vinegar, and ground red pepper; set aside.

**6** After chicken has roasted 50 minutes, brush with half of honey glaze; continue roasting 5 minutes. Brush with remaining glaze; roast about 5 minutes longer. Chicken is done when temperature on meat thermometer reaches 175° to 180°F. and juices run clear when thickest part of thigh is pierced with tip of knife.

**7** Place chicken on warm platter; let stand 10 minutes to set juices for easier carving.

**8** Meanwhile, warm tortillas as label directs. Remove rack from roasting pan. Skim and discard fat from pan. Add chicken broth and *2 tablespoons water* to pan; heat to boiling over medium heat, stirring to loosen brown bits. Stir in hoisin sauce.

**9** Slice chicken and wrap in tortillas with hoisin mixture and green onions. ***Makes 4 main-dish servings.***

Each serving: About 740 calories, 55 g protein, 60 g carbohydrate, 29 g total fat (7 g saturated), 2 g fiber, 154 mg cholesterol, 1405 mg sodium.

# Mexico City Roast Chicken

🐓 🐓 🐓

PREP: 15 MINUTES / ROAST: 1 HOUR

The contrast of warm spices and brown sugar with smoky chipotle chiles in adobo* adds a delicious depth of flavor.

1 whole chicken (about 3½ pounds)
2 tablespoons chipotle chiles in adobo,* finely
   chopped
1 tablespoon brown sugar
1 tablespoon chili powder
1 tablespoon cider vinegar
1 teaspoon ground cumin
2 teaspoons tomato paste
½ teaspoon salt
⅛ teaspoon ground cinnamon

2 jumbo onions (about 12 ounces each), each cut
   into 8 wedges
2 teaspoons vegetable oil
Optional accompaniments: warm flour tortillas,
   shredded lettuce, cilantro leaves, and lime
   wedges

**1** Preheat oven to 450°F. Remove giblets and neck from chicken; refrigerate for use another day. Rinse chicken with cold running water and drain well; pat dry with paper towels.

**2** In small bowl, combine chipotle chiles, brown sugar, chili powder, vinegar, cumin, tomato paste, salt, and cinnamon until blended (mixture will be thick). With fingertips, gently separate skin from meat on chicken breast and thighs. Spread chipotle mixture on meat under skin.

**3** With chicken breast-side up, lift wings up toward neck, then fold wing tips under back of chicken so wings stay in place. With string, tie legs together.

**4** In medium roasting pan (15½" by 10½"), stir onions with oil and ¼ *cup water*. Place chicken, breast side up, in pan.

**5** Roast chicken about 1 hour, stirring onions halfway through cooking time. Chicken is done when temperature on meat thermometer reaches 175° to 180°F. and juices run clear when thickest part of thigh is pierced with tip of knife.

**6** Place chicken on warm platter; let stand 10 minutes to set juices for easier carving.

**7** Meanwhile, with slotted spoon, transfer onions to platter with chicken. Skim and discard fat from drippings in pan. Serve chicken with any pan juices or slice chicken and wrap in warm tortillas with lettuce and cilantro. Serve with lime wedges. ***Makes 4 main-dish servings.***

*Canned chipotle chiles in adobo (smoked jalapeño chiles in a vinegary marinade) are available in Hispanic markets.

Each serving: About 590 calories, 50 g protein, 21 g carbohydrate, 33 g total fat (9 g saturated), 4 g fiber, 159 mg cholesterol, 545 mg sodium.

# Lemon Chicken with Apple Jelly

♥ ♥ ♥

PREP: 25 MINUTES / ROAST: 2 HOURS

1 whole chicken (about 7 pounds)
1 lemon, cut in half
½ teaspoon dried thyme
½ teaspoon coarsely ground black pepper
¼ teaspoon paprika
1¼ teaspoons salt
2 tablespoons apple jelly
1 cup chicken broth, canned or homemade
  (page 11)
1 cup milk
2 tablespoons all-purpose flour

1 Preheat oven to 375°F. Remove giblets and neck from chicken; refrigerate for use another day. Rinse chicken with cold running water and drain well; pat dry with paper towels.

2 Place chicken, breast side up, on rack in medium roasting pan (15½" by 10½"). Rub chicken all over with cut sides of lemon; place lemon halves in cavity of chicken. Lift chicken wings toward neck, then fold them under back of chicken so they stay in place. With string, tie legs together.

3 Rub chicken with thyme, pepper, paprika, and 1 teaspoon salt. Roast chicken 2 hours until temperature on meat thermometer reaches 175° to 180°F. and juices run clear when thickest part of thigh is pierced with tip of knife, basting occasionally with pan drippings for an attractive sheen.

4 About 10 minutes before chicken is done, remove foil. In cup, stir apple jelly with fork until smooth; brush jelly over chicken. Place chicken on warm platter; let stand 10 minutes to set juices for easier carving.

5 Remove rack from roasting pan. Skim fat from drippings in roasting pan. Add broth to drippings, stirring to loosen brown bits; pour into small saucepan. Add milk, flour, and remaining ¼ teaspoon salt and stir until blended. Heat to boiling over high heat, stirring frequently. Reduce heat to low; simmer 2 minutes, stirring constantly.

6 Pour gravy into gravy boat. Serve chicken with gravy. *Makes 6 main-dish servings.*

Each serving: About 665 calories, 67 g protein, 9 g carbohydrate, 38 g total fat (11 g saturated), 0 g fiber, 213 mg cholesterol, 880 mg sodium.

# Mahogany Chicken

♥ ♥ ♥

PREP: 10 MINUTES / ROAST: 1 HOUR 15 MINUTES

Just rub the skin with salt and pepper, then brush with the luscious glaze during the last 30 minutes of cooking time.

1 whole chicken (3½ pounds)
¾ teaspoon salt
½ teaspoon coarsely ground black pepper
2 tablespoons dark brown sugar
2 tablespoons balsamic vinegar
2 tablespoons dry vermouth
Fresh oregano and rosemary for garnish

1 Preheat oven to 375°F. Remove giblets and neck from chicken; refrigerate for use another day. Rinse chicken with cold running water and drain well. Pat dry with paper towels.

2 With chicken breast side up, lift wings up toward neck, then fold them under back of chicken so they stay in place. With string, tie legs together.

3 Place chicken, breast side up, on rack in small roasting pan (14" by 10"); rub with salt and pepper. Roast chicken 45 minutes.

4 Meanwhile, in small bowl, stir brown sugar, balsamic vinegar, and vermouth until sugar dissolves.

5 After chicken has roasted 45 minutes, brush with some glaze. Turn oven control to 400°F. and roast chicken 30 minutes longer, brushing with glaze twice more during roasting, until chicken is a deep brown color, thermometer reaches 180°F., and juices run clear when thickest part of thigh is pierced with tip of knife.

6 Place chicken on warm platter; let stand 10 minutes to set juices for easier carving.

7 Meanwhile, add ¼ *cup water* to roasting pan and heat to boiling over medium heat, stirring to loosen brown bits. Remove pan from heat; skim and discard fat. Serve chicken with pan juices. Garnish with fresh herbs. *Makes 4 main-dish servings.*

Each serving: About 450 calories, 48 g protein, 8 g carbohydrate, 24 g total fat (7 g saturated), 0 g fiber, 154 mg cholesterol, 585 mg sodium.

*Mahogany Chicken* ➤

# Roast Chicken with Olives & Sherry

PREP: 15 MINUTES / ROAST: 1 HOUR

Simple, but full of big Spanish flavor.

1 whole chicken (about 3½ pounds)
12 Mediterranean-style green olives, pitted and finely chopped
1 small shallot, minced
1 garlic clove, minced
1 tablespoon minced fresh parsley leaves
1 tablespoon extravirgin olive oil
½ teaspoon finely grated lemon peel
¼ teaspoon salt
¼ teaspoon coarsely ground black pepper
¾ cup chicken broth
3 tablespoons dry sherry

**1** Preheat oven to 450°F. Remove giblets and neck from chicken; refrigerate for use another day. Rinse chicken with cold running water and drain well; pat dry with paper towels.

**2** In small bowl, stir olives, shallot, garlic, parsley, olive oil, lemon peel, salt, and pepper until mixed. With fingertips, gently separate skin from meat on breast. Rub olive mixture on breast meat under skin.

**3** With chicken breast-side up, lift wings up toward neck, then fold wing tips under back of chicken so wings stay in place. With string, tie legs together. Place chicken, breast side up, on rack in small roasting pan (14" by 10").

**4** Roast chicken about 1 hour. Chicken is done when temperature on meat thermometer reaches 175° to 180°F. and juices run clear when thickest part of thigh is pierced with tip of knife.

**5** Place chicken on warm platter; let stand 10 minutes to set juices for easier carving.

**6** Meanwhile, remove rack from roasting pan. Skim and discard fat from drippings in pan. Add broth and sherry and heat to boiling over medium-high heat, stirring to loosen brown bits from bottom of pan. Serve chicken with pan juices. *Makes 4 main-dish servings.*

Each serving: About 495 calories, 48 g protein, 2 g carbohydrate, 30 g total fat (8 g saturated), 0 g fiber, 154 mg cholesterol, 720 mg sodium.

# Tandoori-Style Roast Chicken

PREP: 15 MINUTES / ROAST: 1 HOUR

A low-fat yogurt coating spiked with lime juice and spices adds zip to skinless chicken.

1 whole chicken (about 3½ pounds), skin removed
1 container (8 ounces) plain low-fat yogurt
½ small onion, chopped
1 tablespoon paprika
2 tablespoons fresh lime juice
1 tablespoon minced, peeled fresh ginger
1 teaspoon ground cumin
1 teaspoon ground coriander
¾ teaspoon salt
¼ teaspoon ground red pepper (cayenne)
Pinch ground cloves

**1** Preheat oven to 450°F. Remove giblets and neck from chicken; refrigerate for use another day. Rinse chicken with cold running water and drain well; pat dry with paper towels.

**2** In blender at high speed, blend all ingredients except chicken until smooth. With breast side up, lift wings up toward neck, then fold wing tips under back of chicken so wings stay in place. With string, tie legs together.

**3** In large bowl, coat chicken inside and outside with yogurt mixture. Place chicken, breast side up, on rack in small roasting pan (14" by 10"). Brush chicken with half of yogurt mixture remaining in bowl; reserve any remaining mixture.

**4** Roast chicken 30 minutes; brush with remaining yogurt mixture. Roast chicken about 30 minutes longer or until temperature on meat thermometer reaches 175° to 180°F. and juices run clear when thickest part of thigh is pierced with tip of knife.

**5** Place chicken on warm platter; let stand 10 minutes to set juices for easier carving. *Makes 4 main-dish servings.*

Each serving: About 320 calories, 45 g protein, 7 g carbohydrate, 12 g total fat (4 g saturated), 0 g fiber, 130 mg cholesterol, 600 mg sodium.

# Roast Chicken Paprikash

🐓🐓🐓

PREP: 15 MINUTES / ROAST: 1 HOUR

Lots of thinly sliced onions are tossed with paprika and roasted in the pan with the chicken until they're soft and tender. Just a bit of sour cream adds a rich finish.

1 whole chicken (about 3½ pounds)
1 tablespoon margarine or butter, softened
1 garlic clove, crushed with garlic press
2 jumbo onions (about 12 ounces each), thinly
  sliced
1 tablespoon paprika
½ teaspoon salt
¼ cup chicken broth
2 tablespoons sour cream

**1** Preheat oven to 450°F. Remove giblets and neck from chicken; refrigerate for use another day. Rinse chicken with cold running water and drain well; pat dry with paper towels.

**2** In cup, mix margarine or butter with garlic. With fingertips, gently separate skin from meat on chicken breast and thighs. Spread garlic mixture on meat under skin.

**3** With breast side up, lift wings up toward neck, then fold wing tips under back of chicken so wings stay in place. With string, tie legs together.

**4** In small roasting pan (14" by 10"), stir onions with paprika, salt, and ¼ cup water. Place chicken breast-side up in pan.

**5** Roast chicken about 1 hour, stirring onions halfway through roasting time. Chicken is done when temperature on meat thermometer reaches 175° to 180°F. and juices run clear when thickest part of thigh is pierced with tip of knife.

**6** Place chicken on warm platter; let stand 10 minutes to allow juices to set for easier carving.

**7** Meanwhile, skim and discard fat from onion mixture in pan. Add chicken broth to onions; heat to boiling over medium heat, stirring to loosen brown bits. Stir in sour cream. Serve chicken with onion mixture. *Makes 4 main-dish servings.*

Each serving: About 590 calories, 50 g protein, 16 g carbohydrate, 35 g total fat (10 g saturated), 3 g fiber, 163 mg cholesterol, 540 mg sodium.

# Roast Chicken with 40 Cloves of Garlic

🐓🐓🐓

PREP: 15 MINUTES / ROAST: 1 HOUR

Roasting renders the garlic soft and golden. Some of the garlic is then mashed into the pan juices; the rest can be spread on crusty bread.

1 whole chicken (about 3½ pounds)
6 thyme sprigs
½ teaspoon salt
¼ teaspoon coarsely ground black pepper
40 garlic cloves (about 2 heads), unpeeled, with
  loose papery skin discarded
1 cup chicken broth, canned or homemade
  (page 11)

**1** Preheat oven to 450°F. Remove giblets and neck from chicken; refrigerate for use another day. Rinse chicken with cold running water and drain well; pat dry with paper towels.

**2** With fingertips, gently separate skin from meat on chicken breast. Place 4 thyme sprigs under skin of chicken breast. Place remaining thyme sprigs inside cavity of chicken. Sprinkle outside of chicken with salt and pepper.

**3** With chicken breast-side up, lift wings up toward neck, then fold wing tips under back of chicken so wings stay in place. With string, tie legs together. Place chicken, breast side up, on rack in small roasting pan.

**4** Roast chicken 30 minutes. Add garlic cloves to pan and roast about 30 minutes longer. Chicken is done when temperature on meat thermometer reaches 175° to 180°F. and juices run clear when thickest part of thigh is pierced with tip of knife.

**5** Place chicken on warm platter; let stand 10 minutes to set juices for easier carving.

**6** Meanwhile, remove rack from roasting pan. With slotted spoon, transfer garlic cloves to small bowl. Skim and discard fat from drippings in pan. Discard skin from 6 garlic cloves; add garlic to roasting pan with chicken broth. Heat broth mixture to boiling over medium heat, stirring to loosen brown bits and mashing garlic with spoon until well blended.

**7** Serve chicken with pan juices and remaining garlic cloves. *Makes 4 main-dish servings.*

Each serving: About 500 calories, 50 g protein, 10 g carbohydrate, 28 g total fat (8 g saturated), 1 g fiber, 157 mg cholesterol, 700 mg sodium.

# Roast Chicken with Creamy Mushroom Sauce

🐓 🐓 🐓

PREP: 15 MINUTES / ROAST: 1 HOUR

Perfectly cooked meat and a classic sauce you make in the same roasting pan—what could be easier?

1 whole chicken (about 3½ pounds)
½ teaspoon salt
¼ teaspoon coarsely ground black pepper
1 package (8 ounces) white mushrooms, each cut into quarters
1 package (3½ ounces) shiitake mushrooms, stemmed and each cut into quarters
1 tablespoon all-purpose flour
1¼ cups chicken broth, canned or homemade (page 11)
2 tablespoons heavy or whipping cream
1 tablespoon chopped fresh parsley leaves

1 Preheat oven to 450°F. Remove giblets and neck from chicken; refrigerate for use another day. Rinse chicken with cold running water and drain well; pat dry with paper towels. Sprinkle chicken with salt and pepper.

2 With chicken breast-side up, lift wings up toward neck, then fold wing tips under back of chicken so wings stay in place. With string, tie legs together. Place chicken, breast side up, on rack in small roasting pan (about 14" by 10").

3 Roast chicken 15 minutes; add mushrooms to roasting pan, and roast chicken about 45 minutes longer. Chicken is done when temperature on meat thermometer reaches 175° to 180°F. and juices run clear when thickest part of thigh is pierced with tip of knife.

4 Place chicken on warm platter; let stand 10 minutes to set juices for easier carving.

5 Meanwhile, remove rack from roasting pan. Skim and discard fat from drippings. In small bowl, with wire whisk, mix flour and ¼ cup chicken broth until smooth; stir into mushrooms in roasting pan. Heat mushroom mixture over medium heat 1 minute, stirring constantly. Slowly stir remaining 1 cup broth into roasting pan; cook, stirring constantly, until mixture boils and thickens slightly, about 5 minutes.

6 Remove pan from heat; stir in cream and parsley. Serve chicken with mushroom sauce. *Makes 4 main-dish servings.*

Each serving: About 565 calories, 50 g protein, 6 g carbohydrate, 37 g total fat (11 g saturated), 1 g fiber, 172 mg cholesterol, 765 mg sodium.

# Granny's Roast Chicken with Rice & Spinach Stuffing

🐓 🐓 🐓

PREP: 40 MINUTES / ROAST: 2 HOURS 30 MINUTES

Rice & Spinach Stuffing (page 131)
1 whole chicken (about 7 pounds)
1 tablespoon vegetable oil
1 teaspoon dried rosemary, crushed
½ teaspoon coarsely ground black pepper
1 teaspoon salt
2 teaspoons grated lemon peel
Pan Gravy (page 142)

1 Prepare Rice & Spinach Stuffing.

2 Preheat oven to 350°F. Remove giblets and neck from chicken; refrigerate for use another day. Rinse chicken with cold running water and drain well; pat dry with paper towels.

3 Spoon some stuffing lightly into neck cavity. Fold neck skin over stuffing; fasten neck skin to back with 1 or 2 skewers. With chicken breast-side up, lift wings up toward neck, then fold under back of chicken so they stay in place. Spoon stuffing into body cavity.* Close by folding skin lightly over opening; skewer closed if necessary. With string, tie legs together.

*Granny's Roast Chicken with Rice & Spinach Stuffing*

**4** Place chicken, breast side up, on rack in roasting pan. In cup, mix oil, rosemary, pepper, salt, and 1 teaspoon grated lemon peel. Rub chicken all over with herb mixture. Roast chicken about 2½ hours, basting occasionally with pan drippings for an attractive sheen, until temperature on meat thermometer reaches 175° to 180°F. and juices run clear when thickest part of thigh is pierced with tip of knife. When chicken turns golden, cover loosely with a tent of foil. Start checking for doneness during last 30 minutes.

**5** Prepare Pan Gravy. Pour into gravy boat. To serve, arrange rice stuffing from casserole around chicken on platter; garnish chicken with remaining 1 teaspoon grated lemon peel. Serve chicken with gravy and stuffing. ***Makes 6 main-dish servings.***

*Bake any leftover stuffing in small covered casserole during last 30 minutes of roasting time.

Each serving: About 800 calories, 70 g protein, 33 g carbohydrate, 42 g total fat (11 g saturated), 2 g fiber, 208 mg cholesterol, 625 mg sodium.

# Roast Chicken with Lemons & Fresh Herbs

PREP: 1 HOUR / ROAST: 2 HOURS

1 whole chicken (about 7 pounds)
2 lemons
1 bunch fresh thyme
1 bunch fresh sage leaves
2 garlic cloves
½ teaspoon paprika
1 tablespoon cornstarch
¼ teaspoon salt
¼ teaspoon coarsely ground black pepper

**1** Preheat oven to 375°F. Remove giblets and neck from chicken; refrigerate for use another day. Rinse chicken with cold running water and drain well; pat dry with paper towels.

**2** Cut 4 thin slices from 1 lemon. Cut remaining lemon in half. Chop enough thyme to measure 1 tablespoon. Carefully push fingers between skin and meat of chicken breast to loosen skin. Place lemon slices and 4 sage leaves under skin. Place garlic cloves, lemon halves and remaining partial lemon, thyme sprigs, and remaining sage leaves inside cavity of chicken (if desired, set aside some thyme sprigs and sage leaves for garnish). Sprinkle chicken with chopped thyme and paprika.

**3** With chicken breast-side up, lift wings up toward neck, then fold wing tips under back of chicken so wings stay in place. With string, tie legs together.

**4** Place chicken, breast side up, on rack in roasting pan. Roast chicken about 2 hours until temperature on meat thermometer reaches 175° to 180°F. and juices run clear when thickest part of thigh is pierced with tip of knife, basting occasionally with drippings.

**5** Place chicken on warm platter; let stand 10 minutes to allow juices to set for easier carving.

**6** Prepare gravy: Remove rack from roasting pan. Pour pan drippings into 2-cup measuring cup (set pan aside); let drippings stand a few seconds until fat separates from meat juice. Skim and discard fat. To meat juice in cup, add *water* to equal 1½ cups liquid. Add meat-juice mixture to roasting pan; stir until brown bits are loosened. Pour meat-juice mixture into small saucepan; stir in cornstarch, salt, and pepper. Over high heat, heat to boiling, stirring occasionally until gravy thickens slightly; boil 1 minute.

**7** Pour gravy into gravy boat. Serve chicken with gravy. *Makes 8 main-dish servings.*

Each serving: About 465 calories, 49 g protein, 3 g carbohydrate, 28 g total fat (8 g saturated), 0 g fiber, 156 mg cholesterol, 220 mg sodium.

# Thyme-Basted Capon

PREP: 20 MINUTES / ROAST: 3 HOURS

Rice & Vegetable Stuffing (page 131)
1 fresh or frozen (thawed) capon (about 7 pounds)
1 tablespoon vegetable oil
1⅛ teaspoons dried thyme
1½ teaspoons salt
½ teaspoon coarsely ground black pepper
2 tablespoons all-purpose flour
1 cup milk

**1** Prepare Rice & Vegetable Stuffing.

**2** Preheat oven to 325°F. Remove giblets and neck from capon; refrigerate for use another day. Rinse capon with cold running water and drain well; pat dry with paper towels.

**3** Spoon stuffing into body cavity.* With string, tie legs together.

**4** Place capon, breast side up, on rack in roasting pan. In cup, mix oil, 1 teaspoon thyme, 1 teaspoon salt, and ¼ teaspoon pepper. Rub capon all over with herb mixture. Roast capon 2½ to 3 hours, basting occasionally with drippings for an attractive sheen, until temperature on meat thermometer reaches 175° to 180°F. and juices run clear when thickest part of thigh is pierced with tip of knife.

**5** Place capon on warm platter; let stand 10 minutes to allow juices to set for easier carving.

**6** Prepare gravy: Remove rack from roasting pan. Pour pan drippings into 1-cup measure (set pan aside); let drippings stand a few seconds until fat separates from meat juice. Skim 2 tablespoons fat from drippings and place in 2-quart saucepan. Skim and discard any remaining fat from drippings. To meat juice in measuring cup, add *water* to equal 1 cup liquid. Add meat-juice mixture to roasting pan; stir until browned bits are loosened.

**7** Stir flour, remaining ½ teaspoon salt, remaining ¼ teaspoon pepper, and remaining ⅛ teaspoon thyme into fat in saucepan. Gradually stir in meat-juice mixture and milk and cook over medium heat, stirring, until gravy boils and thickens slightly. Pour gravy into gravy boat.

**8** To serve, arrange rice stuffing from casserole around capon on platter. Serve capon with gravy and rice stuffing. *Makes 8 main-dish servings.*

*Bake any leftover stuffing in small covered casserole during last 45 minutes of roasting time.

Each serving:  About 750 calories, 62 g protein, 47 g carbohydrate, 33 g total fat (9 g saturated), 3 g fiber, 170 mg cholesterol, 1280 mg sodium.

# Cider-Glazed Turkey with Glazed Apples

❋ ❋ ❋

PREP: 25 MINUTES / ROAST: 4½ HOURS

Chestnut & Apple Stuffing (page 154)
One 14-pound fresh or frozen (thawed) turkey
1 tablespoon vegetable oil
1 teaspoon rubbed sage
½ teaspoon coarsely ground black pepper
1½ teaspoons salt
¼ cup apple cider or apple juice
¼ cup honey
2 medium Golden Delicious apples
2 medium Red Delicious apples
2 tablespoons margarine or butter

**1** Prepare Chestnut & Apple Stuffing.

**2** Preheat oven to 325°F. Remove giblets and neck from turkey; refrigerate for use another day. Rinse turkey with cold running water and drain well; pat dry with paper towels.

**3** Stuff the turkey as directed in "How to Stuff a Turkey," page 155.

**4** Place turkey, breast side up, on rack in large roasting pan. In cup, mix oil, sage, pepper, and salt. Rub turkey with herb mixture. Insert meat thermometer into thickest part of thigh next to body, being careful that pointed end of thermometer does not touch bone. Cover turkey with a loose tent of foil, letting top of thermometer poke through. Roast turkey about 4½ hours; start checking for doneness during last hour of roasting. Turkey is done when thigh temperature on meat thermometer reaches 175° to 180°F. and drumstick feels soft when pressed with fingers protected by paper towels; breast temperature should reach 165° to 170°F.; stuffing should reach 160° to 165°F. (Upon standing, temperature of thigh will rise to 180° to 185°F.; breast, 170° to 175°F.).

**5** About 30 minutes before end of roasting time, remove foil to brown turkey and prepare cider-and-honey glaze: In 1-quart saucepan, heat apple cider and honey to boiling over medium-high heat. Boil 4 to 5 minutes, stirring constantly, until mixture thickens; keep glaze warm.

**6** Prepare apples: Cut each apple into quarters. In 12-inch skillet, melt margarine or butter over medium-high heat. Add apples and cook until golden brown and tender, turning them occasionally. Stir in 1 tablespoon cider-and-honey glaze; toss to coat apples well. Keep apples warm.

**7** About 10 minutes before end of roasting time, brush turkey with remaining glaze; continue roasting. When turkey is done, place on warm large platter; cover with foil to keep warm.

**8** Arrange glazed apples on platter with turkey. Serve turkey with glazed apples and stuffing. *Makes 14 main-dish servings.*

Each serving:  About 860 calories, 77 g protein, 59 g carbohydrate, 33 g total fat (9 g saturated), 7 g fiber, 212 mg cholesterol, 1010 mg sodium.

# BREAD STUFFINGS FOR BIG BIRDS

All of these stuffing recipes make enough to stuff a 12- to 16-pound bird (see also "Easy Corn-Bread Stuffings" on page 162). As a general rule, bread stuffings are better if you have time to let the bread you are using for the stuffing get a bit stale (i.e., dry out a bit). If the bread you buy is still very fresh and moist, spread the slices on the oven racks (*not* on a baking sheet) in a very low oven and let them dry out for about 30 minutes.

Although it's hard to beat the flavor of a stuffing that's been cooked inside a turkey (for guidelines on how to stuff a turkey, consult the box on the opposite page), there is some argument for cooking the stuffing separately. In fact, you might even want to prepare one of these stuffings as a side dish some time when you are not roasting a bird. To bake a stuffing by itself, spoon it into a 13" by 9" glass baking dish. Cover with foil and bake in a preheated 325°F. oven for 45 minutes or until heated through.

*Multigrain Stuffing*

## Moist 7-Grain Bread Stuffing

PREP: 10 MINUTES / COOK: 10 MINUTES

½ cup margarine or butter (1 stick)
4 medium celery stalks, diced
2 medium onions, diced
1 loaf (24 ounces) 7-grain bread or
   white bread, cut into ½-inch cubes
1 medium Granny Smith apple,
   shredded
½ cup chopped fresh parsley leaves
1 teaspoon dried sage
1 teaspoon salt
½ teaspoon coarsely ground black
   pepper

1 In 8-quart Dutch oven or saucepot, melt margarine or butter over medium heat. Add celery and onions and cook until tender, stirring occasionally.
2 Remove Dutch oven from heat. Add bread cubes, apple, ¾ cup water, parsley, sage, salt, and pepper. Toss to mix well. Makes 9 cups stuffing.

EACH ½ CUP: ABOUT 155 CALORIES, 4 G PROTEIN, 21 G CARBOHYDRATE, 7 G TOTAL FAT (1 G SATURATED), 3 G FIBER, 0 MG CHOLESTEROL, 380 MG SODIUM.

## Multigrain Stuffing

PREP: 15 MINUTES / COOK: 20 MINUTES

3 tablespoons margarine or butter
½ bunch celery (about 7 stalks),
   chopped
3 medium onions, chopped
1 teaspoon dried oregano
1 teaspoon coarsely ground black
   pepper
1½ loaves (16 ounces each) multigrain
   bread, cut into ½-inch cubes
¾ cup dark raisins
1 can (14½ ounces) chicken broth or
   1¾ cups homemade (page 11)

1 In 8-quart Dutch oven or saucepot, melt margarine or butter over medium heat. Add celery and onions and cook until golden brown, stirring occasionally.

Stir in ¼ cup water. Reduce heat to low, cover, and continue cooking until celery and onions are very tender.
2 Remove Dutch oven from heat. Add oregano, pepper, bread cubes, raisins, chicken broth, and 1 cup water. Toss to mix well. Makes about 11 cups stuffing.

EACH ½ CUP: ABOUT 120 CALORIES, 4 G PROTEIN, 21 G CARBOHYDRATE, 3 G TOTAL FAT (1 G SATURATED), 3 G FIBER, 0 MG CHOLESTEROL, 265 MG SODIUM.

## Herbed White Bread Stuffing

PREP: 10 MINUTES / COOK: 10 MINUTES

½ cup margarine or butter (1 stick)
½ bunch celery (about 7 stalks),
   chopped
1 large onion, chopped
2 loaves (16 ounces each) white
   bread, cut into ½-inch cubes
⅓ cup chopped fresh parsley leaves
1½ teaspoons rubbed sage
1½ teaspoons salt
1 teaspoon dried thyme
½ teaspoon coarsely ground black
   pepper
3 cups chicken broth, canned or
   homemade (page 11)

1 In 8-quart Dutch oven or saucepot, melt margarine or butter over medium heat. Add celery and onion and cook until tender, stirring occasionally.
2 Remove Dutch oven from heat. Add bread cubes, parsley, sage, salt, thyme, pepper, and chicken broth. Toss to mix well. Makes about 12 cups stuffing.

EACH ½ CUP: ABOUT 145 CALORIES, 3 G PROTEIN, 20 G CARBOHYDRATE, 5 G TOTAL FAT (1 G SATURATED), 1 G FIBER, 0 MG CHOLESTEROL, 535 MG SODIUM.

## Chestnut & Apple Stuffing

PREP: 25 MINUTES / COOK: 30 MINUTES

2 pounds chestnuts
12 cups day-old French bread, cut into
 ½-inch cubes (16-ounce loaf)
6 tablespoons margarine or butter
 (¾ stick)
2 large celery stalks, sliced
1 medium onion, diced
3 large Rome Beauty or Crispin apples
 (about 1¾ pounds), peeled, cored,
 and diced
2 teaspoons poultry seasoning
1 can (14½ ounces) chicken broth or
 1¾ cups homemade (page 11)
1 teaspoon salt

**1** In 3-quart saucepan, heat chestnuts
and enough *water* to cover to boiling
over high heat. Reduce heat to medium;
cover and cook 10 minutes.
**2** Remove saucepan from heat. With
slotted spoon, transfer 3 or 4 chestnuts
at a time from water to cutting board.
Cut each chestnut in half. With spoon
or tip of small knife, scrape out chestnut

meat from its shell (skin will stay in
shell). Chop any large pieces of chestnut
meat; place in large bowl. Discard cooking water. Toss bread cubes with chestnuts.
**3** In same saucepan, melt margarine or
butter over medium heat. Add celery
and onion and cook until vegetables are
golden brown and tender, about 10
minutes. Add diced apples and poultry
seasoning; cook 2 minutes longer, stirring occasionally. Stir in chicken broth,
salt, and *1 cup water*; heat to boiling
over high heat.
**4** Pour hot mixture over chestnut mixture. Toss to mix well. Makes about 12
cups stuffing.

EACH ½ CUP: ABOUT 160 CALORIES, 3 G
PROTEIN, 28 G CARBOHYDRATE, 4 G TOTAL
FAT (1 G SATURATED), 4 G FIBER, 0 MG
CHOLESTEROL, 325 MG SODIUM.

## Rosemary-Sage Stuffing

PREP: 10 MINUTES / COOK: 10 MINUTES

2 tablespoons vegetable oil
4 medium celery stalks, diced
2 medium onions, diced
1½ loaves (16 ounces each) firm
 white bread, cut into ½-inch cubes
2 teaspoons minced fresh sage, or
 ½ teaspoon dried sage
2 teaspoons minced fresh rosemary or
 ½ teaspoon dried rosemary, crushed
1 teaspoon salt

**1** In 8-quart Dutch oven or saucepot,
heat oil over medium heat. Add celery
and onions and cook until tender, stirring occasionally.
**2** Remove Dutch oven from heat. Add
bread cubes, sage, rosemary, salt, and
1¼ cups water. Toss to mix well. Makes
about 10 cups stuffing.

EACH SERVING: ABOUT 110 CALORIES,
3 G PROTEIN, 19 G CARBOHYDRATE, 3 G
TOTAL FAT (0 G SATURATED), 1 G FIBER,
0 MG CHOLESTEROL, 305 MG SODIUM.

## HOW TO STUFF A TURKEY

There are two cavities that can be stuffed in a large bird: the neck cavity and the body cavity. The body cavity is larger and will hold the bulk
of the stuffing. But for either cavity the stuffing should be packed in very
lightly, not crammed in.

**1** Spoon some stuffing lightly into neck cavity. Fold neck skin over stuffing; fasten neck skin to back with 1 or 2 skewers. With turkey breast-
side up, lift wings toward neck, then fold them under back of turkey
so they stay in place.

**2** Spoon remaining stuffing lightly into body cavity.* Close by folding skin over opening; skewer closed if necessary. Depending on brand
of turkey, with string, tie legs and tail together, or push drumsticks under
band of skin, or use stuffing clamp.

*Bake any leftover stuffing in covered casserole during last 30 minutes
of roasting time.

## Mushroom & Sausage Stuffing

PREP: 10 MINUTES / COOK: 15 MINUTES

3 tablespoons olive oil
5 medium celery stalks, chopped
I large onion, chopped
I½ pounds medium mushrooms, finely
    chopped
I½ pounds weisswurst (fully cooked
    veal sausage) or bratwurst, finely
    chopped
I½ loaves (16 ounces each) firm
    white bread, cut into ½-inch cubes
I½ teaspoons salt
3 large eggs

**I** In 8-quart Dutch oven or saucepot,
heal oil over medium heat. Add celery,
onion, and mushrooms and cook until
tender, stirring occasionally.
**2** Remove Dutch oven from heat. Add
weisswurst, bread cubes, salt, eggs, and
I½ cups water. Toss to mix well. Makes
about 12 cups stuffing.

EACH ½ CUP: ABOUT 200 CALORIES, 8 G
PROTEIN, 17 G CARBOHYDRATE, II G
TOTAL FAT (3 G SATURATED), I G FIBER,
44 MG CHOLESTEROL, 470 MG SODIUM.

*Sausage Stuffing*

## Vegetable-Bread Stuffing

PREP: 15 MINUTES / COOK: 15 MINUTES

4 tablespoons margarine or butter
    (½ stick)
4 medium carrots, peeled and finely
    diced
4 medium celery ribs, diced
I large onion, diced
I large red pepper, diced
½ teaspoon salt
¼ teaspoon coarsely ground black
    pepper
I bunch spinach, coarsely chopped
I½ loaves (16 ounces each) oatmeal
    bread, cut into ½-inch cubes
I⅓ cups vegetable or chicken broth

**I** In 8-quart Dutch oven or saucepot,
melt margarine or butter over medium
heat. Add carrots, celery, onion, red
pepper, salt, and black pepper and cook
until vegetables are tender, stirring occasionally. Stir in spinach and cook. stirring,

until spinach wilts.
**2** Remove Dutch oven from heat. Add
bread cubes and broth. Toss to mix well.
Makes about 10 cups stuffing.

EACH ½ CUP: ABOUT 130 CALORIES, 4 G
PROTEIN, 20 G CARBOHYDRATE, 4 G TOTAL
FAT (I G SATURATED), 2 G FIBER, 0 MG
CHOLESTEROL, 375 MG SODIUM.

## Sausage Stuffing

PREP: 10 MINUTES / COOK: 20 MINUTES

I pound sweet Italian-sausage links,
    casings removed
3 medium celery stalks, chopped
I medium onion, chopped
I½ cups chicken broth, canned or
    homemade (page 11)
I½ loaves (16 ounces each) firm
    white bread, cut into ½-inch cubes
¼ cup chopped fresh parsley leaves

**I** In 8-quart Dutch oven, cook sausage
meat, celery, and onion over medium-
high heat until sausage is golden brown
and vegetables are tender, using spoon
to break up sausage.
**2** Add chicken broth, stirring to loosen
brown bits from bottom of Dutch
oven. Stir in bread cubes and parsley
until well mixed. Makes about 12 cups
stuffing.

EACH ½ CUP: ABOUT 145 CALORIES, 5 G
PROTEIN, 15 G CARBOHYDRATE, 7 G TOTAL
FAT (2 G SATURATED), I G FIBER, 15 MG
CHOLESTEROL, 360 MG SODIUM.

# Roast Stuffed Turkey with Spiced Balsamic-Apple Glaze

🐓 🐓 🐓

PREP: 1 HOUR 30 MINUTES / ROAST: 4 HOURS 30 MINUTES

Herbed White Bread Stuffing or Multigrain Stuffing
   (page 154)
One 14-pound fresh or frozen (thawed) turkey
½ teaspoon coarsely ground black pepper
1½ teaspoons salt
½ cup apple jelly
3 tablespoons balsamic vinegar
½ teaspoon ground cinnamon
¼ teaspoon ground cloves
Giblet Gravy (page 142)

**1** Prepare one of the stuffings.

**2** Preheat oven to 325°F. Remove giblets and neck from turkey; reserve for making gravy. Rinse turkey with running cold water and drain well.

**3** Stuff the turkey as directed in "How to Stuff a Turkey," page 155.

**4** Place turkey, breast-side up, on rack in large roasting pan. Rub turkey all over with pepper and 1½ teaspoons salt. Insert meat thermometer into thickest part of thigh next to body, being careful that pointed end of thermometer does not touch bone. Cover turkey with a loose tent of foil, letting top of thermometer poke through.

**5** Roast turkey about 4½ hours; start checking for doneness during last hour of roasting. Turkey is done when thigh temperature on meat thermometer reaches 175° to 180°F. and drumstick feels soft when pressed with fingers protected by paper towels; breast temperature should reach 165° to 170°F.; stuffing should reach 160° to 165°F. (Upon standing, temperature of thigh will rise to 180° to 185°F.; breast, 170° to 175°F.).

**6** While turkey is roasting, prepare giblets and giblet broth for gravy.

**7** About 30 minutes before end of roasting time remove foil from turkey and prepare balsamic-apple glaze: In 1-quart saucepan, heat apple jelly, balsamic vinegar, cinnamon, and cloves to boiling over medium-high heat. Boil about 2 minutes, stirring constantly, until mixture thickens slightly.

**8** About 10 minutes before end of roasting time, brush turkey with apple glaze; continue roasting, brushing with remaining glaze.

**9** When turkey is done, place on large platter; cover with foil to keep warm. Complete Giblet Gravy.

**10** Serve turkey with gravy and stuffing. *Makes 14 main-dish servings.*

Each serving: About 850 calories, 85 g protein, 44 g carbohydrate, 34 g total fat (9 g saturated), 2 g fiber, 270 mg cholesterol, 1390 mg sodium.

---

## GREAT GO-WITHS

### BEETS WITH DILL VINAIGRETTE

PREP: 14 MINUTES / COOK: 30 MINUTES

*6 pounds beets with tops (about 12 medium beets or*
   *4 pounds beets without tops)*
*3 tablespoons cider vinegar*
*2 tablespoons olive oil*
*2 tablespoons chopped fresh dill or 1 teaspoon dried*
   *dill weed*
*2 teaspoons sugar*
*1 teaspoon salt*
*½ small onion, cut into paper-thin slices*

**1** Trim stems and leaves from beets, but leave about 1 inch of stems attached. In 5-quart saucepot, heat beets and enough *water* to cover to boiling over high heat. Reduce heat to low; cover and simmer 30 minutes or until beets are tender. Drain beets; cool until easy to handle. Remove skins. Cut beets into bite-size chunks.

**2** In large bowl, with fork or wire whisk, mix vinegar, olive oil, dill, sugar, and salt. Add onion and beets to vinaigrette. Toss gently to mix. Makes 6 accompaniment servings.

Each serving: About 130 calories, 3 g protein, 21 g carbohydrate, 5 g total fat (1 g saturated), 2 g fiber, 0 mg cholesterol, 520 mg sodium.

# Traditional Roast Turkey with Giblet Gravy

🐓🐓🐓

PREP: 45 MINUTES / ROAST: 3 HOURS 45 MINUTES

Mushroom & Sausage Stuffing (page 156), Vegetable-
  Bread Stuffing (page 156), or Country Sausage &
  Corn-Bread Stuffing (page 162)
One 14-pound fresh or frozen (thawed) turkey
1½ teaspoons salt
½ teaspoon coarsely ground black pepper
Giblet Gravy (page 142)

**1** Prepare any of the 3 stuffings; set aside.

**2** Preheat oven to 325°F. Remove giblets and neck from turkey; reserve for making gravy. Rinse turkey with cold running water and drain well.

**3** Stuff the turkey as directed in "How to Stuff a Turkey," page 155.

**4** Place turkey, breast side up, on rack in large roasting pan. Rub turkey all over with salt and pepper. Insert meat thermometer into thickest part of thigh next to body, being careful that pointed end of thermometer does not touch bone. Cover turkey with a loose tent of foil, letting top of thermometer poke through. Roast turkey about 3 hours 45 minutes; start checking for doneness during last hour of roasting.

**5** While turkey is roasting, prepare giblets and giblet broth for gravy.

**6** To brown turkey, remove foil during last 1 hour of roasting time and baste with pan drippings occasionally. Turkey is done when thigh temperature on meat thermometer reaches 175° to 180°F. and drumstick feels soft when pressed with fingers protected by paper towels; breast temperature should reach 165° to 170°F.; stuffing should reach 160° to 165°F. (Upon standing, temperature of thigh will rise to 180° to 185°F.; breast, 170° to 175°F.).

**7** When turkey is done, place on large platter; cover with foil to keep warm. Complete Giblet Gravy. Serve turkey with gravy and stuffing. *Makes 14 main-dish servings.*

Each serving (with Mushroom & Sausage Stuffing): About 910 calories, 93 g protein, 31 g carbohydrate, 44 g total fat (13 g saturated), 2 g fiber, 345 mg cholesterol, 1275 mg sodium.

# Herb-Rubbed Turkey with Sausage Stuffing

🐓🐓🐓

PREP: 1 HOUR / ROAST: 4 HOURS 15 MINUTES

Sausage Stuffing (page 156)
One 14-pound fresh or frozen (thawed) turkey
1 tablespoon minced fresh rosemary or
  1 teaspoon dried rosemary, crushed
1 tablespoon grated orange peel
2 teaspoons salt
½ teaspoon coarsely ground black pepper
Giblet Gravy (page 142)

**1** Prepare Sausage Stuffing.

**2** Preheat oven to 450°F. Remove giblets and neck from turkey; refrigerate for use another day. Rinse turkey with cold running water and drain well; pat dry with paper towels.

**3** Stuff the turkey as directed in "How to Stuff a Turkey," page 155.

**4** Place turkey, breast-side up, on rack in large roasting pan. In cup, mix rosemary, orange peel, salt, and pepper. Rub turkey all over with herb mixture. Insert meat thermometer into thickest part of thigh next to body, being careful that pointed end of thermometer does not touch bone. Cover turkey with a loose tent of foil, letting top of thermometer poke through. Roast turkey about 4 hours 15 minutes; start checking for doneness during last hour of roasting.

**5** While turkey is roasting, prepare giblets and giblet broth for gravy.

**6** To brown turkey, remove foil during last 1 hour of roasting time and baste with pan drippings occasionally. Turkey is done when thigh temperature on meat thermometer reaches 175° to 180°F. and drumstick feels soft when pressed with fingers protected by paper towels; breast temperature should reach 165° to 170°F.; stuffing should reach 160° to 165°F. (Upon standing, temperature of thigh will rise to 180° to 185°F.; breast, 170° to 175°F.)

**7** When turkey is done, place on large platter; cover with foil to keep warm. Complete Giblet Gravy. Serve turkey with gravy and stuffing. *Makes 14 main-dish servings.*

Each serving: About 830 calories, 88 g protein, 29 g carbohydrate, 37 g total fat (11 g saturated), 2 g fiber, 295 mg cholesterol, 1170 mg sodium.

# THE CHRISTMAS GOOSE

PREP: 2 HOURS / ROAST 3 HOURS

Some tips on successfully roasting goose: Since most geese sold in this country are frozen, allow time for thawing. A 12-pound goose takes at least 2 days to thaw in the refrigerator. You can also thaw the goose in cold water in about 5 hours: Place the bird (in its original wrapping) in a sink with enough cold water to cover, changing the water every half hour. Before roasting, pierce the skin all over with a fork. This will allow the fat to drain during roasting and help crisp the skin. To avoid splatters and spillovers, spoon off fat from roasting pan occasionally during cooking.

*Stuffing:*
*2 tablespoons margarine or butter*
*1 large Granny Smith apple, peeled and chopped*
*1 large celery stalk, diced*
*1 medium carrot, peeled and diced*
*1 small onion, diced*
*½ teaspoon salt*
*¼ teaspoon coarsely ground black pepper*
*¼ teaspoon dried thyme*
*2 cans (14½ ounces each) chicken broth or 3½ cups homemade (page 11)*
*1 package (4 ounces) wild rice*
*1 cup regular long-grain rice*
*1 pound chestnuts*

*Goose:*
*One 12-pound fresh or frozen (thawed) goose*
*1½ teaspoons salt*
*¼ teaspoon coarsely ground black pepper*
*Garnish: small pears or apples and champagne grapes*

**1** Prepare stuffing: In 3-quart saucepan, melt 1 tablespoon margarine or butter over medium heat. Add apple and cook until softened. With slotted spoon, transfer cooked apple to small bowl; set aside.

**2** Add remaining 1 tablespoon margarine or butter to saucepan and melt over medium heat. Add celery, carrot, onion, salt, pepper, and thyme and cook, stirring frequently, until vegetables are golden.

**3** Stir in chicken broth and wild rice; heat to boiling over high heat. Reduce heat to low; cover and simmer 35 minutes.

**4** Stir in white rice; heat to boiling over high heat. Reduce heat to low; cover and simmer 25 minutes longer or until liquid is absorbed and white and wild rices are tender.

**5** Meanwhile, prepare chestnuts: In 4-quart saucepan, heat 1 pound chestnuts and enough *water* to cover to boiling over high heat. Reduce heat to medium; cook 10 minutes. Remove saucepan from heat. With slotted spoon, remove 3 or 4 chestnuts at a time from water to cutting board. Cut each chestnut in half. With tip of small knife, scrape out chestnut meat from its shell (skin will stay in shell). Chop any large pieces of chestnut meat; set chestnut meat aside. Discard cooking water in saucepan.

**6** When rice is done, stir in chestnuts and cooked apple.

**7** Preheat oven to 350°F. Prepare goose: Remove giblets and neck from goose; refrigerate for use another day. Discard fat from body cavity; rinse goose with cold running water and drain well. Pat dry with paper towels.

**8** Fasten neck skin to back with 1 or 2 skewers. With goose breast side up, lift wings toward neck, then fold them under back of goose so they stay in place. Spoon stuffing into body cavity. With string, tie legs and tail together.

**9** Place goose, breast side up, on rack in large roasting pan; with two-tine fork, prick skin in several places to drain fat during roasting. In cup, mix salt and pepper; use to rub over goose. Insert meat thermometer into thickest part of meat between breast and thigh, being careful that pointed end of thermometer does not touch bone. Roast goose 3 hours or until meat thermometer reaches 180° to 185°F.

**10** To serve, place goose on large platter; let stand 10 minutes for easier carving. If you like, garnish platter with small pears or apples and champagne grapes. Makes 8 main-dish servings.

Each serving: About 1270 calories, 87 g protein, 54 g carbohydrate, 76 g total fat (23 g saturated), 5 g fiber, 294 mg cholesterol, 1300 mg sodium.

# Roast Turkey with Rosemary-Sage Stuffing

🐓 🐓 🐓

PREP: 1 HOUR 15 MINUTES / ROAST: 4 HOURS

Rosemary-Sage Stuffing (page 155)
One 16-pound fresh or frozen (thawed) turkey
½ teaspoon coarsely ground black pepper
1½ teaspoons salt
Giblet Gravy (page 142)
Fresh sage and rosemary for garnish

### GREAT GO-WITHS

## SPICED OLIVE RELISH PLATTER

PREP: 15 MINUTES PLUS MARINATING TIME

*1 pound peeled baby carrots*
*2 medium red peppers, cut into 2-inch-long strips*
*½ pound small Mediterranean-style green olives, such as Picholine*
*¾ pound brine-cured black olives, such as Kalamata, pitted and each cut in half*
*1 can (4 to 4½ ounces) chopped mild green chiles, undrained*
*3 garlic cloves, peeled and lightly crushed*
*3 tablespoons extravirgin olive oil*
*1 tablespoon chopped fresh parsley leaves*
*2 teaspoons fennel seeds, crushed*
*1 teaspoon ground red pepper (cayenne)*

**1** In 3-quart saucepan of *boiling water*, cook baby carrots for 3 minutes to blanch. Drain and rinse under cold running water.

**2** In large bowl, combine carrots, red peppers, olives, green chiles and their liquid, garlic, olive oil, parsley, fennel seeds, and ground red pepper. Cover and refrigerate for at least 24 hours. Makes 16 appetizer servings.

Each serving: About 150 calories, 1 g protein, 8 g carbohydrate, 13 g total fat (2 g saturated), 1 g fiber, 0 mg cholesterol, 905 mg sodium.

**1** Prepare Rosemary-Sage Stuffing.

**2** Preheat oven to 325°F. Remove giblets and neck from turkey; reserve for making gravy. Rinse turkey with cold running water and drain well.

**3** Stuff the turkey as directed in "How to Stuff a Turkey," page 155.

**4** Place turkey, breast side up, on rack in large roasting pan. Rub turkey all over with salt. Insert meat thermometer into thickest part of thigh next to body, being careful that pointed end of thermometer does not touch bone. Cover turkey with a loose tent of foil, letting top of thermometer poke through. Roast turkey about 5 hours; start checking for doneness during last hour of roasting.

**5** While turkey is roasting, prepare giblets and giblet broth for gravy.

**6** To brown turkey, remove foil during last 1 hour of roasting time and baste with pan drippings occasionally. Turkey is done when thigh temperature on meat thermometer reaches 175° to 180°F. and drumstick feels soft when pressed with fingers protected by paper towels; breast temperature should reach 165° to 170°F.; stuffing should reach 160° to 165°F. (Upon standing, temperature of thigh will rise to 180° to 185°F.; breast, 170° to 175°F.)

**7** When turkey is done, place on large platter; cover with foil to keep warm. Complete Giblet Gravy.

**8** To serve, garnish platter with fresh herbs. Serve turkey with gravy and stuffing. *Makes 16 main-dish servings.*

Each serving: About 710 calories, 83 g protein, 25 g carbohydrate, 28 g total fat (8 g saturated), 2 g fiber, 270 mg cholesterol, 815 mg sodium.

With all of the other things you have to do to prepare for Thanksgiving or other big family gatherings, you can at least spare yourself the chore of making corn bread from scratch. Try one of these stuffing recipes that call for a good-quality corn-bread stuffing mix.

## SOUTHERN CORN BREAD & HAM STUFFING

PREP: 20 MINUTES / BAKE: 45 MINUTES

½ cup margarine or butter (1 stick)
2 large celery stalks, diced
1 large onion, diced
1 medium red pepper, diced
1 package (14 to 16 ounces) corn-bread stuffing mix
1 package (10 ounces) frozen whole-kernel corn, thawed
½ pound cooked ham, in one piece, diced
1 cup golden raisins
⅓ cup chopped fresh parsley leaves
½ teaspoon coarsely ground black pepper

1 In 8-quart Dutch oven or saucepot, melt margarine or butter over medium heat. Add celery, onion, and red pepper and cook until vegetables are tender, stirring occasionally.

2 Remove Dutch oven from heat. Add corn bread-stuffing mix, corn, ham, raisins, parsley, black pepper, and *3 cups water* to mix well. Use to stuff 12- to 16-pound turkey. Or spoon into 13" by 9" glass baking dish; cover with foil and bake in preheated 325°F. oven 45 minutes or until heated through. Makes about 12 cups stuffing.

Each ½ cup: About 155 calories, 5 g protein, 22 g carbohydrate, 5 g total fat (1 g saturated), 1 g fiber, 6 mg cholesterol, 390 mg sodium.

## COUNTRY SAUSAGE & CORN-BREAD STUFFING

PREP: 45 MINUTES / BAKE 45 MINUTES

1 pound pork-sausage meat
4 tablespoons margarine or butter (½ stick)
3 medium celery stalks, diced
1 large onion, diced
1 medium green pepper, diced

*Country Sausage & Corn-Bread Stuffing*

1 can (14½ ounces) chicken broth or 1¾ cups homemade (page 11)
½ teaspoon coarsely ground black pepper
1 package (14 to 16 ounces) corn-bread stuffing mix
1 cup pecans, toasted and coarsely chopped
¼ cup chopped fresh parsley leaves

1 Heat 12-inch skillet over medium-high heat. Add sausage meat and cook until browned, about 10 minutes, stirring frequently to break up sausage. With slotted spoon, transfer sausage to large bowl.

2 Discard all but 2 tablespoons sausage drippings from skillet. Add margarine or butter, celery, onion, and green pepper and cook, stirring occasionally, until vegetables are browned. Stir in chicken broth, pepper, and *¾ cup water*; heat to boiling, stirring to loosen any brown bits from bottom of skillet.

3 Add vegetable mixture, corn-bread stuffing mix, pecans, and parsley to sausage; mix well. Use to stuff 12- to 16-pound turkey. Or spoon into 13" by 9" glass baking dish; cover with foil and bake in preheated 325°F. oven 45 minutes or until heated through. Makes about 12 cups stuffing.

Each ½ cup: About 165 calories, 4 g protein, 16 g carbohydrate, 9 g total fat (2 g saturated), 1 g fiber, 8 mg cholesterol, 420 mg sodium.

# Roast Turkey with Roasted Sweet Potatoes

PREP: 1 HOUR 15 MINUTES / ROAST: 4 HOURS 45 MINUTES

Southern Corn Bread & Ham Stuffing (opposite page)
One 14-pound fresh or frozen (thawed) turkey
1 tablespoon vegetable oil
¼ teaspoon coarsely ground black pepper
1 teaspoon salt
5 medium sweet potatoes (about 2 pounds), peeled and cut lengthwise into 1-inch-thick wedges
3 tablespoons light brown sugar
2 tablespoons margarine or butter
Pan Gravy (page 142)

**1** Prepare stuffing.

**2** Preheat oven to 325°F. Remove giblets and neck from turkey; refrigerate for use another day. Rinse turkey with cold running water and drain well; pat dry with paper towels.

**3** Stuff the turkey as directed in "How to Stuff a Turkey," page 155.

**4** Place turkey, breast side up, on rack in large roasting pan. Brush turkey with vegetable oil; sprinkle with pepper and salt. Insert meat thermometer into thickest part of thigh next to body, being careful that pointed end of thermometer does not touch bone. Cover turkey with a loose tent of foil, letting top of thermometer poke through. Roast turkey about 4 hours 45 minutes; start checking for doneness during last hour of roasting.

**5** To brown turkey, remove foil during last 1 hour of roasting time and baste with pan drippings occasionally. Turkey is done when thigh temperature on meat thermometer reaches 175° to 180°F. and drumstick feels soft when pressed with fingers protected by paper towels; breast temperature should reach 165° to 170°F.; stuffing should reach 160° to 165°F. (Upon standing, temperature of thigh will rise to 180° to 185°F.; breast, 170° to 175°F.)

**6** Meanwhile, in bowl, toss sweet-potato wedges with brown sugar.

**7** When turkey is done, place on large platter; cover with foil to keep warm. Turn oven control to 425°F. Grease 15½" by 10½" jelly-roll pan well. Place sweet potatoes in pan; dot with margarine or butter. Bake sweet potatoes 30 minutes or until golden and tender, turning them occasionally.

**8** Meanwhile, prepare Pan Gravy. Arrange sweet potatoes on same platter with turkey and serve with gravy. *Makes 14 main-dish servings.*

Each serving: About 880 calories, 82 g protein, 54 g carbohydrate, 36 g total fat (9 g saturated), 3 g fiber, 222 mg cholesterol, 1050 mg sodium.

# Rosemary Roast Turkey Breast

PREP: 20 MINUTES / ROAST: 2 HOURS 30 MINUTES

1 fresh or frozen (thawed) turkey breast (about 6½ pounds)
1½ teaspoons dried rosemary, crushed
1 teaspoon salt
¾ teaspoon coarsely ground black pepper
1 cup chicken broth, canned or homemade (page 11)

**1** Preheat oven to 350°F. Rinse turkey breast with cold running water and drain well. In cup, combine rosemary, salt, and pepper. With hands, rub rosemary mixture all over turkey breast.

**2** Place turkey breast in 13" by 9" metal baking pan. Cover pan loosely with foil. Roast turkey breast 1 hour 30 minutes.

**3** Remove foil. Roast turkey breast 45 to 60 minutes longer, occasionally brushing breast with pan drippings. Start checking turkey breast for doneness during last 30 minutes of cooking. Turkey breast is done when thermometer inserted into breast (being careful that pointed end of thermometer does not touch bone) reaches 170°F.

**4** When turkey breast is done, transfer to warm large platter. Let stand 10 minutes.

**5** Meanwhile, pour chicken broth into drippings in hot roasting pan, stirring to loosen brown bits from bottom of pan. Strain pan-juice mixture into small saucepan; let stand 1 minute. Skim fat and discard. Reheat and serve pan-juice mixture with turkey. *Makes 12 main-dish servings.*

Each serving: About 320 calories, 49 g protein, 0 g carbohydrate, 13 g total fat (4 g saturated), 0 g fiber, 125 mg cholesterol, 390 mg sodium.

# Sage-Roasted Turkey with Sautéed Apples

PREP: 1 HOUR 15 MINUTES / ROAST: 4 HOURS 45 MINUTES

Moist 7-Grain-Bread Stuffing (page 154)
One 14-pound fresh or frozen (thawed) turkey
1 tablespoon vegetable oil
1 teaspoon dried sage
½ teaspoon coarsely ground black pepper
2 teaspoons salt
1 medium potato, peeled and diced
1 large carrot, peeled and diced
1 medium onion, diced
1 medium celery stalk, diced
2 tablespoons honey
3 large Rome Beauty apples
2 large Granny Smith apples
4 tablespoons margarine or butter (½ stick)
1 tablespoon confectioners' sugar

**1** Prepare Moist 7-Grain-Bread Stuffing.

**2** Remove giblets and neck from turkey; reserve for making gravy. Rinse turkey with running cold water and drain well; pat dry with paper towels.

**3** Stuff the turkey as directed in "How to Stuff a Turkey," page 155.

**4** Place turkey, breast side up, on rack in large roasting pan. In cup, mix oil, sage, pepper, and salt. Rub turkey with herb mixture. Insert meat thermometer into thickest part of thigh next to body, being careful that pointed end of thermometer does not touch bone. Cover turkey with a loose tent of foil, letting top of thermometer poke through. Roast turkey about 4 hours 45 minutes; start checking for doneness during last hour of roasting.

**5** While turkey is roasting, prepare giblets and neck to use in gravy: In 3-quart saucepan, heat gizzard, heart, neck, and enough water to cover to boiling over high heat. Reduce heat to low; cover and simmer 45 minutes. Add liver; cook 15 minutes longer. Drain, reserving broth. Pull meat from neck; discard bones. Coarsely chop neck meat and giblets. Cover and refrigerate meat and broth separately.

**6** After turkey has roasted 3 hours, add potato, carrot, onion, and celery to roasting pan, stirring to coat with pan drippings.

**7** To brown turkey, remove foil 20 to 30 minutes before turkey is done and, with pastry brush, brush turkey with honey. Turkey is done when thigh temperature on thermometer reaches 170° to 185°F. and thickest part of drumstick feels soft when pressed with fingers protected by paper towels. (Breast temperature should be 170° to 175°F., stuffing temperature 160° to 165°F.)

**8** Prepare apple garnish: Cut apples crosswise into ½-inch-thick slices. In 12-inch skillet over medium heat, in one-third of margarine or butter, cook one-third of apple slices about 10 minutes or until tender and browned on both sides. Sprinkle with 1 teaspoon of confectioners' sugar. Remove apple slices to plate; keep warm. Repeat 2 more times with remaining margarine, apples, and confectioners' sugar.

**9** When turkey is done, place on warm large platter; keep warm. Prepare vegetable gravy: Remove rack from roasting pan. Skim fat from drippings in pan and discard. Pour pan drippings with vegetables into 4-cup measure or medium bowl. Add reserved giblet broth to roasting pan; stir until brown bits are loosened. To vegetable mixture in cup, add broth and enough water to equal 4 cups.

**10** In blender or in food processor with knife blade attached, blend vegetable mixture, half at a time, until smooth. Pour into 2-quart saucepan. Stir in giblets and neck meat; heat through. Add salt to taste.

**11** Arrange apple slices around turkey on platter. Pour gravy into gravy boat. Serve turkey with gravy and apple slices. *Makes 14 main-dish servings.*

Each serving: About 885 calories, 85 g protein, 44 g carbohydrate, 40 g total fat (10 g saturated), 6 g fiber, 272 mg cholesterol, 1085 mg sodium.

# RELISH ROSTER

## Cranberry-Ginger Relish with Kumquats

In food processor with knife blade attached, blend *1½ packages (12 ounces each) cranberries (about 4½ cups)* until coarsely chopped (or coarsely chop with knife); transfer to medium bowl. Drain syrup from *1 jar (10 ounces) preserved kumquats* into bowl with cranberries. Slice each kumquat in half; remove seeds and chop. Stir kumquats, *½ cup pitted prunes (about 4 ounces)*, chopped, *¼ cup sugar*, and *1 teaspoon grated, peeled fresh ginger* into cranberries. Cover relish and refrigerate at least 1 hour. Makes about 3½ cups.

Each ¼ cup: About 80 calories, 0 g protein, 21 g carbohydrate, 0 g total fat (0 g saturated), 2 g fiber, 0 mg cholesterol, 25 mg sodium.

## No-Cook Fruit Relish

In food processor with knife blade attached, blend *1 large orange*, cut into 8 pieces, *1 package (12 ounces) cranberries, 1 cup pitted prunes, ½ cup walnuts, ½ cup sugar*, and *1 tablespoon grated, peeled fresh ginger* until coarsely chopped. Pour mixture into medium bowl; stir in *1 can (16 ounces) pears in extra-light syrup*, drained and diced. Cover relish and refrigerate at least 1 hour. Makes about 6 cups.

Each ¼ cup: About 70 calories, 1 g protein, 14 g carbohydrate, 2 g total fat (0 g saturated), 1 g fiber, 0 mg cholesterol, 1 mg sodium.

## Warm Cranberry-Pineapple Relish

Drain *2 cans (16 ounces each) pineapple chunks in heavy syrup*, saving ½ cup syrup. In 4-quart saucepan, heat *2 packages (12 ounces each) cranberries, 2 cups sugar, 2 cups dark seedless raisins, 1 tablespoon minced preserved ginger, 2 teaspoons salt, ½ teaspoon ground allspice*, and reserved pineapple syrup to boiling over high heat, stirring occasionally. Reduce heat to low; cover and simmer 10 minutes or until cranberries pop. Add pineapple chunks; continue cooking 5 minutes or until mixture thickens slightly. Serve relish warm (to serve cold, cover and refrigerate). Makes about 8 cups.

Each ¼ cup: About 105 calories, 0 g protein, 28 g carbohydrate, 0 g total fat (0 g saturated), 1 g fiber, 0 mg cholesterol, 150 mg sodium.

## Chopped Fresh Cranberry-Date Relish

In large bowl, with wire whisk or fork, stir *⅔ cup apple jelly* until smooth. In food processor with knife blade attached, chop *1 bag (12 ounces) cranberries*, pulsing on and off several times, until cranberries are smaller than peas (or chop with knife). Add cranberries to jelly. In food processor, chop *1 large Granny Smith apple*, cut into quarters, until the same size as cranberries (or chop with knife). Into bowl with cranberry mixture, stir apple, *1 cup walnuts*, chopped, *1 package (8 ounces) chopped dates*, and *¼ cup apple juice*. Makes about 3½ cups.

Each ¼ cup: About 160 calories, 2 g protein, 29 g carbohydrate, 5 g total fat (0 g saturated), 2 g fiber, 0 mg cholesterol, 7 mg sodium.

## Cranberry-Strawberry Relish

Drain syrup from *1 package (10 ounces) frozen sweetened sliced strawberries*, thawed, into 1-cup measuring cup. Add enough *water* to equal 1 cup liquid. Set strawberries aside. In 3-quart saucepan, heat syrup mixture from strawberries, *½ cup sugar*, and *1 package (12 ounces) cranberries* to boiling over high heat, stirring occasionally. Reduce heat to low; simmer, uncovered, 10 minutes or until cranberries pop. Stir strawberries into mixture. Spoon relish into bowl. Cover and refrigerate until chilled, about 3 hours. Makes about 3 cups.

Each ¼ cup: About 70 calories, 0 g protein, 18 g carbohydrate, 0 g total fat (0 g saturated), 1 g fiber, 0 mg cholesterol, 1 mg sodium.

# Rolled Turkey Breast with Basil Mayonnaise

🐓 🐓 🐓

PREP: 45 MINUTES / ROAST: 1¼ HOURS

Divide and butterfly a whole turkey breast with our simple directions. Serve hot or cold.

ROLLED TURKEY BREAST:

1 whole turkey breast with bones (about
    6 pounds)
2 teaspoons salt
1 teaspoon coarsely ground black pepper
1 jar (12 ounces) roasted red peppers, drained
1½ cups loosely packed fresh basil leaves
1 tablespoon olive oil

BASIL MAYONNAISE:

2 cups loosely packed fresh basil leaves
1 cup light mayonnaise
1 cup reduced-fat sour cream
2 teaspoons fresh lemon juice
¼ teaspoon salt

Basil sprigs for garnish

**1** Prepare Rolled Turkey Breast: Place turkey breast on cutting board, skin side up. With sharp knife, working with 1 side of breast, starting parallel and close to large end of rib bone, cut and scrape meat away from bone and rib cage, gently pulling back meat in one piece as you cut. Repeat with remaining side of breast; discard bones and skin.

**2** To butterfly breast halves: Place 1 breast half, cut side up, on cutting board. With sharp knife, starting at a long side, cut breast horizontally in half, but not all the way through, making sure that meat on other long side stays connected. Spread meat open. Place butterflied breast between 2 sheets of plastic wrap. With meat mallet or rolling pin, pound breast to about ¼-inch even thickness. Repeat with second breast half.

**3** Preheat oven to 350°F. Sprinkle each breast half with ½ teaspoon salt and ¼ teaspoon black pepper. Arrange red-pepper slices evenly over breasts, leaving a 2-inch border all around edges of meat; top with basil leaves. Starting at a narrow end, roll each breast with filling, jelly-roll fashion. With string, tie each rolled turkey breast at 2-inch intervals. Brush rolls with oil and sprinkle with remaining 1 teaspoon salt and ½ teaspoon black pepper.

**4** Place rolls, seam sides down, on rack in large roasting pan (17" by 11½"). Insert meat thermometer into center of 1 roll. Roast turkey rolls about 1 hour and 15 minutes. Turkey is done when temperature on meat thermometer reaches 160°F. Temperature will rise to 165°F. upon standing.

**5** While turkey is roasting, prepare Basil Mayonnaise: In food processor with knife blade attached or in blender, blend basil, mayonnaise, sour cream, lemon juice, and salt until sauce is creamy. Cover and refrigerate sauce until ready to use.

**6** When turkey rolls are done, place on large platter. Let stand 10 minutes to set juices for easier carving if serving warm. If not serving right away, wrap and refrigerate turkey rolls until ready to serve.

**7** To serve, remove strings. Slice turkey rolls into about ¼-inch-thick slices and serve with Basil Mayonnaise. Garnish with basil sprigs. *Makes 12 main-dish servings.*

Each serving: About 320 calories, 45 g protein, 6 g carbohydrate, 12 g total fat (3 g saturated), 2 g fiber, 130 mg cholesterol, 710 mg sodium.

◀ *Rolled Turkey Breast with Basil Mayonnaise*

# Baked Dishes & Skillet Dishes

# Apricot-Glazed Baked Chicken

PREP: 5 MINUTES / BAKE: 50 MINUTES

1 whole chicken (about 3½ pounds), cut into
  quarters
¾ cup apricot preserves
2 tablespoons red wine vinegar
1 teaspoon salt
¼ teaspoon coarsely ground black pepper

**1** Preheat oven to 400°F.

**2** Arrange chicken, skin-side up, in roasting pan; bake 30 minutes.

**3** Meanwhile, in small bowl, mix apricot preserves, vinegar, salt, and pepper.

**4** After chicken has baked 30 minutes, spoon apricot mixture over it and continue baking 15 to 20 minutes, basting occasionally with drippings in pan, until chicken is fork-tender and juices run clear when chicken is pierced with tip of knife. Arrange chicken on platter. ***Makes 4 main-dish servings.***

Each serving: About 565 calories, 48 g protein, 39 g carbohydrate, 24 g total fat (7 g saturated), 1 g fiber, 154 mg cholesterol, 750 mg sodium.

# Baked Chicken & Prunes

PREP: 30 MINUTES / BAKE: 1 HOUR

1 whole chicken (about 3½ pounds), cut up
½ teaspoon salt
1 tablespoon olive or vegetable oil
1 pound small white onions, peeled and each cut in
  half
1 can (14½ ounces) chicken broth or 1¾ cups
  homemade (page 11)
1 tablespoon all-purpose flour
1 cup pitted prunes
¼ cup blanched whole almonds
2 tablespoons brown sugar

**1** Sprinkle chicken pieces with salt. In nonstick 12-inch skillet, heat oil over medium-high heat until very hot. Add chicken and cook until well browned on both sides. With slotted spoon, transfer chicken to shallow 2-quart casserole or 12" by 8" baking dish.

**2** Add onions to skillet and cook until well browned, stirring occasionally.

**3** Preheat oven to 375°F. In small bowl, stir together chicken broth and flour. Add chicken-broth mixture and prunes to skillet; heat to boiling over high heat. Reduce heat to low; cover and simmer 5 minutes or until onions are almost tender.

**4** Spoon onion mixture over chicken in casserole. Sprinkle with almonds, then brown sugar. Bake, uncovered, 45 minutes or until juices run clear when chicken is pierced with tip of knife and onions are tender. Skim fat from sauce in casserole. ***Makes 4 main-dish servings.***

Each serving: About 835 calories, 55 g protein, 44 g carbohydrate, 49 g total fat (13 g saturated), 6 g fiber, 203 mg cholesterol, 940 mg sodium.

# Baked Lime Chicken

PREP: 25 MINUTES / BAKE: 50 MINUTES

2 small limes
1 whole chicken (about 3½ pounds), cut up, skin
   removed
3 tablespoons margarine or butter
¼ cup all-purpose-flour
1 teaspoon salt
½ teaspoon coarsely ground black pepper
2 tablespoons light brown sugar
1 can (14½ ounces) chicken broth or 1¾ cups
   homemade (page 11)

**1** Preheat oven to 400°F. From limes, grate peel and squeeze 2 tablespoons juice. Place chicken in bowl; toss with lime juice.

**2** In medium roasting pan (15½" by 10½"), melt margarine or butter in oven. Remove pan from oven.

**3** On waxed paper, mix flour, salt, and pepper; use to coat chicken pieces. Dip chicken pieces, one at a time, into melted margarine or butter in roasting pan, turning to coat. Arrange chicken, skin-side up, in pan. (Do not use smaller pan and crowd chicken pieces; they won't brown.)

**4** In cup, mix lime peel and brown sugar; sprinkle over chicken pieces. Pour chicken broth into roasting pan and bake, uncovered, 50 minutes, basting chicken with pan juices occasionally, until chicken is tender and juices run clear when pierced with tip of knife.

**5** To serve, arrange chicken on warm platter. Skim fat from drippings in pan if any. Spoon pan juices over chicken. *Makes 4 main-dish servings.*

Each serving: About 370 calories, 42 g 14 g carbohydrate, 15 g total fat (3 g saturated), 0.5 g fiber, 133 mg cholesterol, 1280 mg sodium.

# Chicken with Figs & Lemon

PREP: 25 MINUTES / BAKE: 50 MINUTES

2 medium lemons
¼ cup packed brown sugar
¼ cup white vinegar
1 package (12 to 14 ounces) dried Calimyrna figs
12 medium bone-in chicken thighs, with skin
   (about 4 pounds)
1 teaspoon salt
1 tablespoon minced fresh parsley leaves

**1** Preheat oven to 400°F.

**2** Trim and discard ends from one lemon and cut crosswise into 4 or 5 slices; set aside. Into cup, squeeze juice from remaining lemon (about 2 tablespoons); stir in brown sugar, vinegar, and *¼ cup water.*

### *Last-minute* DINNERS
## CITRUS-GLAZED CHICKEN BREASTS

PREP: 5 MINUTES / BAKE: 20 MINUTES

*4 large refrigerated roasted chicken-breast halves
   (about 2 pounds)
1 small lemon
¼ cup orange marmalade
2 teaspoons soy sauce*

**1** Preheat oven to 450°F. Place chicken-breast halves, skin-side up, in roasting pan.

**2** Bake chicken 20 minutes. Meanwhile, from lemon, grate 1 teaspoon peel and squeeze 1 tablespoon juice. In 1-quart saucepan, heat lemon peel, lemon juice, orange marmalade, and soy sauce over low heat until marmalade melts.

**3** Brush chicken with marmalade mixture frequently during last 10 minutes of cooking time. Makes 4 main-dish servings.

Each serving: About 250 calories, 40 g protein, 15 g carbohydrate, 4 g total fat (2 g saturated), 0 g fiber, 108 mg cholesterol, 1075 mg sodium.

**3** Place figs and lemon slices in bottom of large roasting pan (17" by 11½"); arrange chicken thighs on top. Pour vinegar mixture over chicken; sprinkle with salt. Roast chicken 50 minutes or until golden brown, basting frequently with juices in pan and turning figs if they begin to brown.

**4** With slotted spoon, transfer chicken, figs, and lemon slices to warm platter. Tilt roasting pan and skim fat from meat juice. Pour meat juice over chicken; sprinkle with minced parsley. *Makes 4 main-dish servings.*

Each serving: About 935 calories, 62 g protein, 78 g carbohydrate, 44 g total fat (12 g saturated), 9 g fiber, 224 mg cholesterol, 795 mg sodium.

# Chutney Chicken & Squash

PREP: 10 MINUTES / BAKE: 1 HOUR

2 acorn squash (about 1¼ pounds each)
1 whole chicken (about 3½ pounds), cut up
1 teaspoon salt
1 cup mango chutney, coarsely chopped
2 teaspoons curry powder

**1** Preheat oven to 425°F. Cut each squash lengthwise into quarters, then cut each quarter crosswise in half. Arrange squash and chicken, skin-side up, in large roasting pan (17" by 11½"). Sprinkle with salt. Bake 30 minutes, basting occasionally with drippings in pan, if any.

**2** Mix chutney and curry powder; brush mixture over chicken and squash. Bake 20 to 30 minutes longer until juices run clear when thickest part of chicken is pierced with tip of knife and squash is fork-tender.

**3** Arrange chicken and squash in serving bowl. Pour *½ cup water* into roasting pan, scraping bottom to remove any brown bits; heat through over high heat. Skim fat. Pour pan juices over chicken and squash. *Makes 6 main-dish servings.*

Each serving: About 500 calories, 33 g protein, 53 g carbohydrate, 16 g total fat (4 g saturated), 5 g fiber, 103 mg cholesterol, 940 mg sodium.

# Maple-Glazed Chicken & Pears

PREP: 15 MINUTES / BAKE: 50 MINUTES

2 large bone-in chicken-breast halves (about
    1½ pounds), skin removed
4 large chicken legs (about 3 pounds), skin
    removed
1 tablespoon minced fresh rosemary or
    1 teaspoon dried rosemary, crushed
1½ teaspoons salt
½ teaspoon coarsely ground black pepper
3 large pears, each cut lengthwise in half
¼ cup maple syrup
Boston lettuce leaves

**1** Preheat oven to 425°F. Rub chicken pieces with rosemary, salt, and pepper.

**2** Arrange chicken and pears in large roasting pan (17" by 11½"). Bake chicken and pears 25 minutes. Brush maple syrup on chicken and pears; bake 20 to 25 minutes longer, occasionally brushing chicken and pears with pan drippings.

**3** To serve, line 6 dinner plates with Boston lettuce leaves; top each with a piece of chicken and a pear half. To drippings in roasting pan, add *½ cup hot water*, stirring to loosen any brown bits from pan. Skim and discard fat. Spoon drippings over chicken and pears. *Makes 6 main-dish servings.*

Each serving: About 335 calories, 44 g protein, 25 g carbohydrate, 6 g total fat (2 g saturated), 3 g fiber, 147 mg cholesterol, 740 mg sodium.

# Rosemary-Apricot Chicken

PREP: 20 MINUTES PLUS MARINATING / BAKE: 45 MINUTES

A crowd pleaser to dish up hot or cold, and a perfect picnic dish or potluck supper offering. If you'll have access to a grill for your picnic, bake the marinated chicken at home without the glaze, then reheat it on the grill, brushing with the apricot mixture just before removing it from the heat. Bring along a variety of fully-cooked sausages to put on the fire alongside the chicken.

2 teaspoons salt
1 teaspoon dried rosemary, crushed
½ teaspoon coarsely ground black pepper
4 garlic cloves, crushed with garlic press
3 whole chickens (about 3 pounds each), each cut into quarters, skin removed
½ cup apricot jam
2 tablespoons fresh lemon juice
2 teaspoons Dijon mustard

**1** In cup, mix salt, rosemary, pepper, and garlic. Rub rosemary mixture over chicken quarters; cover and refrigerate in large bowl about 2 hours.

**2** Preheat oven to 350°F. Place chicken quarters, skinned-side up, in 2 large roasting pans (17" by 11½" each) or 2 jelly-roll pans (15½" by 10½" each). Bake chicken 25 minutes on 2 oven racks, rotating pans between upper and lower racks halfway through baking.

**3** Meanwhile, in small bowl, with fork, mix apricot jam, lemon juice, and mustard. Brush apricot mixture over chicken; bake 20 minutes longer, rotating pans after 10 minutes or until juices run clear when thickest part of thigh is pierced with tip of knife. Serve chicken hot, or cover and refrigerate to serve cold later. *Makes 12 main-dish servings.*

Each serving: About 230 calories, 35 g protein, 9 g carbohydrate, 5 g total fat (1 g saturated), 0 g fiber, 114 mg cholesterol, 540 mg sodium.

# Oven-Barbecued Hawaiian Chicken

PREP: 20 MINUTES / BAKE: 50 MINUTES

1 can (8 ounces) crushed pineapple in unsweetened pineapple juice
⅓ cup chili sauce
¼ cup apricot preserves
2 tablespoons brown sugar
2 tablespoons soy sauce
1 teaspoon cornstarch
1 whole chicken (about 3½ pounds), cut up, skin removed

**1** Preheat oven to 400°F. In small bowl, combine crushed pineapple with its juice, chili sauce, apricot preserves, brown sugar, soy sauce, and cornstarch; mix well.

**2** Arrange chicken in medium roasting pan (15½" by 10½") lined with foil. Spoon pineapple mixture over chicken.

**3** Bake chicken 45 to 50 minutes, basting occasionally with pan drippings, until juices run clear when chicken is pierced with tip of knife.

**4** Arrange chicken on large platter and spoon any sauce in roasting pan over chicken. *Makes 4 main-dish servings.*

Each serving: About 365 calories, 42 g protein, 35 g carbohydrate, 6 g total fat (2 g saturated), 1 g fiber, 133 mg cholesterol, 975 mg sodium.

◀ *Rosemary-Apricot Chicken*

# Chicken with Balsamic-Glazed Vegetables

🐓 🐓 🐓

PREP: 15 MINUTES / BAKE: 45 MINUTES

2 medium leeks (about ¾ pound)
2 medium baby eggplants (about ¾ pound) or
   ½ small eggplant
4 large bone-in chicken breast halves (about
   2½ pounds)
2 medium yellow peppers, each cut into quarters
¼ cup balsamic vinegar
1 tablespoon olive or vegetable oil
2 teaspoons sugar
1¼ teaspoons salt
¾ teaspoon coarsely ground black pepper

**1** Cut off roots and trim leaf ends of leeks. Cut leeks lengthwise in half. Rinse leeks with running cold water to remove all sand. Cut each baby eggplant lengthwise in half. (If using regular eggplant, cut into about 3" by 1" strips.)

**2** Preheat oven to 400°F. In large roasting pan (17" by 11½"), arrange the chicken breasts, skin-side up, with leeks, eggplants, cut-sides up, and yellow peppers.

**3** In cup, with fork, mix balsamic vinegar, olive oil, sugar, salt, and black pepper. With pastry brush, brush balsamic-vinegar mixture over chicken and vegetables in roasting pan.

**4** Bake chicken and vegetables 40 to 45 minutes, basting occasionally with pan drippings, until chicken and vegetables are golden and tender and juices run clear when chicken is pierced with tip of knife.

**5** To serve, arrange chicken and vegetables on platter. Into drippings in roasting pan, stir ¼ *cup hot water*, stirring to loosen any brown bits from pan. Skim and discard fat; spoon drippings over chicken and vegetables. *Makes 4 main-dish servings.*

Each serving: About 490 calories, 49 g protein, 16 g carbohydrate, 25 g total fat (7 g saturated), 2 g fiber, 145 mg cholesterol, 880 mg sodium.

# Chicken with Onions & Garlic

PREP: 10 MINUTES / BAKE: 55 MINUTES

1 whole chicken (about 3½ pounds), cut up
1 teaspoon salt
¼ teaspoon coarsely ground black pepper
2 medium red onions
1 whole large garlic bulb
1 tablespoon vegetable oil

**1** Preheat oven to 425°F. Rub chicken with salt and pepper. Place chicken in medium roasting pan (15½" by 10½").

**2** Do not remove skin from onions; cut each onion lengthwise in half; place in bowl. Separate garlic cloves from whole garlic bulb, keeping skin on garlic cloves and removing only loose papery skin. Place garlic in bowl with onions. Toss onions and garlic with oil. Sprinkle garlic cloves over chicken; place onions, cut-side down, in roasting pan around chicken.

**3** Bake chicken, onions, and garlic 50 to 55 minutes until chicken is browned and juices run clear when chicken is pierced with tip of knife, brushing chicken occasionally with pan drippings toward end of cooking time.

**4** To serve, arrange chicken, onions, and garlic on warm platter. *Makes 4 main-dish servings.*

Each serving: About 665 calories, 53 g protein, 12 g carbohydrate, 44 g total fat (12 g saturated), 2 g fiber, 203 mg cholesterol, 785 mg sodium.

## TURKEY LASAGNA

PREP: 35 MINUTES
BAKE: 40 MINUTES PLUS STANDING TIME

*9 lasagna noodles (about 8 ounces)*
*Salt*
*3 tablespoons olive or vegetable oil*
*1 medium onion, minced*
*1 medium head escarole (about ¾ pound), cut into*
  *bite-size pieces*
*2 cups coarsely chopped cooked turkey (about 12*
  *ounces)*
*3 tablespoons all-purpose flour*
*2½ cups milk*
*¼ pound Jarlsberg or Swiss cheese, shredded (1 cup)*
*2 tablespoons chopped fresh parsley leaves*

**1** In large saucepot, prepare lasagna noodles in *boiling salted water* as label directs; drain. Cut each lasagna noodle crosswise in half.

**2** Meanwhile, in 10-inch skillet, heat 1 tablespoon oil over medium heat. Add onion and cook until tender, about 10 minutes. Increase heat to medium-high; stir in escarole and ½ teaspoon salt. Cook 5 minutes longer or until escarole is lightly browned and all liquid evaporates. Remove skillet from heat; stir in chopped turkey.

**3** Preheat oven to 375°F. In 2-quart saucepan, stir together remaining 2 tablespoons oil and flour. Cook, stirring constantly, over medium heat 1 minute. Gradually stir in milk and ½ teaspoon salt and cook, stirring constantly, until sauce boils and thickens. Remove saucepan from heat; stir in ½ cup shredded cheese until cheese melts.

**4** In 8" by 8" glass baking dish, evenly spoon ½ cup cheese sauce. Arrange one-third of lasagna noodles over sauce, overlapping to fit. Top with one-half of turkey mixture. Repeat layering one time. Top with the remaining ½ cup cheese, then with remaining lasagna noodles and remaining cheese sauce. Sprinkle with chopped parsley.

**5** Cover baking dish with foil and bake 30 minutes. Uncover and bake 10 minutes or until hot and bubbly and top is lightly browned. Remove lasagna from oven; let stand 10 to 15 minutes for easier serving. Makes 6 main-dish servings.

Each serving: About 455 calories, 31 g protein, 41 g carbohydrate, 18 g total fat (4 g saturated), 3 g fiber, 70 mg cholesterol, 330 mg sodium.

# Chicken & Pasta Torte

PREP: 40 MINUTES / BAKE: 45 MINUTES

12 ounces lasagna noodles
1 tablespoon olive or vegetable oil
1 medium onion, chopped
1 pound ground chicken
½ teaspoon fennel seeds, crushed
½ teaspoon salt
¼ teaspoon coarsely ground black pepper
¼ teaspoon rubbed sage
1 package (10 ounces) frozen chopped spinach,
  thawed and well drained
1 cup shredded mozzarella cheese (4 ounces)
½ cup grated Parmesan cheese
4 ounces sliced boiled ham, diced
4 large eggs, lightly beaten
2 cups bottled tomato-based pasta sauce,
  preferably with basil

**1** In large saucepot, prepare lasagna noodles in *boiling water* as label directs.

**2** Meanwhile, in 12-inch skillet, heat olive oil over medium heat. Add onion and cook until tender. Increase heat to high; add ground chicken, fennel seeds, salt, pepper, and sage and cook until chicken is lightly browned. Remove from heat; stir in spinach, mozzarella, Parmesan, ham, and eggs.

**3** Drain noodles. Grease well 3-quart round casserole (about 3 inches deep). Preheat oven to 375°F.

**4** Arrange enough lasagna noodles, overlapping slightly, to cover bottom and side of casserole, allowing noodles to extend over edge of casserole. Spoon half of chicken mixture over noodles; top with remaining noodles, then remaining chicken mixture. Bring overhanging lasagna noodles over chicken mixture; press firmly.

**5** Cover casserole. Bake 45 minutes or until hot. Remove casserole from oven and let stand 10 minutes for easier serving. Meanwhile, in small saucepan over low heat, heat pasta sauce until hot.

**6** To serve, with spatula, loosen edge of torte from casserole; invert torte onto large round platter. Top with some pasta sauce. Cut into wedges to serve. Spoon remaining pasta sauce over each serving. *Makes 6 main-dish servings.*

Each serving: About 575 calories, 38 g protein, 54 g carbohydrate, 22 g total fat (8 g saturated), 5 g fiber, 235 mg cholesterol, 1130 mg sodium.

# Glazed Chicken & Onions

PREP: 15 MINUTES / BAKE: 50 MINUTES

½ cup peach or apricot preserves
¼ cup balsamic vinegar
2 teaspoons grated orange peel
1 teaspoon salt
¾ teaspoon coarsely ground black pepper
1 whole chicken (about 3½ pounds), cut into
  quarters
2 medium chicken legs (about 1 pound)
2 large onions, each cut into 6 wedges
Orange slices and orange-peel strips for garnish

**1** Preheat oven to 400°F. In small bowl, mix peach preserves, vinegar, orange peel, salt, and pepper.

**2** Arrange chicken pieces and onion wedges in large roasting pan (17" by 11½"). Spoon peach-preserves mixture over chicken and onions. Bake 45 to 50 minutes, basting occasionally with pan juices, until onions are tender and juices run clear when chicken is pierced with tip of knife.

**3** To serve, place chicken and onions on warm large platter. Garnish with orange slices and orange-peel strips. Skim fat from juices in roasting pan. Serve pan juices with chicken. *Makes 6 main-dish servings.*

Each serving: About 500 calories, 43 g protein, 24 g carbohydrate, 25 g total fat (7 g saturated), 2 g fiber, 140 mg cholesterol, 530 mg sodium.

*Glazed Chicken & Onions*

# Country Chicken Casserole

PREP: 20 MINUTES / BAKE: 40 MINUTES

½ cup all-purpose flour
½ teaspoon coarsely ground black pepper
1¼ teaspoons salt
2 whole chickens (about 3½ pounds each), cut up, skin removed
2 tablespoons vegetable oil
1 large onion, chopped
4 medium celery stalks, cut into 1-inch pieces
1 garlic clove, minced
1 can (28 ounces) tomatoes, drained
1 can (14½ ounces) chicken broth or 1¾ cups homemade (page 11)
3 tablespoons tomato paste
½ teaspoon dried thyme
1 can (15 to 19 ounces) garbanzo beans, rinsed and drained

1 Preheat oven to 400°F. On waxed paper, mix flour, pepper, and 1 teaspoon salt; use to coat chicken pieces. In 12-inch skillet, heat oil over medium-high heat until very hot. Add chicken pieces, half at a time, and cook until browned on all sides, transferring to bowl as it browns.

2 Add onion to skillet and cook over medium-high heat, stirring occasionally, until tender and golden. Add celery and cook until tender-crisp. Stir in garlic and cook, stirring, until garlic begins to brown.

3 Add drained tomatoes, chicken broth, tomato paste, thyme, and remaining ¼ teaspoon salt to skillet. Heat to boiling over high heat; boil 1 minute. Stir in garbanzo beans.

4 Transfer chicken pieces and vegetable mixture to deep 6-quart casserole. Bake, covered, 35 to 40 minutes, until chicken is fork-tender and juices run clear when pierced with tip of knife. Skim fat from pan juices in casserole. Serve pan juices with chicken. *Makes 8 main-dish servings.*

Each serving: About 370 calories, 46 g protein, 21 g carbohydrate, 11 g total fat (2 g saturated), 4 g fiber, 133 mg cholesterol, 1030 mg sodium.

# Honey Chicken with Crumb-Topped Tomatoes

PREP: 30 MINUTES / BAKE: 1 HOUR

4 medium bone-in chicken-breast halves (about 2½ pounds), skin removed
¼ cup Dijon mustard
3 tablespoons honey
2 teaspoons curry powder
1 teaspoon fresh lemon juice
2 large tomatoes, each cut in half horizontally
1 slice firm-textured bread, torn into small pieces
2 tablespoons grated Parmesan cheese
1 tablespoon chopped fresh parsley leaves
¼ teaspoon salt
¼ teaspoon coarsely ground black pepper
Nonstick cooking spray

1 Preheat oven to 375°F. Line 13" by 9" glass baking dish with foil. Place chicken, skinned-side up, in dish.

2 In small bowl, mix mustard, honey, curry powder, and lemon juice. Brush mustard mixture over chicken. Bake chicken, uncovered, 40 minutes.

3 Meanwhile, place tomatoes, cut-side up, in 8" by 8" glass baking dish. In small bowl, stir together bread, Parmesan, parsley, salt, and pepper. Sprinkle crumb mixture over tomato halves. Spray each tomato lightly with nonstick cooking spray.

4 After chicken has baked 40 minutes, place tomatoes in same oven and bake 20 minutes longer or until tomatoes are heated through and chicken is golden brown and juices run clear when pierced with tip of knife.

5 Arrange chicken and tomato halves on 4 dinner plates. Spoon any glaze remaining in baking dish over chicken. *Makes 4 main-dish servings.*

Each serving: About 325 calories, 45 g protein, 23 g carbohydrate, 4 g total fat (1 g saturated), 2 g fiber, 109 mg cholesterol, 720 mg sodium.

# Rosemary Chicken & Vegetables

🐓🐓🐓

PREP: 15 MINUTES / BAKE: 45 MINUTES

4 large bone-in chicken thighs, with skin (about 1¼ pounds)
2 large bone-in chicken-breast halves, with skin (about 1¼ pounds)
1½ teaspoons chopped fresh rosemary or ¾ teaspoon dried rosemary, crushed
1½ teaspoons salt
1 teaspoon coarsely ground black pepper
1 pound medium red potatoes, each cut into quarters
3 medium carrots, peeled and each cut lengthwise in half, then crosswise into 3 pieces
2 medium fennel bulbs (about ¾ pound each), each cut into 6 wedges
5 garlic cloves, unpeeled
1 tablespoon olive or vegetable oil

**1** Preheat oven to 400°F. Arrange chicken pieces in large roasting pan (17" by 11½"). Sprinkle chicken pieces with rosemary, ¾ teaspoon salt, and ¾ teaspoon pepper.

**2** In large bowl, toss potatoes, carrots, fennel, and garlic with olive oil, remaining ¾ teaspoon salt, and ¼ teaspoon pepper until vegetables are well coated. Arrange vegetables around chicken pieces in roasting pan.

**3** Roast chicken and vegetables 40 to 45 minutes, basting occasionally with pan drippings, until chicken pieces and vegetables are golden and tender, and juices run clear when chicken is pierced with tip of knife.

**4** Transfer chicken and vegetables to warm large platter. Skim fat from drippings in roasting pan; spoon drippings over chicken and vegetables on platter. *Makes 4 main-dish servings.*

Each serving: About 605 calories, 48 g protein, 31 g carbohydrate, 31 g total fat (8 g saturated), 5 g fiber, 167 mg cholesterol, 1195 mg sodium.

---

## CREATIVE LEFTOVERS

# CHICKEN CORN-BREAD COBBLER

PREP: 40 MINUTES / BAKE: 20 MINUTES

2 tablespoons vegetable oil
1 pound carrots, peeled and cut into ¼-inch-thick slices
2 large celery stalks, cut into ¼-inch-thick slices
1 large onion, chopped
1 teaspoon salt
10 ounces mushrooms, sliced
1 cup milk
3 tablespoons plus ½ cup all-purpose flour
1 can (14½ ounces) chicken broth or 1¾ cups homemade (page 11)
1 large egg
½ cup yellow cornmeal
1½ teaspoons baking powder
¼ cup shortening
2 cups cubed cooked chicken or turkey (12 ounces)
1 cup frozen peas

**1** In 10-inch skillet with oven-safe handle (or cover skillet handle with heavy-duty foil when baking in oven later), heat oil over medium-high heat. Add carrots, celery, onion, and ½ teaspoon salt and cook until lightly browned, about 10 minutes. Add mushrooms to skillet and cook until vegetables are tender, about 5 minutes.

**2** In 1-cup measuring cup, mix ¾ cup milk and 3 tablespoons flour; stir into vegetables in skillet along with chicken broth. Cook over high heat, stirring constantly, until mixture boils and thickens slightly; boil 1 minute. Remove from heat.

**3** Preheat oven to 400°F. In cup, mix egg and remaining ¼ cup milk. In large bowl, combine cornmeal, baking powder, remaining 1 cup flour, and remaining ½ teaspoon salt. With pastry blender or two knives used scissor-fashion, cut shortening into flour mixture to resemble coarse crumbs; stir in egg mixture until just combined.

**4** Stir chicken and frozen peas into skillet; heat to boiling over high heat. Spoon cobbler mixture over mixture in skillet, leaving a 1½-inch border all around. Bake 15 to 20 minutes until top is firm and golden brown. Makes 4 main-dish servings.

Each serving: About 660 calories, 38 g protein, 58 g carbohydrate, 31 g total fat (8 g saturated), 8 g fiber, 137 mg cholesterol, 1435 mg sodium.

# Three-Pepper Chicken

♦ ♦ ♦

PREP: 25 MINUTES / BAKE: 50 MINUTES

2 whole chickens (about 3½ pounds each), cut up,
  skin removed
2 jumbo onions (1 pound each), each cut into
  6 wedges
2 teaspoons salt
½ cup apple jelly
¼ cup minced, peeled fresh ginger
1 teaspoon hot pepper sauce
2 medium red peppers, each cut lengthwise in half
2 medium yellow peppers, each cut lengthwise in
  half
2 medium green peppers, each cut lengthwise in
  half

**1** Preheat oven to 425°F. In 2 large roasting pans, each
about 17" by 11½" (or in 1 large roasting pan and one
15½" by 10½" jelly-roll pan), arrange chicken pieces
and onion wedges. Sprinkle with salt. Arrange pans on
2 oven racks. Bake chicken and onions 25 minutes,
brushing occasionally with pan drippings.

**2** Meanwhile, in small saucepan, melt apple jelly with
ginger and hot pepper sauce over low heat. Arrange
peppers around chicken in roasting pan. Brush chick-
en, peppers, and onions with jelly mixture. Switch
pans on oven racks; bake 25 minutes longer or until
chicken is nicely glazed and juices run clear when
thickest part of chicken is pierced with tip of knife,
and peppers and onions are tender.

**3** Transfer chicken, peppers, and onions to large platter. To drippings in 1 pan, add ¼ cup hot water, stirring to loosen any brown bits from pan. Stir ¼ cup hot
water into second pan. Skim fat from both pans.
Spoon drippings over chicken, peppers, and onions.
*Makes 10 main-dish servings.*

Each serving: About 315 calories, 34 g protein, 22 g carbohydrate,
10 g total fat (3 g saturated), 2 g fiber, 111 mg cholesterol, 605 mg
sodium.

# Chicken, Rice & Beans Casserole

PREP: 20 MINUTES / BAKE: 40 MINUTES

4 large chicken legs (about 3 pounds), skin
  removed
½ teaspoon paprika (optional)
½ teaspoon salt
½ teaspoon coarsely ground black pepper
1 tablespoon vegetable oil
1 medium onion, chopped
1 medium green pepper, chopped
1 cup regular long-grain rice
1 can (8 ounces) tomato sauce
½ cup pimiento-stuffed olives, each cut in half if
  large
1 can (10½ ounces) garbanzo beans, rinsed and
  drained
1 can (8¾ ounces) red kidney beans, rinsed and
  drained

**1** Sprinkle chicken legs with paprika, salt, and black
pepper.

**2** In 10-inch skillet, heat oil over medium-high heat
until very hot. Add 2 chicken legs at a time and cook
until browned on all sides, transferring chicken legs to
plate as they brown.

**3** Preheat oven to 375°F. Add onion and green pepper
to skillet and cook until tender-crisp. Add rice, stirring
until rice turns opaque. Stir in tomato sauce and *1¼
cups water.* Heat to boiling over high heat.

**4** Spoon rice mixture into 13" by 9" glass baking dish
or 3-quart shallow casserole. Tuck chicken in rice.
Cover baking dish and bake 30 minutes. Gently stir
olives, garbanzo beans, and red kidney beans into rice
mixture. Cover and bake 10 minutes longer or until
beans and olives are heated through, rice is tender, and
juices run clear when chicken is pierced with tip of
knife. *Makes 4 main-dish servings.*

Each serving: About 590 calories, 50 g protein, 62 g carbohydrate,
15 g total fat (3 g saturated), 7 g fiber, 155 mg cholesterol, 1370 mg
sodium.

# Easy Chicken & Eggplant Casserole

PREP: 25 MINUTES / BAKE: 30 MINUTES

Fully-cooked chicken cutlets make this layered casserole a snap to assemble.

1 small eggplant (about 1 pound), cut crosswise
    into ½-inch-thick slices
3 tablespoons olive or vegetable oil
1½ teaspoons salt
1 medium onion, minced
1 can (35 ounces) Italian plum tomatoes
1 tablespoon sugar
1 small head escarole (about 1 pound)
2 packages (14 ounces each) refrigerated, fully-
    cooked breaded chicken cutlets (8 cutlets)
1 package (8 ounces) part-skim mozzarella cheese,
    cut into thin slices

**1** Preheat broiler. In large bowl, toss eggplant slices with 2 tablespoons olive oil and 1 teaspoon salt. Arrange eggplant slices on rack in broiling pan. With pan at closest position to source of heat, broil eggplant slices 8 to 10 minutes, turning once, until tender and lightly browned on both sides. Turn oven control to 400°F.

**2** Meanwhile, in 3-quart saucepan, heat remaining 1 tablespoon oil over medium-high heat. Add onion and remaining ½ teaspoon salt and cook until tender. Add tomatoes with their juice and sugar; with slotted spoon or fork, thoroughly crush tomatoes. Heat to boiling over high heat; boil 1 minute to blend flavors. Remove from heat.

**3** Reserve 8 escarole leaves; coarsely chop remaining escarole. In 13" by 9" glass baking dish, toss chopped escarole and all but 1 cup tomato sauce.

**4** Alternately arrange chicken cutlets, eggplant, cheese, and reserved escarole leaves, slightly overlap-

ping, over tomato-sauce mixture in baking dish; top with reserved tomato sauce. Bake 30 minutes or until sauce is bubbling and cheese begins to brown. *Makes 8 main-dish servings.*

Each serving: About 535 calories, 21 g protein, 35 g carbohydrate, 36 g total fat (9 g saturated), 4 g fiber, 52 mg cholesterol, 1610 mg sodium.

# Country Chicken & Potato Bake

PREP: 15 MINUTES / BAKE: 1 HOUR

2 pounds potatoes, cut into 1½-inch chunks
1 medium onion, finely chopped
2 whole chickens (about 3 pounds, each), cut up
2 teaspoons salt
2 tablespoons chopped fresh rosemary or
    2 teaspoons dried rosemary, crushed
½ teaspoon coarsely ground black pepper
Fresh rosemary for garnish

**1** Preheat oven to 425°F. In large roasting pan (about 17" by 11½"), toss potatoes and onion with chicken pieces, salt, rosemary, and pepper. Arrange the chicken pieces, skin-side up; bake, uncovered, 1 hour or until potatoes are tender and browned and juices run clear when chicken is pierced with tip of knife, basting with pan drippings occasionally.

**2** To serve, skim any fat from pan drippings. Garnish with fresh rosemary. *Makes 8 main-dish servings.*

Each serving: About 590 calories, 46 g protein, 21 g carbohydrate, 35 g total fat (10 g saturated), 2 g fiber, 174 mg cholesterol, 755 mg sodium.

◄ *Country Chicken & Potato Bake*

# Chicken & Vegetables Parmesan

PREP: 25 MINUTES / BAKE: 20 MINUTES

2 tablespoons vegetable oil
2 small zucchini (about 6 ounces each)
½ pound mushrooms, each cut into quarters
¼ teaspoon salt
⅓ cup seasoned dried bread crumbs
¼ teaspoon coarsely ground black pepper
2 tablespoons milk
1 large egg
4 medium skinless, boneless chicken-breast halves
　(about 1¼ pounds)
1 jar (14 to 16 ounces) marinara sauce
1 package (10 ounces) frozen artichoke hearts,
　thawed
2 cups shredded part-skim mozzarella cheese
　(8 ounces)

**1** In nonstick 10-inch skillet, heat 1 tablespoon oil over high heat. Add zucchini, mushrooms, and salt and cook until golden and tender; transfer to bowl.

**2** On waxed paper, mix bread crumbs and pepper. In pie plate, with fork, beat milk and egg slightly. Dip chicken breasts in milk mixture, then in bread-crumb mixture to coat.

**3** Preheat oven to 375°F. In nonstick 12-inch skillet, heat remaining 1 tablespoon oil over medium-high heat until very hot. Add chicken and cook until golden brown on both sides and juices run clear when pierced with tip of knife, 6 to 8 minutes, turning breasts once.

**4** Spoon half of marinara sauce into 13" by 9" baking dish; top with chicken breasts. Spoon remaining sauce over chicken. Arrange cooked vegetables and artichoke hearts in baking dish around chicken. Sprinkle with shredded mozzarella. Bake 15 to 20 minutes, uncovered, until cheese melts and mixture is hot and bubbly. *Makes 4 main-dish servings.*

Each serving: About 545 calories, 55 g protein, 31 g carbohydrate, 24 g total fat (8 g saturated), 8 g fiber, 169 mg cholesterol, 1490 mg sodium.

## GREAT GO-WITHS

# BEET, ORANGE & WATERCRESS SALAD

PREP: 45 MINUTES / COOK: 30 MINUTES

The dressing for this salad can be made up to one day ahead. Washed watercress, wrapped in damp paper towels, can be refrigerated one day ahead, as can the sectioned oranges and cooked and sliced beets. Store them in separate airtight containers in refrigerator.

*10 medium beets (about 2 pounds without tops)*
*4 large oranges*
*¼ cup olive oil*
*¼ cup red wine vinegar*
*1 tablespoon Dijon mustard*
*1 teaspoon sugar*
*¾ teaspoon salt*
*¼ teaspoon coarsely ground black pepper*
*3 bunches watercress (about 12 ounces), tough stems*
　*removed*
*1 medium red onion, thinly sliced*

**1** In 4-quart saucepan, heat beets and enough *water* to cover to boiling over high heat. Reduce heat to low; cover and simmer 30 minutes or until beets are fork-tender.

**2** Meanwhile, from 1 orange, grate 1 teaspoon peel. Cut peel and white pith from all oranges. Holding oranges over large bowl to catch juice, cut segments from between membranes. Place segments in small bowl; set aside. Into juice, with wire whisk or fork, mix olive oil, vinegar, mustard, sugar, salt, pepper, and orange peel.

**3** Drain beets and cool with running cold water. Peel and cut each beet in half, then cut each half into ¼-inch-thick slices.

**4** Add beets, orange segments, watercress, and red onion to dressing; toss to coat. Makes 10 accompaniment servings.

Each serving: About 120 calories, 3 g protein, 17 g carbohydrate, 6 g total fat (1 g saturated), 3 g fiber, 0 mg cholesterol, 270 mg sodium.

# Crispy Chicken with Parmesan Tomatoes

PREP: 20 MINUTES / BAKE: 40 MINUTES

½ cup seasoned dried bread crumbs
2 tablespoons chopped fresh parsley leaves
2 small garlic cloves, minced
4 teaspoons olive or vegetable oil
1 teaspoon coarsely ground black pepper
¼ cup Dijon mustard
4 large bone-in chicken-breast halves, with skin (about 3 pounds)
Nonstick cooking spray
¼ cup grated Parmesan cheese
2 teaspoons dried oregano
½ teaspoon salt
6 medium plum tomatoes (about 1½ pounds), each cut lengthwise in half

**1** Preheat oven to 400°F.

**2** In small bowl, mix bread crumbs, parsley, garlic, olive oil, and ½ teaspoon pepper until blended.

**3** Brush Dijon mustard onto skin side of chicken-breast halves, then coat with bread-crumb mixture, firmly pressing crumb mixture onto chicken.

**4** Spray 13" by 9" glass or ceramic baking dish with nonstick cooking spray. Place chicken, skin-side up, in baking dish. Bake chicken (do not turn) 20 minutes.

**5** Meanwhile, on waxed paper, mix Parmesan, oregano, salt, and remaining ½ teaspoon pepper. Sprinkle Parmesan-cheese mixture over tomato halves. Add tomatoes to baking dish with chicken and bake 15 to 20 minutes longer until coating on chicken is crisp and browned and juices run clear when chicken is pierced with tip of knife. *Makes 4 main-dish servings.*

Each serving: About 540 calories, 61 g protein, 20 g carbohydrate, 22 g total fat (6 g saturated), 3 g fiber, 158 mg cholesterol, 1285 mg sodium.

# Maple-Glazed Chicken & Sweet Potatoes

PREP: 20 MINUTES / BAKE: 45 MINUTES

6 medium sweet potatoes (about 3½ pounds), peeled and cut into 2-inch chunks
1 tablespoon vegetable oil
1½ teaspoons salt
1 whole chicken (about 3½ pounds), cut into quarters
2 large chicken legs (about 1¼ pounds)
1 teaspoon coarsely ground black pepper
1 tablespoon margarine or butter
¼ cup maple syrup
2 tablespoons brown sugar

**1** Preheat oven to 450°F. In large bowl, mix sweet potatoes with oil and ½ teaspoon salt. Place sweet potatoes in 15½" by 10½" jelly-roll pan; set aside.

**2** Tuck wings under chicken breasts. Rub chicken pieces with black pepper and remaining 1 teaspoon salt. Arrange chicken, skin-side up, in large roasting pan (17" by 11½"). Place chicken and sweet potatoes on 2 oven racks. Bake 25 minutes, brushing chicken occasionally with pan drippings.

**3** In small saucepan, melt margarine or butter over low heat; stir in maple syrup and brown sugar until blended. Brush chicken with syrup mixture. Switch pans on oven racks. Bake chicken and sweet potatoes 20 minutes longer or until chicken is nicely glazed and juices run clear when thickest part of chicken is pierced with tip of knife and potatoes are fork-tender.

**4** To serve, place chicken and sweet potatoes on large platter. Spoon off fat from drippings in roasting pan. Over medium heat, heat the drippings in roasting pan with *½ cup water* to boiling; stir until brown bits are loosened. Spoon pan juices over chicken and sweet potatoes. *Makes 6 main-dish servings.*

Each serving: About 675 calories, 47 g protein, 60 g carbohydrate, 27 g total fat (7 g saturated), 6 g fiber, 146 mg cholesterol, 770 mg sodium.

*Chicken Breasts Stuffed with Sun-Dried Tomatoes & Basil*

# Chicken Breasts Stuffed with Sun-Dried Tomatoes & Basil

PREP: 15 MINUTES / BAKE: 40 MINUTES

¼ cup oil-packed sun-dried tomatoes with
   1 tablespoon oil from tomatoes
¼ cup chopped fresh basil leaves
2 tablespoons grated Parmesan cheese
1 teaspoon coarsely ground black pepper
4 medium bone-in chicken-breast halves, with skin
   (about 2 pounds)
½ teaspoon salt

**1** Preheat oven to 425°F. Coarsely chop sun-dried tomatoes. In small bowl, mix chopped basil, sun-dried tomatoes, Parmesan, and ½ teaspoon pepper.

**2** Carefully push fingers between skin and meat of each chicken breast to form a pocket; place some basil mixture in each pocket. Place chicken breasts, skin-side up, in 13" by 9" glass baking dish; brush with oil from sun-dried tomatoes; sprinkle with salt and remaining ½ teaspoon pepper.

**3** Bake chicken 35 to 40 minutes until juices run clear when chicken is pierced with tip of knife, basting occasionally with pan drippings. *Makes 4 main-dish servings.*

Each serving: About 320 calories, 39 g protein, 5 g carbohydrate, 16 g total fat (4 g saturated), 1 g fiber, 105 mg cholesterol, 485 mg sodium.

# Baked Chicken Stuffed with Prosciutto Cream

PREP: 15 MINUTES / BAKE: 45 MINUTES

1 ounce thinly sliced prosciutto, chopped
1 package (3 ounces) cream cheese, softened
2 teaspoons fresh lemon juice
6 medium bone-in chicken-breast halves, with skin (about 3½ pounds)
18 large basil leaves
½ teaspoon salt
½ teaspoon dried basil
½ teaspoon all-purpose flour

**1** Preheat oven to 400°F.

**2** In small bowl, stir together prosciutto, softened cream cheese, and 1 teaspoon lemon juice.

**3** Carefully push fingers between skin and meat of chicken pieces to form a pocket; place 3 large basil leaves and some cream-cheese mixture into each pocket. Place chicken, skin-side up, in medium roasting pan (14" by 10"); sprinkle with salt and dried basil. Bake 35 to 45 minutes until juices run clear when chicken is pierced with tip of knife, basting occasionally with pan drippings.

**4** Transfer chicken to warm platter; keep warm. Pour pan drippings into 1-cup measure; let stand a few seconds until fat separates from meat juice; skim and discard fat. Add enough *water* to measuring cup to make ¾ cup. Add remaining 1 teaspoon lemon juice. Stir flour into meat-juice mixture. Add meat-juice mixture to roasting pan over medium-high heat; stir until brown bits are loosened from pan and mixture boils and thickens slightly.

**5** To serve, pour sauce over chicken. *Makes 6 main-dish servings.*

Each serving: About 345 calories, 45 g protein, 1 g carbohydrate, 17 g total fat (6 g saturated), 0 g fiber, 140 mg cholesterol, 425 mg sodium.

# Cheese-Stuffed Chicken

PREP: 30 MINUTES / BAKE: 45 MINUTES

2 bunches watercress
1 tablespoon olive oil
1 medium onion, minced
1 small carrot, peeled and shredded
¾ cup part-skim ricotta cheese
½ cup shredded Swiss cheese (2 ounces)
¼ cup grated Parmesan or Romano cheese
⅛ teaspoon coarsely ground black pepper
6 medium bone-in chicken-breast halves, with skin (about 3½ pounds)
½ teaspoon salt

**1** Reserve 1 bunch watercress for garnish later. Discard tough stems from second bunch of watercress, then coarsely chop.

**2** In 10-inch skillet, heat oil over medium heat. Add onion and carrot and cook until evenly coated with oil. Cover and cook 5 minutes or until vegetables are just tender, stirring occasionally. Add chopped watercress to skillet; cook, uncovered, until watercress just wilts, about 2 to 3 minutes, stirring frequently. Remove skillet from heat; cool vegetable mixture slightly.

**3** Preheat oven to 400°F. Stir ricotta, Swiss cheese, Parmesan, and pepper into vegetable mixture. Carefully push fingers between skin and meat of chicken breasts to form a pocket, place some stuffing in each pocket. Place chicken, skin-side up, in large roasting pan (17" by 11½"); sprinkle with salt. Bake 45 minutes or until chicken is fork-tender, basting frequently with juices in pan.

**4** To serve, place chicken on warm large platter; pour pan juices over chicken. Garnish with reserved watercress. *Makes 6 main-dish servings.*

Each serving: About 425 calories, 53 g protein, 6 g carbohydrate, 20 g total fat (8 g saturated), 2 g fiber, 143 mg cholesterol, 455 mg sodium.

# EASY BEGGAR'S CHICKEN

PREP: 40 MINUTES PLUS OVERNIGHT MARINATING / BAKE: 2 HOURS

According to legend, the first Beggar's Chicken was made by coating a chicken with wet clay and roasting the mud-encased bird in a wood fire. Here is a considerably more convenient version, in which the chicken is baked in a clay pot (or 5-quart Dutch oven).

1 tablespoon plus ¼ teaspoon salt
2 tablespoons dry sherry or dry white wine
1 whole chicken (about 4 pounds)
1 medium head green cabbage (about 3 pounds)
1 tablespoon vegetable oil
½ pound ground pork
2 green onions, thinly sliced
1 can (8 ounces) sliced bamboo shoots, drained and cut
    into matchstick-thin strips
8 ounces mushrooms, chopped
2 tablespoons soy sauce
2 slices peeled ginger, each about 1 inch in diameter and
    ¼ inch thick

1 In cup, mix 1 tablespoon salt with 1 tablespoon dry sherry. Rub sherry mixture inside and over outside of chicken. Place chicken in bowl; cover and refrigerate overnight.

2 If using clay pot, soak 3-quart clay pot in *cold water* as label directs.

3 Meanwhile, discard tough outer leaves from cabbage; with knife, remove core. Fill 8-quart saucepot three-fourths full with *water*; heat to boiling. Place cabbage in water cut-side up. Using 2 large spoons or forks, gently separate leaves from head of cabbage as outer leaves soften slightly. Transfer 8 large leaves to colander to drain. Chop enough cabbage to equal ½ cup; coarsely cut up any remaining cabbage.

4 In 10-inch skillet, heat oil over high heat until very hot. Add ground pork and green onions and cook until pork is lightly browned. Stir in bamboo shoots, mushrooms, chopped cabbage, soy sauce, remaining 1 tablespoon dry sherry, and remaining ¼ teaspoon salt; cook 1 minute. Remove skillet from heat.

5 Pour off water from clay pot. In clay pot or 5-quart Dutch oven, evenly arrange cut-up cabbage; set aside.

6 With chicken breast-side up, fold wings under back of bird so they stay in place. Spoon pork mixture into body cavity of chicken. Close by folding skin over opening; skewer if necessary. Wrap chicken with cabbage leaves and place, breast-side up, on top of cabbage in clay pot. Add ginger slices. Cover and bake in 400°F. oven 2 hours.

7 Skim fat from liquid. Serve chicken from clay pot or transfer to large deep platter. Serve chicken with cabbage, stuffing, and its broth. Makes 4 main-dish servings.

Each serving: About 730 calories, 69 g protein, 15 g carbohydrate, 43 g total fat (13 g saturated), 6 g fiber, 217 mg cholesterol, 1330 mg sodium.

# Shrimp-Stuffed Chicken Legs

🐓 🐓 🐓

PREP: 30 MINUTES / BAKE: 45 MINUTES

1 pound medium shrimp, shelled, deveined, and
    minced
1 slice white bread, torn into small pieces
1 green onion, minced
1 tablespoon dry sherry
¼ teaspoon ground ginger
1 teaspoon salt
6 medium chicken legs (about 3 pounds)

1 In small bowl, combine shrimp, bread, green onion, sherry, ginger, and ½ teaspoon salt; mix well.

2 Preheat oven to 400°F. Push fingers between skin and meat of each chicken leg to form a pocket; place some stuffing in each pocket. Rub chicken legs with remaining ½ teaspoon salt; place, stuffing-side up, in large roasting pan.

3 Bake chicken legs 40 to 45 minutes until chicken is browned and juices run clear when chicken is pierced with tip of knife, basting chicken occasionally with pan drippings. (To prevent chicken from sticking to pan, move chicken slightly after first 5 to 10 minutes of baking.) *Makes 6 main-dish servings.*

Each serving: About 390 calories, 43 g protein, 3 g carbohydrate, 21 g total fat (6 g saturated), 0 g fiber, 231 mg cholesterol, 635 sodium.

# Stuffed Chicken & Zucchini Casserole

PREP: 30 MINUTES / BAKE: 1 HOUR

2 medium plum tomatoes, seeded and diced
½ cup packed fresh basil leaves, coarsely chopped
2 ounces prosciutto or cooked ham, coarsely chopped
2 tablespoons grated Parmesan cheese
6 medium chicken legs (about 3 pounds)
½ teaspoon coarsely ground black pepper
1¼ teaspoons salt
3 small zucchini (about 6 ounces each), cut into large chunks

**1** Preheat oven to 425°F. In small bowl, mix tomatoes, basil, prosciutto, and Parmesan.

**2** Carefully push fingers between skin and meat of each chicken leg to form a pocket. Spread one-sixth of tomato mixture in each pocket; tuck skin under leg to hold mixture securely in place.

**3** Arrange chicken legs, skin-side up, in one layer in 13" by 9" glass baking dish. Sprinkle chicken with pepper and ¾ teaspoon salt. Bake, uncovered, 30 minutes, brushing chicken occasionally with pan drippings.

**4** Arrange zucchini around chicken legs in baking dish; sprinkle zucchini with remaining ½ teaspoon salt and continue baking 25 to 30 minutes longer or until juices run clear when chicken is pierced with tip of knife and zucchini is tender-crisp.

**5** To serve, skim fat from drippings in dish. *Makes 6 main-dish servings.*

Each serving: About 360 calories, 35 g protein, 4 g carbohydrate, 22 g total fat (6 g saturated), 1 g fiber, 147 mg cholesterol, 825 mg sodium.

# Country Captain

PREP: 50 MINUTES / BAKE: 1 HOUR

2 tablespoons plus 1 teaspoon vegetable oil
2 whole chickens (3½ pounds each), cut up and skin removed
2 medium onions, chopped
1 large Granny Smith apple, peeled and diced
1 large green pepper, diced
3 large garlic cloves, minced
1 tablespoon grated, peeled fresh ginger
3 tablespoons curry powder
½ teaspoon coarsely ground black pepper
¼ teaspoon ground cumin
1 can (28 ounces) tomatoes in puree
1 can (14½ ounces) chicken broth or 1¾ cups homemade (page 11)
½ cup dark seedless raisins
1 teaspoon salt

**1** In 8-quart Dutch oven, heat 2 tablespoons vegetable oil over medium-high heat until hot. Brown chicken in batches, removing pieces to bowl as they brown.

**2** Preheat oven to 350°F. In same Dutch oven, heat remaining 1 teaspoon oil over medium-high heat; cook onions, apple, green pepper, garlic, and ginger 2 minutes, stirring frequently. Reduce heat to medium; cover and cook 5 minutes.

**3** Stir in curry powder, black pepper, and cumin; cook 1 minute. Add tomatoes with their puree, chicken broth, raisins, salt, and chicken pieces; heat to boiling over high heat; boil 1 minute.

**4** Cover Dutch oven and bake 1 hour or until juices run clear when chicken is pierced with tip of knife. *Makes 8 main-dish servings.*

Each serving: About 325 calories, 39 g protein, 21 g carbohydrate, 10 g total fat (2 g saturated), 3 g fiber, 122 mg cholesterol, 710 mg sodium.

# Baked Mushroom-Stuffed Chicken Breasts

PREP: 20 MINUTES / BAKE: 45 MINUTES

½ pound mushrooms, finely chopped
3 medium plum tomatoes, seeded and diced
4 teaspoons soy sauce
¼ cup chopped fresh basil leaves
6 medium bone-in chicken-breast halves, with skin (about 3 pounds)
2 teaspoons dried rosemary, crushed
¼ teaspoon salt

**1** Preheat oven to 450°F.

**2** In nonstick 10-inch skillet, cook mushrooms, tomatoes, and soy sauce over high heat until all liquid evaporates and mushrooms are golden. Remove skillet from heat; stir in basil. Let cool slightly.

**3** Carefully push fingers between skin and meat of chicken-breast halves to form a pocket; place some mushroom mixture into each pocket. Place breasts, skin-side up, in large roasting pan (17" by 11½"); sprinkle with rosemary and salt. Bake 35 to 45 minutes until juices run clear when chicken is pierced with tip of knife. *Makes 6 main-dish servings.*

Each serving: About 260 calories, 38 g protein, 3 g carbohydrate, 10 g total fat (3 g saturated), 1 g fiber, 103 mg cholesterol, 415 mg sodium.

---

## GREAT GO-WITHS

### MANGO SALAD

PREP: 10 MINUTES

*1 large mango*
*2 tablespoons olive oil*
*2 tablespoons white wine vinegar*
*1 teaspoon sugar*
*½ teaspoon salt*
*8 cups loosely packed mixed greens*

**1** Slice long piece of mango from each side of seed; peel mango and cut into bite-size chunks.

**2** In large bowl, mix olive oil, vinegar, sugar, and salt. Toss mango and mixed greens with dressing. Makes 6 accompaniment servings.

Each serving: About 105 calories, 2 g protein, 14 g carbohydrate, 5 g total fat (1 g saturated), 2 g fiber, 0 mg cholesterol, 220 mg sodium.

---

# Baked Herb Chicken

PREP: 20 MINUTES / BAKE: 40 MINUTES

2 tablespoons fresh thyme or 2 teaspoons dried thyme
2 tablespoons chopped fresh rosemary or 2 teaspoons dried rosemary, crushed
1 tablespoon olive or vegetable oil
2 teaspoons paprika
½ teaspoon salt
1 teaspoon coarsely ground black pepper
2 whole chickens (about 3½ pounds each), each cut into quarters

**1** Preheat oven to 425°F. In cup, mix thyme, rosemary, olive oil, paprika, salt, and pepper. With hands, rub chicken quarters with herb mixture.

**2** Place chicken quarters, skin-side up, on rack in large roasting pan. Roast chicken 40 minutes (do not turn) or until golden and juices run clear when pierced with tip of knife. *Makes 8 main-dish servings.*

Each serving: About 435 calories, 48 g protein, 1 g carbohydrate, 26 g total fat (7 g saturated), 0 g fiber, 154 mg cholesterol, 290 mg sodium.

# Spinach-Stuffed Chicken Legs

🐔 🐔 🐔

PREP: 20 MINUTES / BAKE: 50 MINUTES

Our easy way to turn chicken legs into an elegant meal you'll make again and again! Serve with a super-simple Mango Salad (opposite page).

1 package (10 ounces) frozen chopped spinach, thawed and squeezed dry
½ cup packed fresh basil leaves, chopped
¼ cup oil-packed sun-dried tomatoes, chopped
3 tablespoons grated Parmesan cheese
6 large chicken legs (about 4 pounds)
½ teaspoon salt
¼ teaspoon coarsely ground black pepper

**1** Preheat oven to 425°F. In bowl, mix spinach, basil, sun-dried tomatoes, and Parmesan. Carefully push fingers between skin and meat of each chicken leg to form pocket; spread one-sixth of spinach mixture in each pocket.

**2** Arrange chicken, stuffing-side up, in small roasting pan (14" by 10"); sprinkle with salt and pepper. Bake, uncovered, 50 minutes, brushing chicken occasionally with pan drippings, until juices run clear when chicken is pierced with tip of knife.

**3** Arrange chicken on large platter; keep warm. Skim fat from drippings in roasting pan. Add *½ cup water*; heat to boiling over medium heat, stirring to loosen brown bits. Spoon into bowl to serve with chicken. *Makes 6 main-dish servings.*

Each serving: About 395 calories, 42 g protein, 5 g carbohydrate, 22 g total fat (6 g saturated), 2 g fiber, 139 mg cholesterol, 445 mg sodium.

*Spinach-Stuffed Chicken Legs*

# Baked Rosemary Chicken

PREP: 15 MINUTES / BAKE: 35 MINUTES

2 tablespoons all-purpose flour
¼ teaspoon coarsely ground black pepper
¾ teaspoon salt
1 large egg white
¼ cup dried bread crumbs
½ teaspoon dried rosemary, crushed
4 medium bone-in chicken-breast halves (about
   2½ pounds), skin removed
2 tablespoons margarine or butter

**1** Preheat oven to 425°F. On waxed paper, mix flour, pepper, and salt. In pie plate, beat egg white with *1 tablespoon water*. In cup, mix bread crumbs and rosemary. Coat chicken with flour mixture; dip meat side into egg-white mixture. Then sprinkle meat side with bread-crumb mixture; press crumbs firmly onto chicken.

**2** In 13" by 9" metal baking pan, melt margarine or butter in oven; remove pan from oven. Arrange chicken, bread crumb-side down, in melted margarine in pan; bake 25 minutes. Turn chicken over and bake 10 minutes longer or until golden and juices run clear when chicken is pierced with tip of knife. *Makes 4 main-dish servings.*

Each serving: About 300 calories, 45 g protein, 8 g carbohydrate, 8 g total fat (2 g saturated), 0 g fiber, 107 mg cholesterol, 695 mg sodium.

---

## GREAT GO-WITHS

### CARIBBEAN RICE & BEANS

PREP: 5 MINUTES / COOK: 20 MINUTES

½ cup regular long-grain rice
1 tablespoon vegetable oil
1 bunch green onions, cut into 1½-inch pieces
1 large firm banana, cut into ¼-inch-thick slices
1 can (15 to 16 ounces) black beans, rinsed and
   drained

**1** In 2-quart saucepan, prepare rice as label directs but do not use margarine or butter.

**2** Meanwhile, in nonstick 10-inch skillet, heat oil over medium-high heat. Add green onions and cook until golden and tender. Stir in banana and cook until just heated through.

**3** When rice is done, add to skillet with banana mixture. Stir in black beans; heat through. Makes 4 accompaniment servings.

Each serving: About 215 calories, 7 g protein, 38 g carbohydrate, 4 g total fat (1 g saturated), 4 g fiber, 0 mg cholesterol, 185 mg sodium.

---

# Caribbean-Style Baked Chicken

PREP: 15 MINUTES / BAKE: 40 MINUTES

Serve the chicken with Caribbean Rice & Beans (at left). You can make it while the chicken is baking.

1 tablespoon vegetable oil
1 medium onion, chopped
¼ cup apple jelly
½ cup chili sauce
2 tablespoons fresh lime juice
¼ teaspoon ground allspice
¼ teaspoon hot pepper sauce
1 whole chicken (about 3½ pounds), cut into
   quarters, skin removed
1 lime, sliced, for garnish

**1** Preheat oven to 425°F. In 1-quart saucepan, heat oil over medium heat. Add onion and cook until tender and golden. Add apple jelly and cook, stirring constantly, until jelly melts. Stir in chili sauce, lime juice, allspice, and hot pepper sauce until blended. Remove saucepan from heat.

**2** Place chicken quarters, bone-side down, in 13" by 9" metal baking pan. Spoon half of chili-sauce mixture evenly over chicken. Bake 20 minutes. Do not turn chicken. Spoon remaining chili-sauce mixture over chicken; bake 20 minutes longer or until juices run clear when thickest part of chicken is pierced with tip of knife.

**3** Arrange chicken on large platter. Skim fat from pan. Stir *2 tablespoons hot water* into pan, scraping up brown bits. Pour meat juices over chicken. Garnish platter with lime slices. *Makes 4 main-dish servings.*

Each serving: About 370 calories, 42 g protein, 28 g carbohydrate, 9 g total fat (2 g saturated), 1 g fiber, 133 mg cholesterol, 620 mg sodium.

# Italian Chicken & Sausage Casserole

PREP: 15 MINUTES / BAKE: 1 HOUR 5 MINUTES

6 medium red potatoes (about 2 pounds), cut into bite-size chunks
2 garlic cloves, minced
1 whole chicken (about 3½ pounds), cut up
1 pound hot Italian sausage links
1 can (16 ounces) whole tomatoes with tomato puree
1 teaspoon salt
1 teaspoon dried marjoram, crushed
1 bunch broccoli rabe, tough stems discarded

**1** Preheat oven to 375°F. In large roasting pan (17" by 11½"), combine potato chunks, garlic, chicken pieces, sausage links, tomatoes with puree, salt, marjoram, and *½ cup water*. Bake 45 minutes, basting chicken and potatoes occasionally with pan drippings.

**2** Stir in broccoli rabe; cover pan with foil and bake 15 to 20 minutes longer until chicken and vegetables are tender.

**3** Turn chicken pieces skin-side up in pan. Turn oven control to broil. Broil 4 to 5 minutes until chicken skin is browned and crisp. Skim fat from liquid in roasting pan. *Makes 6 main-dish servings.*

Each serving: About 730 calories, 51 g protein, 37 g carbohydrate, 42 g total fat (13 g saturated), 3 g fiber, 178 mg cholesterol, 1175 mg sodium.

# Individual Tex-Mex Chicken Casseroles

PREP: 25 MINUTES / BAKE: 10 MINUTES

1 tablespoon vegetable oil
1 medium onion, diced
2 tablespoons all-purpose flour
1 teaspoon chili powder
1 teaspoon salt
¾ pound skinless, boneless chicken thighs, cut into 1-inch chunks
1 cup milk
1 can (8¾ ounces) creamed corn
1 can (10½ ounces) red kidney beans, rinsed and drained
2 tablespoons chopped fresh cilantro leaves
¼ pound Monterey Jack cheese with jalapeño chiles, shredded (1 cup)
2 cups tortilla chips (2 to 3 ounces)

**1** In nonstick 10-inch skillet, heat oil over medium heat. Add onion and cook until tender. With slotted spoon, transfer onion to bowl.

**2** Meanwhile, on waxed paper, mix flour, chili powder, and salt; use to coat chicken chunks.

**3** Add chicken to skillet and cook until it just loses its pink color throughout. Transfer to bowl with onion.

**4** Stir milk, creamed corn, and kidney beans into skillet; heat to boiling. Stir in chicken and onion, cilantro, and half of cheese; heat through. Remove skillet from heat.

**5** Preheat oven to 375°F. Coarsely break 1 cup tortilla chips and place in bottom of four 10-ounce oven-safe bowls or small casseroles. Place bowls in jelly-roll pan for easier handling. Spoon chicken mixture into bowls; top with remaining shredded cheese. Tuck remaining chips into chicken mixture. Bake 10 minutes or until mixture is hot and bubbly and cheese melts. *Makes 4 main-dish servings.*

Each serving: About 490 calories, 33 g protein, 41 g carbohydrate, 23 g total fat (8 g saturated), 6 g fiber, 109 mg cholesterol, 1240 mg sodium.

# Baked Garlic, Chicken & Shrimp

🐔🐔🐔

PREP: 20 MINUTES / BAKE: 40 MINUTES

Attention, garlic lovers! In this recipe each diner gets a serving of elephant garlic cloves, so named because of their enormous size—one head can weigh up to 1 pound! When roasted, the garlic is sweet and flavorful. (If you can't find elephant garlic, use regular garlic instead.)

1 large head elephant garlic
2 teaspoons plus 1 tablespoon olive or vegetable oil
1 whole chicken (about 3½ pounds), cut up, skin removed
1 tablespoon finely chopped fresh rosemary or 1 teaspoon dried rosemary, crushed
1¼ teaspoons salt
2 teaspoons fresh lemon juice
½ teaspoon coarsely ground black pepper
1 pound large shrimp
Fresh rosemary sprigs for garnish

**1** Preheat oven to 450°F. Separate garlic into cloves, removing any loose papery skin, but do not peel. In large roasting pan (17" by 11½"), toss garlic cloves with 2 teaspoons olive oil. Cover roasting pan with foil and bake garlic 15 minutes.

**2** Meanwhile, cut each chicken-breast piece in half.

**3** In large bowl, mix rosemary, salt, lemon juice, pepper, and remaining 1 tablespoon olive oil; add chicken and toss until well coated. Place chicken in roasting pan with garlic. Bake 15 minutes, uncovered, basting chicken once or twice with drippings.

*Baked Garlic, Chicken & Shrimp*

**4** Meanwhile, with kitchen shears, cut along back of each shrimp, exposing vein, but keeping shell intact. Rinse each shrimp under running cold water to remove vein. Pat shrimp dry with paper towels.

**5** After chicken has baked 15 minutes, add shrimp to chicken mixture, tossing to coat shrimp with drippings in pan. Bake 10 minutes longer, uncovered, or until shrimp turn opaque throughout and juices run clear when chicken is pierced with tip of knife.

**6** To serve, arrange chicken, shrimp, and garlic on platter. Spoon pan drippings over. Garnish with rosemary. *Makes 6 main-dish servings.*

Each serving: About 325 calories, 43 g protein, 17 g carbohydrate, 9 g total fat (2 g saturated), 1 g fiber, 182 mg cholesterol, 680 mg sodium.

# Chicken Mexicana
🐓 🐓 🐓
PREP: 15 MINUTES / BAKE: 45 MINUTES

Serve with Tomato Salsa (page 103).

1 can (4 to 4½ ounces) chopped mild green chiles
½ cup Dijon mustard
1 tablespoon fresh lime juice
½ teaspoon coarsely ground black pepper
⅔ cup dried bread crumbs
⅔ cup yellow cornmeal
1 tablespoon paprika
2 tablespoons coarsely chopped fresh cilantro
   leaves
1¼ teaspoons salt
1 teaspoon dried oregano
2 whole chickens (about 3 pounds each), cut up,
   skin removed
Nonstick cooking spray
2 tablespoons olive or vegetable oil

**1** In small bowl, mix chiles, mustard, lime juice, and pepper until blended. On waxed paper, mix bread crumbs, cornmeal, paprika, cilantro, salt, and oregano.

**2** Preheat oven to 425°F. Evenly brush mustard mixture onto chicken, then coat with bread-crumb mixture, firmly pressing crumb mixture onto chicken.

**3** Spray large roasting pan (17" by 11½") with nonstick cooking spray. Place chicken in roasting pan. With brush, lightly dab olive oil onto chicken.

**4** Bake chicken (do not turn) 40 to 45 minutes until coating is crisp and browned and juices run clear when pierced with tip of knife.

**5** To serve, arrange chicken on large platter. *Makes 8 main-dish servings.*

Each serving: About 325 calories, 37 g protein, 17 g carbohydrate, 9 g total fat (2 g saturated), 1 g fiber, 114 mg cholesterol, 1020 mg sodium.

# Indian-Spiced Chicken
🐓 🐓 🐓
PREP: 10 MINUTES / BAKE: 50 MINUTES

1 container (16 ounces) plain low-fat yogurt
¼ cup hot pepper sauce
2 tablespoons chopped fresh parsley leaves
2 tablespoons fresh lime juice
1¼ teaspoons salt
¼ teaspoon ground ginger
¼ teaspoon ground cardamom (optional)
2 whole chickens (about 3½ pounds each), each
   cut into quarters, skin removed
Lime wedges

**1** Preheat oven to 450°F. In medium bowl, with wire whisk or fork, mix yogurt, hot pepper sauce, parsley, lime juice, salt, ginger, and cardamom, if using, until well blended.

**2** Tuck wings under chicken breasts. Dip chicken quarters in yogurt mixture to coat both sides thoroughly; arrange chicken in 1 layer in large roasting pan (17" by 11½"). Spoon any remaining yogurt mixture over chicken quarters.

**3** Bake chicken, basting once or twice with pan drippings, 50 minutes or until coating is golden brown and juices run clear when thickest part of chicken is pierced with tip of knife, covering loosely with a sheet of foil during last 10 minutes of cooking if coating begins to brown too quickly.

**4** To serve, arrange chicken quarters on warm large platter. Garnish with lime wedges to be squeezed over chicken. *Makes 8 main-dish servings.*

Each serving: About 310 calories, 44 g protein, 4 g carbohydrate, 11 g total fat (3 g saturated), 0 g fiber, 130 mg cholesterol, 720 mg sodium.

# Sage-Baked Chicken

PREP: 25 MINUTES / BAKE: 50 MINUTES

¾ teaspoon coarsely ground black pepper
½ teaspoon rubbed sage
½ teaspoon salt
6 medium chicken legs (about 3¼ pounds)
1 pound medium mushrooms, each cut into quarters
1 tablespoon soy sauce
2 teaspoons all-purpose flour

**1** Preheat oven to 400°F. In small bowl, combine pepper, sage, and salt. Rub chicken legs with sage mixture. Arrange chicken legs in large roasting pan (17" by 11½").

**2** Bake chicken, uncovered, 45 to 50 minutes, basting occasionally with pan drippings, until juices run clear when chicken is pierced with tip of knife.

**3** Meanwhile, in nonstick 12-inch skillet, cook mushrooms over medium-high heat, stirring frequently, until all liquid evaporates. Add soy sauce and cook 1 minute. Set skillet aside.

**4** When chicken is done, transfer to large platter. Skim fat from drippings in roasting pan. In small bowl, combine flour and *1 cup water*. Pour flour mixture into drippings in roasting pan; heat to boiling over medium heat, stirring to loosen brown bits.

**5** Pour drippings mixture from roasting pan into skillet with mushrooms; heat to boiling over high heat. Reduce heat to low; simmer 2 minutes or until gravy thickens slightly.

**6** Spoon mushroom gravy over chicken. *Makes 6 main-dish servings.*

Each serving: About 305 calories, 33 g protein, 5 g carbohydrate, 17 g total fat (5 g saturated), 1 g fiber, 111 mg cholesterol, 475 mg sodium.

# Tandoori-Style Baked Chicken Breasts

PREP: 10 MINUTES PLUS MARINATING / BAKE: 30 MINUTES

A low-fat yogurt marinade packed with spices tenderizes the chicken. Great with rice and grilled onions.

1 container (8 ounces) plain low-fat yogurt
½ small onion, chopped
1 tablespoon paprika
2 tablespoons fresh lime juice
1 tablespoon minced, peeled fresh ginger
1 teaspoon ground cumin
1 teaspoon ground coriander
¾ teaspoon salt
¼ teaspoon ground red pepper (cayenne)
Pinch ground cloves
6 medium bone-in chicken-breast halves (about 3 pounds), skin removed
Lime wedges for garnish

**1** In blender, blend yogurt, onion, paprika, lime juice, ginger, cumin, coriander, salt, ground red pepper, and ground cloves until smooth. Place chicken in medium bowl or zip-tight plastic bag with marinade. Marinate in refrigerator 30 minutes.

**2** Preheat oven to 450°F. Place chicken on rack in medium roasting pan (15" by 10"). Spoon half of marinade over chicken and bake 30 minutes or until juices run clear when pierced with tip of knife. Garnish with lime wedges. *Makes 6 main-dish servings.*

Each serving: About 195 calories, 36 g protein, 5 g carbohydrate, 3 g total fat (1 g saturated), 0 g fiber, 88 mg cholesterol, 415 mg sodium.

*Tandoori-Style Baked Chicken Breasts* ➤

## QUICK CHICKEN POTPIE

PREP: 30 MINUTES / BAKE: 10 MINUTES

*2 tablespoons margarine or butter*
*1½ pounds skinless, boneless chicken breasts, cut*
*    for stir-fry*
*1 small onion, minced*
*2 tablespoons cornstarch*
*¾ cup chicken broth*
*1 package (16 ounces) frozen mixed vegetables*
*    (carrots, cauliflower, green beans, zucchini,*
*    and butter beans)*
*1 cup half-and-half or light cream*
*1 tablespoon Dijon mustard*
*¼ teaspoon dried rosemary, crushed*
*¼ teaspoon salt*
*¼ teaspoon coarsely ground black pepper*
*1 package (8 ounces) refrigerated crescent*
*    dinner rolls*

**1** In 10-inch skillet with oven-safe handle (or cover skillet handle with heavy-duty foil when baking in oven later), melt margarine or butter over medium heat. Add chicken, half at a time, and cook until lightly browned. With slotted spoon, transfer chicken to bowl.

**2** Preheat oven to 400°F. Add onion to skillet and cook until tender. In cup, stir cornstarch and chicken broth until smooth. Add cornstarch mixture, frozen vegetables, half-and-half, mustard, rosemary, salt, and pepper to skillet; heat to boiling, stirring constantly. Stir in chicken. Remove skillet from heat.

**3** Unroll crescent dough on lightly floured surface; separate into 2 rectangles. For each rectangle, pinch perforations to seal and roll dough to measure 11" by 4". Cut each rectangle lengthwise into four 1-inch-wide strips. Use strips to make lattice top over chicken mixture, allowing excess dough to extend over side of skillet. Then, twist excess dough and place around edge of skillet. Bake 10 minutes or until crust is golden brown. Makes 6 main-dish servings.

Each serving: About 395 calories, 32 g protein, 27 g carbohydrate, 17 g total fat (6 g saturated), 2 g fiber, 81 mg cholesterol, 730 mg sodium.

# Chicken in Phyllo Packets

PREP: 40 MINUTES / BAKE: 50 MINUTES

1 tablespoon vegetable oil
1 jumbo onion (1 pound), chopped
1 pound skinless, boneless chicken thighs, coarsely
    chopped
½ teaspoon salt
1 package (10 ounces) frozen chopped spinach,
    thawed and squeezed dry
½ teaspoon grated lemon peel
¼ teaspoon coarsely ground black pepper
½ cup crumbled feta cheese (2 ounces)
Nonstick cooking spray
8 sheets fresh or frozen (thawed) phyllo (about
    17" by 12" each)

**1** In nonstick 12-inch skillet, heat oil over medium-high heat. Add onion and stir until coated with oil. Reduce heat to low; cover and cook until onion is tender and translucent, about 10 minutes.

**2** Add chicken and salt to skillet. Cook until onion and chicken begin to brown, about 10 minutes. Add spinach, lemon peel, and pepper, stirring to mix well; remove skillet from heat. Gently stir in feta cheese.

**3** Preheat oven to 350°F. Spray large cookie sheet with nonstick cooking spray. On work surface, place 1 sheet phyllo with a short side facing you; spray lightly with nonstick cooking spray. Top with another phyllo sheet. Spoon one-fourth of chicken mixture in 6-inch-long log along center of edge of short side facing you; fold long sides toward center over filling. From chicken-mixture side, roll phyllo jelly-roll fashion, to make a packet. Place packet on cookie sheet; spray with nonstick cooking spray. Repeat with remaining phyllo and chicken mixture to make 3 more packets.

**4** Bake phyllo packets 45 to 50 minutes until golden brown. *Makes 4 main-dish servings.*

Each serving: About 390 calories, 30 g protein, 33 g carbohydrate, 16 g total fat (4 g saturated), 3 g fiber, 107 mg cholesterol, 785 mg sodium.

# Chicken Phyllo Pie

### 🐔 🐔 🐔

PREP: 40 MINUTES / BAKE: 20 MINUTES

We top our potpie with light, flaky sheets of phyllo in place of rich pastry dough. And, to cut down even more on fat and calories, we sprayed the phyllo sheets with nonstick cooking spray instead of brushing them with melted butter or margarine.

2 tablespoons olive or vegetable oil

1 pound skinless, boneless chicken breasts, cut into 1-inch chunks

1 small onion, finely chopped

2 tablespoons all-purpose flour

3 medium red potatoes (about ½ pound), cut into 1-inch chunks

2 medium carrots, peeled and sliced

2 medium parsnips, cut into 1-inch chunks

½ teaspoon dried thyme

½ teaspoon salt

¼ teaspoon coarsely ground black pepper

1 can (14½ ounces) chicken broth or 1¾ cups homemade (page 11)

1 package (9 ounces) frozen Italian green beans, thawed

4 sheets fresh or frozen (thawed) phyllo (about 17" by 12" each)

Olive-oil nonstick cooking spray

¼ cup dried bread crumbs

**1** In 4-quart saucepan, heat 1 tablespoon olive oil over medium-high heat until very hot. Add chicken and cook until it just loses its pink color throughout. With slotted spoon, transfer chicken to bowl.

**2** Add remaining 1 tablespoon olive oil to saucepan and heat over medium heat. Add onion and cook until tender and lightly browned. Stir in flour; cook 1 minute. Stir in potatoes, carrots, parsnips, thyme, salt, pepper, and chicken broth; heat to boiling over high heat. Reduce heat to low; cover and simmer until vegetables are tender, about 15 minutes. Stir in frozen Italian green beans; heat through.

**3** Stir chicken into mixture in saucepan; spoon into shallow 1½-quart casserole.

**4** Preheat oven to 375°F. Place 1 sheet of phyllo on work surface; spray lightly with cooking spray; sprinkle with 1 tablespoon bread crumbs. Keeping crumb-side up, gather edges of phyllo to fit top of casserole; gently place phyllo on top of chicken mixture so edge is within rim of casserole. Repeat with remaining phyllo and bread crumbs to cover chicken mixture completely.

**5** Bake potpie 15 to 20 minutes until phyllo is golden brown and chicken mixture is hot. *Makes 4 main-dish servings.*

Each serving: About 440 calories, 33 g protein, 50 g carbohydrate, 12 g total fat (2 g saturated), 8 g fiber, 66 mg cholesterol, 985 mg sodium.

## GREAT GO-WITHS

# CURRIED PEACH & CRANBERRY CHUTNEY

PREP: 5 MINUTES / COOK: 10 MINUTES

Make this sweet-tart chutney up to one week in advance. Reheat before serving or serve cold.

*2 cans (16 ounces each) sliced cling peaches in light syrup, drained and cut up*

*1 jar (8 to 8½ ounces) mango chutney, large pieces cut up*

*1 cup cranberries*

*1 tablespoon sugar*

*½ teaspoon curry powder*

In 3-quart saucepan, combine peaches, chutney, cranberries, sugar, and curry powder; heat to boiling over high heat. Reduce heat to medium and cook, uncovered, 8 to 10 minutes, stirring occasionally until mixture thickens slightly and cranberries pop. Serve sauce warm or cover and refrigerate to serve cold. Makes about 3 cups.

Each tablespoon: About 20 calories, 0 g protein, 5 g carbohydrate, 0 g total fat (0 g saturated), 0 g fiber, 0 mg cholesterol, 2 mg sodium.

# Spicy Deep-Dish Turkey Potpie

🦃🦃🦃

PREP: I HOUR 30 MINUTES / BAKE: 40 MINUTES

2 tablespoons vegetable oil
I large onion, coarsely chopped
1½ pounds lean ground turkey breast
I teaspoon salt
2 tablespoons chili powder
I can (14½ to 16 ounces) stewed tomatoes
I package (10 ounces) frozen lima beans
I can (7¼ to 8 ounces) whole-kernel corn, drained
2 cans (4 to 4½ ounces each) chopped mild green chiles
I teaspoon dried oregano
2 tablespoons cornstarch
3 cups all-purpose flour
I cup shortening
I large egg

**1** In nonstick 12-inch skillet, heat oil over medium-high heat. Add onion and cook until tender. Add ground turkey and ½ teaspoon salt; cook, stirring frequently, until all pan juices evaporate and turkey is browned. Stir in chili powder; cook 1 minute.

**2** Add stewed tomatoes with their liquid, frozen lima beans, corn, green chiles with their liquid, oregano, and *1½ cups water*; heat to boiling over high heat. Reduce heat to medium-low. Simmer, uncovered, 20 minutes. In cup, with fork, mix cornstarch with *2 tablespoons water*. Stir cornstarch mixture into simmering turkey mixture; heat over high heat until mixture boils and thickens. Remove skillet from heat.

**3** Prepare pastry: In large bowl, with fork, stir flour and remaining ½ teaspoon salt. With pastry blender or two knives used scissor-fashion, cut in shortening until mixture resembles coarse crumbs. Sprinkle *6 to 8 tablespoons cold water*, 1 tablespoon at a time, into mixture, mixing lightly with fork after each addition, until dough is just moist enough to hold together. Reserve one-third of dough for decorating pie; wrap with plastic wrap. Divide remaining dough into 2 pieces, one slightly larger; shape each into a ball. On lightly floured surface, with floured rolling pin, roll larger ball of dough into a round 1½ inches larger all around than 9½" by 1½" deep-dish pie plate. Transfer round to plate and ease into plate. Spoon turkey mixture into crust.

**4** Preheat oven to 375°F. Roll smaller ball of dough into 10-inch round. Center round over filling in bottom crust. Trim edges even with pie plate. Cut slits in top crust to allow steam to escape during baking.

**5** Roll out about one-fourth of reserved dough ⅛ inch thick. With 4-inch turkey-shaped cookie cutter or tip of knife, cut out turkey shape, reserving trimmings. Place on small cookie sheet. In cup, with fork, beat egg with *1 tablespoon water*. Brush turkey cutout with some egg mixture. Bake 10 to 12 minutes until golden; cool on wire rack.

**6** Meanwhile, to make double-twist piecrust edge, roll remaining reserved dough and any trimmings into four 16-inch-long pencil-thin ropes. Moisten edge of crust with *water*. Place pastry twists around edge of pie, joining ends together to cover edge completely.

---

## GREAT GO-WITHS

## ZUCCHINI & SQUASH SLAW

PREP: 20 MINUTES

*3 tablespoons olive or vegetable oil*
*1 tablespoon cider vinegar*
*1 tablespoon Dijon mustard*
*1 tablespoon chopped fresh dill or ½ teaspoon dried dill weed*
*1 tablespoon chopped fresh parsley leaves*
*¾ teaspoon salt*
*¼ teaspoon coarsely ground black pepper*
*2 small zucchini (about 8 ounces each), cut crosswise in half, then cut into matchstick-thin strips*
*2 small yellow straightneck squash (about 8 ounces each), cut crosswise in half, then cut into matchstick-thin strips*
*1 bunch or 1 bag (6 ounces) radishes, each cut lengthwise in half*

In large bowl, with wire whisk or fork, mix olive oil, vinegar, mustard, dill, parsley, salt, and pepper. Add zucchini, yellow squash, and radishes; toss to coat. Cover and refrigerate if not serving right away. Makes 6 accompaniment servings.

*Each serving: About 95 calories, 2 g protein, 6 g carbohydrate, 7 g total fat (1 g saturated), 2 g fiber, 0 mg cholesterol, 360 mg sodium.*

**7** Brush top of pie and edge with egg mixture. Bake 35 to 40 minutes until crust is golden and filling is hot. Use turkey cutout to decorate top of pie. *Makes 8 main-dish servings.*

Each serving: About 630 calories, 31 g protein, 57 g carbohydrate, 31 g total fat (7 g saturated), 5 g fiber, 80 mg cholesterol, 725 mg sodium.

# Chicken Popover

🐓 🐓 🐓

PREP: 25 MINUTES / BAKE: 55 MINUTES

3 tablespoons margarine or butter
I teaspoon dried sage
¼ teaspoon coarsely ground black pepper
1¼ cups all-purpose flour
1½ teaspoons salt
I whole chicken (about 3½ pounds), cut up
3 large eggs
1½ cups milk
I teaspoon baking powder
¼ cup chopped fresh parsley leaves

**I** Preheat oven to 400°F. In 15" by 9" baking dish or small open roasting pan, melt margarine or butter in oven. Remove baking dish from oven.

**2** On waxed paper, mix sage, pepper, ¼ cup flour, and 1 teaspoon salt; use to coat chicken pieces. Dip chicken pieces, one at a time, into melted margarine in baking dish to coat both sides; then arrange chicken, skin-side up, in dish. Bake 30 minutes.

**3** In large bowl, with mixer at low speed, beat eggs until frothy; beat in milk until blended. Beat in baking powder, remaining 1 cup flour, and remaining ½ teaspoon salt until batter is smooth. Stir in parsley.

**4** Pour batter over chicken in baking dish. Bake 25 minutes longer or until chicken is tender and popover is puffed and golden brown. Serve immediately. *Makes 4 main-dish servings.*

Each serving: About 915 calories, 62 g protein, 35 g carbohydrate, 56 g total fat (16 g saturated), 1 g fiber, 375 mg cholesterol, 1380 mg sodium.

# Chicken Turnovers

🐓 🐓 🐓

PREP: 45 MINUTES / BAKE: 30 MINUTES

I tablespoon vegetable oil
1¼ pounds ground chicken
I medium onion, finely chopped
I teaspoon salt
¾ teaspoon dried oregano
¼ teaspoon coarsely ground black pepper
I large bunch spinach, coarsely chopped
2 medium plum tomatoes, seeded and diced
I container (8 ounces) part-skim ricotta cheese
I tablespoon fresh lemon juice
I large egg
10 sheets fresh or frozen (thawed) phyllo (about 17" by 12" each)
Nonstick cooking spray

**I** In 12-inch skillet, heat oil over medium-high heat until very hot. Add ground chicken, onion, salt, oregano, and pepper and cook, stirring frequently, until all the liquid evaporates and chicken and onion are golden. Stir in spinach; cook, stirring, until spinach wilts.

**2** Preheat oven to 375°F. In large bowl, mix ground-chicken mixture with tomatoes, ricotta cheese, lemon juice, and egg until well blended.

**3** Arrange phyllo sheets on top of one another; cut stack lengthwise in half. Place strips on waxed paper; cover with slightly damp paper towels to prevent phyllo from drying out. Place 1 phyllo strip on work surface; spray with nonstick cooking spray. Top with another strip.

**4** Place scant ½ cup chicken mixture at end of strip; fold one corner of phyllo strip diagonally over filling so that the short edge meets the long edge of strip, forming a right angle. Continue folding over at right angles, being careful to fold filling securely inside phyllo, until you reach the end of the strip to form a triangular package. Place package, seam-side down, on greased large cookie sheet; spray with nonstick cooking spray.

**5** Repeat with remaining phyllo and filling to make 10 turnovers in all. Bake turnovers 25 to 30 minutes until golden. *Makes 10 turnovers.*

Each turnover: About 230 calories, 17 g protein, 16 g carbohydrate, 11 g total fat (3 g saturated), 3 g fiber, 75 mg cholesterol, 480 mg sodium.

# Light Chicken Drumsticks

### 🐓 🐓 🐓

PREP: 30 MINUTES / BAKE: 40 MINUTES

Removing the skin makes this a much more diet-friendly dish, but using dark-meat drumsticks assures that the flavor level stays high. If you like spicy food, use one of the spicy steak sauces available. For an attractive presentation, but also to act as a side dish, garnish the platter with carrot sticks, celery sticks, and tomato wedges.

Nonstick cooking spray
4 slices firm-textured bread
¼ cup loosely packed parsley leaves
½ cup bottled steak sauce

16 large chicken drumsticks (about 4½ pounds), skin removed
¾ cup honey-crunch wheat germ
1 tablespoon chili powder
½ teaspoon salt
¼ teaspoon ground red pepper (cayenne)
1 large egg white

**1** Preheat oven to 400°F. Spray large roasting pan (17" by 11½") with nonstick cooking spray.

**2** In blender or in food processor with knife blade attached, blend bread with parsley to make coarse bread crumbs and to chop parsley. Place bread-crumb mixture on waxed paper.

**3** Brush steak sauce on 8 chicken drumsticks; dip into bread-crumb mixture to coat. Place in roasting pan.

**4** On another sheet of waxed paper, mix wheat germ, chili powder, salt, and ground red pepper. In pie plate, with fork, mix egg white with *1 tablespoon water*. Toss remaining chicken drumsticks in egg mixture, then

---

## STICKY DRUMSTICKS

PREP: 20 MINUTES / BAKE: ABOUT 35 MINUTES

Have lots of napkins on hand for these delicious oven-barbecued drumsticks. These are guaranteed to be a favorite with the kids in your family, too.

*½ cup apricot preserves*
*¼ cup teriyaki sauce*
*1 tablespoon dark brown sugar*
*1 teaspoon cornstarch*
*1 teaspoon cider vinegar*
*¼ teaspoon salt*
*12 medium chicken drumsticks (about 3 pounds), skin removed*

**1** Preheat oven to 425°F. In large bowl, with wire whisk, mix apricot preserves, teriyaki sauce, brown sugar, cornstarch, vinegar, and salt until blended. Add chicken drumsticks, tossing to coat.

**2** Spoon chicken and sauce into 15½" by 10½" jelly-roll pan. Bake 15 minutes. Remove chicken from oven; with pastry brush, brush chicken with sauce in pan. Cook chicken 15 to 20 minutes longer, brushing with sauce every 5 minutes.

**3** Remove chicken from oven; brush with sauce. Allow chicken to cool on jelly-roll pan 10 minutes

before serving. Place chicken in serving dish; spoon sauce in jelly-roll pan over chicken. Makes 12 main-dish servings.

Each serving: About 115 calories, 13 g protein, 11 g carbohydrate, 2 g total fat (1 g saturated), 0 g fiber, 47 mg cholesterol, 335 mg sodium.

roll in wheat-germ mixture to coat. Place in pan with other drumsticks.

**5** Bake drumsticks 35 to 40 minutes until coating is crisp and golden brown, and juices run clear when chicken is pierced with tip of knife. *Makes 8 main-dish servings.*

Each serving (1 of each kind of drumstick) without vegetable garnish: About 270 calories, 33 g protein, 17 g carbohydrate, 7 g total fat (1 g saturated), 2 g fiber, 106 mg cholesterol, 610 mg sodium.

# Creole Chicken Drumsticks

PREP: 10 MINUTES / COOK: 25 MINUTES

1 tablespoon vegetable oil
8 small chicken drumsticks (about 2 pounds)
1 small green pepper, cut into bite-size pieces
1 medium onion, thinly sliced
¼ pound smoked ham, in one piece, cut into
    ½-inch chunks
1 cup regular long-grain rice
1 can (8 ounces) stewed tomatoes
1 can (14½ ounces) chicken broth or 1¾ cups
    homemade (page 11)
½ teaspoon hot pepper sauce
1 can (3½ ounces drained weight) pitted ripe
    olives, drained

**1** In 12-inch skillet, heat oil over high heat until very hot. Add chicken and cook 5 minutes or until lightly browned, turning occasionally. Push chicken to one side of skillet; add green pepper, onion, ham, and rice. Cook 5 minutes or until rice is lightly browned, stirring often.

**2** Add stewed tomatoes, chicken broth, and hot pepper sauce; heat to boiling over high heat. Reduce heat to medium low; cover and cook 15 minutes or until chicken and rice are tender. Stir in olives; heat through. *Makes 4 main-dish servings.*

Each serving: About 555 calories, 40 g protein, 48 g carbohydrate, 22 g total fat (5 g saturated), 3 g fiber, 137 mg cholesterol, 1340 mg sodium.

# "Fried" Chicken

PREP: 15 MINUTES / BAKE: 45 MINUTES

For our update of Grandma's Southern Fried Chicken, we baked the chicken instead of frying it and removed all the skin first—reducing fat, not flavor. Serve the chicken with any one of the salsas on page 103.

1 container (8 ounces) plain low-fat yogurt
1¼ teaspoons salt
1 cup dried bread crumbs
¾ teaspoon coarsely ground black pepper
4 large bone-in chicken-breast halves (about
    2½ pounds), skin removed
4 large chicken legs (about 2¼ pounds), separated
    into drumstick and thigh, skin removed

**1** Preheat oven to 425°F. In pie plate, mix yogurt and salt. On waxed paper, mix bread crumbs and black pepper. Coat chicken pieces lightly with yogurt mixture, then dip in bread-crumb mixture to coat.

**2** Arrange chicken pieces in single layer in large roasting pan (17" by 11½"). Bake 40 to 45 minutes, without turning, until chicken is fork-tender and juices run clear when chicken is pierced with tip of knife.

**3** When chicken is done, if you like, turn oven control to broil. Broil chicken in roasting pan 4 to 5 minutes until coating is golden brown. *Makes 6 main-dish servings.*

Each serving: About 345 calories, 52 g protein, 16 g carbohydrate, 7 g total fat (2 g saturated), 1 g fiber, 151 mg cholesterol, 830 mg sodium.

# Sesame Chicken Wings

### 🐓 🐓 🐓
PREP: 15 MINUTES / BAKE: 1 HOUR

12 medium chicken wings (about 3 pounds)
3 tablespoons soy sauce
3 tablespoons dry sherry
1 tablespoon grated, peeled fresh ginger
2 teaspoons Asian sesame oil
4 tablespoons maple syrup
1 tablespoon sesame seeds
1 small head romaine lettuce, sliced

**1** Preheat oven to 400°F. In small roasting pan or 13" by 9" baking pan, toss chicken wings with soy sauce, sherry, ginger, sesame oil, and 2 tablespoons maple syrup. Bake 45 minutes, basting often with soy-sauce mixture in pan and adding *water* to pan during baking if mixture looks dry.

**2** After chicken wings have baked 45 minutes, brush with remaining 2 tablespoons maple syrup; sprinkle with sesame seeds. Bake 15 minutes longer or until wings are browned and very tender.

**3** Line platter with romaine lettuce; arrange wings on lettuce. Skim fat from drippings in roasting pan. Pour drippings over wings and lettuce. *Makes 4 main-dish servings.*

Each serving: About 490 calories, 38 g protein, 18 g carbohydrate, 29 g total fat (8 g saturated), 2 g fiber, 109 mg cholesterol, 890 mg sodium.

# Oven-Fried Chicken with Mushroom Gravy

### 🐓 🐓 🐓
PREP: 25 MINUTES / BAKE: 40 MINUTES

¼ cup plus 2 tablespoons all-purpose flour
1 teaspoon salt
½ teaspoon coarsely ground black pepper
¾ cup seasoned dried bread crumbs
1 large egg
2¼ cups milk
1 whole chicken (about 3½ pounds), cut up, skin removed
3 tablespoons vegetable oil
½ pound medium mushrooms, sliced
4 teaspoons soy sauce

**1** Preheat oven to 425°F. On sheet of waxed paper, mix ¼ cup flour, ¾ teaspoon salt, and pepper. On another sheet of waxed paper, place bread crumbs. In pie plate, with fork, beat egg with ¼ cup milk. Coat chicken pieces with flour mixture; dip into egg mixture, then coat with bread crumbs.

**2** Place chicken pieces in large roasting pan (17" by 11½"); drizzle with 2 tablespoons oil. Bake 40 minutes or until chicken is golden and juices run clear when chicken is pierced with tip of knife. Do not turn chicken. Remove pan from oven; keep chicken warm.

**3** Meanwhile, in nonstick 10-inch skillet, heat remaining 1 tablespoon oil over medium-high heat. Add mushrooms and cook until tender and golden and liquid evaporates. Stir in remaining 2 tablespoons flour and remaining ¼ teaspoon salt. Gradually stir in soy sauce and remaining 2 cups milk. Cook, stirring frequently, until mushroom gravy boils and thickens slightly. Pour gravy into gravy boat.

**4** To serve, arrange chicken on warm large platter. Pass mushroom gravy to spoon over chicken. *Makes 6 main-dish servings.*

Each serving: About 400 calories, 35 g protein, 22 g carbohydrate, 19 g total fat (5 g saturated), 1 g fiber, 132 mg cholesterol, 870 mg sodium.

# Easy Oven Meatballs

### 🐓 🐓 🐓

PREP: 20 MINUTES / BAKE: 25 MINUTES

There"s no fuss, no muss, no splatter because you oven-bake these delicious turkey meatballs—in just 25 minutes! Serve them over cooked spaghetti or rice.

2 slices white bread, chopped into fine crumbs
1 tablespoon grated onion
1 pound lean ground turkey breast
1 package (10 ounces) frozen chopped spinach, thawed and squeezed dry
1 teaspoon salt
¼ teaspoon coarsely ground black pepper
1 large egg
3 medium carrots, peeled and thinly sliced

¼ pound mushrooms, cut into ½-inch pieces
1 jar (30 ounces) marinara-style pasta sauce

**1** Preheat oven to 400°F. Grease 13" by 9" metal baking pan. In large bowl, mix bread crumbs and onion with ground turkey, spinach, salt, pepper, and egg.

**2** Shape turkey mixture into 16 meatballs. Place meatballs in pan and bake 25 minutes or until meatballs are lightly browned and cooked through.

**3** Meanwhile, in 3-quart saucepan, heat carrots, mushrooms, pasta sauce, and ½ *cup water* to boiling over high heat. Reduce heat to low; cover and simmer 20 minutes. When meatballs are done, add to sauce; cover and simmer 10 minutes longer to blend flavors and cook vegetables until tender. *Makes 4 main-dish servings.*

Each serving: About 370 calories, 37 g protein, 38 g carbohydrate, 10 g total fat (2 g saturated), 7 g fiber, 124 mg cholesterol, 2130 mg sodium.

*Easy Oven Meatballs*

# No-Crust Mexican Chicken Quiche

PREP: 30 MINUTES / BAKE: 30 MINUTES

1 bunch green onions
2 teaspoons vegetable oil
¾ pound ground chicken
1 tablespoon chili powder
½ teaspoon salt
½ jar (7 ounces) roasted red peppers, drained and cut into thin strips
Nonstick cooking spray
8 large eggs
6 egg whites
1¼ cups reduced-fat (2%) milk
¾ cup shredded Cheddar cheese

**1** Set aside 10 pretty strips of green onion tops for making lattice-top garnish on quiche. Chop enough remaining green onions to equal ½ cup (reserve any remaining green onions for use another day).

**2** In nonstick 10-inch skillet, heat *½ inch water* to boiling over high heat. Add green-onion tops and cook 1 minute. Remove green-onion tops from water and drain on paper towels. Wipe skillet dry with paper towels.

**3** Preheat oven to 400°F. In same skillet, heat oil over medium-high heat. Add chopped green onions and ground chicken and cook, stirring frequently, until pan juices evaporate and green onions are tender. Stir in chili powder, salt, and half of roasted red-pepper strips; cook 1 minute.

**4** Spray 10-inch quiche dish with nonstick cooking spray. Spoon chicken mixture into quiche dish.

**5** In medium bowl, with wire whisk or fork, mix whole eggs, egg whites, milk, and ½ cup cheese; pour over chicken mixture. Sprinkle remaining ¼ cup cheese, then remaining roasted red-pepper strips over quiche. Lay 5 green-onion tops about 1½ inches apart across top of quiche. Lay remaining 5 green-onion tops diagonally across first ones to make a lattice design.

**6** Bake quiche 25 to 30 minutes until knife inserted in center comes out clean. *Makes 6 main-dish servings.*

Each serving: About 315 calories, 28 g protein, 7 g carbohydrate, 19 g total fat (7 g saturated), 1 g fiber, 349 mg cholesterol, 530 mg sodium.

# Parmesan-Coated Oven-Fried Chicken

PREP: 15 MINUTES / BAKE: 35 MINUTES

Olive-oil nonstick cooking spray
½ cup plain dried bread crumbs
¼ cup grated Parmesan cheese
2 tablespoons yellow cornmeal
½ teaspoon ground red pepper (cayenne)
1 egg white
½ teaspoon salt
1 whole chicken (about 3½ pounds), cut up and skin removed
Green onions for garnish

**1** Preheat oven to 425°F. Spray 15½" by 10½" jelly-roll pan with cooking spray.

**2** On waxed paper, mix bread crumbs, Parmesan, cornmeal, and ground red pepper. In pie plate, beat egg white and salt.

**3** Dip each piece of chicken in egg-white mixture, then coat with bread-crumb mixture. Place chicken in pan; spray lightly with cooking spray.

**4** Bake chicken 35 minutes or until coating is crisp and juices run clear when chicken is pierced with tip of knife. Garnish with green onions if you like. *Makes 4 main-dish servings.*

Each serving: About 325 calories, 46 g protein, 14 g carbohydrate, 8 g total fat (3 g saturated), 1 g fiber, 137 mg cholesterol, 660 mg sodium.

*Parmesan-Coated Oven-Fried Chicken* ➤

# Biscuit-Topped Chicken Casserole

🐓 🐓 🐓

PREP: 1 HOUR / BAKE: 30 MINUTES

¼ cup elbow macaroni
2 tablespoons vegetable oil
1¼ pounds skinless, boneless chicken breasts, cut into bite-size chunks
2 medium onions, coarsely sliced
1 medium head green cabbage (2½ pounds), coarsely sliced
¾ teaspoon salt
¼ cup all-purpose flour
1 can (14½ ounces) chicken broth or 1¾ cups homemade (page 11)
1 cup frozen peas
1 jar (4 ounces) pimientos, drained and cut into thin strips
2¼ cups buttermilk baking mix
⅔ cup milk
Parsley leaves
1 egg yolk, slightly beaten

**1** In 2-quart saucepan, in *3 cups boiling water*, cook macaroni until tender. Drain; set aside.

**2** In 12-inch skillet, heat oil over medium-high heat until very hot. Add chicken and cook until lightly browned on all sides. Transfer chicken to plate. Add onions, cabbage, and salt to skillet and cook over high heat until vegetables are browned. Reduce heat to medium-low; cover and cook until vegetables are very tender, about 20 minutes, stirring occasionally.

**3** In cup, mix flour with *½ cup water*; stir into cabbage mixture with chicken broth and *1½ cups water*. Over high heat, cook, stirring constantly, until mixture boils and thickens slightly. Stir in frozen peas, pimientos, cooked chicken, and macaroni. Spoon chicken mixture into 2½-quart casserole.

**4** Preheat oven to 350°F. Prepare buttermilk baking mix for rolled biscuits with milk as label directs but do not bake. Place biscuits on top of chicken mixture in casserole to cover mixture completely. Place 1 parsley leaf on each biscuit. Brush biscuits lightly with beaten egg yolk.

**5** Bake casserole 25 to 30 minutes until biscuits are golden and mixture is hot and bubbly. To prevent overbrowning, cover with foil last 10 minutes. *Makes 6 main-dish servings.*

Each serving: About 510 calories, 32 g protein, 55 g carbohydrate, 18 g total fat (4 g saturated), 8 g fiber, 94 mg cholesterol, 1735 mg sodium.

## *Last-minute* DINNERS
## CHICKEN & SPINACH PIE

PREP: 15 MINUTES / BAKE: 35 MINUTES

*1 tablespoon vegetable oil*
*1 medium onion, diced*
*1 pound ground chicken*
*1 package (10 ounces) frozen chopped spinach, thawed and squeezed dry*
*½ cup bottled Russian salad dressing*
*Two refrigerated pie crusts for 9-inch pie*

**1** In nonstick 10-inch skillet, heat oil over medium heat. Add onion and cook 5 minutes. Increase heat to medium-high, stir in chicken and continue cooking until all liquid evaporates and chicken is golden. Stir in spinach and Russian salad dressing; heat through.

**2** Preheat oven to 425°F. Place 1 pie crust on greased cookie sheet; top with chicken mixture, leaving 1-inch border. Place second crust over filling. Press edges together to seal; flute.

**3** Cut slits in crust to allow steam to escape during baking. Bake pie 30 to 35 minutes until golden. Makes 4 main-dish servings.

Each serving: About 875 calories, 27 g protein, 57 g carbohydrate, 60 g total fat (17 g saturated), 2 g fiber, 122 mg cholesterol, 945 mg sodium.

# Smoked Chicken Turnovers

PREP: 55 MINUTES / BAKE: 20 MINUTES

1 whole large boneless smoked chicken breast (about 1 pound)
⅓ cup light mayonnaise
2 tablespoons sweet pickle relish
¼ teaspoon coarsely ground black pepper
2 tablespoons milk plus additional for brushing turnovers
1 large celery stalk, sliced
2 cups all-purpose flour
¾ teaspoon salt
¾ cup shortening

**1** Remove skin from smoked chicken breast and cut meat into ½-inch chunks. In medium bowl, with fork, mix mayonnaise, relish, pepper, and 2 tablespoons milk. Add chicken and celery; toss to mix well.

**2** In large bowl, mix flour and salt. With pastry blender or two knives used scissor-fashion, cut in shortening until mixture resembles coarse crumbs. Sprinkle *5 to 6 tablespoons cold water*, 1 tablespoon at a time, into mixture, mixing lightly after each addition until dough is just moist enough to hold together. Shape dough into a ball.

**3** Preheat oven to 400°F. On lightly floured surface, with floured rolling pin, roll half of dough into a 12½" by 12" rectangle. From 12½-inch side, cut ½-inch-wide strip; reserve for decorating turnovers. Cut remaining pastry square into four 6-inch squares. Spoon about ⅓ cup chicken filling onto 1 corner of each pastry square, leaving ½-inch border. Brush pastry edges lightly with milk; fold dough diagonally over filling to make triangular turnovers. With fork, firmly press edges together to seal. Place turnovers on ungreased large cookie sheet. Repeat with remaining pastry and filling.

**4** Lightly brush turnovers with milk. Cut reserved pastry strips as desired and use to decorate the tops of turnovers; brush the strips with milk.

**5** Bake turnovers 15 to 20 minutes until crust is golden brown and filling is hot. Serve hot or refrigerate to serve cold later. *Makes 8 turnovers.*

Each turnover: About 395 calories, 15 g protein, 27 g carbohydrate, 25 g total fat (6 g saturated), 1 g fiber, 28 mg cholesterol, 860 mg sodium.

# Spicy Turkey-Vegetable Meat Loaf

PREP: 40 MINUTES / BAKE: 50 MINUTES

Instead of the traditional pork, veal, and beef, we mixed ground turkey with cooked vegetables and added yogurt to keep the loaf moist. The leftovers are great for lunch-box sandwiches.

2 tablespoons vegetable oil
¾ pound mushrooms, finely chopped
2 medium carrots, peeled and finely chopped
1 large onion, finely chopped
1 large celery stalk, finely chopped
1 small red pepper, finely chopped
1¼ teaspoons salt
2 pounds lean ground turkey breast
1 container (8 ounces) plain low-fat yogurt
½ cup chili sauce
¼ cup chopped fresh parsley leaves
1½ teaspoons chili powder
3 slices whole-wheat or white bread, finely chopped

**1** In 12-inch skillet, heat oil over medium-high heat. Add mushrooms, carrots, onion, celery, red pepper, and ½ teaspoon salt and cook until vegetables are tender and well browned, about 20 minutes. Remove skillet from heat; cool slightly.

**2** Preheat oven to 375°F. In large bowl, mix ground turkey, yogurt, chili sauce, parsley, chili powder, and remaining ¾ teaspoon salt until well blended. Stir in vegetable mixture and bread.

**3** In jelly-roll pan, pat turkey mixture into 12" by 5" oval loaf. Bake 50 minutes or until meat thermometer inserted into thickest part of meat loaf reads 165°F. *Makes 8 main-dish servings.*

Each serving: About 250 calories, 32 g protein, 18 g carbohydrate, 5 g total fat (1 g saturated), 3 g fiber, 72 mg cholesterol, 740 mg sodium.

# Turkey & Spinach Meat Loaf

PREP: 20 MINUTES / BAKE: 1 HOUR 15 MINUTES

Serve this meat loaf with Savory Onions & Red Peppers (opposite page).

1 tablespoon vegetable oil
1 medium onion, chopped
1 medium celery stalk, chopped
1 small red pepper, chopped
1 teaspoon salt
½ teaspoon coarsely ground black pepper
1 pound lean ground beef
¾ pound lean ground turkey breast
1 package (10 ounces) frozen chopped spinach, thawed and squeezed dry
½ cup seasoned dried bread crumbs
1 teaspoon dried basil
2 large egg whites

**1** In nonstick 10-inch skillet, heat oil over medium-high heat. Add onion, celery, red pepper, salt, and black pepper and cook until vegetables are tender and golden, stirring occasionally.

**2** Preheat oven to 350°F. In large bowl, mix ground beef, ground turkey, chopped spinach, bread crumbs, basil, egg whites, and vegetable mixture until well blended. In 13" by 9" metal baking pan, shape meat mixture into 8" by 5" loaf, pressing firmly. Bake meat loaf 1¼ hours. *Makes 8 main-dish servings.*

Each serving: About 265 calories, 24 g protein, 10 g carbohydrate, 14 g total fat (5 g saturated), 2 g fiber, 69 mg cholesterol, 595 mg sodium.

# Mushroom-Stuffed Chicken Loaf

PREP: 40 MINUTES / BAKE: 50 MINUTES

¾ pound mushrooms
2 tablespoons vegetable oil
1 medium onion, finely chopped
1 tablespoon soy sauce
3 tablespoons chopped fresh parsley leaves
1½ pounds ground chicken
1½ cups fresh bread crumbs (about 3 slices white bread)
1 teaspoon salt
½ teaspoon coarsely ground black pepper
1½ cups chicken broth, canned or homemade (page 11)
1 tablespoon all-purpose flour

**1** Slice enough mushrooms to equal ½ cup; reserve for mushroom sauce later. Coarsely chop remaining mushrooms.

**2** In nonstick 10-inch skillet, heat 1 tablespoon oil over medium-high heat. Add onion and cook until tender. Add chopped mushrooms; cook over high heat, stirring occasionally, until mushrooms are tender and liquid from mushrooms evaporates, about 10 minutes. Stir in soy sauce and 2 tablespoons chopped parsley. Remove skillet from heat.

**3** Preheat oven to 350°F. In bowl, mix chicken, bread crumbs, salt, pepper, and ¼ cup chicken broth.

**4** In 12" by 8" metal baking pan, form half of chicken mixture into 9" by 5" rectangle. Spoon mushroom mixture in row down center. Top with remaining chicken mixture and shape into 9" by 5" oval loaf.

**5** Bake chicken loaf 50 minutes or until center of chicken loses its pink color, basting occasionally with ¼ cup chicken broth.

**6** Transfer chicken loaf to warm platter; keep warm. Reserve any meat juice in baking pan.

**7** In small saucepan, heat remaining 1 tablespoon oil over medium-high heat. Add reserved sliced mushrooms, stirring occasionally, until liquid from mushrooms evaporates, about 5 minutes. Strain meat juice in baking pan through sieve into mushrooms in saucepan; add remaining 1 cup chicken broth. Heat to boiling over high heat. In cup, with fork, mix flour and *3 tablespoons water* until smooth. Stir flour mixture into mushroom mixture; heat until mixture boils and thickens slightly. Remove from heat; stir in remaining 1 tablespoon parsley. Serve chicken loaf with mushroom sauce. *Makes 8 main-dish servings.*

Each serving: About 215 calories, 17 g protein, 9 g carbohydrate, 12 g total fat (3 g saturated), 1 g fiber, 71 mg cholesterol, 730 mg sodium.

---

## GREAT GO-WITHS

## SAVORY ONIONS & RED PEPPERS

### PREP: 5 MINUTES / COOK: 15 MINUTES

*1 tablespoon olive oil*
*2 large onions, cut into ¾-inch-thick slices*
*2 small red peppers, cut into ½-inch-wide strips*
*¾ teaspoon sugar*
*½ teaspoon dried basil*
*¼ teaspoon coarsely ground black pepper*
*½ teaspoon salt*

**1** In 12-inch skillet, combine oil, onions, red peppers, and *¼ cup water*; heat to boiling over medium-high heat. Reduce heat to low; cover and simmer 5 minutes. Remove cover; cook over medium-high heat until water evaporates.

**2** Add sugar, basil, black pepper, and salt to skillet. Cook, stirring, until vegetables are golden brown and tender and glazed. Makes 8 accompaniment servings.

Each serving: About 40 calories, 1 g protein, 6 g carbohydrate, 2 g total fat (0 g saturated), 1 g fiber, 0 mg cholesterol, 145 mg sodium.

---

# Chicken & Couscous Skillet

### PREP: 10 MINUTES / COOK: 35 MINUTES

1 tablespoon olive oil
12 medium chicken drumsticks (about 3 pounds)
1 medium onion, diced
2 medium green peppers, cut into ½-inch pieces
1 medium red pepper, cut into ½-inch pieces
¼ teaspoon salt
¼ teaspoon coarsely ground black pepper
¼ teaspoon dried thyme
1 can (14½ ounces) chicken broth or 1¾ cups homemade (page 11)
1 package (10 ounces) couscous (Moroccan pasta)
¼ cup chopped fresh parsley leaves

**1** In 12-inch skillet, heat oil over medium-high heat until very hot. Add 6 chicken drumsticks at a time and cook until lightly browned on all sides, transferring drumsticks to plate as they brown.

**2** Add onion, green and red peppers, salt, black pepper, and thyme to skillet and cook over high heat until peppers are tender-crisp, stirring frequently; stir in chicken broth.

**3** Return chicken drumsticks to skillet; heat to boiling over high heat. Reduce heat to low; cover and simmer 15 minutes or until chicken is fork-tender. With tongs, transfer the chicken to a large plate; keep chicken warm.

**4** Stir couscous and parsley into vegetable mixture in skillet. Remove skillet from heat; cover and let stand 5 minutes. Arrange chicken in skillet with couscous. *Makes 6 main-dish servings.*

Each serving: About 470 calories, 36 g protein, 42 g carbohydrate, 16 g total fat (4 g saturated), 3 g fiber, 123 mg cholesterol, 525 mg sodium.

*Turkey Pinwheels*

# Turkey Pinwheels

🦃 🦃 🦃

PREP: I HOUR / BAKE: I HOUR 30 MINUTES

Steamed broccoli would make an colorful side dish for these attractive turkey pinwheels.

2 tablespoons plus 2 teaspoons vegetable oil
I pound carrots, peeled and diced
2 medium onions, diced
I large red pepper, diced
I medium celery stalk, diced
1¼ teaspoons salt
2 tablespoons dried bread crumbs
2 tablespoons grated Parmesan cheese
¼ cup chopped fresh parsley leaves

I skinless, boneless turkey-breast half (about 2½ pounds)
I teaspoon coarsely ground black pepper

**I** In 12-inch skillet, heat 2 tablespoons oil over medium-high heat. Add carrots, onions, red pepper, celery, and ½ teaspoon salt and cook until vegetables are well browned, about 15 minutes, stirring frequently. Add *½ cup water* to skillet; heat to boiling over high heat. Reduce heat to low; cover and simmer 5 minutes or until vegetables are tender. Remove cover; cook until any liquid in skillet has evaporated. Remove skillet from heat.

**2** Stir bread crumbs, Parmesan, and 2 tablespoons chopped parsley into skillet.

**3** Preheat oven to 325°F. On cutting board, holding knife parallel to work surface, and starting from a long side of turkey breast, cut breast horizontally, almost, but not all the way through. Spread breast open to make a butterflied breast. With flat side of meat mallet or small skillet, pound butterflied breast between 2 sheets plastic wrap into a rectangle about 14" by 12".

**4** Spread vegetable mixture evenly over entire turkey breast. Starting from a long side, roll turkey, jelly-roll fashion, to enclose stuffing completely. Tie turkey-breast roll securely with string at 1½-inch intervals; place on rack in small roasting pan.

**5** In cup, mix black pepper, remaining 2 teaspoons oil, remaining ¾ teaspoon salt, and remaining 2 table-spoons parsley; pat over turkey-breast roll. Bake turkey-breast roll 1¼ to 1½ hours, brushing occasionally with any pan drippings, until meat thermometer reaches 170° F.

**6** When turkey is done, transfer to cutting board and discard string. Let turkey-breast roll sit 10 minutes for easier slicing.

**7** To serve, cut turkey-breast roll crosswise into ½-inch-thick slices. Arrange slices on warm platter. *Makes 12 main-dish servings.*

Each serving: About 190 calories, 27 g protein, 11 g carbohydrate, 4 g total fat (1 g saturated), 4 g fiber, 59 mg cholesterol, 350 mg sodium.

---

## GREAT GO-WITHS

### TOMATOES VINAIGRETTE

PREP: 15 MINUTES

To dress the platter up a bit, add 6 ounces crumbled goat cheese or sliced mozzarella cheese.

*3 medium tomatoes (about 1 pound), cut into*
*¼-inch-thick slices*
*3 tablespoons extravirgin olive oil*
*2 tablespoons balsamic vinegar*
*2 tablespoons chopped fresh basil leaves*
*½ teaspoon salt*
*¼ teaspoon coarsely ground black pepper*

Arrange tomatoes on platter. In small bowl, with wire whisk or fork, mix olive oil, vinegar, basil, salt, and pepper. Pour dressing over tomatoes. Makes 4 accompaniment servings.

Each serving: About 115 calories, 1 g protein, 6 g carbohydrate, 11 g total fat (2 g saturated), 2 g fiber, 0 mg cholesterol, 300 mg sodium.

---

# Chicken Skillet with Red Potatoes & Spinach

🐓 🐓 🐓

PREP: 15 MINUTES / COOK: 30 MINUTES

2 tablespoons olive or vegetable oil
4 medium onions, cut into ½-inch-thick slices
2 tablespoons all-purpose flour
1¼ teaspoons salt
1¼ teaspoons dried rosemary, crushed
1 teaspoon coarsely ground black pepper
8 large chicken thighs (about 3 pounds), skin removed
1 pound small red potatoes, cut into 1-inch pieces
¼ cup fresh lemon juice (2 medium lemons)
1 small bunch spinach (about ½ pound), coarsely sliced
¼ cup pitted Kalamata olives, each sliced in half

**1** In nonstick 12-inch skillet, heat 1 tablespoon olive oil over medium-high heat. Add onions and cook until golden brown. With slotted spoon, transfer onions to bowl.

**2** On waxed paper, mix flour, salt, rosemary, and pepper; use to coat chicken thighs.

**3** Heat remaining 1 tablespoon oil in skillet; add chicken and cook over medium-high heat until golden brown on all sides.

**4** Add potatoes, lemon juice, cooked onions, and ¼ *cup water*; heat to boiling over high heat. Reduce heat to low; cover and simmer 20 minutes or until chicken and potatoes are fork-tender and juices run clear when chicken is pierced with tip of knife. Skim off fat from liquid in skillet.

**5** Stir in spinach and olives; cook until spinach just wilts. *Makes 4 main-dish servings.*

Each serving: About 505 calories, 44 g protein, 43 g carbohydrate, 17 g total fat (3 g saturated), 7 g fiber, 160 mg cholesterol, 1105 mg sodium.

# Turkey-Noodle Skillet Dinner

PREP: 15 MINUTES / COOK: 30 MINUTES

8 ounces wide egg noodles
3 tablespoons vegetable oil
3 medium celery stalks, cut into ½-inch-wide slices
1 medium onion, diced
10 ounces mushrooms, each cut into quarters
2 medium carrots, peeled and cut into bite-size pieces
¼ teaspoon coarsely ground black pepper
2 tablespoons plus ¼ cup all-purpose flour
1½ teaspoons salt
1 pound turkey cutlets, cut into 1-inch pieces
½ cup chicken broth
1 quart milk
2 tablespoons grated Parmesan cheese
¼ cup chopped fresh parsley leaves

**1** In large saucepot, prepare noodles in *boiling water* as label directs, but do not use salt in water; drain.

**2** Meanwhile, in nonstick 12-inch skillet, heat 1 tablespoon oil over medium-high heat. Add celery and onion and cook until golden and tender; transfer with slotted spoon to bowl. Add 1 tablespoon oil to skillet and heat. Add mushrooms and cook, stirring frequently, until tender and golden. Transfer to bowl with celery and onions.

**3** Meanwhile, in 1-quart saucepan, in *1 inch boiling water*, heat carrots to boiling. Reduce heat to low; cover and simmer 5 to 10 minutes until carrots are tender; drain.

**4** On waxed paper, combine pepper, 2 tablespoons flour, and ½ teaspoon salt; use to coat turkey-cutlet pieces.

**5** In same skillet, heat remaining 1 tablespoon oil over medium-high heat until very hot. Add turkey pieces and cook, stirring occasionally, until turkey is golden. Transfer to bowl with vegetables.

**6** In small bowl, with fork, mix remaining ¼ cup flour with chicken broth until smooth. Stir flour mixture, milk, and remaining 1 teaspoon salt into skillet.

Cook over medium-high heat, stirring to loosen brown bits, until mixture thickens slightly and boils; boil 1 minute.

**7** Return turkey and vegetable mixture to skillet. Stir in carrots, Parmesan, parsley, and noodles; heat through. *Makes 6 main-dish servings.*

Each serving: About 465 calories, 33 g protein, 49 g carbohydrate, 15 g total fat (5 g saturated), 4 g fiber, 107 mg cholesterol, 855 mg sodium.

# Mexican Skillet Chicken

PREP: 10 MINUTES / COOK: 15 MINUTES

Serve with warmed tortillas.

1½ pounds skinless, boneless chicken breasts, cut into 1½-inch chunks
2 tablespoons all-purpose flour
2 tablespoons vegetable oil
1 teaspoon salt
½ teaspoon ground cumin
¼ teaspoon ground red pepper (cayenne)
½ cup milk
1 can (11 ounces) whole-kernel corn, drained
¼ pound Monterey Jack cheese, shredded (1 cup)
1 can (8 ounces) kidney beans, rinsed and drained
1 cup loosely packed shredded iceberg lettuce
1 small tomato, diced

**1** In medium bowl, toss chicken with flour until well coated.

**2** In 10-inch skillet, heat oil over medium-high heat until very hot. Add chicken, salt, cumin, and ground red pepper and cook until chicken loses its pink color. Add milk and cook, stirring, over high heat until mixture boils and thickens slightly. Stir in corn and shredded cheese; heat through. Remove skillet from heat.

**3** Top center of chicken mixture with kidney beans. Sprinkle lettuce and tomato around edge of skillet. *Makes 6 main-dish servings.*

Each serving: About 320 calories, 35 g protein, 15 g carbohydrate, 13 g total fat (5 g saturated), 3 g fiber, 89 mg cholesterol, 700 mg sodium.

# Turkey & Potato Skillet "Pie"

PREP: 30 MINUTES / COOK: 30 MINUTES

*3 tablespoons vegetable oil*
*4 medium turnips (about 1 pound), shredded*
*1 medium onion, diced*
*2 cups finely chopped cooked turkey*
*½ cup shredded Muenster cheese (2 ounces)*
*2 tablespoons chopped fresh parsley leaves*
*2 tablespoons margarine or butter*
*4 medium potatoes (about 1¼ pounds), very thinly sliced*

1 In nonstick 10-inch skillet, heat 1 tablespoon oil over medium heat. Add turnips and onion and cook until vegetables are tender, stirring occasionally. Transfer vegetables with any liquid to medium bowl; stir in chopped turkey, cheese, and parsley; set aside.

2 In same skillet, melt margarine or butter with remaining 2 tablespoons vegetable oil over medium-high heat. Arrange potato slices in concentric circles, overlapping slices. Cook about 15 minutes or until potatoes are tender and undersides of potatoes are golden. Spoon turkey mixture evenly on top of potatoes; reduce heat to low; cover and cook 15 minutes or until cheese is melted and turkey is heated through.

3 To serve, carefully invert "pie" onto platter; cut into 6 wedges. Makes 6 main-dish servings.

Each serving: About 325 calories, 22 g protein, 23 g carbohydrate, 16 g total fat (4 g saturated), 4 g fiber, 53 mg cholesterol, 205 mg sodium.

# Cabbage-Patch Hash

🐓 🐓 🐓

PREP: 10 MINUTES / COOK: 30 MINUTES

3 tablespoons olive or vegetable oil
1 pound skinless, boneless chicken breasts, cut into 1-inch chunks
¾ teaspoon salt
1 small head green cabbage (about 1 pound), cut into 1-inch pieces
6 medium red potatoes (about 1½ pounds), cut into ½-inch pieces
1 large onion, cut into ½-inch pieces
2 medium green peppers, cut into ½-inch pieces
1 medium red pepper, cut into ½-inch pieces
2 teaspoons chopped fresh rosemary or ½ teaspoon dried rosemary, crushed
½ teaspoon coarsely ground black pepper

1 In 5-quart Dutch oven, heat 1 tablespoon olive oil over medium-high heat until very hot. Add chicken and ¼ teaspoon salt and cook until chicken is lightly browned and just loses its pink color throughout. Transfer chicken to large bowl.

2 Add 1 tablespoon oil to pan and heat over medium-high heat. Add cabbage and ¼ teaspoon salt and cook, stirring quickly and constantly, until cabbage is coated with oil. Stir in *½ cup water*; heat to boiling. Reduce heat to medium; cook cabbage, stirring frequently, until tender-crisp. Transfer cabbage to bowl with chicken.

3 Add remaining 1 tablespoon oil to pan and heat over medium-high heat. Add potatoes, onion, and remaining ¼ teaspoon salt and cook until potatoes are lightly browned. Stir in green and red peppers, rosemary, and black pepper and cook, stirring frequently, until vegetables are tender. Return chicken and cabbage to skillet and heat through. *Makes 4 main-dish servings.*

Each serving: About 415 calories, 32 g protein, 45 g carbohydrate, 12 g total fat (2 g saturated), 7 g fiber, 66 mg cholesterol, 545 mg sodium.

## TURKEY MELT WITH POTATOES, PEPPER & ONION

PREP: 15 MINUTES / COOK: 15 MINUTES

*1 pound medium red potatoes, unpeeled, cut into
    1½-inch pieces*
*1 tablespoon olive oil*
*1 large onion, cut into ½-inch slices*
*1 medium red or green pepper, cut into 1-inch pieces*
*½ teaspoon salt*
*¾ pound cooked turkey, cut into 1-inch chunks
    (about 2 cups)*
*¼ pound Swiss cheese, shredded (1 cup)*

**1** In 2-quart saucepan, heat potatoes and enough *water* to cover to boiling over high heat. Reduce heat to low; cover and simmer 8 to 10 minutes until potatoes are almost tender; drain.

**2** Meanwhile, in nonstick 10-inch skillet, heat olive oil over medium heat. Add onion and red pepper and cook until they begin to brown, stirring occasionally.

**3** Add potatoes and salt. Cook 10 minutes or until potatoes are well browned and vegetables are tender, turning vegetables with spatula occasionally.

**4** Stir in turkey and *¼ cup water*; heat to boiling. Reduce heat to low; cover and cook 10 minutes or until turkey is heated through. During last 3 minutes or cooking time, stir in shredded cheese. Makes 4 main-dish servings.

*Each serving: About 400 calories, 36 g protein, 27 g carbohydrate, 15 g total fat (7 g saturated), 3 g fiber, 92 mg cholesterol, 435 mg sodium.*

# Chicken Shortcake Casserole

PREP: 50 MINUTES / BAKE: 20 MINUTES

1 large red pepper
2 tablespoons olive or vegetable oil
2 medium celery stalks, sliced
1 medium onion, chopped
1½ pounds skinless, boneless chicken breasts, cut
    into bite-size chunks
⅓ cup all-purpose flour
1 cup low-fat (1%) milk
1 large sweet potato (about ¾ pound), cut into
    ½-inch pieces
1 can (14½-ounces) chicken broth or 1¾ cups
    homemade (page 11)
1 package (10 ounces) frozen Fordhook lima beans
1 can (8¾ ounces) cream-style corn
¼ cup minced fresh parsley leaves
1 teaspoon salt
3 tablespoons margarine or butter
1¼ cups buttermilk baking mix

**1** Mince enough red pepper to equal 2 tablespoons; pat dry with paper towel and set aside for shortcake topping. Cut remaining red pepper into ½-inch pieces.

**2** In 12-inch skillet, heat oil over medium-high heat. Add red-pepper pieces, celery, and onion and cook until tender-crisp. Stir in chicken and cook, stirring constantly, until chicken loses its pink color.

**3** In cup, with fork, mix flour with ⅔ cup milk; add to chicken mixture along with sweet potato, chicken broth, frozen lima beans, corn, 3 tablespoons parsley, and salt. Heat to boiling over medium-high heat, stirring occasionally; boil 1 minute. Remove skillet from heat.

**4** Preheat oven to 450°F. In medium bowl, with pastry blender or two knives used scissor-fashion, cut margarine or butter into buttermilk baking mix until mixture resembles coarse crumbs. Stir in remaining ⅓ cup milk, reserved minced red pepper, and remaining 1 tablespoon parsley just until blended.

**5** On floured surface, with floured hands, gently knead dough 5 or 6 times to blend well. Pat lightly to form a ¾-inch-thick round. With knife, cut round into 6 wedges.

6 Spoon chicken mixture into 2½-quart casserole (about 3 inches deep). Arrange shortcake wedges, slightly overlapping, over chicken mixture. Bake, uncovered, 20 minutes or until mixture is bubbly and shortcake wedges are golden brown. *Makes 6 main-dish servings.*

Each serving: About 540 calories, 36 g protein, 60 g carbohydrate, 17 g total fat (3 g saturated), 7 g fiber, 67 mg cholesterol, 1320 mg sodium.

# Skillet Cassoulet

PREP: 20 MINUTES / COOK: 1 HOUR

½ pound kielbasa, cut into small chunks
1 whole chicken (about 3 pounds), cut into
    10 pieces
¾ teaspoon salt
1 small onion, chopped
½ small green pepper, chopped
2 medium carrots, peeled and cut into thin coins
1 can (8 ounces) tomato sauce
1 tablespoon light brown sugar
½ teaspoon dry mustard
½ teaspoon dried thyme
1 can (16 ounces) baked beans
1 can (15 to 19 ounces) white kidney beans
    (cannellini), rinsed and drained

1 In 12-inch skillet, cook kielbasa chunks over medium-high heat until browned on all sides; with slotted spoon, transfer to bowl.

2 Add chicken and salt to skillet and cook over medium-high heat until chicken is well browned on all sides; transfer to bowl with kielbasa.

3 Discard all but 2 tablespoons drippings from skillet. Add onion, green pepper, and carrots and cook 10 minutes or until onion and pepper are tender. Add kielbasa, chicken, tomato sauce, brown sugar, mustard, and thyme. Heat to boiling over high heat. Reduce heat to low, cover, and simmer 20 minutes. Stir in baked beans and white kidney beans and cook 10 to 20 minutes longer or until chicken is tender. *Makes 6 main-dish servings.*

Each serving: About 480 calories, 38 g protein, 34 g carbohydrate, 22 g total fat (7 g saturated), 9 g fiber, 106 mg cholesterol, 1440 mg sodium.

# Chicken & Okra Skillet

PREP: 10 MINUTES / COOK: 1 HOUR

¼ pound thick-sliced bacon
1 whole chicken (about 3 pounds), cut up
3 tablespoons all-purpose flour
1 cup regular long-grain rice
1 can (14½ to 16 ounces) stewed tomatoes
1 cup chicken broth, canned or homemade
    (page 11)
¼ teaspoon ground red pepper (cayenne)
1 package (10 ounces) frozen whole okra

1 In 12-inch skillet, cook bacon over medium-low heat until brown. Transfer bacon to paper towels to drain. Discard all but 1 tablespoon fat from skillet.

2 Add chicken pieces to skillet and cook over medium-high heat until browned on all sides, about 20 minutes. Transfer chicken to large bowl; discard all but 3 tablespoons drippings from skillet.

3 Stir flour into drippings remaining in skillet and cook over medium-low heat, stirring frequently, until mixture is reddish brown, but not burned, about 10 minutes.

4 Meanwhile, prepare rice as label directs.

5 Stir stewed tomatoes, chicken broth, ground red pepper, and *1 cup water* into skillet. Return chicken to skillet and heat to boiling over high heat. Reduce heat to low; cover and simmer 15 minutes, stirring occasionally. Add frozen okra; heat to boiling over high heat, separating okra with fork. Reduce heat to low; cover and simmer 10 minutes or until chicken is fork-tender.

6 Crumble bacon and stir into rice. With large spoon, push chicken pieces and okra to edge of skillet; pile rice into center of skillet. *Makes 4 main-dish servings.*

Each serving: About 760 calories, 50 g protein, 54 g carbohydrate, 37 g total fat (11 g saturated), 4 g fiber, 149 mg cholesterol, 770 mg sodium.

## INDIVIDUAL TURKEY COBBLERS

PREP: 5 MINUTES / COOK: 30 MINUTES

*1 cup buttermilk baking mix*
*½ teaspoon dried thyme*
*⅓ cup plus 1¾ cups milk*
*1 can (10¼ ounces) condensed cream-of-mushroom soup*
*1 package (10 ounces) frozen mixed vegetables*
*1¼ pounds smoked turkey, in one piece, cut into bite-size chunks*

**1** Preheat oven to 425°F. In bowl, mix baking mix, thyme, and ⅓ cup milk just until blended and mixture leaves side of bowl. Spoon dough into 4 mounds onto cookie sheet. Bake 13 to 15 minutes until biscuits are golden.

**2** Meanwhile, in 3-quart saucepan, heat undiluted soup, frozen vegetables, and remaining 1¾ cups milk to boiling over medium-high heat, stirring often. Reduce heat to low, cook until vegetables are tender, about 10 minutes, stirring occasionally.

**3** Stir turkey into soup mixture; heat through. Spoon into four 2-cup bowls; top with biscuits. Makes 4 main-dish servings.

Each serving: About 485 calories, 37 g protein, 42 g carbohydrate, 19 g total fat (7 g saturated), 3 g fiber, 92 mg cholesterol, 2485 mg sodium.

# Chicken & Sweet Potato Blanquette

PREP: 40 MINUTES / BAKE: 50 MINUTES

4 tablespoons all-purpose flour
1¼ teaspoons salt
6 medium chicken legs (about 3½ pounds), skin removed
3 tablespoons olive oil
1 pound small white onions, peeled and each cut in half
¾ pound medium mushrooms, each cut in half
1 cup milk
4 medium sweet potatoes (about 2 pounds), each cut lengthwise in half, then crosswise into 1-inch-wide slices
¼ cup frozen peas
2 tablespoons coarsely chopped fresh dill or 1 teaspoon dried dill weed

**1** On waxed paper, combine 2 tablespoons flour and ¾ teaspoon salt; use to coat chicken legs.

**2** In 8-quart Dutch oven, heat 2 tablespoons oil over medium-high heat until very hot. Add chicken legs, 3 at a time, and cook until golden on both sides; transfer to plate.

**3** Preheat oven to 350°F. Add remaining 1 tablespoon oil to pan. Add onions, mushrooms, and remaining ½ teaspoon salt and cook until golden.

**4** In 2-cup measuring cup, with wire whisk or fork, stir milk, remaining 2 tablespoons flour, and *½ cup water*. Add milk mixture to vegetables in Dutch oven; heat to boiling over high heat, stirring to loosen brown bits from bottom of pan. Add sweet potatoes and chicken to Dutch oven; heat to boiling.

**5** Cover Dutch oven and bake 40 minutes. Add peas; bake 10 minutes longer or until juices run clear when chicken is pierced with tip of knife and vegetables are tender, stirring occasionally. Stir in dill. *Makes 6 main-dish servings.*

Each serving: About 490 calories, 37 g protein, 52 g carbohydrate, 15 g total fat (3 g saturated), 7 g fiber, 127 mg cholesterol, 670 mg sodium.

# Smoked Turkey & Bean Enchiladas

PREP: 20 MINUTES / BAKE: 20 MINUTES

Tomato juice and bottled salsa make an ultraquick sauce for turkey enchiladas.

1 cup tomato juice
2 teaspoons cornstarch
1 jar (12 to 15 ounces) mild to medium salsa
1 tablespoon olive or vegetable oil
1 bunch green onions, thinly sliced
1 tablespoon chili powder
2 cups diced smoked turkey
1 can (15¼ to 19 ounces) red kidney beans, rinsed and drained
1 can (4 to 4½ ounces) chopped mild green chiles, undrained
6 tablespoons sour cream
6 (8-inch diameter) flour tortillas
6 ounces Monterey Jack cheese, shredded (about 1½ cups)
1 small tomato, diced

**1** In 2-quart saucepan, stir tomato juice, cornstarch, and ½ *cup water* until smooth. Cook, stirring, over medium heat until mixture boils and thickens slightly; boil 1 minute. Stir in salsa; pour mixture into 13" by 9" glass baking dish. Set aside.

**2** In nonstick 10-inch skillet, heat olive oil over medium heat. Add half of green onions and cook until tender. Stir in chili powder; cook 1 minute. Stir in turkey, kidney beans, chiles with their liquid, and ¼ *cup water*.

**3** Preheat oven to 350°F. Spread 1 tablespoon sour cream over each tortilla. Sprinkle tortillas with half of shredded cheese. Dividing evenly, spoon turkey mixture in lengthwise strip down center of each tortilla; roll jelly-roll fashion. Place rolled tortillas, seam-side down, in sauce in baking dish; sprinkle with remaining shredded cheese. Cover dish with foil and bake 20 minutes or until cheese melts and enchiladas are heated through.

**4** Sprinkle enchiladas with tomato and remaining green onions. *Makes 6 main-dish servings.*

Each serving: About 430 calories, 25 g protein, 41 g carbohydrate, 19 g total fat (8 g saturated), 6 g fiber, 61 mg cholesterol, 1850 mg sodium.

## GREAT GO-WITHS

### THREE-C SLAW

PREP: 1 HOUR / CHILL: 1 HOUR 30 MINUTES

This refreshing slaw has the unexpected zip of celeriac along with cabbage and just enough carrot to add a hint of sweetness.

*1 cup light mayonnaise*
*½ cup Dijon mustard with seeds*
*½ cup fresh lemon juice*
*2 tablespoons sugar*
*2 tablespoons rice vinegar*
*½ teaspoon salt*
*½ teaspoon coarsely ground black pepper*
*1 medium head green cabbage (3 pounds), thinly sliced*
*3 medium bulbs celeriac (celeryroot),\* about 10 ounces each, peeled and finely shredded*
*1 pound carrots, peeled and finely shredded*

**1** In small bowl, with wire whisk or fork, mix mayonnaise, mustard, lemon juice, sugar, vinegar, salt, and pepper.

**2** Place cabbage, celeriac, and carrots in large bowl. Add dressing and toss to coat well. Cover bowl with plastic wrap and refrigerate at least 1½ hours to allow flavors to blend. Makes 20 accompaniment servings.

*If you can't find celeriac, substitute an additional pound of carrots and ½ teaspoon celery seeds.

Each serving: About 90 calories, 2 g protein, 12 g carbohydrate, 4 g total fat (1 g saturated), 2 g fiber, 4 mg cholesterol, 350 mg sodium.

# Main-Dish Salads

# Chicken-Pinwheel Salad

PREP: 45 MINUTES / COOK: 45 MINUTES

4 teaspoons plus 3 tablespoons olive or vegetable oil
1 small onion, minced
4 large skinless, boneless chicken-breast halves (about 1½ pounds)
1 large bunch basil
12 oil-packed sun-dried tomatoes without salt, finely chopped
1¼ teaspoons salt
2 small zucchini (about 6 ounces each), cut into ¼-inch-thick slices
6 medium red potatoes (about 1½ pounds), cut into ¼-inch-thick slices
3 tablespoons red wine vinegar
¾ teaspoon sugar
¼ teaspoon coarsely ground black pepper
4 large lettuce leaves
2 small tomatoes, cut into wedges

**1** In 1-quart saucepan, heat 2 teaspoons oil over medium heat. Add onion and cook until lightly browned. Stir in *1 tablespoon water* and continue cooking until onion is very tender.

**2** Meanwhile, place the chicken breasts between 2 sheets of waxed paper and with the flat side of a small skillet or meat pounder, pound to a ¼-inch thickness. Chop enough basil to measure 1 tablespoon; reserve remaining basil.

**3** Stir all but 1 tablespoon sun-dried tomatoes into onion in saucepan. Sprinkle both sides of chicken with ½ teaspoon salt. With breast halves boned-side up, spread with onion mixture, then top evenly with some whole basil leaves. Roll each breast half jelly-roll fashion; secure with toothpicks.

**4** In nonstick 12-inch skillet, heat 1 teaspoon oil over medium heat. Add zucchini slices and ¼ teaspoon salt and cook until zucchini is tender and lightly browned. Transfer zucchini to plate. Add 1 teaspoon oil to skillet. Add chicken rolls and cook until lightly browned all over. Reduce heat to low; cover and cook until chicken loses its pink color throughout, about 10 minutes total cooking time. Transfer chicken rolls to cutting board; cool slightly until easy to handle.

## Last-minute DINNERS
## CHICKEN & FRUIT SALAD

PREP: 20 MINUTES

*1 refrigerated roasted whole chicken (about 2¼ pounds)*
*1 medium bunch spinach*
*2 medium pink or white grapefruits, peeled and sectioned*
*2 medium Red Delicious apples, cut into ¾-inch chunks*
*¾ pound seedless green grapes*
*⅓ cup bottled poppy-seed salad dressing*

**1** Remove and discard skin and bones from chicken; tear chicken into bite-size pieces. Chop 1 cup loosely packed spinach leaves; set remaining leaves aside.

**2** In large bowl, combine chicken, chopped spinach, grapefruits, apples, grapes, and salad dressing; toss to coat.

**3** To serve, arrange remaining spinach leaves on platter; spoon chicken salad over spinach leaves. Makes 4 main-dish servings.

Each serving: About 540 calories, 35 g protein, 44 g carbohydrate, 29 g total fat (8 g saturated), 5 g fiber, 154 mg cholesterol, 1110 mg sodium.

**5** Meanwhile, in 2-quart saucepan, heat sliced potatoes and enough *water* to cover to boiling over high heat. Reduce heat to low; cover and simmer 5 minutes or until potatoes are fork-tender. Drain potatoes.

**6** In cup, with fork, mix vinegar, sugar, pepper, chopped basil, remaining 3 tablespoons olive oil, remaining ½ teaspoon salt, and remaining 1 tablespoon sun-dried tomatoes. Set salad dressing aside.

**7** Discard toothpicks from chicken rolls and cut rolls into ½-inch-thick slices. On 4 dinner plates, place sliced chicken on lettuce leaves. Arrange potatoes, zucchini, and tomatoes on plates with chicken. To serve, drizzle dressing over all. Garnish with basil sprigs. *Makes 4 main-dish servings.*

Each serving: About 550 calories, 46 g protein, 46 g carbohydrate, 20 g total fat (3 g saturated), 7 g fiber, 99 mg cholesterol, 950 mg sodium.

# Smoked Chicken Salad with Pears & Arugula

PREP: 20 MINUTES

2 tablespoons red wine vinegar
1 tablespoon Dijon mustard
¾ teaspoon salt
½ teaspoon coarsely ground black pepper
½ teaspoon sugar
⅓ cup olive or vegetable oil
2 bunches arugula, torn
12 ounces spinach, torn
1 can (28 ounces) sliced pears, drained
2 whole large boneless smoked chicken breasts
(about 1½ pounds), skin removed, cut into bite-size chunks
1 jar (7 ounces) roasted red peppers, drained and cut into ¾-inch-wide strips
Shaved Parmesan cheese for garnish

**1** In small bowl, combine vinegar, mustard, salt, black pepper, and sugar. With wire whisk or fork, slowly beat in olive oil until dressing thickens slightly.

**2** Place arugula and spinach in large bowl. Add sliced pears and toss; drizzle dressing over salad greens in bowl. Top with smoked chicken and roasted red peppers. Garnish with shaved Parmesan. *Makes 6 main-dish servings.*

Each serving without cheese: About 325 calories, 23 g protein, 24 g carbohydrate, 16 g total fat (3 g saturated), 4 g fiber, 42 mg cholesterol, 1390 mg sodium.

# Baked Mustard Chicken Salad

PREP: 20 MINUTES / BAKE: 50 MINUTES

1 tablespoon light mayonnaise
2 tablespoons plus 1 teaspoon spicy brown mustard
2 slices white bread, finely chopped
2 tablespoons minced fresh parsley leaves
¾ teaspoon salt
4 medium chicken legs (about 2¼ pounds), skin removed
1 package (10 ounces) frozen Fordhook lima beans
2 tablespoons red wine vinegar
1 tablespoon olive or vegetable oil
¼ teaspoon coarsely ground black pepper
¼ teaspoon sugar
4 cups sliced escarole
1 medium red pepper, cut into thin strips

**1** Preheat oven to 400°F. In small bowl, mix mayonnaise and 2 tablespoons mustard. On waxed paper, mix bread crumbs, parsley, and ½ teaspoon salt. Brush mustard mixture onto smooth side of chicken legs; dip mustard side into bread-crumb mixture to coat.

**2** Place chicken legs, bread-crumb side up, in small roasting pan (14" by 10"). Bake 45 to 50 minutes until coating on chicken is crisp and browned and juices run clear when chicken is pierced with tip of knife.

**3** Meanwhile, prepare lima beans as label directs; cool.

**4** In large bowl, with fork, mix vinegar, olive oil, black pepper, sugar, remaining 1 teaspoon mustard, and remaining ¼ teaspoon salt. Add escarole, red pepper, and lima beans; toss to coat.

**5** To serve, arrange escarole salad and chicken legs on large platter. *Makes 4 main-dish servings.*

Each serving: About 350 calories, 36 g protein, 24 g carbohydrate, 11 g total fat (2 g saturated), 6 g fiber, 118 mg cholesterol, 815 mg sodium.

# Chicken Salad with Croutons and Lemon-Caper Vinaigrette

🐓🐓🐓

PREP: 30 MINUTES / COOK: 15 MINUTES

½ medium head chicory (about 8 ounces), torn
    into 2-inch pieces
I medium head radicchio (about 6 ounces), cut
    into ½-inch slices
I medium head Belgian endive (about 6 ounces),
    cut into thin lengthwise strips
3 tablespoons margarine or butter
½ long loaf (8 ounces) Italian bread, cut into 1-inch
    cubes
I garlic clove, sliced
4 small skinless, boneless chicken-breast halves
    (about I pound)
½ teaspoon salt
I large lemon
2 tablespoons capers, drained and chopped
2 teaspoons Dijon mustard
I teaspoon sugar
¼ teaspoon coarsely ground black pepper
3 tablespoons olive oil

**1** Place chicory, radicchio, and Belgian endive in large bowl.

**2** In nonstick 12-inch skillet, melt 2 tablespoons margarine or butter over medium heat. Add bread cubes and garlic and cook, stirring occasionally, until bread is lightly browned. Discard garlic; transfer garlic croutons to bowl with salad greens. Wipe skillet clean.

**3** Add remaining 1 tablespoon margarine or butter to skillet. Add chicken and ¼ teaspoon salt and cook until chicken is browned on both sides. Reduce heat to medium; cover and cook until chicken is tender and juices run clear when chicken is pierced with tip of knife. Transfer chicken to plate.

**4** From lemon, grate 1 teaspoon peel and squeeze 2 tablespoons juice. In small bowl, combine lemon juice, lemon peel, capers, mustard, sugar, pepper, remaining ¼ teaspoon salt, and any juices from plate with chicken. With wire whisk, slowly beat in olive oil until mixture thickens slightly.

**5** Toss salad greens and garlic croutons with three-fourths of dressing. Arrange salad on 4 dinner plates; top with chicken and drizzle remaining dressing over chicken. *Makes 4 main-dish servings.*

Each serving: About 485 calories, 33 g protein, 37 g carbohydrate, 22 g total fat (4 g saturated), 4 g fiber, 66 mg cholesterol, 1085 mg sodium.

# Curried Chicken Salad

🐓🐓🐓

PREP: 20 MINUTES / COOK: 25 MINUTES

I pound skinless, boneless chicken breasts
I medium onion, cut into quarters
¼ cup mango chutney, chopped
2 medium celery stalks, chopped
I large mango, cut into ½-inch chunks
I medium Granny Smith apple, cut into
    ½-inch chunks
⅓ cup plain low-fat yogurt
¼ cup light mayonnaise
2 tablespoons golden raisins
2 teaspoons curry powder
1½ teaspoons grated, peeled fresh ginger
¼ teaspoon salt
Lettuce leaves

**1** Place chicken breasts in 10-inch skillet. Add onion and enough *water* to cover the chicken; heat to boiling over high heat. Remove skillet from heat; cover skillet and let chicken sit in poaching liquid for 20 minutes or until chicken loses its pink color throughout. Transfer chicken to plate; cool until easy to handle.

**2** In large bowl, combine chutney, celery, mango, apple, yogurt, mayonnaise, raisins, curry powder, ginger, and salt.

**3** When chicken is cool, cut into ½-inch chunks. Add chicken to mixture in bowl; toss to coat. Serve chicken salad on lettuce. *Makes 4 main-dish servings.*

Each serving: About 345 calories, 28 g protein, 41 g carbohydrate, 7 g total fat (2 g saturated), 3 g fiber, 72 mg cholesterol, 535 mg sodium.

*Chicken Salad with Croutons and Lemon-Caper Vinaigrette* ➤

# Chicken Salad with Confetti Relish

### 🐓 🐓 🐓

PREP: 45 MINUTES / COOK: 15 MINUTES

2 tablespoons olive or vegetable oil
1 bunch green onions, chopped
1 medium red pepper, diced
1 can (16 to 17 ounces) whole-kernel corn, drained
1 can (15 to 16 ounces) black beans, rinsed and drained
3 tablespoons white wine vinegar
1¼ teaspoons sugar
¾ teaspoon coarsely ground black pepper
1½ teaspoons ground cumin
1 teaspoon salt
1 medium head romaine lettuce
2 teaspoons all-purpose flour
1 teaspoon chili powder
¼ teaspoon ground red pepper (cayenne)
4 large skinless, boneless chicken-breast halves (about 1½ pounds)

**1** In 3-quart saucepan, heat 1 tablespoon olive oil over medium-high heat. Add green onions and red pepper and cook, stirring occasionally, until vegetables are tender. Remove saucepan from heat; stir in corn, black beans, vinegar, sugar, pepper, 1 teaspoon cumin, and ½ teaspoon salt.

**2** Chop enough romaine lettuce to measure 2 cups; set remaining lettuce aside. Stir chopped romaine into black-bean mixture in saucepan; set relish aside.

**3** On waxed paper, mix flour, chili powder, ground red pepper, remaining ½ teaspoon salt, and remaining ½ teaspoon cumin; use to coat chicken breasts.

**4** In 10-inch skillet, heat remaining 1 tablespoon oil over medium-high heat until very hot. Add chicken breasts and cook 6 to 8 minutes, turning once, until fork-tender and golden brown. Transfer chicken breasts to cutting board. With knife held in slanting position almost parallel to the cutting board, cut each chicken breast crosswise into 4 or 5 slices, almost, but not all the way through breast; fan breast out slightly.

**5** Cut reserved romaine lettuce into 1-inch-wide strips; place on large platter. Arrange chicken and relish on lettuce. ***Makes 4 main-dish servings.***

Each serving: About 425 calories, 49 g protein, 35 g carbohydrate, 11 g total fat (2 g saturated), 8 g fiber, 99 mg cholesterol, 1065 mg sodium.

# Chicken & Barley Salad

### 🐓 🐓 🐓

PREP: 20 MINUTES / COOK: 1 HOUR

1½ cups barley
2 tablespoons soy sauce
2 tablespoons fresh lemon juice
2 tablespoons peach or apricot preserves
1 boneless smoked chicken breast (about 12 ounces), skinned and cut into ½-inch-thick slices
¾ cup coarsely chopped watercress leaves
2 medium nectarines, cut into ½-inch chunks
1 medium celery stalk, thinly sliced

**1** In 4-quart saucepan, heat barley and *7 cups water* to boiling over high heat. Reduce heat to low; cover and simmer 1 hour or until barley is tender. Drain and rinse with cold water; set aside.

**2** In large bowl, stir soy sauce, lemon juice, and peach preserves until blended. Add barley, smoked chicken, watercress, nectarines, and celery; toss to coat. ***Makes 4 main-dish servings.***

Each serving: About 400 calories, 25 g protein, 68 g carbohydrate, 5 g total fat (1 g saturated), 13 g fiber, 31 mg cholesterol, 1240 mg sodium.

# Smoked Chicken & Fresh Mozzarella Salad

PREP: 30 MINUTES

1 bunch basil
3 tablespoons olive or vegetable oil
2 tablespoons fresh lemon juice
2 teaspoons Dijon mustard
1 teaspoon dried oregano
1 teaspoon sugar
¾ teaspoon salt
½ teaspoon coarsely ground black pepper
4 boneless smoked chicken-breast halves (about 1½ pounds)
3 medium tomatoes, sliced
1 pound fresh mozzarella cheese, sliced

1 Finely chop enough basil to make 2 tablespoons; reserve remaining basil for garnish. In small bowl, with fork, mix chopped basil, olive oil, lemon juice, mustard, oregano, sugar, salt, and pepper; set dressing aside.

2 Remove skin from chicken. Holding knife almost parallel to cutting surface, cut each smoked chicken-breast half into thin slices.

3 On large platter, arrange chicken, tomatoes, and mozzarella. Tuck in some basil leaves. To serve, spoon dressing over. *Makes 10 main-dish servings.*

Each serving: About 275 calories, 24 g protein, 3 g carbohydrate, 18 g total fat (9 g saturated), 1 g fiber, 69 mg cholesterol, 1025 mg sodium.

---

## CREATIVE LEFTOVERS

## TEX-MEX COBB SALAD

PREP: 25 MINUTES

Make this with the Rosemary Roast Turkey Breast as suggested below, or use any skinless roast turkey or chicken in its place.

¼ cup fresh lime juice
2 tablespoons chopped fresh cilantro leaves
4 teaspoons olive oil
1 teaspoon sugar
¼ teaspoon ground cumin
¼ teaspoon salt
¼ teaspoon coarsely ground black pepper
1 medium head romaine lettuce (about 1¼ pounds), trimmed and leaves cut into ½-inch-wide strips
1 pint cherry tomatoes, each cut into quarters
¾ pound leftover skinless Rosemary Roast Turkey Breast (page 163), cut into ½-inch pieces (2 cups)
1 can (15 to 19 ounces) black beans, rinsed and drained
2 small cucumbers (6 ounces each), peeled, seeded, and sliced ½ inch thick

1 In small bowl, with wire whisk, combine lime juice, cilantro, olive oil, sugar, cumin, salt, and pepper.

2 Place lettuce in large serving bowl. Arrange tomatoes, turkey, black beans, and cucumbers in rows over lettuce to cover.

3 Just before serving, toss the salad with the dressing. Makes 4 main-dish servings.

Each serving: About 300 calories, 33 g protein, 21 g carbohydrate, 10 g total fat (2 g saturated), 7 g fiber, 66 mg cholesterol, 420 mg sodium.

# Mexican Chicken & Rice Salad

PREP: 10 MINUTES / COOK: 25 MINUTES

2 tablespoons olive oil
1 small onion, chopped
2 cups regular long-grain rice
1 teaspoon turmeric
1¼ teaspoons salt
1 pound skinless, boneless chicken breasts, cut into
   1½-inch chunks
2 tablespoons chili powder
2 cans (15¼ to 19 ounces each) red kidney beans,
   rinsed and drained
1 can (4 to 4½ ounces) chopped mild green chiles,
   drained
2 tablespoons cider vinegar
¼ cup chopped fresh cilantro leaves

**1** In 3-quart saucepan, heat 1 tablespoon olive oil over medium-high heat. Add onion and cook until tender. Stir in rice, turmeric, ¾ teaspoon salt, and *4 cups water*; heat to boiling over high heat. Reduce heat to low; cover and simmer 20 minutes or until rice is tender.

**2** Meanwhile, in nonstick 12-inch skillet, heat remaining 1 tablespoon oil over high heat until very hot. Add chicken and cook until browned on all sides. Stir in chili powder and remaining ½ teaspoon salt; cook 1 minute. Stir in kidney beans and green chiles; cook until chicken loses its pink color throughout and mixture is heated through.

**3** In large bowl, mix cooked rice mixture, chicken mixture, vinegar, and cilantro until blended. *Makes 6 main-dish servings.*

Each serving: About 485 calories, 31 g protein, 72 g carbohydrate, 7 g total fat (1 g saturated), 8 g fiber, 44 mg cholesterol, 885 mg sodium.

# Baby Spinach with Nectarines & Grilled Chicken

PREP: 25 MINUTES / GRILL: 15 MINUTES

There's no waste with baby spinach—it's so tender, you can eat the stems and all.

4 small skinless, boneless chicken-breast halves
   (about 1 pound)
1 teaspoon fresh thyme leaves
¾ teaspoon salt
½ teaspoon coarsely ground black pepper
2 tablespoons olive oil
1 tablespoon balsamic vinegar
½ teaspoon Dijon mustard
1 shallot, minced
2 large ripe nectarines, pitted and sliced
½ English (seedless) cucumber, cut lengthwise in
   half, then thinly sliced crosswise
8 ounces baby spinach
2 ounces crumbled feta cheese (½ cup)

**1** Rub chicken with thyme, ½ teaspoon salt, and ¼ teaspoon pepper. Place chicken on grill over medium heat. Cook chicken about 7 minutes per side or until juices run clear when thickest part is pierced with tip of knife, turning once. Transfer chicken to cutting board; cool until easy to handle.

**2** Meanwhile, in large bowl, with wire whisk, mix olive oil, vinegar, mustard, shallot, remaining ¼ teaspoon salt, and remaining ¼ teaspoon pepper. Stir in nectarines and cucumber.

**3** To serve, cut chicken into ½-inch-thick slices. Toss spinach with nectarine mixture. Arrange salad on 4 plates; top with feta and sliced chicken. *Makes 4 main-dish servings.*

Each serving: About 285 calories, 31 g protein, 15 g carbohydrate, 12 g total fat (3 g saturated), 4 g fiber, 78 mg cholesterol, 730 mg sodium.

*Baby Spinach with Nectarines & Grilled Chicken* ➤

# Sesame Chicken Salad

PREP: 25 MINUTES / BROIL: 10 MINUTES

1½ pounds skinless, boneless chicken breasts
½ teaspoon salt
¼ teaspoon coarsely ground black pepper
3 tablespoons Asian sesame oil
3 tablespoons creamy peanut butter
2 tablespoons soy sauce
2 tablespoons seasoned rice vinegar
1½ teaspoons sugar
1 teaspoon grated, peeled fresh ginger
¼ teaspoon hot pepper sauce
1 garlic clove, finely minced
1 bunch watercress, thick stems removed
1 small red pepper, cut into matchstick-thin strips
½ seedless cucumber, cut into 2½-inch-long matchstick-thin strips
2 green onions, cut into 2½-inch-long matchstick-thin strips

**1** Preheat broiler. Rub chicken breasts with salt, pepper, and 1 tablespoon sesame oil. Place chicken in broiling pan (without rack). With pan at closest position to source of heat, broil breasts 4 minutes on each side or until juices run clear when chicken is pierced with tip of knife. Cool chicken until easy to handle.

**2** Meanwhile, in large bowl, with wire whisk, mix peanut butter, soy sauce, vinegar, sugar, ginger, hot pepper sauce, garlic, remaining 2 tablespoons sesame oil, and *¼ cup water.*

**3** Pull chicken breasts into long, thin strips; toss with sesame dressing.

**4** To serve, line platter with watercress; top with chicken salad. Arrange red pepper, cucumber, and green onion strips on top of salad. *Makes 4 main-dish servings.*

Each serving: About 380 calories, 45 g protein, 9 g carbohydrate, 19 g total fat (3 g saturated), 2 g fiber, 99 mg cholesterol, 1150 mg sodium.

# Raspberry-Chicken Salad with Caramelized Onions

PREP: 30 MINUTES / COOK: 45 MINUTES

4 tablespoons vegetable oil
1 large onion, thinly sliced
4 medium skinless, boneless chicken-breast halves (about 1¼ pounds)
⅓ cup balsamic or red wine vinegar
½ cup orange juice
¾ teaspoon salt
¼ teaspoon coarsely ground black pepper
3 medium oranges
12 ounces spinach, cut into ½-inch-wide slices
1 bunch radishes, thinly sliced
½ pint raspberries

**1** In nonstick 10-inch skillet, heat 1 tablespoon oil over medium heat. Add onion and cook until tender and browned, about 20 minutes. With slotted spoon, transfer onion to small bowl; set aside.

**2** Add chicken breasts to skillet and cook over medium-high heat until browned on both sides. Add vinegar, orange juice, salt, and pepper; heat to boiling over high heat. Reduce heat to low; cover and simmer 10 to 15 minutes until chicken is fork-tender.

**3** Meanwhile, cut and peel white membrane from oranges. Cut out sections between membranes; discard seeds. In large bowl, toss orange sections, spinach, radishes, and raspberries. Arrange spinach mixture on large platter.

**4** With slotted spoon, transfer chicken to plate. Heat liquid in skillet to boiling over high heat, stirring to loosen brown bits from bottom. Reduce heat to low and slowly pour in remaining 3 tablespoons oil, beating vinaigrette with a wire whisk or fork until well mixed.

**5** Cut chicken breasts into ¼-inch-wide strips and tuck into spinach salad. Sprinkle salad with onion and pour warm vinaigrette on top. *Makes 4 main-dish servings.*

Each serving: About 410 calories, 37 g protein, 30 g carbohydrate, 16 g total fat (2 g saturated), 8 g fiber, 82 mg cholesterol, 610 mg sodium.

◀ *Raspberry-Chicken Salad with Caramelized Onions*

# Spinach, Chicken & Feta Salad

PREP: 20 MINUTES / COOK: 25 MINUTES

4 tablespoons olive or vegetable oil
1 medium red pepper, cut into ¼-inch-wide strips
1 medium yellow pepper, cut into ¼-inch-wide
  strips
1½ pounds skinless, boneless chicken breasts, cut
  crosswise into 1-inch-thick strips
1 teaspoon salt
3 tablespoons white wine vinegar
1 teaspoon sugar
½ teaspoon coarsely ground black pepper
12 ounces spinach, tough stems removed
¼ pound feta cheese

**1** In 12-inch skillet, heat 3 tablespoons olive oil over medium-high heat. Add red and yellow peppers and cook until tender and lightly browned, about 10 minutes. With slotted spoon, transfer pepper strips to large bowl.

**2** Add chicken and ½ teaspoon salt and cook until chicken is lightly browned and loses its pink color, about 10 minutes, stirring frequently. With slotted spoon, transfer chicken to bowl with peppers.

**3** Remove skillet from heat. Add vinegar, sugar, black pepper, remaining 1 tablespoon oil, and remaining ½ teaspoon salt, stirring to loosen brown bits from bottom of skillet.

**4** Add spinach and vinegar mixture to bowl with chicken; gently toss to mix. Finely crumble feta onto salad. *Makes 4 main-dish servings.*

Each serving: About410 calories, 45 g protein, 7 g carbohydrate, 22 g total fat (7 g saturated), 2 g fiber, 124 mg cholesterol, 1060 mg sodium.

# Warm & Spicy Asian Chicken Salad

PREP: 15 MINUTES / COOK: 25 MINUTES

1½ pounds skinless, boneless chicken breasts, cut
  into bite-size chunks
1 tablespoon minced, peeled fresh ginger
¾ teaspoon crushed red pepper
1 garlic clove, minced
4 tablespoons soy sauce
½ pound bean sprouts
2 tablespoons plus ¼ cup vegetable oil
½ pound snow peas, strings removed
4 ounces fresh shiitake mushrooms, stems
  discarded and caps sliced
1 can (8 ounces) sliced water chestnuts, drained
2 tablespoons white wine vinegar
2 teaspoons sugar
½ teaspoon dry mustard
½ small head Napa (Chinese cabbage), about 12
  ounces, thinly sliced

**1** Place chicken in bowl; stir in ginger, crushed red pepper, garlic, and 2 tablespoons soy sauce.

**2** Place bean sprouts in bowl. Pour *boiling water* over bean sprouts to cover; let stand 5 minutes; drain.

**3** In nonstick 10-inch skillet, heat 1 tablespoon oil over medium-high heat. Add snow peas and shiitake mushrooms and cook until snow peas are tender-crisp and mushrooms are tender, about 5 minutes. With slotted spoon, transfer to large bowl.

**4** Add 1 tablespoon vegetable oil to skillet. Add chicken, half at a time, and cook until chicken is golden brown on the outside and just loses its pink color throughout, about 5 minutes. Add chicken and water chestnuts to snow-pea mixture.

**5** In small bowl, with wire whisk or fork, mix vinegar, sugar, dry mustard, remaining ¼ cup oil, and remaining 2 tablespoons soy sauce. Add dressing to chicken mixture; toss to mix well.

**6** To serve, toss Napa cabbage with bean sprouts. Arrange Napa mixture on large platter; top with chicken mixture. *Makes 4 main-dish servings.*

Each serving: About 470 calories, 46 g protein, 20 g carbohydrate, 23 g total fat (3 g saturated), 5 g fiber, 99 mg cholesterol, 1155 mg sodium.

## CHICKEN & POTATO SALAD

PREP: 15 MINUTES / COOK: 15 MINUTES

We added lots of vegetables to the chicken, and mixed it all with a low-fat mayonnaise dressing.

*6 medium red potatoes (about 1 pound), each cut into quarters*
*½ pound wax beans or green beans*
*3 cups shredded cooked chicken or turkey, preferably dark meat*
*2 medium plum tomatoes, each cut into thin wedges*
*1 medium zucchini (8 ounces), cut into small chunks*
*½ cup pitted Kalamata olives, each cut in half*
*1 can (13¾ to 14 ounces) artichoke hearts, drained and each cut into quarters*
*⅓ cup milk*
*¼ cup light mayonnaise*
*2 tablespoons chopped fresh parsley leaves*
*1 tablespoon fresh lemon juice*
*1 teaspoon Dijon mustard*
*½ teaspoon salt*
*¼ teaspoon coarsely ground black pepper*

**1** In 3-quart saucepan, heat potatoes and enough *water* to cover to boiling over high heat. Reduce heat to low; cover and simmer 10 minutes or until potatoes are fork-tender. Add wax beans for last 5 minutes of cooking. Drain.

**2** In large bowl, mix cooked potatoes, wax beans, chicken, tomatoes, zucchini, olives, and artichoke hearts.

**3** In small bowl, with fork, mix milk, mayonnaise, parsley, lemon juice, mustard, salt, and pepper until blended. Add to chicken mixture in bowl, tossing to coat well. Makes 6 main-dish servings.

Each serving: About 335 calories, 27 g protein, 24 g carbohydrate, 14 g total fat (3 g saturated), 3 g fiber, 85 mg cholesterol, 585 mg sodium.

# Chicken Salad Olé

PREP: 15 MINUTES / COOK: 15 MINUTES

1 large lime
8 ounces spinach, torn into bite-size pieces
1 small head Boston lettuce, torn into bite-size pieces
2 tablespoons plus ¼ cup olive or vegetable oil
4 large skinless, boneless chicken-breast halves (about 1½ pounds)
¾ teaspoon salt
1 teaspoon Dijon mustard
½ teaspoon sugar
¾ cup bottled medium-hot salsa
¼ cup pitted Kalamata olives, minced

**1** From lime, grate 1 teaspoon peel and squeeze 1 tablespoon juice.

**2** Place spinach and Boston lettuce in large bowl; refrigerate.

**3** In 12-inch skillet, heat 2 tablespoons oil over medium-high heat until very hot. Add chicken breasts and cook 4 to 5 minutes until golden brown. Turn chicken and sprinkle with ½ teaspoon salt. Reduce heat to medium and cook chicken until juices run clear when pierced with tip of knife, about 5 minutes longer. Transfer chicken to plate.

**4** Meanwhile, in small bowl, with wire whisk or fork, mix mustard, sugar, remaining ¼ cup olive oil, remaining ¼ teaspoon salt, and lime juice. Toss dressing with spinach and Boston lettuce in bowl. Place salad on large platter.

**5** Cut each chicken breast diagonally into 3 slices, keeping slices together. Arrange chicken on salad.

**6** Add salsa, olives, and *¼ cup water* to skillet, stirring to loosen any brown bits from bottom, and heat through. Spoon salsa mixture over chicken on salad; sprinkle chicken with grated lime peel. *Makes 4 main-dish servings.*

Each serving: About 430 calories, 41 g protein, 9 g carbohydrate, 25 g total fat (4 g saturated), 2 g fiber, 99 mg cholesterol, 1255 mg sodium.

# Turkey & Pear Salad

### 🐓 🐓 🐓

PREP: 15 MINUTES / COOK: 10 MINUTES

2 pounds turkey cutlets
1 tablespoon margarine or butter
½ cup walnuts, coarsely broken, or blanched whole
  almonds
1 large lemon
4 large pears
¾ cup light mayonnaise
¼ cup milk
¼ teaspoon salt
3 celery stalks, thinly sliced
Lettuce leaves

**1** In 12-inch skillet, heat turkey cutlets and *3 cups water* to boiling over high heat. Reduce heat to low; cover and simmer 5 minutes or until turkey is fork-tender. Cool slightly and cut turkey into thin strips.

**2** Meanwhile, in 1-quart saucepan, melt margarine or butter over medium heat. Add walnuts and cook 5 minutes. With slotted spoon, transfer walnuts to plate; set aside.

**3** From lemon, squeeze juice into shallow bowl. Cut 2 pears into ½-inch chunks; thinly slice remaining 2 pears. Dip pear slices into lemon juice to prevent browning; set aside.

**4** In large bowl, mix mayonnaise, milk, and salt. Add walnuts, pear chunks, turkey, and celery; toss to mix well.

**5** To serve, line platter with lettuce leaves; spoon salad onto lettuce; arrange pear slices around salad. *Makes 6 main-dish servings.*

Each serving: About 445 calories, 40 g protein, 27 g carbohydrate, 20 g total fat (3 g saturated), 4 g fiber, 105 mg cholesterol, 445 mg sodium.

# Smoked Turkey & Fruit Salad

### 🐓 🐓 🐓

PREP: 30 MINUTES

⅓ cup olive or vegetable oil
3 tablespoons white wine vinegar
1 tablespoon Dijon mustard
½ teaspoon salt
½ teaspoon coarsely ground black pepper
½ teaspoon sugar
1 large bunch spinach
1 pound smoked turkey breast, in one piece, torn
  into bite-size strips
½ pound red seedless grapes, each cut in half
4 ounces feta cheese, crumbled (about 1 cup)
1 medium cantaloupe or 2 medium papayas

**1** In large bowl, with wire whisk or fork, mix olive oil, vinegar, mustard, salt, pepper, sugar, and *2 tablespoons water* until dressing is blended.

**2** Thinly slice enough spinach to equal 1 cup; reserve remaining spinach.

**3** To bowl with dressing, add smoked turkey, grapes, sliced spinach, and feta cheese; toss to coat.

**4** To serve, cut rind from cantaloupe; cut cantaloupe into thin wedges. Arrange remaining spinach leaves and cantaloupe wedges on platter; top with smoked-turkey mixture. *Makes 4 main-dish servings.*

Each serving: About 485 calories, 32 g protein, 28 g carbohydrate, 29 g total fat (8 g saturated), 5 g fiber, 73 mg cholesterol, 1865 mg sodium.

*Smoked Turkey & Fruit Salad* ➤

## COUSCOUS "PAELLA" SALAD

PREP: 30 MINUTES

3 tablespoons olive or vegetable oil
3 tablespoons white wine vinegar
¼ cup chopped fresh parsley leaves
½ teaspoon coarsely ground black pepper
¼ teaspoon salt
⅛ teaspoon saffron or ½ teaspoon turmeric
1½ cups frozen peas
1 can (14½ ounces) chicken broth or 1¾ cups
    homemade (page 11)
1 package (10 ounces) couscous (Moroccan pasta)
2 large celery stalks, thinly sliced
1 jar (7 ounces) roasted red peppers, drained and
    cut into 1-inch pieces
¼ cup pimiento-stuffed olives, coarsely chopped
3 ounces smoked ham, cut into matchsticks
3 cups shredded cooked chicken

1 In large bowl, mix olive oil, vinegar, parsley, black pepper, salt, saffron or turmeric, and frozen peas.

2 In small saucepan, heat chicken broth to boiling over high heat. Pour broth into bowl with dressing mixture and stir in couscous; cover bowl with a plate and let stand 5 minutes.

3 Add celery, roasted red peppers, olives, ham, and chicken to couscous and toss well. Makes 4 main-dish servings.

Each serving: About 710 calories, 54 g protein, 68 g carbohydrate, 23 g total fat (5 g saturated), 5 g fiber, 124 mg cholesterol, 1365 mg sodium.

# Honey-Mustard Turkey Salad

PREP: 15 MINUTES

¼ cup Dijon mustard with seeds
1 tablespoon plus 1½ teaspoons honey
1 teaspoon red wine vinegar
1½ pounds smoked turkey breast, in one piece, cut
    into 1-inch chunks
2 large celery stalks, cut into ¼-inch-thick slices
½ cup walnut halves, coarsely chopped
½ pound seedless red grapes

In large bowl, mix mustard, honey, and vinegar. Add turkey, celery, and walnuts to dressing and toss to coat well. Spoon turkey salad onto platter or in large serving bowl and arrange grapes around salad. *Makes 6 main-dish servings.*

Each serving: About 245 calories, 25 g protein, 14 g carbohydrate, 9 g total fat (2 g saturated), 1 g fiber, 48 mg cholesterol, 1320 mg sodium.

# Turkey Cutlet Salad with Toasted Pecans

PREP: 20 MINUTES / COOK: 10 MINUTES

1 pound turkey cutlets
⅓ cup pecan halves, toasted and chopped
1 medium celery stalk, chopped
⅓ cup light mayonnaise
¼ cup dark seedless raisins
½ teaspoon salt
¼ teaspoon coarsely ground black pepper
¼ teaspoon dried dill weed
1 small head leaf lettuce

1 In 10-inch skillet, heat turkey cutlets and *3 cups water* to boiling over high heat. Reduce heat to low; cover and simmer 5 minutes or until turkey is fork-tender.

**2** Drain turkey and cut into bite-sized chunks. In medium bowl, mix turkey with pecans, celery, mayonnaise, raisins, salt, pepper, and dill.

**3** To serve, arrange lettuce leaves on platter; top with turkey salad. *Makes 4 main-dish servings.*

Each serving: About 285 calories, 29 g protein, 12 g carbohydrate, 14 g total fat (2 g saturated), 2 g fiber, 77 mg cholesterol, 510 mg sodium.

### *Last-minute* DINNERS

## CHICKEN WITH PLUM TOMATO DRESSING

PREP: 20 MINUTES

*3 medium plum tomatoes (about 8 ounces), seeded and chopped*
*1 medium dill pickle, finely chopped*
*1 small garlic clove, minced*
*2 tablespoons olive or vegetable oil*
*1 tablespoon chopped fresh basil leaves*
*¼ teaspoon salt*
*⅛ teaspoon coarsely ground black pepper*
*4 large refrigerated roasted chicken-breast halves (about 2 pounds)*
*6 cups mesclun mix*

**1** In medium bowl, combine tomatoes, pickle, garlic, oil, basil, salt, and pepper; mix well.

**2** Discard bones from chicken; cut each chicken-breast half diagonally into 4 slices, keeping slices together.

**3** Arrange salad greens on 4 dinner plates. Place chicken-breast halves on top of salad greens, fanning slices slightly. Spoon tomato sauce over chicken. Makes 4 main-dish servings.

Each serving: About 300 calories, 42 g protein, 9 g carbohydrate, 11 g total fat (2 g saturated), 2 g fiber, 108 mg cholesterol, 1270 mg sodium.

# Chicken Taco Salad

PREP: 10 MINUTES / COOK: 25 MINUTES

2 pounds skinless, boneless chicken breasts
1 medium onion, cut into quarters
¼ cup white wine vinegar
3 tablespoons vegetable oil
1 tablespoon chopped fresh parsley leaves
2 teaspoons chili powder
½ teaspoon salt
⅛ teaspoon crushed red pepper
1 medium head romaine lettuce, cut crosswise into
   ½-inch-wide strips
2 medium tomatoes, cut into ¾-inch chunks
1 medium avocado, cut into ¾-inch chunks
½ bag (10 ounces) tortilla chips
¼ cup pitted Kalamata olives, sliced

**1** Place chicken breasts in 10-inch skillet. Add onion and enough *water* to cover the chicken; heat to boiling over high heat. Remove skillet from heat; cover skillet and let chicken sit in poaching liquid for 20 minutes or until chicken loses its pink color throughout. Transfer chicken to plate; cool until easy to handle.

**2** Meanwhile, in 1-cup measuring cup, with fork, stir together vinegar, oil, parsley, chili powder, salt, and crushed red pepper.

**3** Shred chicken and place in large bowl. Add half of dressing to chicken in bowl; toss to coat. Reserve remaining dressing.

**4** Place lettuce in large serving bowl; mound chicken on center of lettuce. Arrange tomatoes and avocado in concentric circles around chicken. Tuck tortilla chips around edge of salad; sprinkle olives over salad. To serve, toss salad with reserved dressing. *Makes 6 main-dish servings.*

Each serving: About 560 calories, 41 g protein, 38 g carbohydrate, 28 g total fat (5 g saturated), 6 g fiber, 88 mg cholesterol, 665 mg sodium.

# Chicken Niçoise

🐓🐓🐓

PREP: 25 MINUTES / COOK: 35 MINUTES

1 pound skinless, boneless chicken breasts
1 pound small red potatoes, each cut in half
1 tablespoon plus ¼ cup olive oil
1 medium red onion, cut crosswise into thin slices
    and separated into rings
¼ cup fresh lemon juice
2 teaspoons capers, drained
2 teaspoons sugar
½ teaspoon Dijon mustard
¼ teaspoon salt
¼ teaspoon coarsely ground black pepper
3 large eggs, hard-cooked
½ head Boston lettuce
½ head green leaf lettuce
1 package (8 ounces) frozen sugar snap peas,
    thawed
4 medium plum tomatoes, cut into ¼-inch-thick
    slices
¼ cup pitted Kalamata olives, thinly sliced

**1** Place chicken breasts in 10-inch skillet. Add onion and enough *water* to cover the chicken; heat to boiling over high heat. Remove skillet from heat; cover skillet and let chicken sit in poaching liquid for 20 minutes or until chicken loses its pink color throughout. Transfer chicken to plate; cool until easy to handle.

**2** Meanwhile, in 4-quart saucepan, heat potatoes and enough *water* to cover to boiling over high heat. Reduce heat to low; cover and simmer 10 to 12 minutes, until potatoes are fork-tender.

**3** In 10-inch skillet, heat 1 tablespoon oil over medium-high heat. Add onion rings and cook, stirring occasionally, until tender; set aside.

**4** In small bowl, with wire whisk or fork, mix lemon juice, capers, sugar, mustard, salt, and pepper until blended. Gradually add remaining ¼ cup olive oil, whisking constantly, until dressing is blended.

**5** To serve, remove shells from hard-cooked eggs. Cut each egg into quarters. Arrange lettuce on large platter. Arrange chicken strips in center of platter. Arrange potatoes, sugar snap peas, tomatoes, eggs, and sautéed

onion around chicken. Sprinkle with olives. Drizzle salad with dressing; toss to serve. ***Makes 4 main-dish servings.***

Each serving: About 525 calories, 36 g protein, 38 g carbohydrate, 25 g total fat (4 g saturated), 5 g fiber, 225 mg cholesterol, 520 mg sodium.

---

## CREATIVE LEFTOVERS

# SKILLET CHEF'S SALAD

PREP: 35 MINUTES / COOK: 10 MINUTES

*2 tablespoons olive or vegetable oil*
*2 green onions, thinly sliced*
*2 teaspoons all-purpose flour*
*2 teaspoons sugar*
*¼ teaspoon salt*
*¼ cup tarragon or white wine vinegar*
*1 tablespoon Dijon mustard*
*6 cups torn assorted salad greens*
*1 large celery stalk, thinly sliced*
*1 small cucumber, thinly sliced*
*¼ pound baked ham, cut into matchsticks*
*½ pound roast turkey, cut into matchsticks*
*½ pound Jarlsberg or Swiss cheese, cut into*
    *matchsticks*
*3 ounces radishes, thinly sliced*
*1 medium tomato, cut into wedges*

**1** In 12-inch skillet, heat olive oil over medium heat. Add green onions and cook just until tender. Stir in flour, sugar, and salt until smooth. Add vinegar, mustard, and *½ cup water*; cook, stirring, until dressing boils and thickens slightly. Remove skillet from heat.

**2** Toss salad greens, celery, and cucumber in hot dressing in skillet; arrange ham, turkey, cheese, radishes, and tomato wedges on salad-green mixture. Serve directly from skillet. Makes 4 main-dish servings.

Each serving: About 465 calories, 39 g protein, 15 g carbohydrate, 26 g total fat (3 g saturated), 3 g fiber, 96 mg cholesterol, 1010 mg sodium.

---

# INDEX

# CREDITS

Cover: Ann Stratton. Page 10: Mark Thomas. Page 13: Charles Gold. Page 16: Lisa Koenig. Page 20: Beatriz Da Costa. Page 28: Zeva Oelbaum. Pages 33, 36, and 41: Lisa Koenig. Page 44: Mark Thomas. Page 51: Brian Hagiwara. Page 52: Charles Gold. Page 59: Mark Thomas. Pages 62 and 66: Lisa Koenig. Page 70: Ann Stratton. Page 74: Lisa Koenig. Page 81: Brian Hagiwara. Page 85: Lisa Koenig. Page 86: Brian Hagiwara. Page 88: Lisa Koenig. Pages 92, 97, 103, 107, 111, 112, 115, 116, 118, 121: Brian Hagiwara. Page 122: Lisa Koenig. Page 124: Alan Richardson. Page 133: Steven Mark Needham. Page 136: Alan Richardson. Page 140: Lisa Koenig. Page 142: Brian Hagiwara. Page 147: Alan Richardson. Page 150: Lisa Koenig. Pages 154 and 156: Brian Hagiwara. Page 161: Ann Stratton. Page 162: Brian Hagiwara. Page 165: Alan Richardson. Page 167: Mark Thomas. Page 171: Charles Gold. Page 174: Mark Thomas. Page 178: Charles Gold. Pages 182 and 187: Lisa Koenig. Page 191: Steven Mark Needham. Page 194: Lisa Koenig. Pages 197 and 202: Alan Richardson. Page 205: Zeva Oelbaum. Page 207: Alan Richardson. Pages 212 and 223: Charles Gold. Page 224: Lisa Koenig. Page 228: Ann Stratton. Pages 230, 235, and 238: Lisa Koenig.

Special thanks to: Debrah Donahue, Katie Bleacher Everard, Christopher Lilly, Karen Pickus, Catherine Wuenschel

Farberware Classic cookware on page 182 provided by Meyer Corporation

# METRIC CONVERSIONS

## LENGTH

| If you know: | Multiply by: | To find: |
| --- | --- | --- |
| INCHES | 25.0 | MILLIMETERS |
| INCHES | 2.5 | CENTIMETERS |
| FEET | 30.0 | CENTIMETERS |
| YARDS | 0.9 | METERS |
| MILES | 1.6 | KILOMETERS |
| MILLIMETERS | 0.04 | INCHES |
| CENTIMETERS | 0.4 | INCHES |
| METERS | 3.3 | FEET |
| METERS | 1.1 | YARDS |
| KILOMETERS | 0.6 | MILES |

## VOLUME

| If you know: | Multiply by: | To find: |
| --- | --- | --- |
| TEASPOONS | 5.0 | MILLILITERS |
| TABLESPOONS | 15.0 | MILLILITERS |
| FLUID OUNCES | 30.0 | MILLILITERS |
| CUPS | 0.24 | LITERS |
| PINTS | 0.47 | LITERS |
| QUARTS | 0.95 | LITERS |
| GALLONS | 3.8 | LITERS |
| MILLILITERS | 0.03 | FLUID OUNCES |
| LITERS | 4.2 | CUPS |
| LITERS | 2.1 | PINTS |
| LITERS | 1.06 | QUARTS |
| LITERS | 0.26 | GALLONS |

## WEIGHT

| If you know: | Multiply by: | To find: |
| --- | --- | --- |
| OUNCES | 28.0 | GRAMS |
| POUNDS | 0.45 | KILOGRAMS |
| GRAMS | 0.035 | OUNCES |
| KILOGRAMS | 2.2 | POUNDS |

## TEMPERATURE

| If you know: | Multiply by: | To find: |
| --- | --- | --- |
| DEGREES FAHRENHEIT | 0.56 (AFTER SUBTRACTING 32) | DEGREES CELSIUS |
| DEGREES CELSIUS | 1.8 (THEN ADD 32) | DEGREES FAHRENHEIT |